CW01371966

Shakespeare's Syndicate

Shakespeare's Syndicate

*The First Folio, its Publishers, and
the Early Modern Book Trade*

BEN HIGGINS

OXFORD
UNIVERSITY PRESS

OXFORD
UNIVERSITY PRESS

Great Clarendon Street, Oxford, OX2 6DP,
United Kingdom

Oxford University Press is a department of the University of Oxford.
It furthers the University's objective of excellence in research, scholarship,
and education by publishing worldwide. Oxford is a registered trade mark of
Oxford University Press in the UK and in certain other countries

© Ben Higgins 2022

The moral rights of the author have been asserted

First Edition published in 2022

All rights reserved. No part of this publication may be reproduced, stored in
a retrieval system, or transmitted, in any form or by any means, without the
prior permission in writing of Oxford University Press, or as expressly permitted
by law, by licence or under terms agreed with the appropriate reprographics
rights organization. Enquiries concerning reproduction outside the scope of the
above should be sent to the Rights Department, Oxford University Press, at the
address above

You must not circulate this work in any other form
and you must impose this same condition on any acquirer

Published in the United States of America by Oxford University Press
198 Madison Avenue, New York, NY 10016, United States of America

British Library Cataloguing in Publication Data

Data available

Library of Congress Control Number: 2021945531

ISBN 978–0–19–284884–0

DOI: 10.1093/oso/9780192848840.001.0001

Printed and bound by
CPI Group (UK) Ltd, Croydon, CR0 4YY

Links to third party websites are provided by Oxford in good faith and
for information only. Oxford disclaims any responsibility for the materials
contained in any third party website referenced in this work.

For my brilliant family: Mum, Dad, Amy, and Rob
Most of all, for my grandfather, John Gent

Contents

Acknowledgements	ix
List of Figures	xi
List of Tables	xiii
List of Abbreviations	xv
Note on Transcription and Citation Conventions	xvii
Introduction	1

PART 1 'PRINTED BY ISAAC JAGGARD, AND ED. BLOUNT. 1623.'

1. 'Master *William Shakesperes* workes': Edward Blount at the Black Bear — 41
2. 'Prudentia': The Jaggard Publishing House — 79

PART 2 'J. SMITHWEEKE, AND W. ASPLEY, 1623.'

3. A Minor Shakespearean: William Aspley at the Parrot — 125
4. 'Under the Diall': John Smethwick in St Dunstan's Churchyard — 170

Epilogue — 211

Appendix 1: The Letters of Edward Blount	221
Appendix 2: The Publications of William and Isaac Jaggard	237
Appendix 3: The Wholesale Locations of Shakespeare's Books, 1593–1640	242
Bibliography	251
Index	277

Acknowledgements

This book began as a doctoral project at the University of Oxford supervised by Tiffany Stern. It is a pleasure to acknowledge the great debt I owe to her intellectual guidance and to her ongoing support and friendship. That doctorate was funded by the Arts and Humanities Research Council and without the help of that organization could never have been completed, let alone emerged as a book. Adam Smyth and Lukas Erne had the dubious task of examining my thesis and did so with tremendous care and generosity. I am grateful to them both for their support and expertise as this book has emerged from its earlier form.

Several friends and colleagues read parts of this material along the way and many more helped the project along with insightful conversation. Among these generous souls I would like to thank Peter W. M. Blayney, Giles Bergel, Jakub Boguszak, Olivia Chappell for her reading and for much more besides, Heather Doherty, Hugh Gazzard, Adam G. Hooks, Katherine Hunt, Alice Leonard, Zachary Lesser, Amy Lidster, Laurie Maguire, Daniel McAteer, Peter McCullough, Kirk Melnikoff, Timothy Michael, Dianne Mitchell, Andy Murphy, Katie Murphy, Emma Smith, Tiffany Stern, Georgina Wilson, and Henry Woudhuysen.

I wrote this book during lectureships based at Lincoln College and then at Corpus Christi College in Oxford. It is a pleasure to thank both institutions for their hospitality during this time and the students I taught who helped clarify my ideas. I would particularly like to thank my English colleagues at both colleges: at Lincoln, Daniel McCann, Peter McCullough, Timothy Michael, and Henry Woudhuysen; and at Corpus, Hannah Lucas, Helen Moore, and David Russell. The English Faculty at Oxford, particularly the early modern contingent under the leadership of Lorna Hutson, has provided an excellent community in which to think through this material. For inspirational teaching that shaped my work at an earlier stage I would like thank Pascale Aebischer, Andy Brown, Nick McDowell, and Philip Schwyzer, all at Exeter University.

Some of the research for this book was carried out during fellowships at the Folger Library in Washington, DC and the Huntington Library in San Marino; my thanks to the staff of both libraries. Many other libraries supported me along the way, but my particular thanks to Sarah Wheale and the rest of the staff at the Bodleian Library. Georgina Wilson was a tremendous help both during a stint as a research assistant and more broadly in many discussions about early modern books. My research was also greatly helped by the generosity and friendship of Peter W. M. Blayney, who shared unpublished material with me throughout the process. Some of what follows may vex him; I hope he also finds something to enjoy. Adam Smyth has been a source of inspiration and guidance throughout both this project and more broadly the tiring march through academic precarity.

An alternative kind of research for this book involved speaking to other scholars about their experiences of overhauling a doctoral thesis. Everyone I spoke to offered valuable insight that informed my own process, including Claire M. L. Bourne, Alex da Costa, Bart van Es, Nicholas Hardy, Jeffrey Todd Knight, Laurie Maguire, Daniel Sawyer, Adam Smyth, Whitney Trettien, and Daniel Wakelin among others. Adam G. Hooks, I think, saw some echo of intellectual problems he had earlier solved and made time to talk and offer encouragement at several important moments. I am grateful to all of those I spoke with for reflecting on their experiences. Some of those conversations about writing first books are now published in the *Paper Kingdoms* interview series at: www.benjaminhiggins.co.uk.

I would also like to thank Ellie Collins, Karen Raith, and Henry Clarke at Oxford University Press for guiding this project through the publication process and for choosing my two anonymous readers, who improved the manuscript immensely. Both readers scrutinized the manuscript with meticulous care, down to the minutiae of edition sheets and imprint addresses. Reader One did all of this twice and followed up with fresh material after their duties were over. I am grateful to them both for modelling how peer review should be done. It goes without saying that all remaining slips are my own.

This book had a different kind of beginning in a ramshackle printing workshop in Bexhill-on-Sea, where on lunch breaks from journalism I learned how to print from an elderly man named Bill Addison. Together he and I made a book of poetry, using his utterly disorganized cases of metal type and a giant Heidelberg platen press. With tremendous patience Bill would set down his work on that week's church programmes or restaurant menus and guide me in setting another few lines. If you have never seen a mechanized Heidelberg running it is quite something: a huge flywheel spins with tremendous force and a chunk of metal about the size of a small car comes alive. Little windmill arms snatch up a sheet of paper, whirl it into the platen, and then yank it away, moving at a rate of two or three impressions a second. The sheer bulk and power of the thing brings an aura of death into the room. The stack of blank paper on the right is hurled through its transformation and becomes a pile of printed sheets on the left. As each sheet lands, a rubber nozzle sneaks in a quick puff of chalk to prevent the kinds of offset ghosts that now haunt the Jaggard Quartos. The whole thing is a kind of crazy, mesmeric word-factory. Somewhere in the image of Bill, white hair flying, leaning on the arm of his press as it clatters through another of our poems, is a seed of this book.

My last and deepest thanks go to my family for their patience, love, and support: to my mum, Alison, my dad, Colin, my sister, Amy, my brother, Rob, and my grandfather, John Gent.

List of Figures

0.1 William Shakespeare, *Mr. William Shakespeares Comedies, Histories, & Tragedies* (1623), sig. πA1v and πA1+1r, RBD EL SH15M 1623, Free Library of Philadelphia   4

0.2 Robert West, *The West Prospect of the Church of St Ethelbergh* (1736), Gough Maps vol. 20, fol. 29b, Bodleian Libraries, University of Oxford   8

0.3 William Shakespeare, *Mr. William Shakespeares Comedies, Histories, & Tragedies* (1623), sig. 3b6r, RBD EL SH15M 1623, Free Library of Philadelphia   12

0.4 *Register D*, p. 69, TSC/1/E/06/03, The Stationers' Company Archive   21

1.1 *Catalogus universalis pronundinis Francofurtensibus vernalibus...* (1624), sig. D4v, MS Ashmole 1057(10), Bodleian Libraries, University of Oxford   43

1.2 Michel de Montaigne, *The essayes* (1603), translated by John Florio, sig. Z3r, L. L. e. 13, Worcester College, Oxford   55

1.3 *Liber Computi Pro Pauperibus*, fol. 115v, TSC/1/G/01/04/07, The Stationers' Company Archive   60

1.4 Jan van Belcamp, 'The Great Picture' (1646), detail of triptych right hand panel, Abbot Hall, Lakeland Arts Trust, England   76

2.1 Justinus, *The historie of Justine*, translated by G. W. (1606), sig. A2r, Fol. Delta. 124, Bodleian Libraries, University of Oxford   95

2.2 *The fierie tryall of Gods saints* (1611), sig. F4v, 4° C 110(7) Th., Bodleian Libraries, University of Oxford   96

2.3 William Shakespeare, *Mr. William Shakespeares Comedies, Histories, & Tragedies* (1623), sig. πA1+1r, STC 22273 Fo.1 no.01, Folger Shakespeare Library   100

2.4 R. White, *The Royal Exchange of London* (1671), Gough Maps vol. 19, fol. 21, Bodleian Libraries, University of Oxford   115

3.1 *Register C*, fol. 63v, TSC/1/E/06/02, The Stationers' Company Archive   126

3.2 *Register D*, p. 440. TSC/1/E/06/03, The Stationers' Company Archive   135

3.3 John Marston and John Webster, *The Malcontent* (1604, STC 17481), sig. B1v, Malone 252 (4), Bodleian Libraries, University of Oxford   140

3.4 John Marston and John Webster, *The Malcontent* (1604, STC 17481), sig. B1v, STC 17481 copy 1, Folger Shakespeare Library   141

3.5 *The whole volume of statutes at large* (1587), flyleaf, copy in private ownership   149

LIST OF FIGURES

3.6 John Boys, *An exposition of the dominical Epistles and Gospels... the spring-part* (1615), sig. A1r, Antiq.e.E.1615.2 (2), Bodleian Libraries, University of Oxford   154

3.7 John Boys, *An exposition of the festivall Epistles and Gospels... the first part* (1613), sig. A1r, Vet. A2 e.473 (6), Bodleian Libraries, University of Oxford   155

3.8 John Boys, *The workes of John Boys Doctor in Divinitie* (1629 [i.e., 1630]), engraved title page, Vet. A2 d.2, Bodleian Libraries, University of Oxford   159

3.9 John Boys, *The autumne part from the twelfth Sunday after Trinitie* (1613), sig. L3v, Vet. A2 e.171 (4), Bodleian Libraries, University of Oxford   164

4.1 Robert West, *The South East Prospect of the Church of St. Dunstan in the West* (1737), Gough Maps vol. 20, fol. 29b, Bodleian Libraries, University of Oxford   171

4.2 The sites of London from which Shakespeare's books were offered for wholesale between 1593 and 1640 inclusive   182

4.3 The sites of publication and wholesale of the first three quartos of *Romeo and Juliet*   192

4.4 The sites of London from which Shakespeare's books were offered for wholesale between 1593 and 1622 inclusive   200

4.5 The sites of London from which Shakespeare's books were offered for wholesale between 1623 and 1640 inclusive   201

4.6 William Shakespeare, *Mr. William Shakespeares Comedies, Histories, and Tragedies* (1632), sig. 3d4r, Phi.F.3.8, Corpus Christi College, University of Oxford   209

A.1 Detail from *Edward Blount to Sir Dudley Carleton, 26 April 1615*, SP 14/80, fol. 136b, The National Archives, Kew   222

A.2 Detail from *Edward Blount to Sir William Trumbull, 6 July 1621*, Additional MS 72361, fol. 110v, The British Library   222

A.3 Detail from *Edward Blount to Christopher Browne, 15 August 1631*, Additional MS 78683, fol. 73v, The British Library   222

List of Tables

1.1	Publishing outputs in edition sheets of the twelve stationers involved in negotiations for the First Folio in their first decade of activity, ordered by average size of publication	50
1.2	Prefatory addresses written by the twelve stationers who owned the right to print one or more of Shakespeare's plays in 1623	66
3.1	Entry of William Shakespeare's work into the Stationers' Register, 1593–1622, ordered by chronology	133
3.2	Entry of William Shakespeare's work into the Stationers' Register, 1593–1622, organized by stationer	137
A1	Jaggard publications	238
A2	Chronological locations	243

List of Abbreviations

Arber	*A Transcript of the Registers of the Company of Stationers of London, 1554–1640*. Edited by Edward Arber. 5 vols (London: The Stationers' Company, 1875–84)
BL	The British Library, London
DEEP	*Database of Early English Playbooks*. Edited by Alan B. Farmer and Zachary Lesser. Created 2007. http://deep.sas.upenn.edu
ESTC	*English Short Title Catalogue*, http://estc.bl.uk
LMA	London Metropolitan Archives, London
ODNB	*Oxford Dictionary of National Biography*, www.oxforddnb.com
OED	*Oxford English Dictionary*, www.oed.com
SCA	The Stationers' Company Archives, London
STC	*A Short-Title Catalogue of Books Printed in England, Scotland, & Ireland and of English Books Printed Abroad, 1475–1640*. Edited by A. W. Pollard and G. R. Redgrave. 2nd edn, rev. W. A. Jackson, F. S. Ferguson, and Katharine F. Pantzer. 3 vols (London: The Bibliographical Society, 1976–91)
TNA	The National Archives, Kew
Wing	*Short-Title Catalogue of Books Printed in England, Scotland, Ireland, Wales, and British America, and of English Books Printed in Other Countries, 1641–1700*. Edited by Donald Goddard Wing. 2nd edn, rev. and enl. John J Morrison and Carolyn Nelson. 4 vols (New York: Modern Language Association of America, 1982–98)

Note on Transcription and Citation Conventions

I retain original spelling and punctuation for quotations from primary sources in both print and manuscript, with the following exceptions: I have modernized *i/j* and *u/v*, changed the long s (∫) to short, and amended '*vv*' to '*w*'. For early printed books, *STC* and *Wing* numbers have been included throughout, and the place of publication is London unless otherwise stated.

When dealing with manuscript sources, I have expanded and italicized contractions (m^r becomes m*aste*r). Any interpolations are marked with square brackets; insertions are signalled \with slashes/. When quoting from editions of manuscripts (for example, Jackson's transcriptions of records from the stationers' court) I retain the conventions of the edition. The letters of Edward Blount are presented under their own conventions as appendix one, and any quotes from the letters are taken from the appendix. Much of the material in the archives of the Stationers' Company has now been digitized, and with this in mind citations for this material supply references for Arber and also for the *Literary Print Culture* database where relevant.

Chapter four features several maps of London in the mid-seventeenth century. With permission of The Bibliographical Society, these maps are based on that which is used in *STC*, vol. 3, insert between pp. 246–7 ('London in December 1666'), which is itself based on a combination of John Leake's survey (1666) and John Ogilby's *Large and accurate map of the city of London* (1676). Readers can easily move between the maps in this book and that found in the *STC*.

Introduction

'All Poets,' the ballad writer Martin Parker wrote in 1641, 'Have by their Works eternized their names.'[1] Part of what Parker seems to have had in mind when he wrote, as the following lines of his poem make clear, was the title page of the folio collection of William Shakespeare's plays. The book which has come to be called the 'First Folio' was published in 1623 before being reprinted in a second edition in 1632, nine years before Parker's poem, and perhaps reissued again in 1641.[2] Both early editions of Shakespeare's Folio used the same striking design on their title pages: one that featured Shakespeare's name printed in large letters above his now-famous portrait. Remembering other memorable examples of authorship in print, Parker went on to name Shakespeare alongside Philip Sidney, Michael Drayton, George Wither, and Ben Jonson as writers who had all 'thought good, | To have their names in publike understood'.[3]

Centuries later, the writers of Parker's miniature canon enjoy different status. But many readers unfamiliar with George Wither will recognize the title page of Shakespeare's collected works, or *Mr. William Shakespeares Comedies, Histories & Tragedies*, to give the book its full title. What other book more powerfully symbolizes literary authorship? If alive today, those who made the Folio in the early 1620s would surely be delighted with—if a little baffled by—the success of their venture. The book itself envisages a long life in its opening few pages. When 'Time dissolves thy *Stratford* Moniment', wrote the poet Leonard Digges, thinking of the bust that can still be seen in Holy Trinity Church, it is 'thy Workes' by which Shakespeare's name will live. 'This Booke' Digges continued, 'When Brasse and Marble fade, shall make thee looke | Fresh to all Ages'.[4] Early modern print is filled with examples of such hopeful appeals, but in this case Digges' valorization turned out to be prescient. His poem anticipates our own tremendous cultural investment in Shakespeare's Folio, a book which supplies the only known texts for eighteen Shakespeare plays and which updates or revises ten others in important ways. Despite the fact that it lacks any of the poetry and a few plays, the First Folio is unquestionably the single most important document in the history of the

---

[1] Martin Parker, *The poet's blind mans bough* (1641, Wing P443), sig. A4r.
[2] William B. Todd, 'The Issues and States of the Second Folio and Milton's Epitaph on Shakespeare' in *Studies in Bibliography* 5 (1952): pp. 81–108.
[3] Parker, *Blind mans bough*, sig. A4v.
[4] Leonard Digges, 'To the Memorie of the deceased Authour Maister W. Shakespeare' in William Shakespeare, *Mr. William Shakespeares Comedies, Histories, & Tragedies* (1623, STC 22273), sig. πA5+1r.

Shakespearean text. For this reason, the Folio is probably also the single most studied book in literary history. Can there be anything left to say?

This book offers a new account of the First Folio and of early modern publication by focusing on those who made the volume. We already have a detailed understanding of how this book was printed.[5] But, as the rest of this introduction explores, the physical labour of composing and distributing metal type, of inking formes and pulling impressions, is only one of the ways in which a book like the Folio was 'made'. The chapters that follow this introduction are organized around the key personalities of the Folio's publication: the four book-trade businesses, each led by a particular bookseller or printer, that were directly involved in creating the book. This group collectively formed a 'syndicate', or publishing partnership, to produce the Folio, meaning that they shared the costs of the book's publication and took on various other responsibilities described below.[6] Collectively these chapters form an extended close reading of the Folio's imprint and colophon, the two marginal texts found at the beginning and end of the volume and in which these figures are named. The structure of this book, then, takes its bearings from the event of the Folio's publication. Yet if on one level this book promises a narrow focus on the year 1623 and the arrival of the Folio, the content of the chapters themselves unsettles that historical fixity by looking both backwards and forwards through the careers of the Folio's makers, exploiting a tension between the Folio as a material product that belongs in its finished form to October or November of 1623, and as an idea that emerged from and went on to influence the overlapping histories of the book trade and Shakespearean print. In the chapters that follow this introduction, the Folio's imprint and colophon become interpretive keys that direct us towards named personalities and also to the institutional concerns those texts inscribe through their ritualistic observance of the details of publication.

By situating the First Folio in the lives and interests of the book-trade figures who made it, I pursue two related goals. First, I seek to illuminate our understanding of how this landmark volume was made and what that process involved

---

[5] The key works on the First Folio form a fascinating history of their own. They include: Edwin Willoughby, *The Printing of the First Folio of Shakespeare* (Oxford: The Bibliographical Society, 1932); W. W. Greg, *The Shakespeare First Folio: Its Bibliographical and Textual History* (Oxford: Clarendon Press, 1955); Charlton Hinman, *The Printing and Proof-Reading of the First Folio of Shakespeare*, 2 vols (Oxford: Clarendon Press, 1963); Peter W. M. Blayney, *The First Folio of Shakespeare* (Washington, DC: Folger Shakespeare Library, 1991); Hinman and Blayney's introductions to *The Norton Facsimile: The First Folio of Shakespeare*, 2nd edn (New York and London: W. W. Norton & Company, 1996); Anthony James West, *The Shakespeare First Folio: The History of the Book*, 2 vols (Oxford: Oxford University Press, 2001); Emma Smith, *The Making of Shakespeare's First Folio* (Oxford: Bodleian Library, 2015) and *Shakespeare's First Folio: Four Centuries of an Iconic Book* (Oxford: Oxford University Press, 2016).

[6] 'Syndicate' is an anachronistic term in this context but one that captures the shared economic investment made by these stationers. In the early seventeenth century the word meant a council or official committee 'appointed for some specific duty'. It was only in the nineteenth century that it acquired an explicitly capitalist dimension, when it came to mean a group of partners joining together 'for the promotion of a particular enterprise' or to finance 'a scheme requiring large resources of capital', especially one that sought 'control of the market in a particular commodity': 'syndicate, n.,' *OED* def. 2, 3a.

from the perspective of its publishers. But secondly, I use the centrality of the Folio to modern literary and bibliographical studies as licence to explore some new ways to think about early modern publication more broadly. I start at the beginning of the Folio itself and with the pages that lodged in Parker's mind (see Figures 0.1A and 0.1B). This opening, which so powerfully conveys literary authorship, seems the ideal place to challenge our focus on Shakespeare, and to notice instead that the single personality championed by these pages is underpinned by a quiet cast of makers.

The Opening Pages

The first thing we see is the portrait. Tiny script in the bottom left corner supplies a trace of the man who engraved it, a Dutch immigrant artist who signed his name and who tells us what he did and where: 'Martin Droeshout: Sculpsit. London'. Droeshout was young when he made this engraving, an up-and-coming member of London's immigrant artistic community. He must have worked from a picture of the dead Shakespeare, perhaps supplied by one of the playwright's theatrical friends. He worked carefully and may have printed it himself, considering that he twice made tiny corrections to the shading after checking early impressions.[7] Printing an engraved plate like this involved warming the metal over a brazier before using a linen cloth to work ink down into the scratched lines, then using more cloths and finally the hand itself to sweep off excess ink each time an impression was required. For 'a picture in this kinde', wrote Thomas Powell in 1661, 'a thousand Copies may be taken of it (by the help of a Rolling-Press) in a few hours space', though for a relatively detailed portrait like this Powell's judgement seems ambitious.[8]

The portrait has a special status: the engraved plate is the only part of this book that was used in the printing of all four editions of the Folio that appeared over the seventeenth century (in 1623, 1632, 1663–4, and 1685).[9] This fact grants material continuity to books that collectively share no other physical trace: there is a stability to Shakespeare's gaze that endures despite other alterations that see the four Folios present 'Shakespeare' in different ways (rearranged poems; the

---

[7] Blayney, *First Folio* 1991, p. 18. On Droeshout, see June Schlueter, 'Droeshout, Martin, the younger (b. 1601, d. in or after 1640), engraver,' *Oxford Dictionary of National Biography* (Oxford: Oxford University Press, 2004; online edn, 2018 [accessed 3 December 2019]). For an alternative view that the artist may have been Martin Droeshout the Elder, uncle to his younger namesake, see Smith, *Making*, pp. 122–4.

[8] Thomas Powell, *Humane industry* (1661, Wing P3072), sig. G7v. For the process of printing engraved copperplates in the seventeenth century see Roger Gaskell, 'Printing House and Engraving Shop: A Mysterious Collaboration' in *The Book Collector* 53.2 (2004): pp. 213–51.

[9] A. M. Hind, *Engraving in England in the Sixteenth and Seventeenth Centuries*, 3 parts, Part 2: 'The Reign of James I' (Cambridge: Cambridge University Press, 1955), pp. 354–9.

To the Reader.

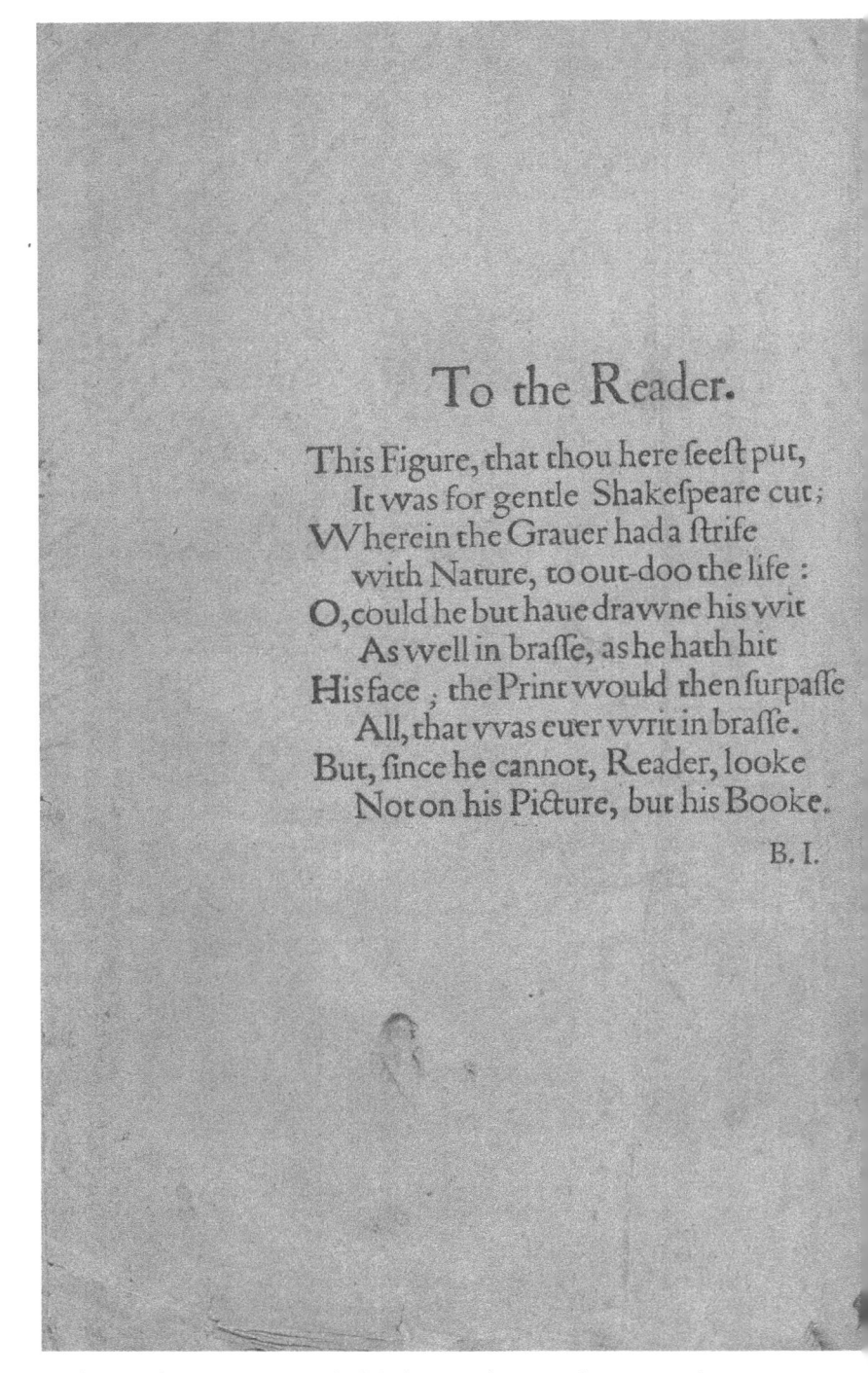

This Figure, that thou here seest put,
　　It was for gentle Shakespeare cut;
Wherein the Grauer had a strife
　　with Nature, to out-doo the life :
O, could he but haue dravvne his vvit
　　As well in brasse, as he hath hit
His face ; the Print would then surpasse
　　All, that vvas euer vvrit in brasse.
But, since he cannot, Reader, looke
　　Not on his Picture, but his Booke.

　　　　　　　　　　　　　B. I.

Figures 0.1A and 0.1B The opening spread of Shakespeare's First Folio. Image of copy owned by the Free Library of Philadelphia (sig. πA1v and πA1+1r), shelfmark: RBD EL SH15M 1623. Credit: Rare Book Department, Free Library of Philadelphia.

Mr. WILLIAM
SHAKESPEARES
COMEDIES,
HISTORIES, &
TRAGEDIES.

Published according to the True Originall Copies.

Martin Droeshout: sculpsit London

LONDON
Printed by Isaac Iaggard, and Ed. Blount. 1623.

addition of new plays). Passed between a sequence of owners, the plate somehow escaped the tumult of the Great Fire in 1666 and was last used for the Fourth Folio in 1685, long after those involved in its making had died. Its image tends to be criticized by scholars who see it as clumsy, but in the poem on the opposite page Ben Jonson takes a different view. He praises the portrait (so if we take him at his word, Jonson saw the plate before writing his poem), and remembers Droeshout when he suggests that 'the Graver had a strife' to get Shakespeare's likeness down accurately. A few lines further on, Jonson describes engravings as being 'writ' onto their metal plates, encouraging us to think of Droeshout as another kind of 'author' of this book. Throughout the poem the pronouns bounce between identifying first Droeshout and then Shakespeare:

> O, could he but have drawne his wit
> As well in brasse, as he hath hit
> His face; the Print would then surpasse
> All, that was ever writ in brasse.
> But, since he cannot, Reader, looke
> Not on his Picture, but his Booke.[10]

In its repetitions of 'he' and 'his' the poem drags us back and forth between the engraver and the playwright, muddling the pair as subjects of the verse. If Droeshout could have drawn Shakespeare's wit, Jonson tells us, as well as he has captured the author's face, then the print would be better. However, since no etching can capture inward faculties like wit and creativity, we must look instead 'Not on his Picture, but his Booke'. The book in this line is inarguably Shakespeare's, but 'his Picture' seems to include both Droeshout and Shakespeare. The ambiguity of that referent reminds us that books are dependent on 'their makers and suppliers' as well as on their authors.[11]

Jonson's treatment of the portrait troubles its status in other ways. He invites us first to notice the picture but then dismisses it, rhetorically distancing it from the 'Booke' itself. In doing so, Jonson leaves the portrait hovering uncertainly on the fringes of the Folio. Like Jonson's poem, the portrait belongs to that class of material that the theorist Gérard Genette would term a 'peritext', meaning a part of the book that acts as a threshold between the text within and the world without.[12] Genette argued that peritexts shape the reading experience and one of the ways Jonson's poem manages this is by urging us to turn away from the portrait

---

[10] Ben Jonson, 'To the Reader' in Shakespeare, *Comedies, Histories, & Tragedies*, sig. πA1v.

[11] D. F. McKenzie, 'The London Book Trade in 1644,' in Peter McDonald and Michael F. Suarez, S. J. eds, *Making Meaning: "Printers of the Mind" and Other Essays* (Amherst, MA: University of Massachusetts Press, 2002), p. 128.

[12] Gérard Genette, *Paratext: Thresholds of Interpretation*, trans. Jane E. Lewin (Cambridge: Cambridge University Press, 1997), pp. 4–5.

and arrive at the substance. But where does the book properly begin? Most likely Jonson means that we should jump ahead to the 'tempestuous noise of Thunder and Lightning' which launches the first play, *The Tempest*, but if so then Jonson also asks us to skip over his own second and much longer poem which appears in the preliminaries.[13]

It is relatively unusual to find a poem like Jonson's on this verso of an early modern book. The page opposite the title page was usually left blank, occasionally spurring readers (John Donne was one) to add their own literary compositions.[14] One reader has done just this with the Folio copy that was presented to the Bodleian Library before being lost and then recovered in ways that have been brilliantly recounted by Emma Smith.[15] This copy is missing the leaf that features Jonson's lines, and on a replacement is the following manuscript poem, probably written during the eighteenth century:

> An Active Swain to make a Leap was seen
> Which sham'd his Fellow Shepherds on the Green,
> And growing Vain, he would Essay once more,
> But lost the Fame, which he had gain'd before;
> Oft' did he try, at Length was forc'd to yeild
> He Stove in Vain, —he had himself Excell'd:
> So Nature once in her Essays of Wit,
> In Shakespear took the Shepherd's Lucky Leap
> But over-straining in the great Effort,
> In Dryden, and the rest, has since fell Short.[16]

The efficacy of this short poem has to do with its being written on this leaf, opposite this portrait. We expect writing in this space to address Shakespeare, and so the poem plays with us by initially seeming to criticize its subject. Our first impression is that Shakespeare must be the 'Active Swain' who, trying a little too hard and 'growing Vain', has now 'lost the Fame, which he had gain'd before'. Over its first six lines, then, the poem seems excitingly to repurpose this space of veneration as the perfect site for an arch critique. A few lines later, though, it becomes clear through a fairly strained comparison that Nature itself is the clumsy swain, and Shakespeare is the 'Lucky Leap' of creation, an 'Essay of Wit' that outdid all others, leaving exhausted Nature only able to sputter out 'Dryden, and the rest'. The poem turns out to be working within the poetics of these opening pages, not

---

[13] Shakespeare, *Comedies, Histories, & Tragedies*, sig. πA1r.
[14] Joshua Eckhardt, *Religion around John Donne* (University Park, PA: Penn State University Press, 2019), p. 61, pp. 68–9.
[15] Smith, *Four Centuries*, pp. 70–88.
[16] Front flyleaf of Bodleian Library Arch. G c.7. A version of Jonson's own poem is copied underneath. The book can be viewed online at *The Bodleian First Folio*: https://firstfolio.bodleian.ox.ac.uk/.

8 SHAKESPEARE'S SYNDICATE

Figure 0.2 The title pages of new books pinned up outside a bookshop in Bishopsgate, London. Detail of 'The West Prospect of the Church of St Ethelbergh' (Robert West, 1736). Credit: Bodleian Libraries, University of Oxford, Gough Maps vol. 20, fol. 29b. Used under Creative Commons licence CC-BY-NC 4.0.

against them: it becomes a conventional response to a tradition instigated by Jonson's own verse, though it adds the twist of using Shakespeare to attack the writer John Dryden (1631–1700) and a later generation of literary heroes.

The title pages of new books were commonly pinned up in public spaces around early modern London (see Figure 0.2), which means they tended to do all the work of marketing the book, rather than relying on verse on a neighbouring page.[17] Fleeting encounters with such title pages, skewered or pasted up in public view, probably composed the majority of the earliest readings of the Folio—very far from the kind of sustained attention we devote to Shakespeare's work today. This practice of book advertising materially enacts Jonson's rhetorical separation of portrait and book. So, to adopt Genette's terms again, the title page becomes both peritext and 'epitext', meaning an element of the book located outside the physical volume.

Title-page pictures like Droeshout's were particularly eye-catching. The author Ralph Austen suggests as much when fretting about how best to market his own book, *A Treatise of fruit-trees* (1653), which featured an engraving of an orderly garden on its title page. Presumably worried about the cost of printing this image, Austen wondered whether 'Title Pages printed without the Plate' should be

---

[17] Tiffany Stern, *Documents of Performance in Early Modern England* (Cambridge: Cambridge University Press, 2009), pp. 50–62. In the poet Thomas Campion's telling it is only 'one leafe'—the title page—of his book that is destined to be pinned up 'like a riders cloke' in Paul's Churchyard: *Observations in the Art of English Poesie* (1602, STC 4543), sig. A4v.

'affixed in seuerall places'; ultimately though, he and his publisher felt there was no need: 'some few Title Pages (with the Plate)' that were 'set up in some few, fittest places' would serve.[18] If extra copies of the Folio title page served as the kind of 'carefully posted' advertisements that in 1678 the bookseller Francis Kirkman described as being 'not a little proud to see' as he strolled around London admiring his own work, then Jonson's deictic insistence in his poem on the situatedness of the portrait becomes more complicated.[19] It is an image 'that thou here seest put', which of course asks readers to notice what they hold in their hands. But the fixity of that 'here' breaks down if the portrait was also found in the city's advertising spaces: the bookshops, playhouses and taverns; the stocks and the inns of court—and perhaps even further afield across England.[20] The lively energy of early modern print, its dual habits of fragmentation and motion, means that the title page here evades Jonson's poetic control: it travels between interpretive contexts, commanding attention by itself but also introducing the book to which it was (usually) physically attached. For those early readers who glimpsed the title page posted up in London, Jonson's lines supplied the first new material of the book, forming a kind of call-and-response with the engraving that allows Shakespeare's rival to form our first impression of the playwright as 'gentle Shakespeare', a man of natural 'wit', if not of Jonsonian learning.

Present in a different way in these opening pages are the unseen workmen who positioned and inked the type, who pulled the press and lifted off the printed sheets. The inky fingermarks of these workmen add an occasional spectral presence to some pages of the Folio, but for the most part the figures who assembled the book belong to that large cadre of absent or invisible labour on which the early modern book trade relied: the wives, widows, and apprentices, the type founders and paper merchants, the pressmen and the compositors whose nimble skill with metal type is registered only through the absence of any human trace. Similarly both present and absent are the many stationers who had earlier

---

[18] *Ralph Austen to Samuel Hartlib, 14 June 1653*, Hartlib Papers (https://www.dhi.ac.uk/hartlib), 41/1/34A. The book in question is *A Treatise of fruit-trees* (1653, Wing A4238). An earlier indication of what Droeshout's fee for the portrait may have been is supplied by Matthew Parker, Archbishop of Canterbury, who in 1574 paid forty-four shillings (just over two pounds) for an engraved map to be printed in a quarto edition of John Caius, *De antiquitate Cantebrigiensis Academiæ* (1574, STC 4345). The sum covered 'the copper to grave in' (12s), colouring (2s), and the fee paid 'to him for carving it' (30s). Plomer's judgement is that the book cost Parker a little over fifteen pounds to print, making the engraving a significant proportion of the overall cost, though it is not clear how many copies were printed: Henry R. Plomer, 'The 1574 Edition of Dr. John Caius's *De Antiquitate Cantebrigiensis Academiæ Libri Duo*' in *The Library* S4, VII.3 (1926), pp. 253–68 at p. 257.

[19] Francis Kirkman, *The unlucky citizen* (1673, Wing K638), sig. N2r. For a recent account of the discursive possibilities of early modern title pages see Lucy Razzle, '"Like to a title leafe": Surface, Face, and Material Text in Early Modern England', in *Journal of the Northern Renaissance* 8 (2017). http://northernrenaissance.org, consulted 23 September 2020.

[20] At least by 1653, the title pages of new books (if not the books themselves) were sent from London to Oxford for advertising purposes. Austen, who lived in Oxford, was disappointed not 'to have seene more Title Pages the last week from London' *Ralph Austen to Samuel Hartlib, 6 June 1653*, Hartlib Papers, 41/1/32A.

published Shakespeare's books, rhetorically invoked through the Folio's claim, printed above the portrait, to supersede earlier publications by offering 'the True Originall Copies' of the plays.[21] This claim relies on a different way of understanding the temporality of this volume: though in one sense the book belongs to 1623, in another way it continually ruptures this singularity, reaching back into the past in order to locate itself in the present.

The following pages of the Folio feature other contributors. The remaining preliminary leaves include two addresses signed by leading members of Shakespeare's theatre company, John Heminge and Henry Condell. One of these prefaces is directed to the book's aristocratic patrons, William and Philip Herbert, the Earls of Pembroke and Montgomery, while the other is addressed to readers of the book. There is the 'Names of the Principall Actors' page, complete with its list headed by Shakespeare himself, and four more laudatory verses. All this paratextual material has been quarried many times by scholars for the ways in which it fashions Shakespeare's authorial persona through a mesh of 'financial contracts and affective ties'.[22] The pages that create 'Shakespeare' as we know him do so in part by relying on the multiple agencies and reputations of its contributors.

Beneath the portrait of Shakespeare on the title page is the imprint: a simple statement that provides key information about the book, including the city in which it was made, the names of two of its leading publishers, and the date of its production:

LONDON
Printed by Isaac Jaggard, and Ed. Blount. 1623.

These two figures—the stationers Isaac Jaggard, who in late 1623 had just buried his father William and taken control of his family's printing and publishing business, and Edward Blount, an elder statesman of the book trade who was nearing the end of his career—were instrumental to the publication of Shakespeare's collected works. Though the imprint states that they 'printed' the book, this term is meant loosely; it tells us that they were responsible for the book's production, rather than suggesting these two figures laboured at a printing press themselves. Yet

---

[21] Important overviews of Shakespeare's printed work are provided by Andrew Murphy, *Shakespeare in Print: A History and Chronology of Shakespeare Publishing*, 2nd rev. edn (Cambridge: Cambridge University Press, 2021). John Jowett, *Shakespeare and Text* (Cambridge: Cambridge University Press, 2007); David Scott Kastan, *Shakespeare and the Book* (Cambridge: Cambridge University Press, 2001); Lukas Erne, *Shakespeare as Literary Dramatist*, 2nd edn (Cambridge: Cambridge University Press, 2013); *Shakespeare and the Book Trade* (Cambridge: Cambridge University Press, 2013). Comprehensive bibliographic work focusing on the Folio includes Eric Rasmussen and Anthony James West, *The Shakespeare First Folios: A Descriptive Catalogue* (Basingstoke: Palgrave Macmillan, 2012); West, *The Shakespeare First Folio*.

[22] Margreta de Grazia, *Shakespeare Verbatim: The Reproduction of Authenticity and the 1790 Apparatus* (Oxford: Clarendon Press, 1991), pp. 14–48 at p. 23.

these stationers did not only oversee the practical side of this book's construction; they also 'made' the book in other ways that *Shakespeare's Syndicate* explores. What is more, the imprint works in partnership with another marginal feature of the Folio, the colophon, which is found at the very end of the book and which states that the Folio was:

> Printed at the Charges of W. Jaggard, Ed. Blount, J. Smithweeke, and W. Aspley, 1623.

Here listed is the complete team of four businesses (or five individual stationers, given the brief resurrection of Isaac Jaggard's father William) who were responsible for the 'charges' of the book and who form the key personalities of *Shakespeare's Syndicate*. In a strictly industrial sense, the 'charges' identified here were the costs of the Folio's production: the expenses involved in buying paper, securing the rights to print the plays, and organizing the labour.[23] However the term also—if we consider 'charge' as a verb—reminds us that the Folio emerged at the will and command of these men. This latter sense of the word seems to have been present in book production since at least the late Elizabethan period: the large folio *Loci communes*, or printed commonplaces, of Peter Martyr was printed in 1583 'at the costs and charges' of its syndicate of four publishers; a psalter of 1565 was printed at 'the command and expensis' of its publisher; John Donne's *Poems* (1633) arrived via the 'charge and paines' of the stationer John Marriot.[24] The blurring together of financial and wilful concerns in such language alerts us to the fact that buried in the dry terminology of the Folio's colophon is the idea that we owe what is perhaps the most important book in the Western literary canon not only to the financial resources of this group of stationers but also to their sheer volition, to their 'constant will to publish' as King Lear puts it, overwhelmed by the need to divide his kingdom among his daughters.[25]

Pictured in Figure 0.3 is the final page of the Folio, where the names of these stationers appear after the closing lines of *Cymbeline* in which the British king celebrates the end of the Roman invasion. 'Publish we this Peace | To all our Subjects,' Cymbeline declares.[26] The presence of the colophon invites an alternative reading of these words, one in which a pun on 'peace' and 'piece' celebrates the finished Folio being sent into the world as well as the restoration of peace in

---

[23] For a summary of these costs see Blayney, *First Folio* 1991, pp. 25–32.
[24] Pietro Martire Vermigli, *The common places of the most famous and renowmed* [sic] *divine Doctor Peter Martyr* (1583, STC 24669), sig. *6r *Heir follouis. Ane compendeous buke, of Godly psalmes* (Edinburgh, 1565, STC 2996.3); John Marriot, 'The Printer to the Understanders' in John Donne, *Poems, by J. D.* (1633, STC 7045), sig. A1v. For similar examples see Georgette de Montenay, *A booke of armes* (1619, STC 18046); Nicolas de Nicolay, *The navigations, peregrinations and voyages* (1585, STC 18574), sig. ¶3v.
[25] Shakespeare, *Comedies, Histories, & Tragedies*, sig. 2q2r.
[26] Shakespeare, *Comedies, Histories, & Tragedies*, sig. 3b6r.

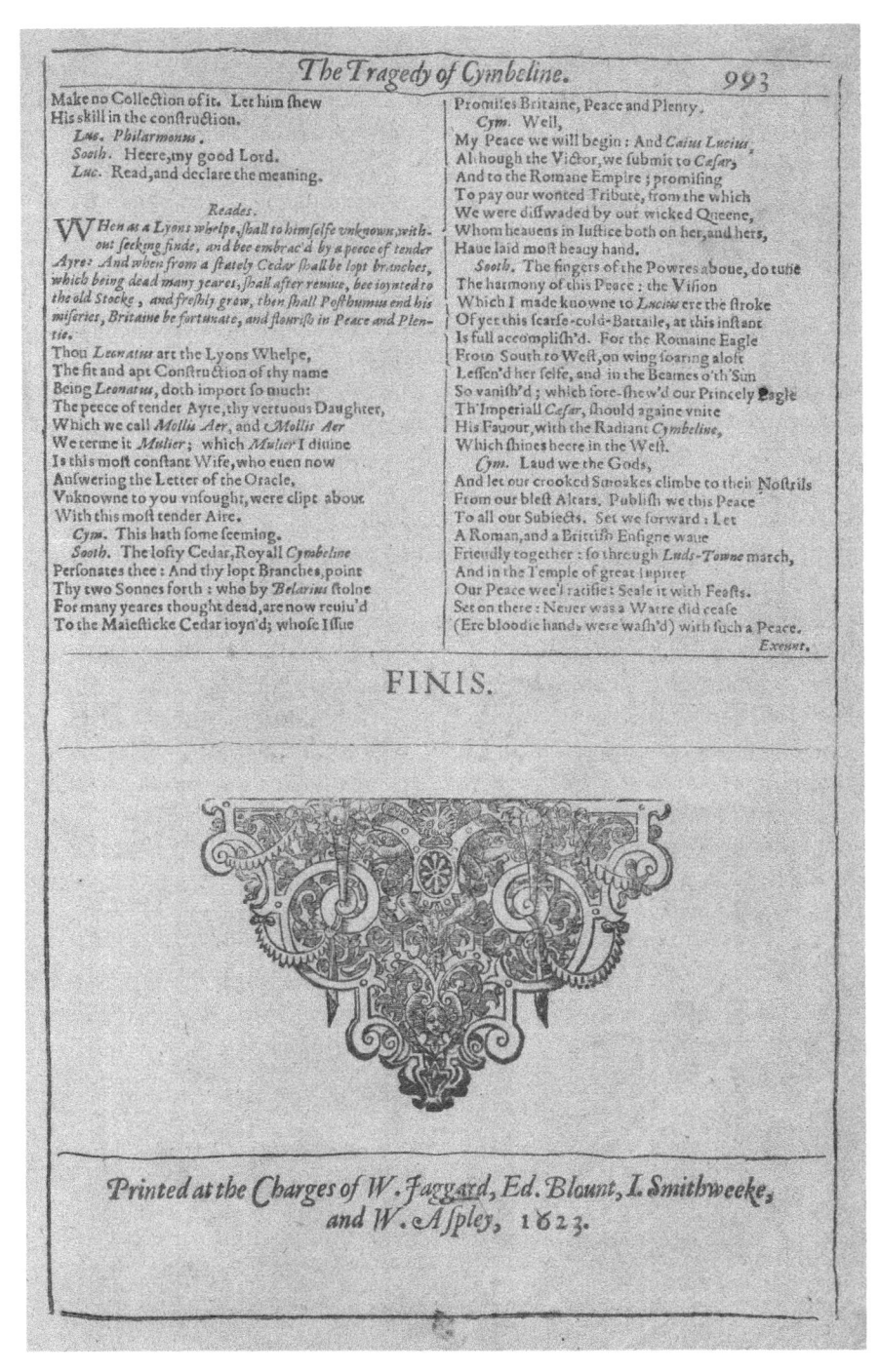

Figure 0.3 The final printed page of *Cymbeline* in the First Folio, featuring the book's colophon (sig. 3b6r). Image of copy owned by the Free Library of Philadelphia, shelfmark: RBD EL SH15M 1623. Credit: Rare Book Department, Free Library of Philadelphia.

Britain. That more playful reading of 'piece' for 'peace' seems to echo across this final page: the Soothsayer thanks the 'fingers of the Powres above' who 'do tune | The harmony of this Peace'; Cymbeline ends the play with his tired yet triumphant pronouncement that he has never before seen 'such a Peace'. The boundaries of the play-world become porous for a moment, and open to the material in which that world is housed. Shakespeare's characters seem to congratulate the book in which they belong—and perhaps the reader who has made it to the end.[27] A little further up the same page, the Roman ambassador Caius Lucius commands his soothsayer to 'Read, and declare the meaning' of a prophecy which holds the key to the play's happy resolution. The final stage direction (*'Exeunt'* aside) is that the character *'Reades'*. Centred in its own line, this direction concludes both play and Folio with an act of literary interpretation, dramatizing the scenario in which the book's readers participate. At the foot of the page, after the *'Exeunt'* has dispersed the play's characters and a bold 'FINIS' has concluded the book's drama, the Folio publishers congregate in discrete reminder of their achievement.

We study the characters of Shakespeare's plays as part of our work to make meaning from his texts, but it is only recently that much attention has been paid to those who published his work. Just an ornament and a few printed borders separate Cymbeline and the soothsayer from the Folio publishers, but those slender boundaries have organized our critical gaze such that in the history of scholarship on Shakespeare's Folio the stationers have appeared only in minor roles. They tend to surface when scholars wonder who might have first had the idea to make the Folio: some have suggested Isaac Jaggard while others prefer Edward Blount, a figure whose work, in the words of one critic, had 'a profound impact on English cultural life' and made him 'the most important publisher of the early seventeenth century'.[28] By consensus John Smethwick and William Aspley belong in supporting roles—incidental characters who were in the right place at the right time—while a history of critical disapproval that began in the

---

[27] Emma Smith finds that readers who began the Folio in a linear fashion were almost always defeated. With the exception of the resolute William Johnstoune, whose copy is now in the library of Meisei University in Japan, Smith finds that readers gave up their ambitious reading projects in favour of dipping into 'textual hotspots': *Four Centuries*, pp. 121–82. For Valerie Wayne's view that *Cymbeline* was placed at the end of the Folio, probably by the publishers, to serve as 'a peroration for the entire volume' see: 'The First Folio's Arrangement and its Finale' in *Shakespeare Quarterly* 66.4 (2015): pp. 389–408, at pp. 391 and 408. Helen Smith finds another Folio moment where the surfaces of the book come into focus: for Smith, Othello's question 'Was this faire Paper?' (sig. 2v2r), sets the 'epistemological status of paper in doubt': '"A unique instance of art": The Proliferating Surfaces of Early Modern Paper' in *Journal of the Northern Renaissance* 8 (2017), par. 9. http://www.northernrenaissance.org, consulted 11 August 2019.
[28] Gary Taylor, 'Blount [Blunt], Edward (*bap.* 1562, *d.* in or before 1632)' in *Oxford Dictionary of National Biography* (Oxford: Oxford University Press, 2004; online edn, 3 January 2008 [accessed 1 November 2019]). For the suggestion that Isaac Jaggard masterminded the Folio venture see: Peter W. M. Blayney, 'Introduction to the Second Edition' in Shakespeare, *The Norton Facsimile*, xxviii; Sonia Massai, *Shakespeare and the Rise of the Editor* (Cambridge: Cambridge University Press, 2007), pp. 118, 161.

14 SHAKESPEARE'S SYNDICATE

nineteenth century has cast William Jaggard as the villain: an 'infamous pirate, liar, and thief', as one outraged bibliographer memorably put it.[29] But recent work is testing the conventional boundaries between literary interpretation and book history, modelling a critical practice that grants dramatic character a fresh equivalency with stationer, or with ornament, page, or typeface, in order to explore new ways of thinking about literary works. So perhaps now is the right time to ask: who were these publishers, and how did they come to make Shakespeare's book?

The Folio Syndicate

The four businesses that financed the Folio began at roughly the same time in late-sixteenth-century London.[30] After their apprenticeships, the stationers concerned were all first active in the 1590s, the same decade in which Shakespeare's own career in print began with the first edition of his narrative poem *Venus and Adonis* (1593). On the face of it, one of the striking things about the Folio is that it represents the only time this group collaborated.[31] For the previous twenty-five years or so in which these stationers had been active, each had pursued his own separate interests. But despite those disparate histories, the London book trade was not large enough for its citizens to retain anonymity. Throughout the 1590s there were (very roughly) 250 books a year printed in London. The total number of printing houses was strictly limited: in 1583 there were twenty-three printing houses in the city; in 1600 the figure was twenty-two; in 1615 there were nineteen.[32] Given the scale of the industry at this time, it is no surprise to discover that these stationers crossed paths long before 1623, even if they had never made a book together.

Some of the links between the Folio publishers came about through their shared status as members of the Stationers' Company—the organization that

---

[29] Algernon Charles Swinbourne, *Studies in Prose and Poetry* (London: Chatto & Windus, 1894), p. 90.

[30] For an overview of the Folio syndicate see Eric Rasmussen, 'Publishing the First Folio' in Emma Smith ed., *The Cambridge Companion to Shakespeare's First Folio* (Cambridge: Cambridge University Press, 2016), pp. 18–29.

[31] There were many kinds of publishing partnerships in the early seventeenth century though it is difficult to recover much detail about what they involved. This complicated forum of collaborations eventually gave way in the later seventeenth century to the rise of 'congers', in which large groups of stationers took more formalized control over the costs of printing and wholesaling. For accounts of book-trade partnerships from the early seventeenth century see: James Raven, *The Business of Books: Booksellers and the English Book Trade 1450–1850* (New Haven and London: Yale University Press, 2007), pp. 41–5; John Barnard, 'The Financing of the Authorised Version 1610–1612: Robert Barker and "Combining" and "Sleeping" Stationers', in *Publishing History* 57 (2005): pp. 5–52.

[32] John Barnard and Maureen Bell, 'Statistical tables' in John Barnard and D. F. McKenzie eds, *The Cambridge History of the Book in Britain: Volume IV 1557–1695* (Cambridge: Cambridge University Press, 2002 [paperback edn 2014]), pp. 779–84; Arber I.248; III.699 (this list of 1615 does not include the King's Printing House). On the capacities of the book trade see Mark Bland, 'The London Book-trade in 1600' in David Scott Kastan ed., *A Companion to Shakespeare* (Oxford: Blackwell Publishing, 1999), pp. 450–63.

controlled book production in England following its incorporation by royal charter in 1557.³³ In 1611, for example, four of the five Folio stationers (Isaac Jaggard was then only sixteen and not yet a freeman of the company) were 'clothed' in Stationers' Hall. This prestigious ceremony, which happened roughly every few years, saw a select group of stationers promoted into the powerful ranks of the liverymen. William Jaggard, John Smethwick, and William Aspley were all clothed on the same day—6 July—while Edward Blount was clothed by himself, in a one-off ceremony that took place a few weeks earlier.³⁴ Their promotion suggests this cohort of stationers came of age just as Shakespeare's own writing career moved towards its close. In 1614, when Edward Blount came into a valuable second share in the Stationers' Company livery stock, that share was passed on by election to John Smethwick, leaving us to wonder whether the circulation of such professional capital was assisted by amiable relations between those involved.³⁵ As these figures took on more responsibility within the Stationers' Company they encountered one another more often, though this was mostly towards the end of their careers. In 1626, for example, Blount and Aspley were appointed by the Court of Assistants to arbitrate 'matters in Controu'sye' concerning an apprentice of the bookseller Robert Allott, who would eventually take over Blount's share of the Shakespeare estate for the Second Folio of 1632.³⁶ By 1630, Aspley, Blount, and Smethwick were all members of the Court of Assistants, meaning that for a while these three booksellers met regularly as part of a group of senior stationers who kept order in the company.³⁷

Suggestive traces hint at other forms of relationship between members of this syndicate. A copy of an expensive folio advice book, published by Blount and now in the Folger Library, was bound using waste sheets of a book that was published by Smethwick. Combined with another example that embodies the opposite arrangement (whereby a copy of a Smethwick book now in the Bodleian Library is found wrapped in waste sheets of an Edward Blount publication), these traces could suggest the two booksellers traded copies of one another's stock.³⁸ One explanation for this mingling of printed matter is that booksellers typically

---

³³ The definitive history of the company's early formation is Peter W. M. Blayney, *The Stationers' Company and the Printers of London 1501–1557*, 2 vols (Cambridge: Cambridge University Press, 2013 [paperback edn 2015]).
³⁴ SCA, *Call of the Livery Book Volume 1*, TSC/1/C/01/06/01, pp. 3–4.
³⁵ William A. Jackson ed., *Records of the Court of the Stationers' Company, 1602–1640* (London: The Bibliographical Society, 1957), p. 70. Smethwick's own yeoman's share fell in part to Nathaniel Butter, who later supplied the right to print an impression of *King Lear* to the Folio publishers.
³⁶ Jackson ed., *Records of the Court*, p. 191. ³⁷ Jackson ed., *Records of the Court*, pp. 218–20.
³⁸ Robert Dallington, *Aphorismes Civill and Militarie* (1613, STC 6197), Folger Library shelfmark STC 6197 Copy 1, which was published by Blount, is wrapped in sheet C of 'The Lost Sheepe is Found' from *Three Sermons by Master Henry Smith* (1616, STC 22742) published by John Smethwick. Similarly, G. Delamothe's *The French Alphabet* (1639, STC 6550), Bodleian Library shelfmark 8° B 287 Linc., published by John Smethwick, is wrapped in sheet B of William Alexander, *A Paraensis to the Prince* (1604, STC 346), published by Edward Blount.

exchanged stock with chosen colleagues in order to offer a wider range of titles. When they did so, the books often arrived as loose sheets, unfolded and unbound, so that customers could express their own binding preferences ('if the Booke please you' wrote Blount in 1620, 'come home to my Shop, you shall have it bound ready to your hand').[39] Flimsier texts were bound swiftly and cheaply by being wrapped in a paper or vellum cover and stab-stitched with thread along the spine; for longer books, readers could opt for something more substantial in sheep or calf leather and boards, perhaps with decoration.[40] In many cases, the binder used printed waste to line the spine and binding in order to strengthen the book's structure. In a bookseller's shop, the obvious source of such waste was the leftover or damaged sheets of an unsold edition. A copy of another Smethwick book survives having been bound in just such waste sheets of a title that was printed by William Jaggard.[41] The relationship between waste sheets and host text embodied by these books may suggest the kinds of links described by Adam Smyth, in which the circulation of unwanted paper makes visible 'certain professional or even familial networks' that would otherwise remain obscure.[42]

Some of this group collaborated or responded to one another in their publishing projects. William Aspley worked with Edward Blount on several titles of moral philosophy, including the successful *Of Wisdome*, by the Frenchman Pierre Charron, friend to Michel de Montaigne, whose essays Blount also published. *Of Wisdome* proved successful enough that in 1621 the London bookseller Thomas Piper wrote to the Oxford stationer Thomas Huggins to warn him that 'I can not buie charoone at m*aste*r Asplies under 4s'; startled by the price, Piper told his colleague that he 'durst not send it at *that* rate till I know your minde' (in the same letter, Piper also tells us that Blount's edition of 'Mountaignes Essaies' was at that time 'exceeding scarse' in London).[43] Following Blount's publication of Christopher Marlowe's popular poem *Hero and Leander* (1598), William Jaggard published a translation of the Greek poet Musaeus's version of the same story. Blount financed a sixth edition of Marlowe's poem in 1613, which may have encouraged Jaggard to

---

[39] 'To the Reader' in William Cavendish[?], *Horæ subseciuæ* (1620, STC 3957), sig. A3r–v.

[40] On early modern binding see David Pearson, *English Bookbinding Styles, 1450–1800: A Handbook* (New Castle, DE: Oak Knoll Press, 2014); Stuart Bennett, *Trade Bookbinding in the British Isles 1660–1800* (London: The British Library, 2004); Aaron T. Pratt, 'Stab-Stitching and the Status of Early English Playbooks as Literature' in *The Library* 16.3 (2015): pp. 304–28.

[41] Michael Drayton, *Poems: by Michael Drayton Esquire* (1610, STC 7220), Bodleian Library shelfmark J-J Drayton f.12, is bound in waste sheets from John Davies, *A discouerie of the state of Ireland* (1613, STC 6349).

[42] Adam Smyth, 'The Scale of Early Modern Studies' in *English Literary Renaissance* 50.1 (2020): pp. 145–52, at p. 151.

[43] *John Pyper to Thomas Huggins, March 23, 1620* [1621], manuscript papers bound into a copy of Gervase Babington, *The works of the Right Reverend Father in God, Gervase Babington* (1637), Huntington Library shelfmark 28116. Aspley and Blount formed publishing partnerships for three other titles in their early careers: Jose de Acosta's *The naturall and Morall Historie of the East and West Indies* (1604, STC 94); Lodowick Bryskett's *A discourse of civill life* (1606, STC 3959); and Thommaso Buoni's *Problemes of beautie and all humane affections* (1606, STC 4103; reissued in 1618).

publish his alternative in 1616, packaged with a preface which praised that 'excellent Poem, of Maister *Marloes*'.[44] Jaggard also worked with Edward Blount on one authorial collection prior to the Folio: a title Jaggard owned that was written by the Elizabethan clergyman Edward Dering was included in a larger volume of Dering's *Workes* (1614), the publication of which was led by Blount. One year after Shakespeare's Folio was finished, John Smethwick published an edition of a poem that he probably acquired from William Aspley. This work, a love poem entitled *Philos and Licia*, seems indebted to Shakespeare's own popular epyllion *Venus and Adonis*; its arrival in 1624 suggests the Folio collaboration both emerged from, and further enabled, this wider culture of textual traffic.[45]

Archival records of these stationers' biographies occasionally reveal other links, sometimes tantalizingly close to the Folio's production. William Jaggard had a brother who also worked in the book trade: John Jaggard, a bookseller based in Fleet Street alongside John Smethwick (both Johns surface regularly in the parish archives of St Dunstan in the West). John Jaggard died in March 1622, around the time that William was printing the Folio comedies. After John's death, his orphans were supported by one Edward Mabbe.[46] Listed as a co-surety alongside Edward Mabbe is 'Joha*nn*es Jaggard Stac*i*oner', which, given the circumstances, seems likely to be a clerk's slip for 'William Jaggard' (there was no other John Jaggard active as a stationer at this time). It is also likely, though not certain, that Edward Mabbe was the brother of James Mabbe, whose poem on the 'memorie of M. W. *Shake-speare*' is found among the Folio preliminaries.[47] We know that James Mabbe was a close friend of Edward Blount, but this note hints at other links between the Mabbes and the Jaggards, and so it reinforces our sense that the industry of early modern book production was shaped by the social and familial relations of its members.

A final caution applies to all four members of this syndicate: none of them were 'publishers' in the way that we understand that word today. That is, they were not dedicated solely to financing book production. In the language of the day William and Isaac Jaggard were printers, a role that saw them and their workforce carry out the labour of making books that were often financed by others (though in chapter two I show the Jaggards were also a significant publishing force). John

---

[44] 'To the Commune Reader' in George Chapman trans., *The Divine Poem of Musæus* (1616, STC 18304), sig. A7v–8r.

[45] *A Pleasant and Delightfull Poeme of Two Lovers, Philos and Licia* (1624, STC 19886). The right to copy for this work was first entered by William Aspley on 2 October 1606, but either Aspley did not publish an edition or no copies survive: Arber III.330. No subsequent transfer between Aspley and Smethwick was recorded in the Stationers' Register, so it is possible that a silent intermediary was involved. Another post-Folio transaction saw 'mist*r*ess Jaggard' (the widow of John Jaggard, brother to William) transfer titles to John Smethwick on 24 February 1625: Arber IV.151; SCA, *Register D*, p. 113.

[46] *Wardmote Inquest Book, St Dunstan in the West*, LMA CLC/W/JB/044/MS03018/001, fol. 105v; *Court of Orphans Recognizances 1590–1633*, LMA CLA/002/05/001, fol. 255v.

[47] I. M., 'To the memorie of M. W. *Shake-speare*' in Shakespeare, *Comedies, Histories, & Tragedies*, sig. πA6r. The initials are generally accepted to identify Mabbe.

Smethwick, William Aspley, and Edward Blount were all booksellers, meaning they carried out a much wider range of activities than publishing alone.[48] Those who ran bookshops in early modern London sold a range of retail books, of course, probably alongside prints, maps, ink, quills, and an associated cultural bricolage that in the case of the bookseller Thomas Dewe, tenuously linked to the Shakespeare canon through his publication of *The troublesome raigne of John King of England* (1622), extended to cookery moulds.[49] We know that booksellers carried out a range of quasi-editorial activities for the books they sponsored, but in 1601 it was also possible for a passing visitor to 'sup and lye' for the night at Blount's bookshop, having first 'borrowed Bluntes cloake', transforming the Black Bear into something like a boarding house, albeit one well stocked with reading material.[50] Other evidence shows that bookshops could act as post offices. An amicable letter written by the same Leonard Digges whose poem features in the opening pages of the Folio contains a note urging its recipient, 'Master Philip Washington' to 'sende the inclosed to Ned Blounte' in 1631; it is just one of many letters that implicate bookshops in networks of exchange.[51] The wider activities of Blount in particular are recorded in his own correspondence, supplied in an appendix to this book. These letters show Blount acted as a broker of currency exchanges and circulated books and manuscripts alongside gossip and the letters of his friends. We could easily push this range of book-anchored activities further: at various times in the late sixteenth and seventeenth centuries we can find authors using the bookshops of their publishers as a base from which to offer tuition for shipbuilding; language-learning techniques; advice on cookery; and singing classes (Tuesdays and Thursdays, between 10 a.m. and 12 noon).[52]

---

[48] On the various activities of early modern bookshops see Ben Higgins, "The Book-sellars Shop': Browsing, Reading, and Buying in Early Modern England' in Adam Smyth ed., *The Oxford Handbook of the History of the Book in Early Modern England* (Oxford: Oxford University Press, forthcoming 2022); Gary Taylor, 'Making Meaning Marketing Shakespeare 1623,' in Peter Holland and Stephen Orgel eds, *From Performance to Print in Shakespeare's England* (Basingstoke: Palgrave Macmillan, 2006), pp. 55–72.

[49] Amid the preliminaries of a book of recipes, one page advertises that those 'desirous of any of the Moulds mentioned in the Booke' may find them 'at the shoppe of *Thomas Dewe* in St. *Dunstons* Church-yarde': John Murrell, *A delightfull daily exercise for ladies and gentlewomen* (1621, STC 18302), sig. A7r.

[50] Folger Library MS V. b. 187, fol. 5v. Thanks to Peter W. M. Blayney for pointing me towards this manuscript.

[51] British Library Lansdowne MS 841, fol. 30v. Other letters in the same volume were left at bookshops for collection (see ff. 14, 25).

[52] In 1614, carpenters were invited to learn shipbuilding techniques from the author and mariner Tobias Gentleman, who offered his instruction 'at M. *Nathaniel Butters*, a Stationers Shop': *Englands Way to Win Wealth* (1614, STC 11745), sig. G3v. Towards the end of the sixteenth century in 1575, another author, Claudius Hollyband, could be found 'teaching in Paules Churcheyarde', offering Italian lessons 'by the signe of the *Lucrece*', meaning he taught either in or beside the bookshop of his printer and publisher, the stationer Thomas Purfoot (Diego de San Pedro, *The pretie and wittie historie of Arnalt & Lucenda* [1575, STC 6758], sig. π1r); see also the French lessons offered by G. Delamothe from bookshops (*The French alphabeth* [1592, STC 6545.5], sig. B1r); the recipe writer Hannah Woolley supplies valuable evidence of women readers visiting bookshops in her book *The Ladies*

All this to say that when in this book I refer to the Jaggards, Blount, Aspley, and Smethwick as the syndicate of Folio 'publishers', I do so in the narrow sense of this being the team that financed Shakespeare's plays in partnership, but with the understanding that publishing and bookselling businesses also relied on a range of other social and commercial practices, many of which I touch on in the chapters of this book.

Assembling the Collection

One major challenge of making the Folio was the need to gather Shakespeare's writings and to secure the necessary permissions for their printing. By the early 1620s, many different stationers owned some part of Shakespeare's literary estate.[53] These ownership claims usually depended on a stationer having at some point entered the play into the Stationers' Register (all register entrances relating to Shakespeare are listed in chapter three, which explores the interpretive consequences of this scattered ownership of literary property).[54] The Folio syndicate itself could collectively claim ownership of just nine of the thirty-six Shakespeare plays that were eventually included in the volume, which meant that publishing the First Folio involved significant negotiations.

The Jaggards owned none of Shakespeare's plays before they began work on the Folio, but they had some luck during the process. It seems that during the printing the Jaggards realized they could legitimately claim the rights to *As You Like It*

Directory (1662, Wing W3281), which includes a preface to 'all LADIES & GENTLEWOMEN' that invites readers to consult Woolley herself 'where you find these Books are to be sold' (A3v–4r). After the Restoration in 1661, the author of a new music book offered singing tuition 'at Joseph Cranfords House a Stationer, at the Signe of the Gun near the West End of St-Pauls Church': Hartlib Papers, 8/66A–B.

[53] What it meant to 'own' an early modern text and the ways in which stationers could defend their property are explained by Peter W. M. Blayney, 'The Publication of Playbooks', in John Cox and David Scott Kastan eds, *A New History of Early English Drama* (New York: Columbia University Press, 1997), pp. 394–405. For the ownership of Shakespeare's plays see Greg, *Shakespeare First Folio*, pp. 58–75. Greg's account of the plays' textual history and status is now dated, but his summary of the ownership claims for individual plays remains valuable. Hinman, *Printing and Proofreading*, vol. 1, pp. 24–30 offers a slightly different account. More recently, James J. Marino discusses the ownership of several Folio plays in *Owning William Shakespeare: The King's Men and their Intellectual Property* (Philadelphia, PA: University of Pennsylvania Press, 2011), pp. 125–33. See also Blayney, *First Folio* 1991, pp. 17–23; Smith, *Making*, pp. 140–3.

[54] The Stationers' Register is the name given by modern scholars to a series of manuscripts in the Stationers' Company archives, parts of which were transcribed by Edward Arber in the late nineteenth century (Arber, vols I–V). Among other things, these manuscripts contain 'register entries': dated records written by the company clerk of a named stationer paying a fee to enter a particular title in order to protect their 'right to copy', meaning the stationer's right to print that title. The Stationers' Register thus preserves an early form of copyright for written works, though with some important differences from the version later enshrined by the Copyright Act of 1710 (see Blayney, 'Publication of Playbooks', 398–405). Recently Blayney has pointed out that the material contained in these manuscripts, particularly the earlier volumes, is more various than we have realized: 'If It Looks Like a Register…' in *The Library* 20.2 (2019): pp. 230–42. See also Giles Bergel and Ian Gadd eds, *Stationers Register Online*: https://stationersregister.online.

through inheritance. The title, or 'right to copy', for this comedy had first been entered into the Stationers' Register in 1600 by a printer named James Roberts.[55] A few years later in around 1606 William Jaggard took over Roberts' printing house, which seems to have enabled Jaggard to claim *As You Like It* along with the rest of Roberts' property.

Edward Blount owned the title to two plays—*Pericles* and *Antony and Cleopatra*—both of which he entered into the Stationers' Register on the same day in May of 1608.[56] But Blount does not seem to have much cared about either work. The first edition of *Pericles* was published in 1609 by another bookseller named Henry Gosson. There is no record of the right to copy being transferred between the two stationers, but neither is there any record that Blount felt his rights had been breached, and so it looks as though Blount was happy to let the play go; it eventually ended up in the hands of Thomas Pavier. For reasons that we do not fully understand, *Pericles* was not ultimately included in the Folio collection (an omission that has, as Emma Smith notes, haunted the play's critical reception ever since).[57] Neither did Blount publish *Antony and Cleopatra*. Instead, he set the play aside in a way that suggests that he forgot about it entirely. In November of 1623, during the final stages of the Folio's printing, Blount and Isaac Jaggard registered their ownership of sixteen Shakespeare plays that had not previously been protected (Figure 0.4). These sixteen plays are listed in the Stationers' Register in the order in which they appear in the Folio itself: 'Anthonie & Cleopatra' is found in the 'Tragedies' section of the entry between 'Mackbeth' and 'Cymbeline', and so Blount and Jaggard must have considered this title to be an unguarded property.[58] However the fee beside this entry (seven shillings, written in a different ink and thus probably at a different moment from the creation of the list) is the sum owed for fourteen plays, not sixteen. Peter Blayney has explained this discrepancy by suggesting that a search of the earlier registers discovered that Blount already owned *Antony and Cleopatra*, and that this was also the moment when the Jaggards realized they had a plausible claim to *As You Like It* through James Roberts' earlier entry.[59]

---

[55] SCA, *Register C*, unfoliated flyleaf; Arber III.37. *As You Like It* was one of four plays entered together and bracketed with the note requiring them 'to be staied', meaning the titles were reserved in some way. Several things about this entry remain mysterious: see Evelyn May Albright, 'To be Staied' in *PMLA* 30.3 (1915): pp. 451–99; William Shakespeare, *As You Like It*, edited by Juliet Dusinberre (London: Arden Shakespeare, 2006), pp. 120–5.

[56] SCA, *Register C*, fol. 167v; Arber III.378.

[57] Smith, *Making*, p. 14. Possible reasons for the exclusion of *Pericles*—none of which seem entirely convincing—include difficulties in securing the right to print; objections to the quality of the text; or the fact that the play was only partly Shakespearean, being a work written in collaboration with George Wilkins. The printers of the Second Folio (Thomas and Richard Cotes) owned the rights to *Pericles* when F2 was published in 1632, but still chose not to include the play in this second edition (see fn. 116 on p. 208).

[58] SCA, *Register D*, p. 69; Arber IV.107. [59] Blayney, *First Folio* 1991, pp. 18–21.

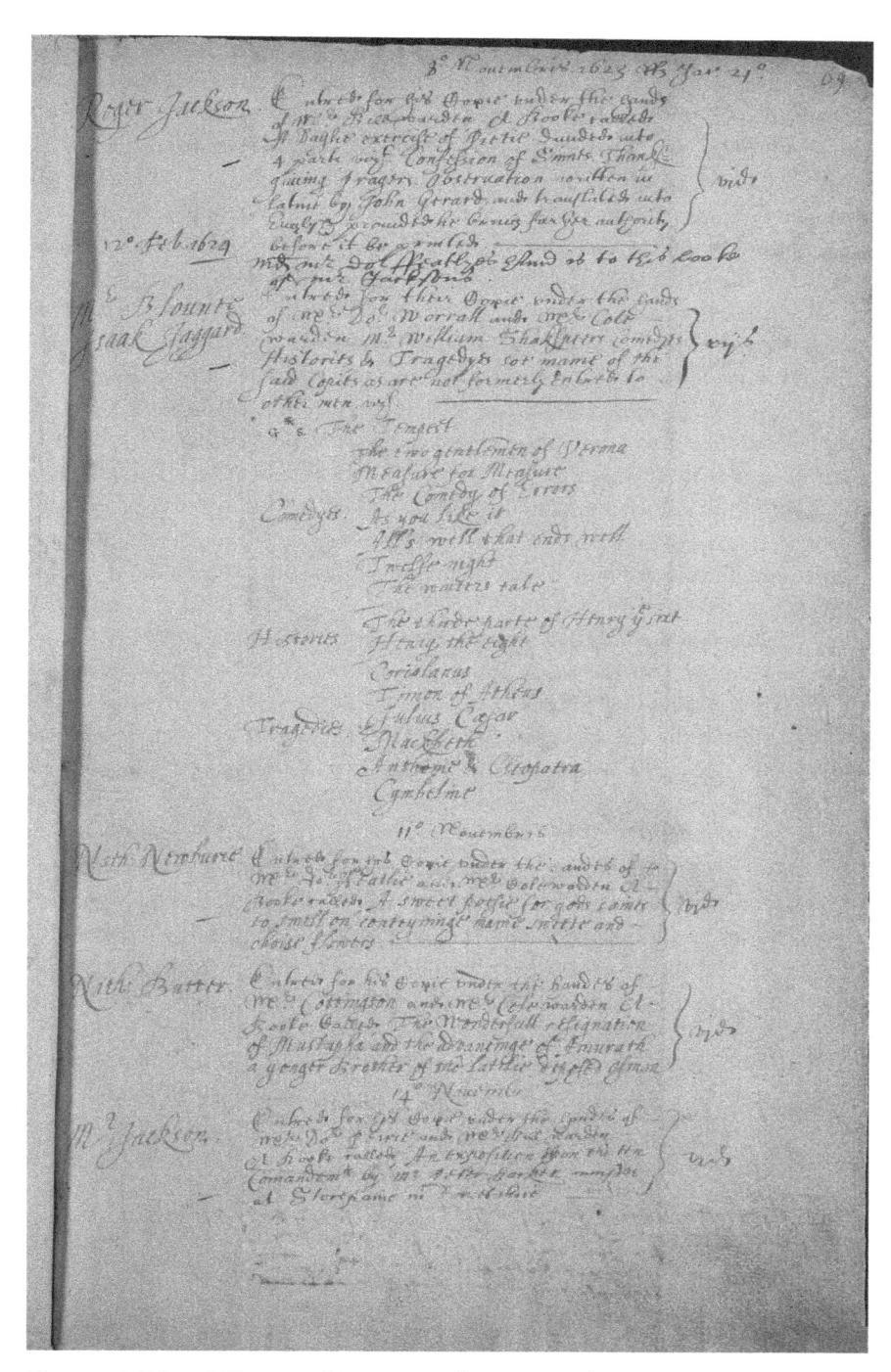

Figure 0.4 Edward Blount and Isaac Jaggard's entrance of sixteen Shakespeare plays in the Stationers' Register on 8 November 1623. Image of SCA, *Register D*, p. 69. Credit: The Stationers' Company Archive.

So the two leading businesses jointly accounted for just three plays, one of which they chose not to include. John Smethwick, who owned the rights to four plays, held more of Shakespeare's work than Blount and the Jaggards combined. The three titles he clearly owned were *Hamlet*, *Romeo and Juliet*, and *Love's Labour's Lost*, all of which he acquired from the estate of a bookseller named Nicholas Ling in 1607. In the same entry Smethwick also acquired the right to print 'The taminge of A Shrewe' from Ling, which technically identifies an anonymous play by that title but which probably also gave Smethwick the right to print the Shakespearean work *The Taming of the Shrew*.[60] The final member of the syndicate, William Aspley, held the right to copy for both *2 Henry IV* and *Much Ado About Nothing*. Aspley registered both plays in 1600 in partnership with the bookseller Andrew Wise.[61] The pair jointly published one edition of each title later that year before Wise died (or at least, disappeared from the documentary record), leaving Aspley with full ownership of two plays that, like Blount, he then put aside and chose not to publish, focusing his career on other ventures discussed in chapter three.

If we combine the titles owned by members of the syndicate with the plays that are listed in the entry of November 1623 then we reach a total of twenty-two plays: not far off two-thirds of the Folio's contents. None of the sixteen plays listed in the November entry had previously been printed (including *The Tempest*, *Twelfth Night*, *Julius Caesar*, and *Macbeth*, among others). To acquire these manuscripts the syndicate must have dealt with Shakespeare's theatre company, which had, in 1619, secured particular control over its work through an order forbidding any of its plays from being printed 'wthout consent'.[62] As far as we can tell, gaining that consent from the King's Men created no difficulties. The Folio has clear support from the theatre: the book's two opening addresses are signed by leading members of the company, and one of these addresses—that which is headed '*To the great Variety of Readers*'—urges readers to buy the volume. The salesmanship of this address has generated consistent speculation about its authorship. Alfred Pollard, for example, wondered whether, despite the neatly printed ascription to '*John Heminge*' and '*Henrie Condell*', the address was written by Edward Blount.[63] But lobbying for sales may have been in the interests of the theatre. Perhaps the King's Men acquired a number of copies as part of their agreement to provide manuscripts, or perhaps they hoped that sales of the Folio

---

[60] SCA, *Register C*, fol. 161r; Arber III.365. For the relationship between the two *Shrew* plays see William Shakespeare, *The Taming of the Shrew*, edited by Barbara Hodgdon (London: Methuen, 2010), pp. 7–18.
[61] SCA, *Register C*, fol. 63v; Arber III.170.   [62] Jackson, *Records*, p. 110.
[63] Alfred W. Pollard, *Shakespeare Folios and Quartos: A Study in the Bibliography of Shakespeare's Plays 1594–1685* (London: Methuen and Company, 1909), p. 122. For a summary of attributions see Francis X. Connor, 'Preliminaries in the First Folio' in William Shakespeare, *The New Oxford Shakespeare: The Complete Works Critical Reference Edition*, 2 vols, edited by Gary Taylor, John Jowett, Terri Bourus, and Gabriel Egan (Oxford: Oxford University Press, 2017), vol. 2, pp. lxxi–lxxxiii at lxxii.

would encourage interest in performances of the plays, mobilizing the kinds of back-and-forth dynamics between bookshop and playhouse suggested by Thomas Middleton in his play *The Roaring Girle* (1611). Middleton's preface to this play anticipates the printed book being allowed both 'chamber-roome at your lodging' and also 'Gallery roome at the play-house', making clear that he envisages the reader carrying the quarto to a performance, perhaps of Middleton's own play.[64] As Tiffany Stern suggests, printed plays may have reminded audiences of 'fine performances in the past' and perhaps also 'advertised forthcoming productions'.[65] It is difficult to imagine readers balancing a copy of the roughly 900-page Folio on their knees in a theatre (except perhaps for those who sat in the private spaces above the stage of the Globe, an area Ben Jonson described as 'the lords roome'), but even so an impressive new collection of plays may well have excited fresh interest in Shakespeare and the repertory of the King's Men.[66]

Having dealt with each other and with the King's Men, the members of the Folio syndicate still needed to collect fourteen last titles, each of which had already been printed or claimed. These fourteen titles were owned by eight other stationers, meaning the Folio syndicate negotiated with each of these figures to secure a one-off right to include their play or plays in a single edition of the Folio.[67]

Very little evidence survives to help us understand what these discussions involved (though chapter three includes parallel examples of stationers gathering titles for a collected works with varying outcomes). However occasional references in the stationers' archives invite some speculation. In February of 1613, a stationers' court set out a decree relating to the 'Buyinge of imp^{r}ssions', which tells us that if the 'owner of a copy, shall sell a whole impression of a booke or copy to any freeman or brother of the companie' then the original owner of the title was forbidden to 'prynt the same booke or copie againe' without reaching an agreement with those that had 'bought thympression'.[68] This decree describes stationers

---

[64] 'To the Comicke, Play-readers, Venery, and Laughter' in Thomas Middleton, *The Roaring Girle* (1611, STC 17908), sig. A3r.

[65] Tiffany Stern, 'Watching as Reading: The Audience and Written Text in Shakespeare's Playhouse' in Laurie Maguire ed., *How to Do Things with Shakespeare: New Approaches, New Essays* (Oxford: Blackwell, 2008), pp. 136–59 at p. 139.

[66] Ben Jonson, 'Every Man out of his Humour' in *The workes of Benjamin Jonson* (1616, STC 14752), sigs. G1r–P4r, at I6v.

[67] These eight other stationers, together with the plays they owned, were Arthur Johnson (*The Merry Wives of Windsor*); Lawrence Hayes (*The Merchant of Venice*); Thomas Dewe (?*King John*); Matthew Law (*Richard II, 1 Henry IV, Richard III*); Thomas Pavier (*Henry V, 2* and *3 Henry VI*, and ?*Titus Andronicus*); Henry Walley (*Troilus and Cressida*); Nathaniel Butter (*King Lear*); and Thomas Walkley (*Othello*). The question marks represent claims that are less clear but probably held. The final title was *A Midsummer Night's Dream*, which, to use Greg's term, was 'derelict', meaning it had no registered owner following the death of the bookseller Thomas Fisher.

[68] Jackson, *Records*, p. 57. For modern bibliographers an *impression* is all the copies of an *edition* that were printed at any one time. This technical definition of an impression recognizes that it was possible for work on a single edition to be paused, meaning one edition could in theory contain multiple impressions. But throughout the handpress period metal type that was used to print a book was almost never left standing in a forme, both because printers constantly needed the type for other work

buying an entire edition (or 'whole impression') of ready printed books from a printer or publisher wholesale, rather than leasing the right to print a text in a collection. But the wording of the decree may also suggest that the owner of the copy was only forbidden from printing his book again 'vppon any such impression' actually being printed, which could imply that the decree also sought to regulate a slightly different situation, whereby one stationer bought the right to print an impression from the owner of the copy.[69] If correct, that interpretation would bring us a little closer to the Folio scenario. In either case, the main purpose of the decree was the same: it sought to protect the stationer who bought an impression (whether that word identified physical copies or also stretched to include a conceptual impression-to-be) from dealing with unexpected competition for their sales.

If this decree does not quite cover the situation in which the Folio syndicate found itself, the rules it established around the sale of impressions nevertheless help us understand the concerns stationers brought to such negotiations. If the syndicate established similar terms with the eight stationers from whom they leased the right to print a play, then those terms could explain some oddities in the history of Shakespeare's books that have puzzled scholars either side of the Folio's publication. After a gradual decline of interest in Shakespeare's writing, there was a sudden flurry of new editions in the early 1620s. Three new editions of Shakespeare plays appeared in 1622, and a fourth—the *Troublesome Reign of King John*—was attributed to Shakespeare on its title page. Two of these editions were published by the bookseller Matthew Law, a stationer who initially withheld three of Shakespeare's bestselling titles from the Folio syndicate: the first part of *Henry IV*, and both *Richard II* and *Richard III* (Hinman found that the Folio's printing was disrupted in these sections, suggesting problems in the negotiations with Law).[70] It seems likely that Law's editions of both *1 Henry IV* and *Richard III* in 1622 were printed alongside the Folio negotiations, perhaps because Law felt that if there was any chance of reaching an agreement with the syndicate, he should make the most of his titles before a contract required him not to reprint the plays for a period of time. The bookseller Thomas Walkley's edition of *Othello* (1622) may similarly have been published with the aim of capitalizing on his property before leasing an impression to the syndicate. The appearance of these early 1620s Shakespeare quartos further complicates the temporality of the Folio's publication: they are both standalone editions and probably also the visible

---

and because in 1587 the Stationers' Company restricted the use of such 'standing formes' to protect the livelihoods of compositors. The upshot is that despite the modern difference between the two terms, 'impression' and 'edition' mean broadly the same thing throughout the early modern period.

[69] Buying the right to print 'one Impression onely' of titles owned by the Stationers' Company was relatively common: Arber III.101, 157, 213, 251, 284; Jackson, *Records*, p. 484.

[70] Hinman, *Printing and Proof-Reading*, vol. 2, p. 523. For a summary see Ben Higgins, 'Printing the Folio,' in Emma Smith ed., *The Cambridge Companion to Shakespeare's First Folio* (Cambridge: Cambridge University Press, 2016), pp. 30–47.

INTRODUCTION   25

signals that a larger venture was underway. The only Shakespeare quartos published in the immediate years after the Folio's publication were the undated fourth editions of *Romeo and Juliet* (1623) and *Hamlet* (1625), financed by John Smethwick. Given that all of Smethwick's other Shakespeare quartos are clearly dated, these two less forthcoming title pages may record Smethwick's attempt to evade any restrictions agreed during the Folio negotiations about the printing of individual plays.[71]

The syndicate formed under the dual pressures of securing the necessary titles and sharing the expenses of the venture. So how much would these negotiations have cost? When booksellers bought the right to print an impression of a title from the Stationers' Company itself, they usually paid a fee to the company's poor fund. So in 1615, the bookseller John Budge paid the Stationers' Company forty shillings to publish an edition of John Foxe's writings, the right to copy for which was owned by the company; for every further impression, Budge was told, 'he shall pay to the Company 40ˢ more'.[72] That fee of forty shillings, or two pounds, is repeated elsewhere in similar contexts, but it also varied, perhaps because the value of an impression depended on the number of copies printed (and so the expected profits), and also on the perceived value of the title.[73] In January 1604, for example, the company charged the bookseller Cuthbert Burby four pounds for 'one Impression onely' of a title he needed to finish a collected *Workes* of the clergyman Richard Greenham; at other times, the company simply asked for a standard royalty fee of sixpence in the pound (or 2.5 per cent) from the stationer's profits to be given to the company's poor fund.[74] And money was not the only form of capital at stake: in negotiating such deals, stationers sometimes used payment in kind, rather than cash, whereby a certain number of copies of the finished book were promised in exchange for the right to print.[75]

The situation faced by members of the Folio syndicate was complicated by having to deal with various sharp-minded individuals rather than with the Stationers' Company itself. In addition to the vexed dealings with Matthew Law, just a few of the earliest copies of the Folio to be sold are missing an entire play. The publishing

---

[71] For the dates of the undated fourth quartos of *Hamlet* and *Romeo and Juliet*, see: R. Carter Hailey, 'The Dating Game: New Evidence for the Dates of Q4 *Romeo and Juliet* and Q4 *Hamlet*,' in *Shakespeare Quarterly* 58.3 (2007): pp. 367–87. Hailey considers the absence of dates at pp. 385–7.

[72] Jackson, *Records*, p. 76.

[73] In 1640 the bookseller William Sheares paid forty shillings for an impression of a book by Thomas More; in 1636 Mary Allott, the bookseller widow of Robert Allott, paid six pounds for 'leaue to print 3. Impressiones' of *The mirrour of martyrs*: Jackson, *Records*, pp. 337, 484.

[74] Arber III.251. Burby's fee was repeated seven years later when the bookseller William Welby sought the same permission (Arber III.452). The printer 'Mʳ Coates' paied £3, 6s, 6d for 'leaue to print an Impression of Latymeres sermones' in 1636 (Jackson, *Records*, p. 484); Elizabeth Purslowe paied just one pound for an impression of *The gentile craft* in 1640 (Jackson, *Records*, p. 489). For examples of the 'sixpence in the pound' model as a tax on buying an impression see Arber III.103, 284, 371.

[75] Jackson, *Records*, p. 67. In 1611 the bookseller Edward White 1 agreed to give another bookseller, Alice Gosson, twenty-five copies of Luis de Granada's *Of prayer and meditation* (1611, STC 16911.5) in exchange for the right to publish an impression: Jackson, *Records*, p. 49.

team only managed to come to terms with Henry Walley, the owner of *Troilus and Cressida*, after the book was finished, meaning that some readers bought a Folio that contained thirty-five plays (which is the number of titles listed on the 'catalogue' page of the book's contents) before the publishers hastily added the thirty-sixth.[76] Two decades later, such fractious discussions were repeated for the 1647 folio edition of the collected plays of Francis Beaumont and John Fletcher, Shakespeare's successors as the lead dramatists for the King's Men. This time the book's publisher, Humphrey Moseley, was forthcoming about the effort it took to gather the various plays. ''Twere vaine to mention the *Chargeablenesse* of this Work,' Moseley grumbled, before continuing:

> those who own'd the *Manuscripts*, too well knew their value to make a cheap estimate of any of these Pieces, and though another joyn'd with me in the *Purchase* and Printing, yet the *Care & Pains* was wholly mine, which I found to be more then you'l easily imagine, unlesse you knew into how many hands the Originalls were dispersed.[77]

The labour of gathering an authorial corpus from 'many hands' belonged to Moseley, who thus created that corpus in ways the Folio syndicate earlier achieved for Shakespeare. Moseley tells us that a publishing partner (the stationer Humphrey Robinson) 'joyn'd with me' to share some of the costs, but he also makes clear that the rest of the work—'more then you'l easily imagine'—was his alone. The Folio publishers had to barter and leverage their social and professional credit in similar ways to complete their collection. The '*Care & Pains*', as Moseley put it, for this protracted, risky, and at times hostile run of negotiations was ultimately in the hands of the four businesses listed above who paid for the book, probably primarily Edward Blount and the Jaggards.

It seems likely that Blount and the Jaggards led negotiations because the documentary evidence we have for the making of the Folio consistently foregrounds the involvement of their businesses while Aspley and Smethwick appear only in the book's colophon.[78] This sense that the syndicate had a two-tier arrangement would have shaped other facets of the collaboration. Though all the businesses

---

[76] Blayney, *First Folio* 1991, pp. 17–23.

[77] 'The Stationer to the Readers', in Francis Beaumont and John Fletcher, *Comedies and Tragedies written by Francis Beaumont and John Fletcher* (1647, Wing B1581), sig. A4v.

[78] The first evidence of the Folio being planned is an advert from 1622, placed in the catalogue of the Frankfurt Book Fair by Isaac Jaggard: *Catalogus uniuersalis pro nundinis Francofurtensibus autumnalibus*…(1622, STC 11329.8). A second advert for the Folio was taken out in 1624 by Edward Blount: *Catalogus universalis pronundinis Francofurtensibus vernalibus*…(1624, STC 11330.2). Both adverts are discussed in chapter one, as is the fact that most authors of the preliminary verses can be connected to Blount in various ways. It was also Edward Blount, together with Isaac Jaggard, who entered the sixteen plays in the Stationers' Register as described above. Other than the Folio's imprint and colophon, one final scrap of evidence foregrounds William Jaggard's role. A manuscript note on the title page of one copy of the Folio records that the book was gifted to its owner by William Jaggard in

were responsible for the 'Charges' of the book, as the colophon records, they may have contributed different amounts. There are examples of co-published books where each partner was required to 'beare their ratable partes of all charges', meaning that each paid according to their stake in the venture; the number of copies each syndicate member finally received would also have been in proportion to their investment.[79] Being the leading figures may have involved one final advantage for Blount and the Jaggards: a reference from 1584 tells us that when any book was published in partnership, 'The printer shall deliu' the wast' sheets of the book 'to the best of ye pten's' (or partners), in order that those involved could use this waste 'to make vp those [copies] yt be vnpfect'.[80] If this order held in 1623, then it was probably Blount and Isaac Jaggard who were best placed to offer the kinds of 'perfecting' services for damaged or incomplete Folio copies that are hinted at in the accounts of a Gray's Inn student named John Buxton. Having bought his Shakespeare Folio at some point before 1627, Buxton that year paid six shillings 'for the changing of Shak-spheares works for on that is perfect', leaving behind an imperfect copy in need of correction.[81]

As I suggest in chapter four, the physical spaces to which a book belonged could contribute to the value and meaning of that book. In the Jaggard printing house, the 750-odd copies that made up the first edition of Shakespeare's Folio were accountable to correctors and proofreaders.[82] Once finished, the gradual dispersal of the edition began, perhaps in surprising ways. It was a rule of the Stationers' Company, reaffirmed in 1622, that 'euery workman that worketh vpon anie Booke' was owed a copy of that book.[83] Some master printers opted to pay their compositors and pressmen extra money in lieu of this privilege, known as 'copy money', but in a happy rebuttal to traditional stories about the Folio's reception, which emphasize the book's success with 'noblemen and commoners of standing', this rule suggests that the earliest figures to have claimed a copy of the finished Folio were those who physically laboured over the book's creation.[84] Copies of the edition would then have been divided between the four businesses

---

1623. In a Latin note, the herald Augustine Vincent describes Jaggard as the 'Typographi', or the 'printer' of the book (Figure 2.3 on p. 100. This copy is now Folger Library STC 22273 Fo.1 no.01).

[79] W. W. Greg and E. Boswell eds, *Records of the Court of the Stationers' Company 1576 to 1602 from Register B* (London: The Bibliographical Society, 1930), p. 43 (three stationers collaborating on an edition in 1592 in a ratio of 2:1:1). See also the three partners responsible for 'ratable charges' for an edition of 1599 (p. 67), and a list from 1595 which distributes copies of an edition among the ten stationers who financed it: two were to receive 200 copies and eight received 100 (p. 51).

[80] Greg and Boswell eds, *Records of the Court*, p. 16.

[81] David McKitterick, '"Ovid with a Littleton": The Cost of English Books in the Early Seventeenth Century' in *Transactions of the Cambridge Bibliographical Society* 11.2 (1997): pp. 184–234 at p. 215.

[82] Estimates for how many copies of the First Folio were printed have ranged between 250 and 1,500 copies. Modern scholars follow Peter W. M. Blayney's judgement of about 750. For a summary see West, *The Shakespeare First Folio* vol. 1., p. 4.

[83] Jackson, *Records* 148. See also D. F. McKenzie, *The Cambridge University Press 1696–1712: A Bibliographical Study*, 2 vols (Cambridge: Cambridge University Press, 1966), vol. 1, pp. 74–5.

[84] West, *The Shakespeare First Folio*, vol. 1, p. 6.

that acted as wholesalers. It was at this point that members of the syndicate would stock their own shelves, exchange copies with other booksellers, and offer the book for sale to customers. As the rest of this introduction shows, the ways in which the Folio syndicate curated this final transition from production to reception held rich potential to influence the book's success.

Reading Early Modern Publication

In 1650, the French letter-writer Jean-Louis Guez de Balzac learned that his collected works had been published by the famous Dutch house run by the Elsevier family. Delighted, de Balzac wrote to his new publisher:

> I have been made a part of the immortal republic. I have been received in the society of demi-gods. In effect, we all live together at Leyden under the same roof. Thanks to you, sometimes I am a neighbor of Pliny; sometimes I find myself beside Seneca, sometimes above Tacitus and Livy.[85]

De Balzac was not the only figure to admire the Elsevier books. 'On my coffin, when in the grave' wrote the Cambridge physician Sir William Browne in his will, 'I desire may be deposited, in its leather-case or coffin, my Pocket Elzevir Horace'.[86] What both de Balzac's excitable letter and Browne's sepulchral request remind us of, in their different ways, is how powerful the brand of an early modern publisher could be. De Balzac was enthralled by his membership of a group formed by the Elsevier imprint. He understood that admission to this 'immortal republic' conferred a kind of associative, co-textual glory. For Browne, writing much later towards the end of the eighteenth century, his Elsevier volume deserved its own 'coffin' within Browne's own casket. The Elsevier name seems as important as that of Horace (this equivalency in Browne's will between author and publisher is found in several early modern examples).[87] We have no way of

---

[85] David W. Davies, *The World of the Elseviers 1580–1712* (The Hague: Martinus Nijhoff, 1954), p. 150. At the same place Davies points out a similar response from the poet Gilles Ménage in 1663: 'Elsevier, my sweet glory [...] the friends of learning value and seek your charming productions; book lovers throng to your shop'. See also Andrew Pettegree, 'A Whole New World? Publishing in the Dutch Golden Age', in Alexander S. Wilkinson and Graeme J. Kemp eds, *Negotiating Conflict and Controversy in the Early Modern Book World* (Leiden: Brill, 2019), pp. 73–87, at pp. 76–8. For the humanist scholar Erasmus' belief that publication by the Aldine Press would grant his writing 'immortality' see Richard McCabe, *'Ungainefull Arte': Poetry, Patronage, and Print in the Early Modern Era* (Oxford: Oxford University Press, 2016), p. 214.

[86] The anecdote is sometimes (understandably given its sepulchral ethos) attributed to the prose stylist Sir Thomas Browne but see Hugh James Rose ed., *A New General Biographical Dictionary*, 12 vols (London: B. Fellowes et. al., 1848), vol. 5, p. 113.

[87] Edward Blount's name can be found in several places—written on the spine of a book, or in the inscription on the first leaf of a manuscript work, or in entries that record books in an inventory—where we might expect the name of the work's author. For examples of this in both print and

knowing how Shakespeare felt about his own publishing syndicate, or at the prospect of finding himself a neighbour, on the shelves of Edward Blount, for example, of Michel de Montaigne, sometimes above Christopher Marlowe and Miguel de Cervantes, but as scholars have increasingly shown in recent years, a book's publisher could matter to both authors and readers, even if the houses involved were not as grand as the Dutch Elseviers.

Amid a vibrant field that has taken its cue from D. F. McKenzie and explored the different roles played by members of the early modern book trade—whether printers, binders, or press licensers—scholars have paid particular attention to the interpretive potential of publishers.[88] Much of this work was inspired by Zachary Lesser's book *Renaissance Drama and the Politics of Publication*, which examined how in financing an edition, a publisher did not 'merely bring a commodity to market' in an inert and neutral way, 'but also imagines, and helps to construct, the purchasers of that commodity and their interpretations of it'.[89] Lesser's work led to significant developments within Shakespeare studies as scholars working against the traditions of formalist New Criticism explored ways in which publishers shaped the meanings of early modern books. The field continues to grow: Adam G. Hooks has provided a compelling, 'bio-bibliographic' account of Shakespeare's printed work by attending to 'the ways in which particular poems and plays were bought and sold within particular bookshops at particular times'.[90] Kirk Melnikoff has traced the range of bookish activities carried out by Elizabethan publishers (acquiring copy, translating texts, compiling collections,

---

manuscript see Belton House Library NT 3058918; Huntington Library 475778; Durham Cathedral Library Hunter MS 130; Edinburgh University Library, MS H-P. Coll. 401, fol. 103r-v; Rosenbach Museum and Library, MS 239/18, pp. 8 and 23–6; and Heidi Brayman Hackel, *Reading Material in Early Modern England: Print, Gender, and Literacy* (Cambridge: Cambridge University Press, 2005), p. 266.

[88] D. F. McKenzie, *Bibliography and the Sociology of Texts* (Cambridge: Cambridge University Press, 1999); Peter D. McDonald and Michael F. Suarez eds, *Making Meaning: 'Printers of the Mind' and Other Essays* (Amherst, MA: University of Massachusetts Press, 2002).

[89] Zachary Lesser, *Renaissance Drama and the Politics of Publication* (Cambridge: Cambridge University Press, 2004), p. 17. Other important studies in this field include the two collections edited by Marta Straznicky: *Shakespeare's Stationers: Studies in Cultural Bibliography* (Philadelphia, PA: University of Pennsylvania Press, 2012); *The Book of the Play: Playwrights, Stationers, and Readers in Early Modern England* (Amherst, MA: University of Massachusetts Press, 2006); Massai, *Rise of the Editor*; Erne, *Literary Dramatist*; Erne, *Book Trade*; Jane Kidnie and Sonia Massai eds, *Shakespeare and Textual Studies* (Cambridge: Cambridge University Press, 2015); Jean-Christophe Mayer, *Shakespeare's Early Readers: A Cultural History from 1590–1800* (Cambridge: Cambridge University Press, 2018); Claire Bourne, *Typographies of Performance in Early Modern England* (Oxford: Oxford University Press, 2020); Amy Lidster, *Publishing the History Play in the Time of Shakespeare: Stationers Shaping a Genre* (Cambridge: Cambridge University Press, 2022).

[90] Adam G. Hooks, *Selling Shakespeare: Biography, Bibliography, and the Book Trade* (Cambridge: Cambridge University Press, 2016), p. 30. Jason Scott-Warren uses a similar critical model to reconstruct the life of Richard Stonley, whose purchase of a copy of *Venus and Adonis* in 1593 provides the earliest known record of one of Shakespeare's books being bought: *Shakespeare's First Reader: The Paper Trails of Richard Stonley* (Philadelphia, PA: University of Pennsylvania Press, 2019).

writing prefaces), and showed how they nurtured 'a native literary culture'.[91] If *Shakespeare's Syndicate* builds on the prehistory of the publishing scene in England so carefully established by Lesser, Melnikoff, and others, then it also looks forward to recent work by Emma Depledge and Peter Kirwan, who examine the Interregnum and beyond to suggest how 'stationers shaped Shakespeare's authorial afterlife'.[92] Their edited collection examines the ways in which Shakespeare was reconstituted as a writer in the decades after the publication of the First Folio.

Amid this increasing attention on publishers and publication, Shakespeare's Folio has largely been avoided in recent years. The major exception to this is the work of Emma Smith, whose focus on the Folio over the past decade has brilliantly enriched our understanding of this book and its readers.[93] More broadly, our reluctance to think about the Folio as a publication event probably relates to what has been called '#FolioFatigue': the weary sense, familiar to most early modernists, that after the exhaustive analytical and enumerative work of the twentieth century, this book has been done to death. Accordingly, some of the most exciting recent work on Shakespeare's texts has deliberately turned away from the folio editions of the seventeenth century and instead embraced the early quarto and octavo editions. Both Faith Acker and Jane Kingsley-Smith, for example, have assembled fascinating accounts of Shakespeare's *Sonnets* (in their first edition of 1609 and beyond), while Tara Lyons and Zachary Lesser attend in different ways to the interpretive possibilities of early quarto editions of Shakespeare's plays.[94] It may be the case, Hooks suggests, that by the middle of the seventeenth century, Shakespeare's status and reputation 'rested securely on *Pericles* and the early narrative poem *The Rape of Lucrece*' rather than being tethered to the Folio.[95]

But our turn away from the Folio also highlights a problem of critical method, which is that much work on the book trade is framed by the study of a single agent. For example, one of the most powerful tools used to think about publishers so far is the notion of specialization. As both Lesser and Melnikoff note, publishers often specialized in certain types of book, which can generate fresh

[91] Kirk Melnikoff, *Elizabethan Publishing and the Makings of Literary Culture* (Toronto, ON: University of Toronto Press, 2018), p. 19.

[92] Emma Depledge and Peter Kirwan eds, *Canonising Shakespeare: Stationers and the Book Trade, 1640–1740* (Cambridge: Cambridge University Press, 2017), p. 1. See also Depledge, *Shakespeare's Rise to Cultural Prominence* (Cambridge: Cambridge University Press, 2018).

[93] Smith, *Making*; *Four Centuries*; Smith ed., *Cambridge Companion*. Smith also led the Bodleian Library's Folio digitization project: *The Bodleian First Folio*, https://firstfolio.bodleian.ox.ac.uk/.

[94] Faith D. Acker, *First Readers of Shakespeare's Sonnets, 1590–1790* (Abingdon: Routledge, 2021); Jane Kingsley-Smith, *The Afterlife of Shakespeare's Sonnets* (Cambridge: Cambridge University Press, 2019); Tara Lyons, 'Serials, Spinoffs, and Histories: Selling "Shakespeare" in Collection before the Folio' in *Philological Quarterly* 91.2 (2012): pp. 185–220; Zachary Lesser, *Ghosts, Holes, Rips and Scrapes: Shakespeare in 1619, Bibliography in the Longue Durée* (Philadelphia, PA: University of Pennsylvania Press, 2021).

[95] Adam G. Hooks, 'Royalist Shakespeare: Publishers, Politics and the Appropriation of *The Rape of Lucrece* (1655)' in Depledge and Kirwan eds, *Canonising Shakespeare*, pp. 26–37, at p. 26.

interpretative findings as scholars explore the ways in which a work may originally have been 'read' and thus shaped by its producer as well as its consumers.[96] One virtue of this work is that it enables scholars to offer readings of a text at the scale of the edition, and so promises access to an excitingly wide-reaching sense of the market for Shakespeare's books (a position which suggests that part of a reading's value lies in the size of the community that in some sense participates in that reading, and so contrasts with the vivid case study of an isolated, copy-specific encounter). At the same time, specialization relies on linking an edition to the intention of an individual book-trade agent. Shakespeare's Folio—and all collaboratively published books—wonderfully frustrate this approach. Whose intention should we pursue? The Folio represents much of the book trade in that it was a fundamentally plural and collaborative venture; there is no clearly '"dominant" or "preferred" reading' here to recover.[97] Thinking about the Folio's publication requires a critical approach that somehow remains open to this collaboration, just as scholars in other areas have moved away from individual actors or authors to explore the significance of theatre companies or literary coteries. The First Folio syndicate was no theatre company—for one thing, the unique nature of this book trade collaboration precludes thinking about the kind of 'special characteristics' which gave a company its collective identity over time—but the publication of the Folio itself was a kind of ensemble work.[98]

So how should we read a collaborative publication? One way to envisage the complexities of that question for the Folio is to consider the tension between the edition as a single conceptual category and the material reality of that edition as four bundles of printed sheets that were distributed between members of the syndicate. What is the relationship between these four piles of finished Folios? If we allow that publishers could, through their personal currency and professional standing, transform the meanings of a book, then we might imagine that each pile becomes its own 'edition'. Wrested out of the broader conceptual category of the edition, the Folios owned by each syndicate member were relocated and to some extent 'remade' within the personal economies of their bookshops, in ways described below. At the same time, each pile belonged to a larger whole, as the imprint and colophon record. Co-published books thus seem to fall between the sturdy critical categories on which much book-trade work relies.

The simplest way forwards might be to offer four different readings of the First Folio, one for each of the publishing businesses involved. This method would

[96] Lesser, *Renaissance Drama*, pp. 26–51; Melnikoff, *Elizabethan Publishing*, pp. 70–6.
[97] Lesser, *Renaissance Drama*, p. 18, quoting Stuart Hall, 'Encoding/Decoding' in Stuart Hall, Dorothy Hobson, Andrew Lowe, and Paul Willis eds, *Culture, Media, Language: Working Papers in Cultural Studies, 1972–79* (London: Routledge in association with the Centre for Contemporary Cultural Studies, University of Birmingham, 2005), pp. 117–27.
[98] Scott McMillin and Sally-Beth MacLean, *The Queen's Men and their Plays* (Cambridge: Cambridge University Press, 1998), p. xii.

generate something like a list of publishing intentions for the Folio: four readings, each of which might draw its critical force from the interpretive communities clustered around those bookshops (who might be familiar with an 'Edward Blount book' or a 'William Aspley book', and so on). But the list model is not the tactic I have chosen. The chapters that follow are based around the personalities named in the Folio's imprint and colophon, but in each case I have sought to join focused work on each stationer with a wider theme that cuts across all their lives and which situates the stationer in a network or a collective category. Rather than treating each figure as a separate case study, the method I have chosen relies where possible on thinking about these stationers in relation to one another and to their book-trade peers. For example, chapter one on Edward Blount explores what it means to describe an early modern book like the Folio as 'literary' and suggests ways that Blount's own strategies—when considered alongside those of his fellow stationers—may have contributed to the creation of this quality. I point out that his investment habits and use of prefatory addresses were, to judge from the surviving material, markedly different from the other stationers involved in the Folio negotiations. The chapter on William Jaggard explores the scale of his publishing work compared to his peers and considers the nature of textual legitimacy; the final two chapters address the problem of gathering a dispersed corpus of writings and the significance of place to the process of publication and sale. The result is, I hope, a way of thinking about stationers that offers ways forwards for this field of research by moving between the case study and a larger sense of these figures as a community. The chapters converge in productive ways on the Folio's publication while resisting the idea that any of these stationers can supply us with a definitive reason for 'why *that* play was published *then*', to use Peter Blayney's influential phrase.[99] This book keeps the individual in focus but crucially argues that their particular tactics and strategies are most clearly revealed through comparison to their peers.

Ultimately, the involvement of multiple stationers in the First Folio encourages us to turn away from our habit of understanding a work—in either its composition or production—through the agency of a single centred consciousness, and instead consider the possibilities of a networked model of literary production. There is no single story about the publication of this book—or if there is, then it is the story of multiple stories, not only those I offer here. This way of working with the interplay of book-trade agent and literary production has the advantage that it acknowledges the plurality of interpretive possibility that is a condition of reading itself.

---

[99] Blayney, 'Publication of Playbooks', p. 391. The phrase surfaces in many subsequent works, e.g. Lesser, *Renaissance Drama*, pp. 10, 16.

Publishers as Merchants of Belief

The publishing syndicate was responsible for the social and cultural circuitry through which Shakespeare's Folio emerged into the world. Who had these businesses spoken to about the Folio as it was being made, for example? Which readers visited their bookseller, as Samuel Pepys did in 1667, to learn amongst other gossip that 'Several good plays are also likely to be abroad soon'?[100] How did news of the Folio's arrival travel through the networks of letter-writing in which booksellers were often embedded, and through which they advertised 'newe titles from England' and 'booke[s] of worth come forthe this tearme' to their overseas contacts?[101] Which other members of the London—and regional—book trade struck deals with the Folio syndicate to stock copies in their own bookshops? In what manner did copies begin to travel abroad to the continent?[102] These questions all bring us back to the networks ranged around the members of the Folio publishing syndicate.

Most importantly, the book's publishers determined how seriously the Folio was taken: how much *belief* readers invested in it. This kind of belief is a tricky thing to pin down and leaves no obvious literary trace. Yet its influence is strikingly visible today. The environment within which Shakespeare's publishers worked had parallels with our modern situation. Then, as now, readers struggled to cope with the sheer volume of text in circulation that was brought about by tremendous technological change. From Robert Burton's despairing diagnosis of 1621 that he lived amid 'a vast *Chaos* and confusion of bookes' to the ludic adventurer Thomas Coryate's complaint about 'the unmeasurable abundance' of print 'in this learned age', all-too familiar anxieties about the amount of choice facing readers and about the quality and credibility of the material produced can be found in many sources from Shakespeare's time.[103] '[T]he truth is,' wrote John Goodwin in 1640, 'that many Bookes of worth and value indeed, had need of

---

[100] Entry for 10 August 1667: Samuel Pepys, *The Diary of Samuel Pepys*, edited by Robert Latham and William Matthews, 11 vols (London: HarperCollins, 2000 [first published 1971]), vol. 8, p. 380.

[101] *Henry Featherstone to William Trumbull, 5 March 1621*: BL Additional MS 72360, fol. 131; *Edward Blount to William Trumbull, 9 May 1623*: BL Additional MS 72365, fol. 130r (see letter six in appendix one).

[102] For an early account of a copy of the Folio being sent overseas, see Anthony James West, 'The First Shakespeare First Folio to Travel Abroad: Constantine Huygens's Copy' in Owen Williams and Caryn Lazzuri eds, *Foliomania! Stories behind Shakespeare's Most Important Book* (Washington, DC: The Folger Shakespeare Library, 2011), pp. 40–4. Rich accounts of early readership of the Folio are provided by Smith, *Four Centuries* and (for Shakespeare's works more broadly) Mayer, *Shakespeare's Early Readers*.

[103] Robert Burton, *The anatomy of melancholy* (1621, STC 4159), sig. A6v-7r; Thomas Coryate, *Coryats Crudities* (1611, STC 5808), sig. B2r. Complaints about abundance were common in the period. Particularly colourful examples include R. W., *Martine Mar-Sixtus* (1591, STC 24913), sig. A3r-4v; Robert Crofts, *The way to happinesse on earth* (1641, Wing C7007), sig. F6v-7r; Anon, *The clergyes bill of complaint* (1643, Wing C4644), sig. A2r. For a scholarly account of the effects of abundance in print see Ann Blair, *Too Much to Know: Managing Scholarly Information before the Modern Age* (New Haven, CT: Yale University Press, 2010).

some further recommendation, in one kinde or other, unto men, then their owne worth.' Without such means to recommend them, Goodwin wrote, valuable literature would 'suffer obscurity, and neglect at the hands of men'.[104]

We can think about Shakespeare's publishers as the 'further recommendation' that Goodwin wistfully imagined: figures who structured the field of literary production by determining what was important and what was not and by investing the texts they sponsored with their own personal resources of credibility. The significance of this role is increasingly clear today, when our relationship to a publisher—from the *New York Times* to Facebook—not only will determine whether or not we encounter a piece of information in the first place but also now critically informs our assessment of that material's importance and veracity. If the author is a 'principle of thrift in the proliferation of meaning', to borrow Michel Foucault's influential formulation, meaning a figure who helps us to organize, limit, and understand an otherwise vertiginous field of discursive possibility, then so too is the publisher a figure who, often in ways that are only semi-visible, shapes our encounters with texts and regulates the meanings we make from them.[105]

As the industry of book production grew across Europe, booksellers were joined by other agents and institutions who became implicated in such hierarchies of importance and who nudged readerly taste in one direction or another. By the eighteenth century, these agents included those who reviewed books in newspapers and magazines or sold them in auction houses; those who wrote poems promoting other works; those who awarded literary pensions or distributed patronage. For institutions we might look to the libraries that collected books or the schools in which they were taught. Collectively these agents form what the cultural theorist Pierre Bourdieu called the 'literary field': a space characterized by the struggle for control of literary values.[106] But when Shakespeare's Folio was published, much of the symbolic power to influence reading habits belonged to publishers, who, through their work of sifting manuscripts, ratifying some and dismissing others, earned reputations that over time did themselves become part of the ways in which readers encountered their books. In other words, the personalities of the early modern book trade helped readers decide what to read and how to approach a work, in ways that formed a precondition—or a type of 'preknowledge', to use Roger Chartier's term—to any future interpretation of the text.[107] As Adrian Johns has commented '[t]he name of the Stationer on a book's title page could tell a prospective reader as much about the contents as could that

---

[104] John Goodwin, *The saints interest in God* (1640, STC 12031), sig. B5v–6r.
[105] Michel Foucault, 'What Is an Author?' in Josué V. Harari ed., *Textual Strategies: Perspectives in Post-Structuralist Criticism* (Ithaca, NY: Cornell University Press, 1979), pp. 141–61, at p. 159.
[106] Pierre Bourdieu, *The Field of Cultural Production*, edited by Randal Johnson (Cambridge: Polity Press, 1993).
[107] Roger Chartier, 'Texts, Printing, Readings' in Lynn Hunt ed., *The New Cultural History* (Berkeley, CA: University of California Press, 1989), pp. 154–75, at p. 167.

of the author.'[108] Thinking with the language of Bourdieu, we could describe this power as the 'symbolic capital' of the Folio publishers, meaning their ability to confer a kind of consecratory value on a text through the association of their name and repute.[109] Within the early modern book trade, the language of 'credit' was often used to articulate similar ideas about the economy of personal reputation.[110]

The primary textual embodiments of this power and of the syndicate's presence were the Folio's imprint and colophon. These brief texts thus hover between two important realms of meaning: they both record information about a book's production and also, as critics are increasingly realizing, they shaped a book's reception. In their in-between status (not quite belonging to the main text, nor being a straightforwardly material feature like typography or format) imprints and colophons flicker between what the textual scholar Jerome McGann would call a book's 'linguistic' and 'bibliographic' codes.[111] The primary purpose of an imprint was, as Peter Blayney has pointed out, to advertise to members of the book trade who it was that had published an edition and the wholesale address from which copies of that edition could be acquired.[112] Colophons performed a similar role, usually repeating some of the information found in an imprint and occasionally, as with the Folio, supplementing it in some way. Given this industrial purpose, we have tended to think about imprints and colophons as inert statements that belonged to 'the realm of dull fact', but recent work has challenged the idea that they operated within a readerly blind spot, demonstrating that they could also be creatively rich texts that exposed both readers and stationers to a 'surprising range of literary and cultural concerns'.[113] Helen Smith quotes Thomas Nashe, whose prose work *The terrors of the night* undermines the idea that retail customers

---

[108] Adrian Johns, *The Nature of the Book* (Chicago, IL: University of Chicago Press, 1998), p. 147. On the value of personal relationships within the early modern book trade—'a face-to-face society, in which personal trust underpinned business confidence'—see James Raven, 'The Economic Context' in John Barnard and D. F. McKenzie eds, *The Cambridge History of the Book in Britain: Volume IV 1557–1695* (Cambridge: Cambridge University Press, 2002), pp. 568–82, with the quote at p. 571.

[109] Bourdieu, *Field of Cultural Production*, p. 75. Bourdieu's work on forms of capital is developed in *Distinction: A Social Critique of the Judgement of Taste*, trans. by Richard Nice (Abingdon: Routledge Classics, 2010).

[110] On credit see Craig Muldrew, *The Economy of Obligation: The Culture of Credit and Social Relations in Early Modern England* (Basingstoke: Palgrave Macmillan, 1998); Ceri Sullivan, *The Rhetoric of Credit: Merchants in Early Modern Writing* (London: Associated University Presses, 2002). Bourdieu (in translation) also adopts the term, e.g. *Field of Cultural Production*, p. 78.

[111] Jerome J. McGann, *The Textual Condition* (Princeton, NJ: Princeton University Press, 1991); *A Critique of Modern Textual Criticism* (Chicago, IL: University of Chicago Press, 1983).

[112] Blayney, 'Publication of Playbooks', p. 390. Blayney revisits imprints in *The Stationers' Company*, vol. 1, pp. 36, 76. For a classic overview of imprint wording see: M. A. Shaaber, 'The Meaning of the Imprint in Early Printed Books', in *The Library* S4, 24.3-4 (1944): pp. 120–41. See also Shef Rogers, 'Imprints, Imprimaturs, and Copyright Pages', in Dennis Duncan and Adam Smyth eds, *Book Parts* (Oxford: Oxford University Press, 2019), pp. 51–64.

[113] Helen Smith, '"Imprinted by Simeon such a signe": Reading Early Modern Imprints' in Helen Smith and Louise Wilson eds, *Renaissance Paratexts* (Cambridge: Cambridge University Press, 2011), pp. 17–33, at p. 17. Smith explores how an imprint 'calls into being the social and spatial topographies

ignored imprints. Scolding those who read only superficially, rather than delving into the contents of a book, Nashe wrote:

> a number of you there bee, who consider neither premisses nor conclusion, but piteouslie torment Title Pages on everie poast: never reading farther of anie Booke, than Imprinted by *Simeon* such a signe.[114]

For Nashe, the imprint of a book, found at the foot of a title page, marked the limits of a casual reader's gaze. We might think, then, that the imprint occupied a privileged space at the end of a reader's initial visual sweep, lingering on in their minds the way that the final poem in a collection stays with us after we have closed the book. The idea that readers attended to imprints also lies behind the Cavalier poet Aston Cokain's verse of 1658:

> You Printers, and the Stationers do raise
> Unto your selves a fame, if not a praise:
> For be the Authour what he will, you give
> Stamps of your Names on's Book, and with him live.[115]

Regardless of who the author was, Cokain points out, stationers nearly always included the 'Stamps of your Names' on their title pages, and so they promoted themselves as much as those who wrote books. Title pages gave life to stationers just as they did for authors, even if, as these lines suggest, the 'fame' of a book's printer or publisher did not necessarily entail praise.

This readerly interest in imprints probably explains why they grew over the later seventeenth century to accommodate little adverts and notices as well as the key details of publication. A reissued edition of Thomas Middleton's play *The Changeling* (1668), for example, features an imprint that advertised the book as being sold at Thomas Dring's bookshop 'at the *White Lyon*': this was a shop, the imprint continued, 'Where you may be Furnish'd with most sorts of *Plays*'.[116] Dring's addition was relatively terse, but by the end of the century some imprints

---

of London even as it describes them' in *Grossly Material Things: Women and Book Production in Early Modern England* (Oxford: Oxford University Press, 2012), p. 149.

[114] Thomas Nashe, 'To Master or Goodman Reader, generally dispersed East or West' in Nashe, *The terrors of the night* (1594, STC 18379), sig. A4r. Quoted by Smith in 'Imprinted', p. 17.

[115] Sir Aston Cokain, *A Chain of Golden Poems* (1658, Wing C4894), sig. O2r. The public association between a stationer and their books cut both ways: it could bring the 'fame' described by Cokain but was also a mechanism for accountability. It was this latter reason that motivated John Milton to argue that the name of a book's stationer was more important than that of its author when he suggested that 'no book be Printed, unlesse the Printers and the Authors name, or at least the Printers' appear: *Areopagitica* (1644, Wing M2092), sig. F1r.

[116] Thomas Middleton, *The Changeling* (1668, Wing M1982), sig. A1r.

featured mini-catalogues of newly published works complete with their prices.[117] The imprint of the First Folio has lost its significance over time (perhaps partly because it is not clear if—and how—modern editions should mediate this information) but was nevertheless a critical feature of the book's original publication. Both the Folio's imprint and its colophon, *Shakespeare's Syndicate* argues, are neglected sites of rhetorical significance and cultural conditioning, 'quasi-magical', as Bourdieu puts it, in their ability to shape the Folio's early reception.[118]

The rest of this book responds in various ways to the Folio's imprint and colophon. While the imprint belongs to the busy semiosis of the Folio title page, the colophon seems a more private statement, one that is less exposed to public gaze.[119] Given that the Folio itself foregrounds Edward Blount and the Jaggards, in the first half of this book I am more directly attentive to the historical characters— textual, biographical, and bibliographical—of these two businesses, while in the second half chapters on the final two stationers hew less closely to the lives of William Aspley and John Smethwick and instead use both stationers to exemplify certain themes. Chapter one begins with Edward Blount and his decision to advertise the First Folio at the Frankfurt Book Fair in 1624. Rather than promoting the *Comedies, Histories, & Tragedies*, as the Folio is named on its title page, Blount instead advertised copies of 'Master *William Shakesperes* workes'.[120] This subtle alteration, which marketed the Folio within the classical tradition of the *opera* of a significant author, was a typically deft manoeuvre from a bookseller who, more than any other from his generation of stationers, is consistently connected with ideas of literary publishing. This first chapter uses Blount to argue that the Folio's 'literary' status was generated from within a bookshop, as well as inhering in Shakespeare's authorial ability.

Chapter two moves to the Jaggard printing house and publishing bookshop in Barbican and considers how the Jaggards have featured in narratives about the 'legitimacy' of Shakespeare's books. Against a long history of viewing the Jaggard printing house as a shady establishment, the involvement of which in the First Folio is hard to explain, this chapter repositions William Jaggard as an authoritative printer-publisher. Rather than seeing William Jaggard as a book-trade 'pirate',

---

[117] For examples of imprint adverts see Francis Manning, *The generous choice* (1700, Wing M486), sig. A1r; Samuel Tuke, *The adventures of five hours* (1704), sig. A1r; Thomas Dogget, *The country-wake: a comedy* (1696, Wing D1828), sig. A1r. It was not only books that were advertised: the bookseller Richard Wellington's edition of G. Hartman's *The family physitian* (1696, Wing H1003) used its imprint to advertise a 'variety of Physical medicines' also sold at Wellington's bookshop 'at the *Lute* in St *Paul's Church-Yard*' (sig. A1r).

[118] Bourdieu, *Cultural Production*, p. 81.

[119] Lotte Hellinga argues colophons also addressed readers: '"Less than the Whole Truth": False Statements in 15th-Century Colophons' in Robin Myers and Michael Harris eds, *Fakes and Frauds: Varieties of Deception in Print & Manuscript* (Winchester: St Paul's Bibliographies, 1989), pp. 1–29. See also Alfred W. Pollard, *An Essay on Colophons with Specimens and Translations* (Chicago, IL: The Caxton Club, 1905), pp. 91–122; Rogers, 'Imprints, Imprimaturs'.

[120] *Catalogus universalis pronundinis Francofurtensibus vernalibus*, sig. D4v; see Figure 1.1 on p. 43.

as the New Bibliographers had it, early readers of the Folio were more likely to associate the Jaggard house with books that were destined for libraries: encyclopaedic in scope and authoritative in content. The starting point of chapter three on William Aspley is his critical status as a 'secondary' or minor Shakespearean. The chapter uses Aspley to explore the challenge of gathering a dispersed corpus of writing, and argues that the process by which Shakespeare's theatrical manuscripts leaked in ones and twos out of the theatre and into the hands of many different 'minor' booksellers and printers underpins the bibliographic creativity and fertility of the playwright's books. The model of literary authority established for Shakespearean print was, this chapter argues, enabled by the very lack of centralized control that led to stationers like Aspley owning just a small part of the playwright's literary estate.

The final chapter examines the different sites of London from which Shakespeare's books were financed and sold. Uniquely among the Folio syndicate, John Smethwick worked from a bookshop that was based down Fleet Street in the churchyard of St Dunstan in the West, a site that was on the western edge of the City of London at some distance from the central book-trade hub of Paul's Cross Churchyard. Bringing together recent work on the spaces of the London book trade, this chapter asks whether we can read Shakespeare's literary life by following the journeys of his books across the city. After the arrival of the Folio, this chapter shows, Shakespeare's work drifted westwards across London, where those titles that prevailed despite Shakespeare's fading popularity found their resting place in and around this alternative churchyard in which Smethwick's bookshop was found.

In 1641, the religious writer Laurence Womock, chaplain to a baron named William Paget, placed a prominent dedication to his aristocratic patron at the front of his latest work. 'This advantage I shall procure from your name' wrote Womock, 'that I shall have the credit to be read, and to bee beleeved.'[121] In *Shakespeare's Syndicate*, I take my cue from Womock's hopeful articulation of the value that was added to his book through the name of its sponsor, and examine the role of Shakespeare's publishers in shaping our own beliefs about what has become one of the most important books in the world. It is a tribute to these stationers that the success of the First Folio has resulted in their own presences being almost entirely effaced. *Shakespeare's Syndicate* recovers these figures and adds them to the ongoing history of Shakespeare in print.

---

[121] Laurence Womock, 'To the Right Honourable William Lord Paget' in *Beaten oyle for the lamps of the sanctuarie* (1641, Wing W3338), sig. A2v.

PART 1

'PRINTED BY ISAAC JAGGARD, AND ED. BLOUNT. 1623.'

1
'Master *William Shakesperes* workes'
Edward Blount at the Black Bear

'Playes' or 'workes'?

In 1624, Shakespeare's Folio was advertised at the spring Frankfurt Book Fair. This bustling market was the centre of the European book world. Booksellers from many countries frequented the stalls, browsing the latest titles, gleaning trends from bookish colleagues. Authorial reputations could be made in this vibrant forum of commerce, amid baskets of spectacles, pickpockets, and wandering comedians.[1] Having a book sold at Frankfurt mattered to English authors because it increased their shot at European renown. In 1622, the astronomer Thomas Lydiat was furious to discover that, although the Stationers' Company had promised him, after 'holding my nose to the grindstone' that 'my books should be put in the catalogue' at Frankfurt, having got hold of a copy he found no listing. His publishers flatly refused to send his books to the Fair and instead, Lydiat complained, had dumped the copies 'at a common Inn: where they have lain ever since at my charges; and they and I together have abyden the obloquy of the world.'[2]

The advert for Shakespeare's Folio appeared towards the back of the Fair's official catalogue, in a section reserved for English books. There had been just one prior sales notice for the Folio which appeared in another Frankfurt catalogue, this time an earlier edition from 1622.[3] These two adverts were placed by different

---

[1] On spectacle sellers and other hawkers at the Frankfurt Book Fair, see James Westfall Thompson, *The Frankfort Book Fair: The Francofordiense Emporium of Henri Estienne* (Chicago, IL: The Caxton Club, 1911), pp. 58–61. See also: Angela Nuovo, *The Book Trade in the Italian Renaissance*, trans. Lydia G. Cochrane (Leiden: Brill, 2013), esp. Part VII 'Fairs', pp. 281–94; Max Spirgatis, 'Englische Litteratur Auf Der Frankfurter Messe Von 1561–1620' in *Beitrage Zur Kenntnis des Schrift-, Buch- und Bibliothekswesens* 7 (1902), pp. 37–89.

[2] MS Bodl. 313., fol. 66v–67v, quotes at fol. 67r and 67v (see also fol. 33r). In this case the book in question may have been *Solis et lunae periodus* (1620, STC 17046), a work of chronology printed by William Stansby, but Lydiat's papers record a history of disillusionment with the Stationers' Company that began with John Bill's production of Lydiat's first book in 1605.

[3] The earlier advert is in *Catalogus uniuersalis pro nundinis Francofurtensibus autumnalibus…* (1622, STC 11329.8), sig. D4v; the second, pictured below, is in *Catalogus universalis pronundinis Francofurtensibus vernalibus…* (1624, STC 11330.2), sig. D4v. Both adverts are discussed by Adam G. Hooks, *Selling Shakespeare: Biography, Bibliography, and the Book Trade* (Cambridge: Cambridge University Press, 2016), pp. 100–2, and David Scott Kastan, *Shakespeare and the Book* (Cambridge: Cambridge University Press, 2001), pp. 60–1.

members of the publishing syndicate and they contain some suggestive differences between how the two businesses envisaged Shakespeare's writing. The first notice, which is the earliest trace we have of the Folio being planned, was placed by Isaac Jaggard, then a young man of twenty-seven, on behalf of the Jaggard printing and publishing house:

> Playes, written by M. *William Shakespeare*, all in one volume, printed by *Isaack Jaggard*, in fol.[4]

The printing of the Folio probably began somewhere in the middle of 1622, around the time that this advert was placed. In other words, Jaggard's notice was advance publicity for a book that was still coming together. The advert is not descriptive but aspirational—it offers a sort of simplified vision for what the Folio would be, one as yet uncorrupted by the testy reality of actually printing the book. The advert foregrounds the genre of plays, and so it suggests that a decision had already been made not to include Shakespeare's poetry. It also supplies Shakespeare's name in full and proudly stresses the novelty of the book's bibliographic status in offering a collection 'all in one volume' (a selling point we might expect the Folio's printer to promote). The book-trade figure named is '*Isaack Jaggard*', which has led some scholars to wonder if the younger Jaggard controlled the making of this book, though our separation of Isaac from his father William may reveal more about our critical investment in the Folio than the workings of an early modern printing house.[5]

The second entry in the Frankfurt catalogue came two years later and described the Folio as the work of the bookseller Edward Blount, the subject of this chapter, who was then a book-trade veteran aged sixty-two. This advert (Figure 1.1) presents the same book in a slightly different way: 'Master *William Shakesperes* workes, printed for *Edward Blount*, in fol.'[6]

Gone was the bibliographically descriptive 'all in one volume', and gone too was the label of 'Playes'. Instead, what starts the entry is Shakespeare's name, promoted from a parenthetical clause in Jaggard's notice, together with the expanded version of his title as a gentleman: he is 'Master' William Shakespeare here. The syntax establishes a possessive relationship between author and work in ways that had already appeared at earlier moments of Shakespeare's career: *Shake-speares sonnets* (1609), for example, or the 1608 first edition of *King Lear*, advertised on

---

[4] *Catalogus uniuersalis...* (1622, STC 11329.8), sig. D4v.
[5] On the likelihood that Isaac Jaggard was probably the mastermind of the Folio venture see: Peter W. M. Blayney, 'Introduction to the Second Edition' in Charlton Hinman ed., *The Norton Facsimile: The First Folio of Shakespeare*, 2nd ed. (New York and London: W. W. Norton & Company, 1996), p. xxviii; Sonia Massai, *Shakespeare and the Rise of the Editor* (Cambridge: Cambridge University Press, 2007), p. 161. On this separation of Isaac and William in the critical tradition see chapter two, pp. 84–5.
[6] *Catalogus universalis...* (1624, STC 11330.2), sig. D4v.

> The Englifh Dictionary, or an interpreter of hard Englifh words, by *H. C.* Gent. printed for *Edmund Weauer*, in 8.
> *Pilgub Euangelica*, or a Commentary on the Reuelation of Saint *Iohn*, by Doctor *Symonds*, printed for *Edmund Weauer*, in 4.
> Abrahams faith, that is, the old Religion, wherein is proued that the Religion now publikely taught and defended by order in the Church of England is the onely true, Catholike, ancient and vnchangeable faith of Gods Elect: and the pretenfed Religion of the Sea of Rome is a falfe, baftard, new, vpftart, hereticall and variable fuperftitious deuice of man. By *Iofias Nichols*: printed for *Edmund Weauer* in 4.
> Mafter *William Shakefperes* workes, printed for *Edward Blount*, in fol.
> Shifts and euafions vfed by Mafter *Arnox* the Iefuit, a Treatife wherein the caufes why he refufeth to anfwer to 17. queftions made by the Minifters of the Church of *Paris*, are examined, &c. by *Peter D. Moulin*, printed for *Nathaniel Newbery*.
> A Catechifme made by Mafter *Daniel Votier*, Minifter of Gods Word, printed for *Nathaniel Newbery*.
> The

Figure 1.1 Edward Blount's advert for the First Folio in the Frankfurt catalogue of 1624: Image of *Catalogus universalis pronundinis Francofurtensibus vernalibus…* (STC 11330.2), sig. D4v. Credit: Bodleian Libraries, University of Oxford, MS Ashmole 1057(10). Used under Creative Commons licence CC-BY-NC 4.0.

its title page as *M. William Shak-speare: his True Chronicle Historie of the life and death of King Lear*.[7] Perhaps more telling is that Blount's advert promotes the Folio as the 'workes' of its author. Unlike Jaggard's advert, this was not a speculative title: the Folio was finished by this point, which means that Blount's wording contradicts the book's printed title of *Comedies, Histories, & Tragedies*. The different styling also means that Blount's advert was out of step with any marketing that relied on the 'posting' of the Folio's title page in public spaces throughout London, and perhaps also at the fair in Frankfurt.[8] These changes were not driven by pressures of space—there are plenty of longer titles in the Frankfurt catalogue, including those directly above and below Blount's listing for Shakespeare. The publisher Edmund Weaver's edition of *Abrahams faith*, for example, records each one of the author Josias Nichols' fulminating adjectives against Roman Catholicism: a 'false, bastard, new, upstart, hereticall and variable superstitious device'. In the face of Nichols' litany, Blount's laconic phrase seems a deliberate deviation from the Folio's title page.

---

[7] William Shakespeare, *Shake-speares sonnets* (1609, STC 22353); *M. William Shak-speare: his True Chronicle Historie of the life and death of King Lear* (1608, STC 22292). On this possessive style of titling in early modern drama see Zachary Lesser and Peter Stallybrass, 'Shakespeare between Pamphlet and Book, 1608–1619' in Margaret Jane Kidnie and Sonia Massai eds, *Shakespeare and Textual Studies* (Cambridge: Cambridge University Press, 2015), pp. 105–33, at pp. 105–12.

[8] This practice is discussed in the introduction (pp. 8–9). Blount's wording of 'workes' is present on the 'Names of the Principall Actors' page in the preliminaries.

How might we understand these changes? Why did Blount reconfigure the book? It was not uncommon for stationers to 'rebrand' old books with new titles. This was the fate of Blount's only other Shakespearean publication: the poetical miscellany *Loves Martyr*, published in 1601 and containing the marginal Shakespeare poem 'The Phoenix and the Turtle', as well as its coda 'Threnos'.[9] Despite featuring work by Ben Jonson, George Chapman, and John Marston as well as Shakespeare the miscellany failed to sell. In 1611 the same printed sheets, presumably lost in the same 'obloquy of the world' as Lydiat's books, were repackaged by the stationer Matthew Lownes with a new title page that rebranded the miscellany as a verse history: *The Annals of Great Britain [...] wherein may be seene all the antiquities of this Kingdome*.[10] Lownes's title reframed the verse as antiquarian, rather than lyric, but his rebranding still seems to have failed. Forlorn copies of 'The Annals of great Brittaine' were hopefully touted by Lownes at Frankfurt in 1624, nearly a quarter of a century after their original publication.[11] 'Stationers,' as the poet John Taylor shrewdly pointed out, 'their olde cast Bookes can grace, | And by new Titles paint a fresh their face', but that did not always guarantee they would sell.[12] But this kind of rebranding tended to happen only when the original title had become stale, which could not have been the case with Blount's Folio advert, given that it appeared just a few months after the book's original publication.

Rather than a resuscitation attempt, then, what is at stake in these two Frankfurt adverts are two alternative visions of the Folio, each linked to a different member of the publishing team and each embodying a different set of concerns. The first reveals a young printer's bibliographic conception of the Folio; the second shows the twist it received from a more experienced hand to introduce Shakespeare to an urbane European readership. By turning to that label of 'workes', Blount marketed Shakespeare within the classical tradition of the *opera* of a significant author. This was a bibliographical line of descent that carried greater cultural status than a collected book of 'playes', as Ben Jonson famously discovered to his cost when his own collection of poems and plays—*The workes of Benjamin Jonson* (1616)—drew the mockery of contemporary critics.[13]

---

[9] Robert Chester and others, *Loves martyr: or, Rosalins complaint* (1601, STC 5119).

[10] As if to advertise the secondary status of this reissued book, the new title page featured a glaring misprint, calling the poem 'The Anuals of Great Britain'. For more on the reissue of old printed sheets 'conjured out of the dust of a publisher's stockroom', see Kirk Melnikoff, *Elizabethan Publishing and the Makings of Literary Culture* (Toronto, ON: University of Toronto Press, 2018), pp. 57–60.

[11] *Catalogus universalis pro nundinis Francofurtensibus autumnalibus de anno M.DC.XXIIII* (1624), sig. E4r. This catalogue has no STC number. A copy of it is bound as item eleven in a volume that contains several other Frankfurt catalogues: Bodleian Library MS Ashmole 1057.

[12] John Taylor 'A Comparison betwixt a *Whore* and a *Booke*' in *A Common Whore* (1622, STC 23742.5), sig. B6v–7r.

[13] Ian Donaldson, *Ben Jonson: A Life* (Oxford: Oxford University Press, 2011), pp. 324–7.

The Frankfurt advertisement reveals some important coordinates of Blount's career. The advert suggests this bookseller's investment in continental culture; an astute awareness of the possibilities of bibliographic branding; and an uncanny eye for which authors to promote and which to suppress. These qualities underpin both Blount's success and his subsequent failure in the book trade. This stationer published books that have become central works within the Western literary tradition; for some critics, he practically invented England's 'first Great Books course'.[14] Blount mixed English vernacular writing—such as poetry by Christopher Marlowe, the *Basilikon Doron* of James I (anglicized from its original Scots), or the plays of John Lyly—with highlights from European literary developments to create a powerful publishing imprint. It was Blount who introduced English readers to the *Essayes* of Michel de Montaigne (translated by Blount's friend John Florio), and to Miguel de Cervantes's picaresque novel *Don Quixote*, as well as publishing monumental dictionaries of European languages. The publisher's impressive inventory has led many scholars to identify Blount as a key figure in the development of a vernacular literary tradition at the start of the seventeenth century—not least because of his involvement in the publication of Shakespeare's Folio.[15]

This chapter explores the idea that Blount was a 'literary' publisher. Our ideas about the literary status of writing tend to focus on authorship. One way to think about Blount, then, is that he was a kind of talent-spotter: someone who, with baffling prescience, discovered figures whose work remains valued today, figures like Shakespeare, Montaigne, or Marlowe. In this chapter I move away from the author to argue that Blount himself—through his book-trade strategies and practices—participated in the creation of the same literary values that we imagine him to have identified elsewhere. Rather than suggesting that Blount was 'particularly likely to be attracted' to Shakespeare's Folio because it was 'a literary project', I want instead to explore some of the ways in which Blount's involvement was itself a marker of literary status.[16] The first part of the chapter considers

---

[14] Kastan, *Shakespeare and the Book*, p. 62. For Blount's biography, see Gary Taylor, 'Blount [Blunt], Edward (*bap.* 1562, *d.* in or before 1632), bookseller and translator,' *Oxford Dictionary of National Biography* (Oxford: Oxford University Press, 2004; online edn, 2008) [accessed 12 November 2019].

[15] The Shakespearean editor Edmond Malone may have been the first to single out Blount as 'a bookseller of eminence' in his *Supplement to the edition of Shakspeare's plays published in 1778 by Samuel Johnson and George Steevens*, 2 vols (1780), vol 2, p. 183. The nineteenth-century Shakespearean scholars Alexander Dyce, Bolton Corney, and John Payne Collier believed they had proved that 'Edward Blount was the real editor of the first folio Shakespeare': *Bolton Corney to John Payne Collier, 25 March 1858* (Folger Shakespeare Library MS Y. c. 622). Phoebe Sheavyn described him as 'a genuine lover of literature': 'Writers and the Publishing Trade, Circa 1600,' in *The Library* S2.7 (1906): pp. 337–65, at p. 340. More recently, Gary Taylor has offered a fascinating account of Blount as 'England's greatest literary critic' in William Shakespeare, *The New Oxford Shakespeare: The Complete Works Critical Reference Edition*, 2 vols, edited by Gary Taylor, John Jowett, Terri Bourus, and Gabriel Egan (Oxford: Oxford University Press, 2017), vol. 2, p. xlvi.

[16] Kastan, *Shakespeare and the Book*, pp. 61–2. The bookseller Humphrey Moseley tends to be positioned as Blount's successor. For some, Moseley's work represents 'the central literary achievement of

Blount's books as investments and asks how the financial dynamics of publishing might be involved in the creation of a proto-literary realm. I then show that Blount returned to ideas of taste in his work and that he was an unusually public figure within the book trade.[17] Finally I ask how the social relations that clustered around Blount's bookshop buttressed the books that he published. Throughout, the chapter argues that Blount's publishing house at the Black Bear was a crucial forum in early seventeenth-century culture. In this bookshop, I argue, economic positioning, cultural fluency, and social influence combined to create a figure whose financial investment in Shakespeare's Folio may have been outstripped by his symbolic ability to legitimate the book as an important collection of the playwright's 'workes'.

'what ever you do, Buy'

Buy the book, urges the address 'To the great Variety of Readers' in the Folio's first few pages: 'what ever you do, Buy.' Its emphasis on the transaction is present from the opening lines:

> From the most able, to him that can but spell: There you are number'd. We had rather you were weighd. Especially, when the fate of all Bookes depends upon your capacities: and not of your heads alone, but of your purses.[18]

The address says: this is a book for everyone, no matter your ability to read and write. But then it dismisses the inclusive approach in favour of a pragmatic appeal to money; the readership's literacy is superseded by its wealth. Further down the page, the address measures reading and judgement in financial units: 'Judge your sixe-pen'orth, your shillings worth, your five shillings worth at a time' it continues, 'But, what ever you do, Buy.'[19] The typical cost of an early modern playbook was sixpence, so here the address seems to say: 'read one play, two plays, or even ten plays at a time—we do not care, as long as you buy the book.'

---

mid-seventeenth-century England': David Scott Kastan, 'Humphrey Moseley and the Invention of English Literature' in Sabrina Alcorn Baron, Eric N. Lindquist, and Eleanor F. Shevlin eds, *Agent of Change: Print Culture Studies after Elizabeth L. Eisenstein* (Amherst and Boston, MA: University of Massachusetts Press, 2007), pp. 105–24, at p. 113.

[17] On early modern stationers as cultural 'tastemakers' see Andie Silva, *The Brand of Print: Marketing Paratexts in the Early English Book Trade* (Leiden: Brill, 2019), pp. 18–39.

[18] John Heminge and Henry Condell, 'To the great Variety of Readers' in William Shakespeare, *Mr. William Shakespeares Comedies, Histories, & Tragedies* (1623, STC 22273), sig. A3r.

[19] Heminge and Condell, 'To the great Variety of Readers' in Shakespeare, *Comedies, Histories, & Tragedies*, sig. A3r.

The Folio cost about fifteen shillings for an unbound copy, which was around a year's pay for a London labourer at this time.[20] Adding a binding to that, whether vellum or leather, could cost anything from one shilling upwards. It was, as Peter Blayney puts it, 'by far the most expensive playbook that had ever been offered to the English public'.[21] The book's cost related to the amount of paper it required: around 227 'edition sheets' (the number of printed sheets required for each ideal copy of the book).[22] Adding to the worries of early modern booksellers, readers commonly treated bookshops as though they were libraries, settling in on 'a stoole and a cushion' and lighting up a pipe, according to Thomas Dekker, fostering anxieties about the customer who 'reades awhile, but nothing buyes at all'.[23] A young Thomas Hobbes apparently enjoyed nothing better during his time in Oxford than to 'goe to the booke-binders' shops, and lye gaping on mappes'.[24]

As if to ward off such thrifty readers, the Folio continually demands to be bought. Publishing books could be risky, in part because all the capital needed to finance an edition was invested before any single copy could be sold for a return.[25] Booksellers responded to the financial challenges of their trade in different ways, and their strategies influenced their reputations. George Wither's well-known caricature of a stationer, written in 1624, portrayed a mercenary figure who thought only of his own profits: 'What booke soever he may have hope to gaine by,' Wither wrote, 'he will divulge.'[26] Similar suspicions about a stationer's relationship to profit are found in other accounts from this time: John Payne's sketch

---

[20] Peter W. M. Blayney, *The First Folio of Shakespeare* (Washington, DC: Folger Shakespeare Library, 1991), pp. 25–9; Jeremy Boulton, 'Wage Labour in Seventeenth-century London' in *Economic History Review* 49.2 (1996): pp. 268–90, at p. 288.

[21] Blayney, 'Introduction to the Second Edition' in Hinman ed., *The Norton Facsimile*, p. xxviii.

[22] The figure of 227 edition sheets is based on the collation provided by W. W. Greg, *A Bibliography of the English Printed Drama to the Restoration*, 4 vols (London: The Bibliographical Society, 1939–59), vol. 3, p. 1109. This figure varies slightly: Carter Hailey finds the Folio required 229 edition sheets in 'The Best Crowne Paper', Owen Williams and Caryn Lazzuri eds, *Foliomania! Stories behind Shakespeare's Most Important Book* (Washington, DC: The Folger Shakespeare Library, 2011), pp. 8–14 at p. 14.

[23] Thomas Dekker, *The pleasant comodie of patient Grisill* (1603, STC 6518), sig. C1r; *The guls horne-booke* (1609, STC 6500), sig. D2r; 'To the generall Readers' in Thomas Churchyard, *The mirror of man, and manners of men* (1594, STC 5242), sig. A2v. On reading in bookshops see Ben Higgins, '"The Book-sellars Shop": Browsing, Reading, and Buying in Early Modern England' in Adam Smyth ed., *The Oxford Handbook of the History of the Book in Early Modern England* (Oxford: Oxford University Press, forthcoming 2022).

[24] John Aubrey, 'The Life of Mr. Thomas Hobbes', quoted in Thomas Hobbes, *Leviathan*, edited by David Johnston, 2nd edn (London and New York: W. W. Norton, 2020), p. 478.

[25] On the economics of book publishing, see James Raven, 'The Economic Context' in John Barnard and D. F. McKenzie eds, *The Cambridge History of the Book in Britain: Volume IV 1557–1695* (Cambridge: Cambridge University Press, 2014), pp. 568–82; Zachary Lesser, *Renaissance Drama and the Politics of Publication* (Cambridge: Cambridge University Press, 2004), pp. 26–36; Shanti Graheli ed., *Buying and Selling: The Business of Books in Early Modern Europe* (Leiden: Brill 2019).

[26] George Wither, *The schollers purgatory* (1624, STC 25919), sig. H4r. On this text and the light it sheds on the early modern book trade see Joseph Loewenstein, 'Wither and Professional Work' in Arthur F. Marotti and Michael D. Bristol eds, *Print, Manuscript, & Performance: the Changing Relations of the Media in Early Modern England* (Columbus, OH: Ohio State University Press, 2000), pp. 103–23.

of stationers 'of two sortes' from 1597 features an avaricious bookseller who financed 'huge heapes or cartlodes of fond and folyshe bookes' only to line his pockets.[27] For Wither, some of the moral force of these criticisms may relate to a sense of personal injury in dealings with the Stationers' Company, but in other ways the values behind these criticisms can be traced back to the Latin etymology of 'to publish': *publicare*, meaning 'to make openly knowne, to cause to bee openly cried', often by a town crier or messenger.[28] This definition reminds us that every act of publication was in effect an imposition on civic attention, a claim for the significance and value of the text.

At the same time, booksellers faced inarguable economic realities. As the introduction made clear, the livelihood of a bookseller did not depend solely on the texts they published, but if a publisher consistently worked more for 'the publike advantage, then to his owne commodity', as Wither put it in his description of the idealized 'honest Stationer', then he risked the collapse of his business.[29] That phrase, 'the publike advantage', suggests the language used in early modern society to articulate motivations that today we might describe as ideological, in the sense that they resist the hegemony of financial capital. We could parse such motivations as literary, religious, political, or perhaps scholarly, but for Wither and others they were imagined through humanistic values of citizenship and the commonweal. The virtuous bookseller was a 'Chapman of Arts', who prioritized 'the curious appetite of the Soule' over his own finances.[30] This idealized vision of the proper motivations for publishing appears elsewhere: Thomas Lydiat aspired to publish his books 'for the greater good' of 'my Country, and the Commonweale of good learning'.[31] The antiquary John Aubrey, in a note to the possible printers of his manuscript 'Naturall Historie of Wiltshire', was both hopeful that his work would make 'a glorious Volumne' and also pragmatic: 'I doe never expect to see it donne', Aubrey wrote, because printing the book would entail 'no inconsiderable charge \expence/' and '\So few/ Men have the Hearts to doe publi*que* good.'[32] But books intended for 'publi*que* good' could be expensive and were not guaranteed to fly off the shelves. 'Learning hath gained most by those Books, by which the

---

[27] John Payne, *Royall exchange* (1597, STC 19489). Payne's 'Prynters of two sortes' heading is in his contents leaf (sig. A4v). He describes the 'wyse and worshipfull' stationer, who makes books that are 'necessarie for church and common welthe' and 'for the mayntenans of laws and civill order', and their venal counterparts, who collaborate with 'seducing secretaries or pennslaves' to make books that serve the flimsy interests of 'rude readers' (D4r–v).

[28] Thomas Elyot, *Bibliotheca Eliotæ* (1559, STC 7663), sig. 3N3v.

[29] Wither, *schollers purgatory*, sig. H2v.   [30] Wither, *schollers purgatory*, sig. H3r, H2v.

[31] *Thomas Lydiat to the Archbishop of Canterbury, 2 July 1634*, Bodleian Library MS Bodl. 313, fol. 21r. There is an alternative formulation in Lydiat's petition to King Charles I, in which Lydiat asks for permission to travel into foreign lands and gather books that he could then publish for the 'propagation and increase of Good Learning' (fol. 25r). See also the travel writer Christopher Farewell's similar judgement that some booksellers 'become able, not onely for their private Families' but also become 'Common-wealths men': *An East-India colation; or a discourse of travels* (1633, STC 10687), sig. F1v–2r.

[32] Bodleian MS. Aubrey 2, fol. 177v.

Printers have lost,' the parliamentarian minister John Goodwin wrote ruefully in 1655, 'whereas foolish Pamphlets have been most beneficial to the Printers.'[33]

Edward Blount took an unusual approach to these competing economic imperatives of profit and 'the publike advantage'. The stereotypical 'mercenary stationer' tended to be associated with ideas of plurality and ephemerality: texts that required minimal investment and so exposed their publishers to little risk while offering reliable sales, such as ballads, chapbooks or newsbooks, almanacs (brought under Stationers' Company monopoly in 1603), and poetry pamphlets. Many early modern booksellers began their careers by investing in shorter books of this kind, which would not tie up much capital in printing-house labour and paper costs, and produced a relatively speedy return. Table 1.1 uses the metric of the 'edition sheet' to compare the first decade of Blount's publishing work with the same period in the careers of the eleven other stationers who were involved in the negotiations for the First Folio plays in the early 1620s.[34]

What does the table reveal? Other than showing us the range of behaviours and investment strategies adopted by early modern publishers as they began their careers, the table also offers different ways of thinking about what it meant for a stationer to be 'productive'. If productivity means 'number of editions' then the table is comfortably led by Thomas Pavier (seventy-three editions) and Nathaniel Butter (eighty-four). Here the idea for both Butter and Pavier seems to have been to publish little and often, maintaining a high work rate and visibility by producing many books of roughly pamphlet-length. Butter has an average of around eleven or twelve edition sheets for each book, while Pavier is around seven sheets (a little more if we discount his collaborations; a little less if we include them).

Yet if Butter and Pavier's work suggests ideas of plurality and ephemerality, then Edward Blount embodies the opposite values of discrimination and

---

[33] John Goodwin, *A fresh discovery of the high-Presbyterian spirit* (1655, Wing G1167), sig. F1r. Goodwin's examples include the Antwerp humanist printer-publisher Christopher Plantin's polyglot bible, which 'sunk and almost ruined his Estate', and the English scholar Sir Henry Savile's edition of John Chrysostom, which apparently cost Savile £8,000 and famously failed to sell. The problem was as old as printing itself: in a 1530 preliminary poem the printer Robert Copland complained that 'morall bokes stoned styll vpon the shelfe' while 'Tyfles and toyes' are 'the thynges so sought': Geoffrey Chaucer, *The assemblie of foules* (1530, STC 5092), sig. A1v, quoted and discussed in Alexandra Gillespie, *Print Culture and the Medieval Author: Chaucer, Lydgate, and their Books 1473–1557* (Oxford: Oxford University Press, 2006) pp. 122–5.

[34] Edition sheets are a standard measure for the cost of book production in the absence of information about press runs. As Joseph A. Dane and Alexandra Gillespie point out, the cost of a book 'is a direct function of the cost of the paper it contains': 'The myth of the cheap quarto', John N. King ed., *Tudor Books and Readers: Materiality and the Construction of Meaning* (Cambridge: Cambridge University Press, 2010), pp. 25–45, at p. 31. These stationers represent all of the early modern stationers with a registered interest in Shakespeare's drama in 1623, but this criteria means they are not all fair comparisons. Notably, Henry Walley (owner of *Troilus and Cressida*) was only active for two years; Thomas Dewe (who had a claim on the right to print *King John* through his publication of the anonymous related play *The Troublesome Raigne of John King of England* in 1622) for just five. A full list of which stationer owned what is supplied in the introduction on p. 23; the ownership of the plays is discussed further in chapter three.

Table 1.1 Publishing outputs in edition sheets of the twelve stationers involved in negotiations for the First Folio in their first decade of activity, ordered by average size of publication.

Stationer	First decade of publication	No. of editions	All Editions (including 'sold by') Total edition sheets	All Editions (including 'sold by') Average size of book	Collaborative Publications Treated as Equal Shares Total edition sheets	Collaborative Publications Treated as Equal Shares Average size of book	No. of collaboratively published editions
Edward Blount	1594–1603	13	510.75	39.3 sheets	500.5	38.5 sheets	1
Arthur Johnson	1602–1611	40	907	22.7 sheets	591.75	14.8 sheets	15
William Aspley	1599–1608	36	481	13.4 sheets	326	9 sheets	19
Thomas Dewe	1621–1625	20	262.75	13.1 sheets	189	9.5 sheets	3
Nathaniel Butter	1604–1613	84	1044.5	12.4 sheets	933	11.1 sheets	11
William Jaggard	1594–1603	10	106.5	10.7 sheets	91	9.1 sheets	3
Thomas Walkley	1618–1627	31	304	9.8 sheets	285.25	9.2 sheets	3
Henry Walley	1609–1610	10	85.5	8.6 sheets	40	4 sheets	10
John Smethwick	1599–1608	19	160	8.4 sheets	131	6.9 sheets	7
Thomas Pavier	1600–1609	73	540.5	7.4 sheets	501.5	6.9 sheets	8
Matthew Law	1595–1604	22	162.5	7.4 sheets	139	6.3 sheets	4
Lawrence Hayes	1617–1626	1	6	6 sheets	6	6 sheets	0

Notes: Variant states and reissues have been removed, except for reissues of an edition that was published in the same year by another stationer, which I have treated as a collaborative publication. I have included books that were only 'sold by' the stationer concerned, interpreting this as some kind of publishing partnership, which means that the 'All Editions' columns probably overestimate the amount of sheets these stationers published individually. All of Henry Walley's imprints also name the bookseller Richard Bonian. Thomas Pavier's total includes ESTC S123140 (not in the STC) and STC 16681.5 (not attributed to him by the STC but for which he owned the right to copy). Nathaniel Butter's total includes STC 18285 (STC vol. 3, p. 294). William Jaggard includes STC 24627a.6, which survives only in an imperfect copy of six leaves, meaning his total is incomplete. I have not included *Basilikon Doron* (1603, STC 14354) for either Blount or Matthew Law, although both were among the consortium of stationers who had minor shares in the project (Arber II.835).

Source: Author, STC, ESTC, and EEBO.

substance. For one thing, Blount was particularly careful about which books he chose. The thirteen editions he published put him among the bottom few booksellers of this group if we adopt the 'number of editions' metric (only William Jaggard, who was also a printer, and Lawrence Hayes, who financed just one edition, published less). At the same time, the average size of a Blount book in this decade was significantly higher than any other stationer at close to forty sheets. That average is dragged upwards by a few books in particular (two of which are discussed below) and several of Blount's publications were small (he financed five editions that were below ten sheets). But the point is that he was also willing to speculate on much larger work, so much so that his total average not only leads this group of stationers, it is also considerably higher than the mean length of any book from this time across the trade as a whole. Looking at everything printed in London during the five years from 1614 to 1618, David L. Gants has found the average length of any book was 21.4 edition sheets long.[35] Most of the stationers listed here fall well below that average, but Blount nearly doubles it.

Second after Blount is the bookseller Arthur Johnson, whose average book was around twenty-three sheets. But both Johnson and the bookseller with the third-largest average, William Aspley, were in the regular habit of forming publishing partnerships (it was one such partnership that brought Aspley his Shakespeare titles). These partnerships mitigated the risk involved in financing large texts, and Johnson's average drops to around fifteen sheets if we remove his collaborations while Aspley drops from just over thirteen sheets to nine. To judge from the admittedly imperfect evidence of imprints and colophons, Blount almost never worked with another stationer in his early years. His second book—a selection of court music—probably involved some form of collaboration with the music printer Thomas East, but the only other evidence of Blount forming a partnership in this time is his 1/15th share in the official 1603 edition of King James's advice book *Basilikon Doron*: an endeavour in which his participation suggests privileged membership of an exclusive group, rather than a risky venture with shared costs.[36]

By sheer number of edition sheets printed, the most prolific figure of this cohort was Nathaniel Butter, whose total of just over 1,044 suggests a wholly different order of productivity. It may be no coincidence, though, that the model of

---

[35] David L. Gants, 'A Quantitative Analysis of the London Book Trade 1614–1618' in *Studies in Bibliography*, 55 (2002): pp. 185–213, at p. 187. Gants also notes that over half of all publishers working in the same period averaged less than 10 edition sheets a year (p. 202). Using a different measure, Alan B. Farmer and Zachary Lesser found that between 1609 and 1611, *most* speculatively published books were about 10.5 sheets long (the length of an average quarto playbook). They find that the average length of any speculatively published book in these three years was a little over thirty sheets, but point out this average is skewed by multiple editions of the Geneva Bible, among other works, and suggest the *median* (rather than the mean) gives a better sense of what most stationers were doing: 'The Popularity of Playbooks Revisited' in *Shakespeare Quarterly* 56.1 (2005): pp. 1–32, at 24–5.

[36] Arber II.835.

relying on many short pamphlets would later make Butter among the most persistently reviled stationers from this period. From 1621 Butter began to publish weekly coranto newsbooks, often in partnership with his fellow bookseller Nicholas Bourne, for which Butter drew criticism from many quarters. Ben Jonson thought that Butter's 'hunger and thirst after publish'd pamphlets' equated to a 'weekly cheat to draw mony'.[37] Similarly for John Fletcher, Butter was 'some lying stationer' who looked 'as if butter would not melt in his mouth'.[38] The poet Abraham Holland grew sick of looking around Paul's Cross and seeing 'such *Butter* everie weeke besmeare | Each publike post, and Church dore'.[39] In their distaste for the overt pursuit of capital, these attacks on Butter and his work echo the sentiments expressed by Wither and Payne.

In contrast to Butter's model, Blount was among the most selective booksellers of this group and was unusually ready to finance larger books. His willingness to accept economic risk suggests one way to think about Blount's 'literariness': to judge from the evidence of edition sheets, he was simply less in thrall to the market than Butter and the rest of his bookselling peers. For the cultural theorist Pierre Bourdieu, this 'denial of the "economy"' is the main condition necessary for a publisher to accumulate cultural capital.[40] A publisher who wants to influence cultural values must demonstrate that their decisions are not governed solely by financial profits, reaching instead for a kind of 'art for art's sake' mentality. By avoiding conventionally popular genres of book like sermons or news pamphlets, by exercising careful principles of selection, and by being willing to publish texts that both involved considerable financial risk and were intellectually valuable, Blount established a powerful position within the marketplace of literary production.

---

[37] Jonson's note 'To The Readers' from which these quotes are taken appears between acts two and three (sig. E2v) of *The Staple of Newes* in his folio collection published in 1631 that begins with *Bartholmew fayre: a comedie* (STC 14753.5). See also Anthony Parr ed., *The Staple of News* (Manchester: Manchester University Press, 1988), pp. 91–2.

[38] 'The Faire Maide of the Inn', in Francis Beaumont and John Fletcher, *Comedies and tragedies written by Francis Beaumont and John Fletcher Gentlemen* (1647, Wing B1581), sig. 7F4v.

[39] Abraham Holland, 'A Continued Inquisition against Paper-Persecuters', in John Davies, *A scourge for paper-persecutors* (1625, STC 6340), sig. [2]A4r. The pun on Butter's name is a variant which in some copies reads as 'Batter'. That Holland had Nathaniel Butter in mind is suggested by his lines on the previous page about the churchyard walls being 'Butter'd with weekely Newes compos'd in Pauls'. See also the poet Richard Brathwait's comments that the newsbooks Butter published 'live not long; a weeke is the longest in the Citie'; once their brief interest had faded, 'they melt like *Butter*': *Whimzies: or, a new cast of characters* (1631, STC 3591), sig. B9v. Andrew Pettegree suggests that the 'particular ridicule' afforded Butter was in no small measure down to the puns afforded by his name: *The Invention of News: How the World Came to Know about Itself* (New Haven, CT: Yale University Press, 2014), p. 259.

[40] Pierre Bourdieu, *The Field of Cultural Production* (Cambridge: Polity Press, 1993), p. 102. See also p. 75, 'The disavowal of the "economy"'. For Bourdieu there is an inverse relationship between forms of capital, whereby those who are 'rich in cultural capital and (relatively) poor in economic capital' find themselves in opposition to those who are 'rich in economic capital and (relatively) poor in cultural capital', p. 185.

Two particularly large books from these years demonstrate the ways in which Blount's work anticipated an elite readership. The first was John Florio's Italian-English folio dictionary *A Worlde of Wordes* (1598), a work that, at 121 edition sheets (roughly twelve times the number needed for a playbook), was a larger investment than almost any other title in table 1.1.[41] In addition to the amount of paper it required, the dictionary (with its small, long primer typeface and crowded pages) also involved significant typesetting labour. Blount entered the right to copy for this 'most copious and exacte' dictionary in 1596, at which point he had published only one other book.[42] Moreover, a few years after *A Worlde of Wordes*, Blount published Florio's English translation of the *Essayes* of Michel de Montaigne (1603). The *Essayes*, another folio publication, was larger still than Florio's dictionary: at 167 edition sheets, it was the single largest book from the sample studied here, and it was again solely financed by Blount.

How does a book both anticipate and encode a particular readership? Price is one obvious mechanism, and both the dictionary and the *Essayes* excluded all but the affluent. '[P]oore men' as the author James Maxwell noted in 1611 'have too little money to buy big bookes.'[43] Early prices on surviving title pages suggest that a copy of the *Essayes* cost somewhere between five and ten shillings, which helps to explain why the book is known to have been popular within aristocratic households.[44] The dictionary would have cost a little less, but not much. Both the cost and size of a book could be more expressive than we might initially realize.[45] Expensive books seem to demand a certain seriousness of readerly intent, whereby the outlay influenced what Rita Felski has recently described in a different context as the 'mood' of reading: something that 'colors the texts we read, endows them with certain qualities, places them in a given light'.[46] Similarly the size of a book extends into the spaces of reading: a large book could not be carried around in a pocket or easily taken to a tavern or playhouse. Instead, expensive

---

[41] There are two larger books: Arthur Johnson's edition of Zacharias Ursinus, *The summe of Christian religion* (1611, STC 24537) was 142.5 sheets, but here the imprint records a collaboration between Johnson and the publisher Humphrey Lownes. The only larger book from the 359 editions featured in the table is Montaigne's *Essayes*, which was also published by Blount and is discussed below.

[42] Arber III.60; SCA, *Register C*, fol. 8v.

[43] James Maxwell, 'To the Right Honourable, Sir William Craven & Sir John Arnot' in *The golden art* (1611, STC 17700), sig. A4r.

[44] William M. Hamlin, *Montaigne's English Journey: Reading the Essays in Shakespeare's Day* (Oxford: Oxford University Press, 2013), pp. 167, 244.

[45] On the cultural implications of size, see Arthur F. Marotti, *Manuscript, Print, and the English Renaissance Lyric* (Ithaca, NY: Cornell University, 1995), pp. 286–90; Roger Chartier, 'Texts, Printing, Readings' in Lynn Hunt ed., *The New Cultural History* (Berkeley, CA: University of California Press, 1989), pp. 154–75, esp. 167–8. On the relationship between the size of a book and its cost, status, and readership, see Steven K. Galbraith, 'English Literary Folios 1593–1623: Studying Shifts in Format', in John N. King ed., *Tudor Books and Readers: Materiality and the Construction of Meaning* (Cambridge: Cambridge University Press, 2010), pp. 46–67, and Dane and Gillespie, 'cheap quarto', pp. 25–45 in the same volume.

[46] Rita Felski, *The Limits of Critique* (Chicago, IL: University of Chicago Press, 2015), p. 21.

folios seem destined for institutional contexts, to be pored over in libraries or other sites of Foucauldian power and import.

Each edition followed the usual protocols of including various paratextual dedications and commendations. Three woodcut altars frame the names of six aristocratic patrons at the start of the *Essayes*; the two editions collectively feature nine dedicatory sonnets, each printed in large type on its own page and cushioned within a spacious margin.[47] Blount and Florio also produced a selection of bespoke presentation copies for both editions. Copies of the dictionary were given to various prominent statesmen and religious figures with personalized inscriptions by Florio, while several gift copies of the *Essayes* bear manuscript corrections and additions in Florio's careful hand.[48] Florio's additions included local corrections of words and spellings, but also material that amplified Montaigne's work by adding new sentences, delicately tucked into the bottom of the printed page, offering revised thoughts in a way that replicated the pattern of corrections, deletions, and augmentations that characterized Montaigne's own writing process (see Figure 1.2).[49] There is a sense from these copy-specific traces that Florio and Blount designed these editions as cultural events.

But what secured success for both editions was the fact that each constituted a dazzling intervention in a significant intellectual and cultural field. There was a 'concerted attempt' in the late sixteenth century to naturalize 'major Italian literary forms into English', together with particular interest in learning Italian among aristocratic and royal households.[50] Florio himself later recalled that he had

---

[47] Sonia Massai discusses these altars: 'Edward Blount, the Herberts, and the First Folio', in Marta Straznicky ed., *Shakespeare's Stationers: Studies in Cultural Biography* (Philadelphia, PA: University of Pennsylvania Press, 2012), pp. 132–46, at pp. 133–6.

[48] For the dictionary: Folger Library STC 11098 Copy 1 is inscribed by Florio to Elizabeth Carey, Lady Berkeley (addressed by Florio as 'la sra Elisabeta Bartley'); York Minster Library VII.K.2 is inscribed by Florio to Tobias Matthew, then the Bishop of Durham; a copy now in private ownership that was gifted to the statesman Sir Thomas Egerton, Lord Keeper of the Great Seal, contains manuscript additions by both Florio and his friend the neo-Latin playwright Matthew Gwinne (for an image of Gwinne's sonnet, see *Catalogue of Distinguished Printed Books Autograph Letters and Manuscripts, the Property of the Newberry Library, Chicago Sold by Order of the Trustees consequent upon the accession of The Louis H. Silver Collection*, 8–9 November 1965 [Sotheby & Co, 1965], 47). The copy in St John's College, Cambridge (shelfmark G.8.9) is also likely to be a presentation copy. For the *Essayes*, Hamlin notes six presentation copies with longhand corrections by Florio: *Montaigne's English Journey*, p. 250. Other of Blount's books from around this time also survive in presentation copies: in 1599, Blount published George Silver's swordfighting manual, *Paradoxes of defence* (STC 22554), and a presentation manuscript with coloured illustrations was given to the Earl of Essex (British Library Additional MS 34192). British Library C. 82. b. 13 may be a presentation copy of a slightly later Blount book, Pierre Charron's *Of wisdome: three bookes* (1608, STC 5051), which was co-published with William Aspley. The copy has the arms of Henry, Prince of Wales on its binding, to whom the book is dedicated.

[49] On authorial corrections in printed books see Adam Smyth, *Material Texts in Early Modern England* (Cambridge: Cambridge University Press, 2018), pp. 104–10. For authorial presentation manuscripts, see Henry Woudhuysen, *Sir Philip Sidney and the Circulation of Manuscripts 1558–1640* (Oxford: Clarendon Press, 1996), pp. 88–103.

[50] Jason Lawrence, *'Who the Devil Taught Thee So Much Italian?': Italian Language Learning and Literary Imitation in Early Modern England* (Manchester: Manchester University Press, 2005), p. 15.

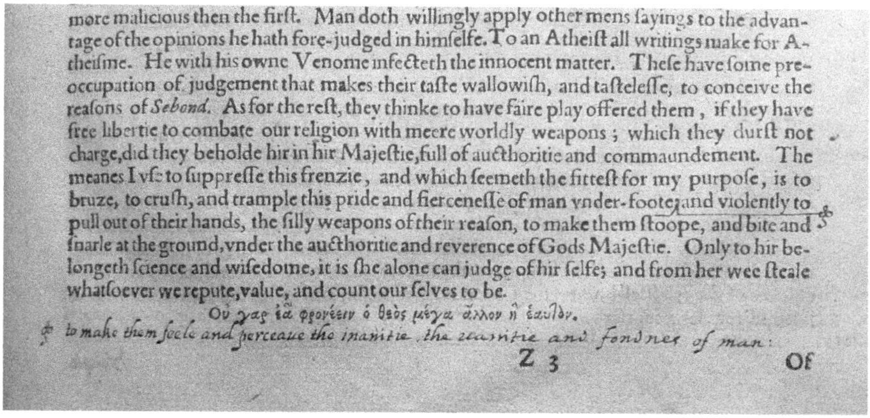
more malicious then the firſt. Man doth willingly apply other mens ſayings to the advantage of the opinions he hath fore-judged in himſelfe. To an Atheiſt all writings make for Atheiſme. He with his owne Venome infecteth the innocent matter. Theſe have ſome preoccupation of judgement that makes their taſte wallowiſh, and taſteleſſe, to conceive the reaſons of *Sebond*. As for the reſt, they thinke to have faire play offered them, if they have free libertie to combate our religion with meere worldly weapons; which they durſt not charge, did they beholde hir in hir Majeſtie, full of aucthoritie and commaundement. The meanes I vſe to ſuppreſſe this frenzie, and which ſeemeth the fitteſt for my purpoſe, is to bruze, to cruſh, and trample this pride and fierceneſſe of man vnder-foote, and violently to pull out of their hands, the ſilly weapons of their reaſon, to make them ſtoope, and bite and ſnarle at the ground, vnder the aucthoritie and reverence of Gods Majeſtie. Only to hir belongeth ſcience and wiſedome, it is ſhe alone can judge of hir ſelfe; and from her wee ſteale whatſoever we repute, value, and count our ſelves to be.

Οὐ γὰρ ἐᾷ φρονέειν ὁ θεὸς μέγα ἄλλον ἢ ἑαυτόν.

to make them feele and perceaue the inanitie, the vanitie and fondnes of man:

Z 3 Of

Figure 1.2 An example of Florio's careful manuscript additions to a copy of Montaigne's *Essayes* (1603, sig. Z3r), expanding Montaigne's thoughts on religious argument. The mark on the right margin shows the note's position in '*An Apologie of* Raymond Sebond'. Image of the copy owned by the library of Worcester College, Oxford, shelfmark L. L. e. 13. Image courtesy of the Provost and Fellows of Worcester College.

tutored 'Two Queenes, and the most eminent subjects of this land' including 'fower Earles, and three lords'.[51] *A Worlde of Wordes* galvanized Italian-English lexicography; its compendium of 46,000 entries is described by its modern editor as 'nothing short of trailblazing and astounding'.[52] The *Essayes* also emerged within, and transformed, an established intellectual context. English readers had known Montaigne's writing since at least as early as 1595, when the stationer Edward Aggas registered (though without ever publishing) 'The Essais of Michaell Lord of Mountene'.[53] And the essay form itself was on the brink of becoming popularized. Three editions of Francis Bacon's own *Essayes* had appeared (in 1597 and 1598), as had the *Essayes* of Sir William Cornwallis in 1600.[54] It was Montaigne's work, though, which emerged as the epitome of the form. For both *A Worlde of Wordes* and Montaigne's *Essayes*, Blount risked a significant amount of capital to publish a major work that irrevocably altered its generic and formal fields.

See also John Gallagher, *Learning Languages in Early Modern England* (Oxford: Oxford University Press, 2019).

[51] *John Florio to Lionel Cranfield, Lord High Treasurer, 1621*: Kent Archives, U269/1.

[52] Hermann Haller ed., *John Florio: A Worlde of Wordes A Critical Edition* (Toronto, ON: University of Toronto Press, 2013), p. xvi.

[53] Arber III.50; SCA, *Register C*, fol. 3v.

[54] Several less well-known efforts also appeared around this time, including the *Essaies, or rather Imperfect offers* of the otherwise unknown Rob Johnson (1601, STC 14695), and the clergyman Daniel Tuvill's *Essaies politicke, and morall* (1608, STC 24396).

Blount's interest in large and expensive books, the publication of which could be promoted as of intellectual worth and as beneficial to the 'publike advantage', became a distinguishing feature of his career. More impressive folios followed, including second editions of both Florio's dictionary (1611) and the *Essayes* of Montaigne (1613). His ambitious publishing strategies probably contributed to his growing visibility in the book trade. In 1600, Blount was himself the recipient of a playful dedication from a fellow publisher. A poem by Christopher Marlowe was dedicated by the stationer Thomas Thorpe 'to his kind, and true friend: Edward Blunt', offered 'in the memory of that pure Elementall wit *Chr. Marlow*' to be 'rais'd in the circle of your Patronage'.[55] The tone of Thorpe's dedication is light-hearted—it has been called a 'Churchyard in-joke'—but it nevertheless placed Blount in the privileged position of patronizing a literary work.[56] Around this time, too, various archival traces suggest that Blount had relationships with privileged communities. In 1596 he received payment from Henry Percy, Earl of Northumberland, for stocking Percy's library with books; shortly afterwards Blount is also found listed in the account books of Prince Henry, after he was chosen by royal warrant to supply 'certen bookes' for 'the furnishing of the Princes Library'.[57] His work seems to have caught the eye of an influential roster of clients, and other evidence from his career suggests he continued to move in such circles. It was Blount who acted as the surety when the clergyman Henry Parry, a favourite of the previous monarch, Queen Elizabeth, was given his first bishopric in 1607; in the same year Blount can be found underwriting another church appointment organized by William Herbert, the Earl of Pembroke, to whom, along with his brother Phillip Herbert, the First Folio would later be dedicated.[58]

Financing the First Folio

How was Blount's approach to investment at stake in the publication of Shakespeare's Folio? We cannot know with any detail how the costs of the Folio were divided between Blount and the rest of the Shakespeare syndicate, only that it was 'at the charges' of the stationers named in the imprint and colophon. Yet if, as seems likely, Blount was one of the leading financiers, then several critics have noticed that publishing Shakespeare led to problems. Perhaps, as Blount's

---

[55] Thomas Thorpe, 'To His Kind, and True Friend: Edward Blunt' in Lucan, *Lucans first booke*, trans. Christopher Marlowe (1600, STC 16883.5), sig. A2r–v.

[56] András Kiséry, 'Companionate Publishing, Literary Publics, and the Wit of Epyllia: The Early Success of *Hero and Leander*' in Kirk Melnikoff and Roslyn L. Knutson eds, *Christopher Marlowe, Theatrical Commerce, and the Book Trade* (Cambridge: Cambridge University Press, 2018), pp. 165–81, at p. 170.

[57] *Sixth Report of the Royal Commission on Historical Manuscripts* (London: HM Stationery Office, 1877), p. 227; TNA E 351/2793.

[58] TNA E 334/14, fol. 87v, 89r. Blount is also found underwriting other appointments at fol. 85v, 132v, and 211v.

biographer Gary Taylor has put it, his investment in the Folio was 'not a rational economic decision'.[59] Rather than launching a vibrant new phase of Blount's career, the Shakespeare Folio looks to have heralded a collapse of Blount's business at the sign of the Black Bear. A steady rhythm of new publications in the years leading up to the Folio dried up, and after 1623 Blount published nothing for several years. Taylor also notes that Blount's importation of books from Europe stopped: port records show that Blount took delivery of unbound books from the continent several times in 1621, but that he disappeared from the next surviving port book for 1625–6.[60] Blount eventually resurfaced in 1628 when he published John Earle's book of witty character sketches, *Micro-cosmographie*, a short duodecimo of just nine edition sheets that proved highly popular. He published a final handful of titles before his death a few years later, but his business never fully recovered.

This faltering end to a career that launched with such ambition has puzzled scholars and has been linked to theories about the Folio's early reception. Critics have considered whether, if Blount was indeed the Folio's major investor, he overstretched himself by investing in Shakespeare. Perhaps, rather than the Folio being an immediate success, the book was in fact a disappointment that failed to sell and so damaged Blount's business. Marta Straznicky for one has wondered whether Blount's decline was related to 'an ill-judged investment in the Shakespeare folio', and others have echoed her concern that the fate of Blount's business may register an equivocal early response to the Folio.[61] New evidence offers a different explanation for the decline of the Black Bear and further highlights Blount's commitment to investing in new cultural forms.

This evidence appears in the form of a Court of Chancery case that came to a head in the final stages of the Folio's production, with hearings in October and November of 1623. At stake was a large sum of money: Blount was owed as much as £2,000 by his brother-in-law, one Roger Roydon. Having pursued this debt

---

[59] Gary Taylor, '*Comedies, Histories, & Tragedies* (and Tragicomedies and Poems): Posthumous Shakespeare, 1623–1728', in Gary Taylor, John Jowett, Terri Bourus, and Gabriel Egan eds, *The New Oxford Shakespeare: The Complete Works Critical Reference Edition*, 2 vols (Oxford: Oxford University Press, 2017), vol. 2, pp. xvii–lxix, at p. lii.

[60] Taylor, 'Tragicomedies and Poems', p. lii. Each of Blount's deliveries was for 'one quarter maund unbound bookes': *Port of London accounts 1620-1*, TNA E 190/24/4, fol. 43v, 124v, and 138r (quote from 43v). A 'maund' was a woven or occasionally wooden container used to transport goods. See also *Port of London accounts 1625-6*, TNA E 190/31/3.

[61] Marta Straznicky, 'What Is a Stationer' in Marta Straznicky ed., *Shakespeare's Stationers: Studies in Cultural Bibliography* (Philadelphia, PA: University of Pennsylvania Press, 2012), pp. 1–16, at p. 313 (n. 33). Gary Taylor points out that both Blount and Aspley look to have had business trouble after the Folio: 'Making Meaning Marketing Shakespeare 1623' in Peter Holland and Stephen Orgel eds, *From Performance to Print in Shakespeare's England* (Basingstoke: Palgrave Macmillan, 2006), pp. 55–72, at p. 61. Taylor elaborates his argument about the Folio's poor initial reception in 'Tragicomedies and Poems', pp. xlix–lviii. See also Emma Smith, *The Making of Shakespeare's First Folio* (Oxford: Bodleian Library, 2015), p. 117; Kastan, *Shakespeare and the Book* (Cambridge: Cambridge University Press, 2001), pp. 62–3.

through various courts for several years, events reached a crisis for Blount at almost exactly the same time that we think the Folio was finished and had arrived on the shelves of London's bookshops. A little context is needed to interpret this case in terms of Blount's investment in Shakespeare. The debt did not originate with Blount. Instead it was created by a fellow bookseller, Richard Bankworth, who shortly before his death in 1612 had loaned £1,000 to his brother-in-law on the understanding that it would be repaid with interest by 1616.[62] However, Bankworth died only a few months after handing over the money, and his widow Elizabeth remarried Edward Blount, who thus inherited this sizeable sum—if it could be recovered. In 1616, when Roydon failed to return the loan, Blount launched legal action. The documents in which these events are recounted—a bill of complaint, and the entry books belonging to the clerks of the Court of Chancery who followed the case—describe how Blount first turned to the court system in Shropshire, where Roydon lived, but found the jury 'very partiall for Roiden'.[63] Blount then appealed to another court, this time in Wales, with no better luck. Stress is laid throughout the accounts on the importance of the debt: it is said that, in its pursuit, Blount 'expended diverse great somes of money, but hitherto could get noe fruict or benefit'.[64] On 16 October 1623—one week after Blount watched at Stationers' Hall as the company clerk carefully listed the sixteen unregistered Shakespeare plays collected by Blount and Isaac Jaggard, and at the same time, according to Charlton Hinman's timetable, that the final pages of *Cymbeline* were being printed—a court clerk recorded that the debt still 'resteth unpaid'.[65] Moreover, the clerk noted that Blount 'hath done his utmost endeavors to get in the said debt and hath spent above £150 in charges' to no avail.[66] The significance of Blount's expenditure is brought home by noting that the total cost of publishing the First Folio was probably around £250; another comparison is provided by the annual rent on Blount's perfectly located bookshop in Paul's Cross Churchyard, which was described in a deed of sale from 1627 as being

---

[62] Details of the case are primarily taken from three related documents: Blount's Bill of Complaint to the Court of Chancery (TNA C 3/333/25), and two statements by the court clerks in the Entry Books of Decrees and Orders (TNA C 33/145, fol. 415v–416r; TNA C 33/147, fol. 663r–v). The debt is also mentioned in the will of Richard Bankworth, Blount's son-in-law, who died in 1621, leaving his portion of the debt to 'my loving father in lawe Edward Blount': TNA PROB 11/138/543. The documents discuss an earlier case heard in the Welsh Court of Great Sessions, but I have been unable to trace a relevant reference in the index sequence for the civil records of the Chester circuit (containing Denbigh, where Blount's case was heard) between 1617 and 1622. A Roger Roydon of Denbigh—perhaps the same man—appears multiple times in the docket rolls in connection with another case in July and September 1620: *Great Sessions Docket Rolls*: National Library of Wales, Great Sessions 8/5, pieces 17 and 19.

[63] TNA C 33/145, fol. 415v.   [64] TNA C 3/333/25.

[65] Charlton Hinman's summary of the timetable of the printing of the Folio is in: *The Printing and Proof-Reading of the First Folio of Shakespeare*, 2 vols (Oxford: Clarendon Press, 1963), vol. 2, pp. 519–29. The late arrival of *Troilus and Cressida* leaves that play hovering uncertainly at the end of this timetable, completed somewhere around the end of October or beginning of November 1623. TNA C 33/145, fol. 416r.

[66] TNA C 33/145, fol. 416r.

around £8.[67] Elsewhere in the court documents, the money owed was described as 'the cheefest means lefte [Blount's family] for their porcons & mayntenance'.[68]

The saga dragged on over the end of 1623. In November, Blount took his case before a London court and won a concession: Roydon agreed to pay Blount £1,400, and offered valuable lands in Wales as a guarantee that he would in fact make good on the payments. A survey of these lands was ordered, but in April 1624 surveyors returned disastrous news. Roydon had led them around lands that did not belong to him, waving airily at fields he did not possess and claiming a surety he did not have. At this point, Blount approached Chancery, and declared himself to 'utterly be defrauded & defeated'.[69] The last document I have found concerning the case is Blount's Bill of Complaint, submitted to Chancery and dated July of 1624. In it, Blount complained that he and his wife (the 'orators' of the bill) had been undone by Roydon and his associates, who were:

> \not contented with your orators said losse But/ having a purpose to deceave your said orators & to defraude & defeate them of the said debt did [act] by practise & combynacion betweene themselves to that end and purpos[e][70]

At this point, the records run out, hiding the outcome of the case. We need to be careful how we interpret the language of financial ruin that runs through this evidence. After all, Blount would hardly portray the debt as immaterial when making the case for its recovery. But other evidence from Blount's biography suggests that he never recovered the money. The records of the Stationers' Company record his financial difficulties from 1618, when he was threatened with losing his part in the English Stock over an undisclosed sum.[71] His debts are noted again later that year, and he was soon forced to sell his shares in the company's English Stock in order to pay off further debt. Other of his money troubles are recorded through the 1620s.[72] A newly discovered Blount letter dated 1631 and discussed below adds a little more colour to his biography shortly before his death, but, in a somewhat poignant epitaph, the final mention of Blount in the Stationers' Company archives is for a payment from the poor fund, recorded in March of 1633 (Figure 1.3). He was probably already dead by this point: the payment

---

[67] Assuming an edition size of 750 copies, Blayney is 'reasonably certain' that a single Folio cost the publishers about 6s 8d, including all costs for paper, securing the copy, and labour: *The First Folio*, p. 26. Blount's rent is noted in *Husting Roll 303, Item 40*: LMA CLA/023/DW/01/302. The deed describes the stationer Thomas Man's purchase of Blount's bookshop at the sign of the Black Bear and Francis Constable's shop at the Sign of the Crane. Both properties were sold freehold for £320; their joint annual rent is given as £16. See also Peter Blayney, *The Bookshops in Paul's Cross Churchyard* (London: The Bibliographical Society, 1990), pp. 26–7.

[68] TNA C 3/333/25.   [69] TNA C 3/333/25.

[70] TNA C 3/333/25. The document is damaged at one end; my interpolations are in square brackets.

[71] William A. Jackson ed., *Records of the Court of the Stationers' Company, 1602–1640* (London: Bibliographical Society, 1957), p. 100.

[72] Jackson ed., *Records*, pp. 105, 106, 146, 152, 180.

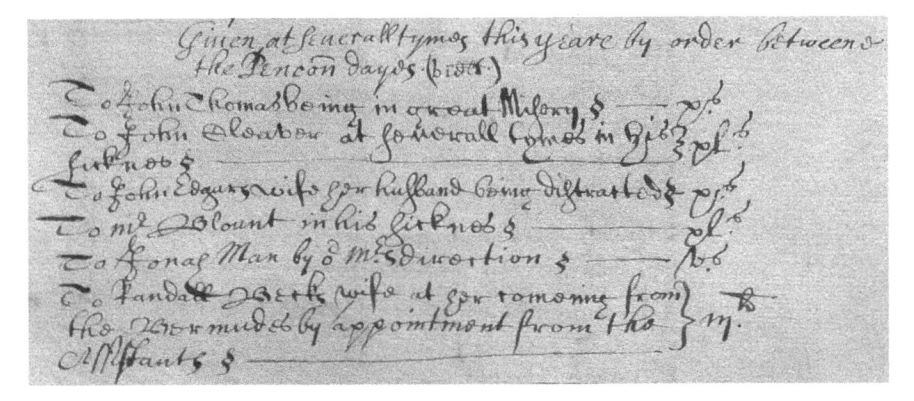

Figure 1.3 Money paid to Blount 'in his sicknes' by the Stationers' Company (five lines up). Image of SCA, *Liber Computi Pro Pauperibus*, fol. 115v. Credit: The Stationers' Company Archive.

appears not in the regular list of pensioners but amid a small huddle of names tacked onto the bottom of the list, recording moneys 'Given at severall tymes this yeare'—meaning in the twelve months from the start of the legal year in March 1632. Unlike the regular entries in the poor fund, which simply list a name and the sum given, these extra six names among which Blount appears have a few words added in explanation for the gift, offering us the briefest of biographical glimpses into the lives of these troubled stationers. John Thomas received ten shillings 'being in great Misery'; John Edgar's wife was given ten shillings 'her husband being distracted'; Randall Beck's wife collected three pounds 'at her comeing from the Bermudes by appointment'. Amid this evocative list, the clerk recorded forty shillings given to 'M*aster* Blount in his sicknes'.[73]

With this biographical evidence of Blount's financial difficulties in mind, the well-known entry of November 1623, in which Blount and Isaac Jaggard claimed ownership of the unregistered titles of Shakespeare's plays (see p. 21), marks another turning point in Blount's career. It was after this entry that Blount began to sell valuable titles for which he owned the right to copy, rather than register new ones. A few months after learning the results of the disastrous survey in Wales, Blount sold the right to publish Christopher Marlowe's popular epyllion *Hero and Leander*, which by 1623 had appeared in eight editions since he had first financed it in 1598. At the same time, Blount also sold his shares in John Ryder's popular English-Latin *Dictionary* and continued the trend by signing over the rights to John Earle's book of character sketches *Micro-cosmographie* a few months

---

[73] SCA, *Liber Computi Pro Pauperibus, 1608–1676*, fol. 115v. In a mark of their differing fortunes since publication of the Shakespeare Folio, the accounts were signed off by William Aspley as warden of the Stationers' Company (fol. 117r). See also W. Craig Ferguson, 'The Stationers' Company Poor Book, 1608–1700,' *The Library* Series 5, 31.1 (1976), pp. 37–51.

after buying the manuscript.[74] Finally, in June of 1630, in an act that may mark the moment at which discussions began for work on the second edition of Shakespeare's Folio (1632), Blount sold 'all his estate and right in the Copies' of the Shakespearean titles he had registered with Jaggard to his successor at the Black Bear, the bookseller Robert Allott.[75]

The lengthy tussle between Blount and his brother-in-law unsettles the critical view that readers passed over Shakespeare's Folio in ways that created problems for one of the book's chief investors. If indeed Blount was a leading figure in the Folio syndicate, then he had more to worry about in the early 1620s than the fate of Shakespeare's book. More broadly, Blount's evident financial difficulties invite us to reconsider his decision to publish Shakespeare at all. Given that his business seems to have been on the brink of collapse, we might expect a cautious approach to his publishing work. Instead, he invested in a project that, in collecting the professional plays of an author in folio format, broke new ground within the book trade with no clear guarantee of success. Blount's financial difficulties may also have driven the formation of the publishing syndicate, so that costs could be shared between the four business. Perhaps, just as with Florio, Montaigne, and other of his authors, we can interpret Blount's gamble on the Shakespeare Folio as further evidence of his commitment to publish authors he believed would satisfy 'the curious appetite of the Soule', in George Wither's words.

The timing of these circumstances means that we could view Shakespeare's Folio as a remarkably fortunate book, one that just evaded the forces that were gradually closing the door of Blount's bookshop. One month before Blount and Jaggard registered Shakespeare's manuscripts, Blount paid sixpence to register Ben Jonson's translation of the Latin prose romance *Argenis*, which was never subsequently printed.[76] It may be the case, as is usually thought, that this manuscript was one of those lost in the fire that engulfed Jonson's library in 1623—the 'three Books not afraid | To speake the Fate of the *Sycilian* Maid', of which Jonson laments the loss in his poem 'An Execration Upon Vulcan'—but perhaps not.[77] Given that Blount had registered the manuscript, it might seem odd for him to then hand it back to its author. Perhaps, then, the *Argenis* marks the point at which both Jonson's energy and Blount's finances ran out, ending the bookseller's ability to promote new work.

---

[74] Arber IV.126, 127, 202; SCA, *Register D*, p. 88, 89, 168. See also Blount's sale of the titles to work by two of his friends: Robert Dallington's *Aphorismes civill and militarie*, and James Mabbe's translation of *The rogue* (IV.206).

[75] Arber IV.243; SCA, *Register D*, p. 209. The memorandum of this assignation in the Stationers' Register is dated 16 November 1630 but describes a note of sale written 'in master Blountes hand' and dated 26 June 1630.

[76] Arber IV.105; SCA, *Register D*, p. 67.

[77] Ben Jonson, *Ben: Jonson's Execration Against Vulcan* (1640, STC 14771), sig. B3r. I am here thinking with Adam Smyth's challenge to a literal reading of Jonson's book list. He wonders whether Jonson's list is 'bibliography as a to-do list, the titles not quite fictions, but hopes, things somewhere in the pipeline': Smyth, *Material Texts*, p. 65.

Edward Blount and the Publication of Taste

We could also locate Blount's 'literariness' in his preoccupation with issues of taste. In various ways Blount used the technologies of print to influence categories of value and judgement. Most straightforwardly, he did this by publishing titles that engaged with cultural debate. Moreover, his work demonstrates a commitment to particular communities of writers and to consistent positions within literary debates.

One such debate concerned the place of rhyme in English literary culture at the turn of the century. In 1602 the bookseller Andrew Wise found time amid a busy period of Shakespeare publishing to finance a book by the poet and musician Thomas Campion called *Observations in the Art of English Poesie*.[78] Campion's biographer describes the *Observations* as the last of the 'forlorn Elizabethan attempts' to impose classical order on the increasingly sprawling field of English poetry.[79] The text contains Campion's views on metre, scansion, and especially on rhyme: it was a 'childish titillation' in Campion's view, which artificially limited a poet's choices and crushed their imaginative range. Moreover rhyme's technical simplicity tempted too many to write verse, creating as many poets 'as hot sommer flies'.[80]

The *Observations* is perhaps best known for the response it prompted from the court poet Samuel Daniel, whose own verse—in *Musophilus*, for example, or *The Civil Wars*—typically leaned heavily on rhyme. Blount published Daniel's rejoinder as *A Defence of Ryme* (1603).[81] The *Defence* rejected 'my adversary' Campion's dated views on poetry and argued that while rhyme could be tiresome, in an 'eminent spirit' it was a tool that carried poetry 'beyond his power to a far happier flight'.[82] Critics generally feel that Daniel easily answered Campion's fusty critique.

The debate lingers on a relatively narrow issue within English literary history but suggests something important about Blount's work. If we think about the *Defence* as a 'Samuel Daniel' book, then its publication by Blount seems odd. Daniel had an unusually strong relationship with the bookseller Simon Waterson, who, just the previous year, had published an impressive folio edition of the writer's collected *Workes* and who owned the right to copy for almost all of Daniel's

---

[78] Wise was among the most important of Shakespeare's publishers. For more on this bookseller, including his publishing partnership with William Aspley which saw the two stationers jointly finance the first editions of *Much Ado About Nothing* (1600) and *2 Henry IV* (1600), see pp. 125–8.

[79] David Lindley, 'Campion, Thomas (1567–1620), poet and musician,' *Oxford Dictionary of National Biography* (Oxford: Oxford University Press, 2004; online edn, May 2006) [accessed 27 November 2019].

[80] Thomas Campion, *Observations in the art of English poesie* (1602, STC 4543), sigs. A7r, A6v.

[81] Samuel Daniel, 'A Defence of Ryme,' in *A Panegyric Congratulatory* (1603, STC 6259).

[82] Daniel, 'Defence of Ryme', sig. G6r. On the debate see Richard Helgerson, *Forms of Nationhood: The Elizabethan Writing of England* (Chicago, IL: University of Chicago Press, 1994), pp. 19–62; Gavin Alexander ed., *Sidney's 'The Defence of Poesy' and Selected Renaissance Literary Criticism* (London: Penguin Books, 2004), pp. lxvii–lxxi.

titles.[83] But for Blount, the text's authorship may have been less important than its contribution to an ongoing argument about English literary culture. The stationer had already contributed to this quarrel by publishing a related statement in the first edition of John Florio's dictionary. After the title page and dedications of *A Worlde of Wordes*, six more preliminary pages are given over to an earlier version of this same bad-tempered tussle over the quiddities of vernacular literature.[84] These pages feature an epistle 'To the Reader', signed by Florio, in which he rails at some unnamed opponents. The epistle—a bewildering piece of verbal stunt-pilotry—begins with typically Florian exuberance:

> I begin with those notable Pirates in this our paper-sea, those sea-dogs, or lande-Critikes, monsters of men, if not beastes rather then men; whose teeth are Canibals, their toongs adder-forkes, their lips aspes-poyson, their eies basiliskes, their breath the breath of a grave, their wordes like swordes of Turkes, that strive which shall dive deepest into a Christian lying bound before them.[85]

This is fun stuff if we allow ourselves to be blown along by the sheer vigour of Florio's prose. Florio's anonymous critics mutate from men into beasts and then beyond; they are pirates, sea-dogs, monsters, asps. There is a kind of underlying logic to his chaotic language, because it concentrates on the organs of speech and critical utterance: teeth become cannibals (perhaps because critics devour the written material on which they rely); tongues flicker and become serpentine; words are Turkish swords carving up helpless Christians. Florio's enemies are transformed into a monstrous chimera whose practice of exegesis becomes poison and death.

Who are Florio's enemies? It is not at all clear from the epistle, but the author's biographer has shown this writing is embedded within the same literary communities who quarrelled about rhyme in 1602-3. Florio's main target was Hugh Sanford, secretary to the Earl of Pembroke (Florio himself only goes so far as 'H. S.', glossed as 'Huffe Snuffe, Horse Stealer, Hob Sowter, Hugh Sot, Humfrey Swineshead, Hodge Sowgelder').[86] Florio tells us that one of Sanford's associates had insulted

---

[83] Daniel's biographer notes that 'All but one or two of Daniel's editions (more than twenty in thirty years) were published by Waterson': John Pitcher, 'Daniel, Samuel (1562/3–1619), poet and historian,' *Oxford Dictionary of National Biography* (Oxford: Oxford University Press, 2004; online edn, September 2004) [accessed 27 November 2019]. Blount and Waterson were linked in ways that reach beyond Daniel: in 1611, the pair stood as sureties for the orphans of the important Elizabethan publisher William Ponsonby, who had been Blount's former master in the book trade: LMA CLA/002/05/001, fol. 33v.

[84] The most detailed account of this dispute is found in Frances Yates, *John Florio: The Life of An Italian in Shakespeare's England* (Cambridge: Cambridge University Press, 1934), pp. 188–212.

[85] John Florio, 'To the Reader' in *A worlde of wordes* (1598, STC 11098), sig. A5v.

[86] Yates, *John Florio*, pp. 192–214; Florio, 'To the Reader' in *A worlde of wordes*, sig. A5v. Yates transcribes the epistle in an appendix.

a good sonnet of a gentlemans, a friend of mine, that loved better to be a Poet, then to be counted so, [and] called the auctor a rymer, notwithstanding he had more skill in good Poetrie, then my slie gentleman seemed to have in good manners or humanitie.[87]

Here is back-and-forth of the kind that we might enjoy today in the letters pages of a literary magazine; Frances Yates imagines Florio standing 'with set teeth and rapier drawn'.[88] The 'rymer' (a scornful term) has been identified as Samuel Daniel, so Florio is telling us here that Sanford—or his friend—had previously insulted Florio's own friend. It is perhaps not surprising that Florio was worked up here: Daniel was his brother-in-law and the pair were fellow students at Oxford in the early 1580s. Identifying the various bristling personalities shows that Blount's publication of Daniel's *Defence* was his second intervention in a series of related arguments about the nature of English poetry. Both the dictionary and the *Defence* make claims from the same side of this debate, suggesting that Blount was committed to a particular vision for the future of vernacular literature.[89]

If Florio's epistle and Daniel's *Defence* suggest Blount's interest in certain literary disputes, then they also demonstrate the ways in which ideas about literature were constituted within communities. Blount's professional commitment to these debates is inextricable from his social loyalty to the circle of authors around Daniel and Florio. The dictionary's epistle emerged from within a distinct literary scene. 'Let *H.S.* hisse, and his complices quarrell,' wrote Florio, 'I have a great faction of good writers to bandie with me.'[90] These 'good writers' probably included Matthew Gwinne, another of Blount's authors; Florio may also have had the witty prose writer Thomas Nashe in mind. This group of influential and cosmopolitan authors worked with shared ideas about English writing. Ranged against Florio and his friends, Sanford and his 'complices' were aligned with Campion, and seemingly with some unnamed contemporary playwrights: 'Let *Aristophanes* and his comedians make plaies,' Florio tells us, 'and scowre their mouthes on *Socrates*.'[91] Aristophanes (the Greek playwright whose caricature of Socrates may have contributed to the philosopher's death) is a cipher here of course, and while we do not know the particular dramatist Florio had in mind, we nevertheless get the sense that the argument involved writers of various literary forms.

But perhaps the epistle's ambiguity is part of the point; we are not the readers Florio had in mind. In that sense, the dictionary's preface is an example of what András Kiséry has described as the 'disclosure of privileged discourse': the trick of promising access to something exclusive—such as a row about literary

---

[87] Florio, 'To the Reader' in *A worlde of wordes*, sig. A5v.   [88] Yates, *John Florio*, p. 212.
[89] The *Defence* named 'Maister *Hugh Samford*' in its concluding pages, enmeshing the text in this fractious social framework: Daniel, 'Defence of Ryme', sig. H6v.
[90] Florio, 'To the Reader' *A worlde of wordes*, sig. A6r.
[91] Florio, 'To the Reader' *A worlde of wordes*, sig. A6r.

culture—while simultaneously withholding full meaning.[92] The obscurity of Florio's language is part of the way that it generates this exclusivity and preserves the coterie within the publicity of print. Having the money to buy a copy of the dictionary did not necessarily grant a reader access to everything within its pages. The dictionary's epistle thus enacts, in its complicated language of hide-and-reveal, a hierarchical dynamic similar to that which hack writers would exploit after the Restoration by publishing 'keys' that promised to reveal the specific personalities alluded to by texts like Jonathan Swift's *Tale of Tub* (1704) or Alexander Pope's *The Dunciad* (1728). Both the dictionary and the *Defence* begin to show us Blount's participation in the contestations and manoeuvres by which literary hierarchies were constructed.[93]

Blount also intervened in cultural discussion in more personal ways. Kirk Melnikoff has shown that stationers increasingly added prefatory statements to their books towards the end of the sixteenth century.[94] However, as Table 1.2 shows, not all booksellers were interested in this form of writing. Most of the twelve stationers involved in the negotiations for the First Folio never wrote—or at least, never wrote and signed—a preliminary address of any kind. Stationers like Thomas Pavier, John Smethwick, and Matthew Law were alert to the potential of preliminary matter to shape their books. Around half of Pavier's books contained a preliminary address of some kind, as did around two-thirds of Law's books and three-quarters of those financed by Smethwick. But these stationers did not add their own voices to the polyphonous envelope of texts that 'define and shape' the rest of a printed book.[95]

At the other end of the scale, Edward Blount's books embody his presence more clearly and consistently than anyone else from this cohort of stationers. His nineteen signed preliminary addresses mean that slightly less than one in five of Blount's editions or issues featured his written contribution. Perhaps that figure is slightly misleading, given that five of those nineteen addresses are the same text: Blount's dedication to the literary patron Sir Thomas Walsingham, printed at the start of fresh editions of Christopher Marlowe's popular poem *Hero and Leander*. But even if we restrict the count to unique addresses, Blount is still left with thirteen signed prefatory statements (and one that he probably wrote but left

---

[92] Kiséry, 'Companionate Publishing', p. 168.

[93] Other of Blount's books engaged directly with ideas of taste and cultural value: Thomasso Buoni's *Problemes of beauty* contains a passage on aesthetics, which among other things considered how it was that language and poetry could be beautiful: Buoni, *Problemes* (1618, STC 4103.5), sig. B12r.

[94] Kirk Melnikoff, *Elizabethan Publishing and the Makings of Literary Culture* (Toronto, ON: University of Toronto Press, 2018), pp. 39–45. See also Franklin B. Williams, *Index of Dedications and Commendatory Verses in English Books Before 1641* (London: Bibliographical Society, 1962).

[95] Heidi Brayman Hackel, *Reading Material in Early Modern England: Print, Gender, and Literacy* (Cambridge: Cambridge University Press, 2005), p. 88. On preliminary addresses see also Richard McCabe, *Ungainefull Arte: Poetry, Patronage, & Print in the Early Modern Era* (Oxford: Oxford University Press, 2016), pp. 73–87.

66 SHAKESPEARE'S SYNDICATE

Table 1.2 Prefatory addresses written by the twelve stationers who owned the right to print one or more of Shakespeare's plays in 1623

Publisher	No. of editions and issues checked	No. of editions and issues with any preface	No. of signed prefaces by stationer (including initials)	No. of unsigned probable prefaces by stationer
Edward Blount	97	86 (89%)	19	1
Thomas Walkley	82	31 (38%)	5	0
Nathaniel Butter	612	271 (44%)	3	11
William Jaggard	88	64 (73%)	3	4
Thomas Dewe	24	24 (100%)	0	2
William Aspley	110	76 (69%)	0	1
Matthew Law	90	61 (68%)	0	1
Henry Walley	11	8 (73%)	0	1
Thomas Pavier	189	96 (51%)	0	0
John Smethwick	100	76 (76%)	0	0
Arthur Johnson	89	75 (82%)	0	0
Lawrence Hayes	2	1 (50%)	0	0

Notes: To compile this table I have reviewed all STC entries for these stationers using a mixture of EEBO and inspection of physical copies. I include both editions and issues because reissues sometimes included new prefatory material. That being said, a reissued stationer epistle has not been counted as a separate preface. New editions that reproduce an old epistle are counted. Excluding variant states and impressions, I have checked a total of 1,495 editions and issues and was unable to check fifty-eight editions and issues. This material comprises the known publishing careers of these stationers with the exceptions of Thomas Walkley and Nathaniel Butter, whose publishing work extends beyond the dates of the STC; the later stages of their careers have not been checked. John Smethwick published one book beyond the STC (Wing L2336) which has been checked. A 'preface' here includes any dedicatory epistle or address to the reader. Some of the 'probable unsigned' prefaces are ambiguous, though I have erred towards caution. From 1621 many of Nathaniel Butter's publications are his coranto newsbooks. Those newsbooks I have been unable to access have been checked using Folke Dahl's *A Bibliography of English Corantos and Periodical Newsbooks 1620-1642* (London: The Bibliographical Society, 1952), in which Dahl makes clear that he has been attentive to 'the numerous "editorial notices" to be found in the newsbooks' (pp. 25–6). These notices hover somewhere between an address to the reader and an editorial introduction, but they have been checked where possible. None that I have seen are signed by Butter, but in a few cases where Butter's authorship seems likely I have included the notice in his count of probable prefaces. My list of William Jaggard's publications is found as an appendix to this book. The signed (and unsigned) prefaces are as follows: Edward Blount: STC 17413, 5624, 11634, 6200, 6201, 7274, 17417, 17418, 17419, 3957, 4917, 288 (contains two signed addresses), 17420, 7439 [reissued as 7440], 7440.2, 14830.7, 17088 (contains two signed prefaces) (STC 13541). Thomas Walkley: STC 1670, 1682, 16927, 22305, 11079.5. Nathaniel Butter: STC 6427, 11189 (STC 22385, 22386, 18507.51A, 18507.77, 23009, 23519.5, 23525.3 [reissued as 23525.4], 23525.5, 18507.277, 18507.337, 18507.343). William Jaggard: STC 13502, 14343, 10717 (STC 6062 [reissued as 6062.2], 17936.5, 3172, 24756). Thomas Dewe: (STC 21609, 24630). William Aspley: (STC 22393). Matthew Law: (STC 17917). Henry Walley: (STC 22332).

unsigned): comfortably more than any other figure from this group even without applying that more stringent filter to his peers.[96] In contrast to the distinct visibility of Blount's signature we might compare the inverse ratio of Nathaniel Butter, who signed three statements and left behind eleven more anonymous addresses that he probably also wrote but never signed. The implication is that although Butter knew the value of prefatory matter, his name carried less meaning. It is worth noticing, too, that Blount's books began with preliminary addresses of any kind more often than was typical for this cohort, suggesting that his books were, by and large, implicated in the complex economies of exchange, patronage, and interpretation activated by the front matter of a book to a greater extent than any of these stationers with the exception of Thomas Dewe.

Data concerning prefaces or edition sheets can seem unyielding, but it helps us to see something like the bibliographic personality of these booksellers. Shakespeare's stationers envisaged their books in different ways and tracking these differences (of investment habits, of paratext) can supply us with variables for thinking about the arrival of a book into the world. If, as Philip Tromans has recently shown, the opening pages of books were of particular interest to readers browsing in bookshops, thumbing through preliminary leaves as they decided whether to buy, then encountering the opinions of 'Ed. Blount' or 'Edw. Blount', as he consistently signed himself, was a relatively familiar accompaniment to many book-buying trips.[97]

These signed prefaces by Blount often foreground his judgements about the texts he introduced. In their easy confidence in assessing the worth of authors

---

[96] In their relatively large number, Blount's signed paratexts also suggest his restless pursuit of new material. Setting aside the success of *Hero and Leander*, Blount tended to prioritize the publication of new titles, which meant he was also continually *designing* books from scratch, and so creating opportunities to include himself in a book's packaging. Other stationers (for example William Aspley and particularly John Smethwick) relied more on republishing popular titles. And because such reprinted books tended to replicate the format and structure of the previous edition, this business model was inherently less open to an evolving prefatory presence (on the static nature of republished titles see Alan B. Farmer and Zachary Lesser, 'Vile Arts: The Marketing of English Printed Drama, 1512–1660,' in *Research Opportunities in Renaissance Drama* 39 (2000): pp. 77–165).

[97] Philip Tromans, 'The Business of Browsing in Early Modern English Bookshops' in Shanti Graheli ed., *Buying and Selling: The Business of Books in Early Modern Europe* (Leiden: Brill, 2019), pp. 111–35. Blount's visibility in print begins to explain the many references to this bookseller that lie scattered in the records of the early seventeenth century. Further to those cited above, letters written by the poet Robert Herrick from Cambridge show that it was through '*Master* Blunt book seller in Paules Church yarde' that Herrick received his quarterly allowance from his uncle Sir William Herrick: *Robert Herrick to Sir William Herrick, January 1617*, Bodleian MS Eng. c. 2278, fol. 17. It was also specifically to 'Mr Blunt' that the West Country preacher John Downe turned in 1624 when, 'having not acquaintance' in the London book trade, he sought a sponsor for the manuscript of a well-received sermon: George Ornsby ed., *The Correspondence of John Cosin, D.D. Lord Bishop of Durham: Together With Other Papers Illustrative of his Life and Times*, 2 vols (Durham: Andrews & Co for the Surtees Society, 1869–72), vol. 1, p. 20. When the poet John Taylor wrote in 1614 that he intended to 'scramble up into Pauls *Churchyard*' where he hoped 'my lines might please' like 'Butter to a Fleming' or 'Honey to a Beare', he may playfully allude to two different kinds of cultural presence among the booksellers: Nathaniel Butter (who published Taylor's book), and Blount's bookshop under the sign of the Black Bear: 'To neyther Monarch, nor Miser' in *Taylors water-worke* (1614, STC 23792), sig. A2r.

and titles, Blount's writings provide heuristics or frames of interpretation that continue to affect how we read his authors today. The bookseller's twin addresses that preface John Lily's *Sixe court comedies* (1632), for example, are for Leah Scragg an 'exercise in literary criticism'.[98] Blount lingers over the literary qualities of Lily's writing ('Witie, Comicall, Facetiously-Quicke'); he tells us that Lily is 'a Rare and Excellent Poet', and that 'Our Nation are in his debt, for a new English'.[99] James Bednarz has read Blount's edition of the poetry miscellany *Loves Martyr* as similarly indebted to the stationer's 'literary judgement and artistic distance'.[100] There are other examples of this kind from Blount's work: his preface to a history of Portugal, for example, in which he described the text as 'excellently written' and 'a faithfull, elegant, sinewie, and well digested historie'; or his preface to a book of essays which may have been the work of a young Thomas Hobbes.[101] For the latter Blount explained how he had come by the essays:

> having heard [the manuscript] commended, I was curious to see and reade them over; and in my opinion (which was also confirmed by others, judicious and learned) supposed if I could get the Copie, they would be welcome abroad. My friends courtesie bestowed it freely upon me.[102]

Once again Blount's subjective appraisal, this time bolstered by the 'judicious and learned' authority of his learned friends, is calmly offered as the rationale for publication. His preface anticipates a possible criticism of the essays: they might seem too long to the average reader, 'because most that have written in that way, have put them in lesse roome'. Such a criticism could be answered, Blount suggested, with the following response:

> if the fault grow by multiplicity of words, repetition, or affected variation of Phrases, then your dislike is well grounded. But when you have read, and finde the length to have proceeded from the matter and variety, of it, I know, your opinion will easily alter.[103]

Possible challenges are anticipated and defused with an argument built on literary-critical grounds. Features of style, including tautology, repetition, and

---

[98] Leah Scragg, 'Edward Blount and the History of Lylian Criticism,' *Review of English Studies* 46.181 (1995): pp. 1-10.
[99] John Lyly, *Sixe court comedies* (1632, STC 17088), sig. A2r, A5r-v.
[100] James Bednarz, 'Contextualising 'The Phoenix and Turtle': Shakespeare, Edward Blount and the Poetical Essays Group of *Love's Martyr*,' *Shakespeare Survey* vol. 67 (2014): pp. 131-49, at p. 133.
[101] Edward Blount 'To the Most Noble and Aboundant president both of Honor and Vertue, Henry Earle of Southampton' in Gerolamo Constaggio, *The historie of the uniting of the kingdom of Portugall to the crowne of Castill* (1600, STC 5624), sig. A2r. The possible Hobbes essays were published as William Cavendish[?], *Horæ subseciuæ* (1620, STC 3957).
[102] Edward Blount, 'To the Reader' in *Horæ subseciuæ*, sig. A2v.
[103] Blount, 'To the Reader' in *Horæ subseciuæ*, sig. A3r.

pleonasm are offered as valid categories of complaint, yet 'the matter and variety' of the work will, it is argued, persuade even the most sceptical reader.

Blount's surviving letters, collected in appendix one, also register his confidence in moderating cultural taste.[104] In sending a newly printed history book abroad to the ambassador Sir William Trumbull in Brussels in 1623, Blount described it as 'A booke of muche esteeme here and the only booke of worth come forthe this tearme'.[105] His statement offered authoritative judgement on the output of the English book trade in the most recent legal term, and although Blount was deferential to his correspondent, asking him to 'exscuse my boldness in this', he nevertheless reiterated his ability to enact trustworthy value judgements when he reassured Trumbull that 'if ought els come forthe worthye your view' then 'I will not fayle to send it'.[106] The letters establish a mutual language of value and taste between Blount and Trumbull, enabling the bookseller to act as a trusted filter for his client and revealing how a publisher's judgement could influence the circulation of books and domestic news through diplomatic networks across the continent.[107]

Perhaps the clearest thing to emerge from Blount's prefaces is the realization that the printed book promoted the voice of its publisher alongside that of its author. As the architect of the edition, the publisher could fold their views into the reading experience, if they chose. A final example: on a copy of *Hero and Leander* now held in the British Library, an early reader has jotted a couplet after Blount's preface to Walsingham. Beneath Blount's initials, the reader has added:

> twas happye in his busken Muse
> [bu]t unhappye in his life and death.[108]

What does this brief reflection on Marlowe tell us? Perhaps nothing new. It suggests he was happiest when composing tragic literature (a 'buskin', or actor's boot,

---

[104] Blount also delved into wider cultural traffic: in 1614 the publisher imported artwork from Venice to London for the ambassador Sir Dudley Carleton, mentioned below. The letter-writer John Chamberlain mentions Blount several times in his correspondence, noting that the stationer traded in various exotic commodities: seeds, news gazettes, and treacle— 'the best you can meet with': Norman McClure ed. *The Letters of John Chamberlain*, 2 vols (Philadelphia: The American Philosophical Society, 1939), vol. 1, pp. 484, 489, 544, 557–8, 613; vol. 2, pp. 30, 171, 287. We get here a sense of what in a different context Jason Scott Warren has described as a marketplace of 'cultural bricolage': *Shakespeare's First Reader: The Paper Trails of Richard Stonley* (Philadelphia, PA: University of Pennsylvania Press, 2019), p. 32.

[105] BL Additional MS 72365, fol. 130r (letter six in appendix one). Blount's five letters to Trumbull were discovered by Gary Taylor, who discusses them in 'Blount [Blunt], Edward' and in 'Making Meaning Marketing Shakespeare 1623,' in *From Performance to Print in Shakespeare's England*, edited by Peter Holland and Stephen Orgel (Basingstoke: Palgrave Macmillan, 2006), pp. 55–72.

[106] BL Additional MS 72365, fol. 130r; see also fol. 116r (letter seven).

[107] For a similar relationship between a bookseller and a high-status customer see: Jason Scott-Warren, 'News, Sociability, and Bookbuying in Early Modern England: The Letters of Sir Thomas Cornwallis' in *The Library* 1.4 (2000): pp. 381–402, at p. 395.

[108] Christopher Marlowe, *Hero and Leander* (1613, STC 17418), sig. A2r, British Library shelfmark C.57.i.45. The page has been cropped at the margin, obscuring a few letters of line two.

was a byword for tragic style) and not well adjusted to a rounder life. But if we read this note differently, not as a scrap of Marlowe biography but for what it tells us about the reader's momentum through the start of the book, then it records a pause prompted by Blount's epistle. In his printed address the stationer lingers on Marlowe's death. Blount explains that although the poet's 'breath-lesse body' has been brought 'to the earth', the poem is published as part of 'farther obsequies due unto the deceased'. The stationer seeds some of the language of the couplet: Marlowe is the 'unhappy deceased Author', and though 'buskin' does not feature Blount describes the poem as an 'unfinished tragedy'.[109] This reader's sparse summary of Marlowe's literary life and chaotic death was cued by Blount's own meditation on 'the man, that hath bin deare unto us'. In this particular copy, the annotation's elegiac mood complements the other side of the opening, where the poem begins with its own reminder of a tragic conclusion: 'ON *Hellespont* guilty of true loves blood...'.[110] To judge from the sample studied here, most booksellers shied away from the chance to make readers pause like this, and to supply the mood and ideas carried forwards into the poem. Others, like Blount, embraced the exposure and influence afforded by prefaces of this kind to frame the reading experience and to arbitrate public taste.

'my good freind master Mabb': Blount's Publishing Circle

The idea that communities could influence taste suggests a final way to think about Blount's bookshop as a site of literary production in early modern London. Under Blount's tenure—and perhaps even before—the Black Bear cultivated an important network of social and professional relations.[111] This particular bookshop and publishing house brings to mind Elizabeth Eisenstein's account of the 'international houses' kept by master printer-publishers of the sixteenth century: sites that built networks and established cultural attitudes.[112] The brief quotation

---

[109] Marlowe, *Hero and Leander* (1613, STC 17418), sig. A3r.
[110] Marlowe, *Hero and Leander* (1613, STC 17418), sig. A2r-v.
[111] András Kiséry gives an account of the Black Bear as an institution that in the 1590s organized a variety of agentive forces and 'completed, joined, combined, isolated, and shaped' the literary estate of Christopher Marlowe: 'An Author and a Bookshop: Publishing Marlowe's Remains at the Black Bear' in *Philological Quarterly* 91.3 (2012): pp. 361–92, at p. 375.
[112] Eisenstein argues that the printing and publishing businesses owned by figures like Christophe Plantin, Aldus Manutius, and André Wechel offered 'a meeting place, message center, sanctuary, and cultural center all in one': Elizabeth Eisenstein, *The Printing Revolution in Early Modern Europe*, 2nd rev. edn (Cambridge: Cambridge University Press, 2012), pp. 112–16, at p. 112. *Printing Revolution* summarizes Eisenstein's classic earlier study, *The Printing Press as an Agent of Change: Communications and Cultural Transformations in Early Modern Europe*, 2 vols in 1 (Cambridge: Cambridge University Press, 1980). The equivalent section about the role of printing houses in the earlier work can be found at pp. 136–59. For an account from a later period of Romantic-era bookshops in London as 'sites for the arbitration of cultural value' see David Fallon, 'Piccadilly Booksellers and Conservative Sociability' in Kevin Gilmartin ed., *Sociable Places Locating Culture in Romantic-period Britain* (Cambridge: Cambridge University Press, 2017), pp. 70–94, at p. 79.

which heads this section is from another of Blount's letters to Trumbull, in which the publisher reports a happy evening of May 1623 spent drinking with three of his friends: the author Robert Dallington, whose work Blount published several times; one 'Doctor Fox'; and finally 'my good freind master Mabb', meaning the translator James Mabbe, another of Blount's authors and the probable author of a poem in the preliminaries of the Shakespeare Folio. The letter describes a convivial scene in which writers socialize with their publisher: they send a cheery toast to their mutual friend the ambassador, and discuss a possible travel plan to visit him in Brussels:

> yesternight [Mabbe] did remember your health in a glasse of Canarrye, which righted by Doctor Fox, master Rob: Dallington and my self. This morning [Mabbe] is gone for Oxford. And hath made half a promise to see Bruxells this sommer if his Gout will give him leave. And hath prevailed with me to keepe him companye in that Journeye.[113]

Far from the sorts of exploitative, hard-headed relations sometimes imagined by New Bibliography to have governed the ways in which early modern stationers related to their authors, this letter suggests genuine friendship between these writers and their publisher. The usual critical opposition between self-interested and mercantile stationer and creative but beleaguered author breaks down, dissolving in a convivial evening of drink and half-made promises of future travel. The letter challenges us to reconceive the publishing bookshop as a generative site that enabled and sustained writers, as much as it profited from them.

Other evidence demonstrates that Blount cultivated a network of influential writers, travellers, and patrons that extended across Europe.[114] To the known surviving Blount letters we can now add another, written by Blount in August 1631, this time not just speculating about European travel plans but actually written from Paris.[115] Though the letter does not supply a name for the dignitary Blount visited, it was probably Sir Isaac Wake, the English ambassador at Paris. Being 'but newly arrived', Blount tells us, 'my Lord will not lett me stirr from him', but Blount finds a little space to write nonetheless.[116] He goes on to discuss future travel plans: with several others, he will travel with Wake to 'see the King and Cardinall' at Monceaux, meaning Louis XIII and Cardinal Richelieu. Blount was by this point largely absent from the world of publishing but the social and diplomatic connections he had cultivated from within the world of book production were clearly still active: in an earlier stage of his career, Wake had been secretary to Sir

---

[113] British Library Additional MS 72365, fol. 116r (letter seven in appendix one).

[114] Gary Taylor provides a summary of Blount's European connections over his career: 'Tragicomedies and Poems', p. xlviii.

[115] *Edward Blount to Christopher Browne*: BL Additional MS 78683, fol. 73r. See letter eight in appendix one.

[116] BL Additional MS 78683, fol. 73r.

Dudley Carleton, on whose behalf Blount had imported artwork from Venice in 1614.[117]

Throughout his career, Blount's books emerge from within a framework of culturally associative relations similar to those that surface in his correspondence. The same names recur on title pages and in preliminary matter, complimenting one another's work and establishing consensus. What we could call Blount's 'publishing circle' was a forum of creative energy, just as a theatre company was, or a coterie community of readers and writers. Just as particular roles in plays were written for certain actors, so too particular books might have been conceived of as more or less suitable to the interventions of members of this publishing circle. Title pages and paratexts aside, Blount's letters convey a sense of the community surrounding his bookshop. In June of 1621, he wrote to Sir William Trumbull:

> Concerning that manuscript I sent you, mentioned in yours; may it please you to give your self what satisfaction you thinke fitt; for in my love of your worthe I sent it to that end. So that when you filled your desyre eyther by reading or Coppying it you wilbe pleased to returne it by some trusty messinger because I have not any coppye therof, and yett have promised .2. or .3. freinds the reading[.][118]

The letter tells us that a unique ('I have not any coppye') but unnamed manuscript was sent to Trumbull in Brussels. Blount tries to retrieve the text because he has 'promised .2 or .3. freinds the reading'. The following month, another manuscript—perhaps the same one—is called for return in a different Blount letter to the same correspondent:

> I intreate you wilbe pleased to returne that manuscript which I sent you by Thorpe for I had promised the viewe thereof to .2. or 3 of my especiall good freindes before I sent it you, and they doe Call upon me dayly for the performing of my promise. Therfore if you have read it or Coppied it, you shall doe me a favour in returning the same, with your Censure.[119]

Both in their direct subject (the retrieval of a text) and through the figures who move in and out of focus in the background ('Thorpe', the 'especiall good freindes'), these letters reflect the society of Blount's bookish activities. We could roughly reconstruct the journeys of this unnamed text: it was sent from London

---

[117] Blount was paid for 'Assurance of Pictures' and 'for the taking up, clensing and delivering them to the Earle of Sommersett at whithall': TNA SP 14/80, fol. 183r. Two letters from Blount to Carleton in 1615 further demonstrate the bookseller's connection to this circle (letters one and two in appendix one).

[118] BL Additional MS 72361, fol. 68r (letter three in appendix one).

[119] BL Additional MS 72361, fol. 109r (letter four in appendix one).

to Brussels, carried by 'Thorpe' (perhaps the stationer Thomas Thorpe, publisher of Shakespeare's *Sonnets*). And now it awaits return by 'some trusty messenger' before being lent out again to other friends. The movement of a text, its social velocity, exposes it to replication and to endorsement and critique: Blount expects that Trumbull will copy it and specifically asks for his 'Censure'. Trumbull later confirmed he would give his opinion 'bothe of matter and style' of the text.[120] Presumably the two or three expectant friends were ready to offer similar judgement. Circulation of this kind seems one way for a text to gather visibility and acquire an audience in its pre-print life; it probably also helped a text to accrue the kinds of written commendations so commonly found in Blount's prefatory matter (a process that brings to mind the readers' reports on which modern peer review relies). The bookseller's premises here is no staid retail environment. Instead, it organizes and unifies the views of a disparate community, establishing a consensus that reaches through London and into parts of Europe. This is bookshop as manuscript reading room, as hub of exchange; a site, as Gary Taylor has put it 'which both attracts and structures reiterated social performances'.[121]

No book from among Blount's inventory embodies the publisher's intellectual and literary community better than Shakespeare's Folio. The Ben Jonson poem discussed in the introduction which addresses the engraved portrait of Shakespeare is one of two appearances by Jonson in the Folio's first pages. The second is Jonson's famous poem, 'To the memory of my beloved', to which we owe several influential descriptions of Shakespeare. He is, in Jonson's lines, the 'Soule of the Age!', and the 'Sweet Swan of *Avon*!'; it is Jonson who groups Shakespeare with a miniature canon of vernacular authors: the deceased playwright outshines John Lyly 'or sporting *Kid*, or *Marlowes* mighty line'; he is said to surpass Geoffrey Chaucer, Edmund Spenser, and Francis Beaumont. Finally, being Jonson, we also get the best-known assessment of Shakespeare's educational abilities: that he had 'small *Latine*, and lesse *Greeke*'.[122] The descriptions belong to Jonson, of course, but in another way they probably also come from Blount. As preliminary verses, Jonson's poems were that form of praise that was 'Beg'd by the *Stationer*', as the playwright James Shirley put it, 'with strength of Purse'.[123] Shirley had in mind stationers who paid for commendations, but it seems likely that the community around the Black Bear generated such endorsements through social and affective ties as much as economic means.

---

[120] BL Additional MS 72364, fol. 125r (letter five in appendix one). Trumbull's willingness to offer critique is quoted back at him in another Blount letter.
[121] Taylor 'Making Meaning', p. 56.
[122] Ben Jonson, 'To the memory of my beloved, The AUTHOR Mr. William Shakespeare' in Shakespeare, *Comedies, Histories & Tragedies*, sig. A4r–v. On the personalities of the Folio preliminaries see Emma Smith, *The Making of Shakespeare's First Folio* (Oxford: Bodleian Library, 2015), pp. 87–110.
[123] James Shirley, 'To his worthy Friend Master Richard Brome, upon his Comedie, called, *A Jouiall Crew*' in Richard Brome, *A joviall crew, or, The merry beggars* (1652, Wing B4873), sig. A4r.

It is Blount and Jonson who share the strongest links among the Folio personalities. These two poems about Shakespeare represent their seventh professional interaction.[124] The pair first collaborated for the poetry miscellany *Loves martyr* (1601), in which Blount promoted Jonson beside Shakespeare as the '*best and chiefest of our* moderne writers'.[125] Closer to the Folio, Jonson wrote a preliminary poem for Blount's edition of the picaresque Spanish novel *The Rogue* (1622/3); in its opening pages Jonson's poem appears alongside verses by several other familiar names, including Leonard Digges, another Folio contributor, and two poems by 'I. F.', probably John Florio.[126] Jonson's poem in *The Rogue* praises the translator, Blount's drinking partner James Mabbe, in high terms, addressing him as 'Friend' and '*English-Rogue*':

> Such Bookes deserve Translators, of like coate
> As was the *Genius* wherewith they were wrote;
> And this hath met that one, that may be stil'd
> More then the Foster-father of this Child[.][127]

Books demand translators that match the quality of their authors, the poem tells us. And in this case, the translator has become a fresh parent of the work. Immediately opposite Jonson's poem in *The Rogue*, Blount saved the last address for himself: 'After so much as you have read heere' he petitioned, 'let it be my minute, to be heard in a line or two for my selfe.'[128] He seems to preside over *The Rogue*'s preliminary material as a conductor over an orchestra. It was probably Blount, then, who procured some of the key statements that shaped the future of Shakespearean biography and criticism.

Most of the remaining personalities that feature in the Folio's first pages can be traced to Blount in ways that similarly remind us of the ability of books to consolidate communities. Sonia Massai has read the Folio's dedication to William and Philip Herbert, the Earls of Pembroke and Montgomery, as an attempt to associate Shakespeare's writing with the literary coterie of the 'Sidney-Herbert-Montgomery patronage network'.[129] More relevantly to this chapter, Massai also establishes a genealogy of dedications to the Herbert brothers which

---

[124] John Smethwick and William Aspley each published one of Jonson's books; neither William nor Isaac Jaggard published any.

[125] Robert Chester and others, *Loues martyr* (1601, STC 5119), sig. Z2r. Shakespeare's poems are on Z3v–4v; Jonson ends the collection on 2A3v–2A6r. The two authors bookend the collection, being the first and last named poets.

[126] Both poems praise Mabbe and his translation, and one points out that *The Rogue* has already met with great success 'in *Italy* and *France*'.

[127] Ben Jonson, 'On the Author, Worke, and Translator' in Mateo Aleman, *The rogue* (1622/3, STC 288), sig. A4v. Mabbe was another Trumbull correspondent: BL Additional MS 72364, fol. 90–1.

[128] Edward Blount, 'The Printer to the *Discreet* and *Curious* Reader' in Aleman, *The rogue*, sig. A5r.

[129] Sonia Massai, 'Edward Blount, the Herberts, and the First Folio', p. 139.

can be traced back through Blount's work and into the work of his master, William Ponsonby. The point here is not only that ideas of taste and literary production are constituted from within communities such as the circle around the Herbert family, but also that such notions of taste inhere within book-trade genealogies and that the credit of any such relationship was bound up with its longevity. To Massai's work on this patronage network, we can add the evidence of Blount's proximity to the Herbert family suggested by the 'Great Picture' triptych of 1646 that now hangs in Abbot Hall. This portrait shows Lady Anne Clifford, the wife of Philip Herbert, surrounded by books at three different stages of her life. What is particularly striking about the triptych, as has often been noted, is the level of detail afforded to the books. Little paper labels painted on the edges of the volumes carefully identify each title for the viewer, and amid this display of literacy are several books either published by or associated in other ways with Blount.[130] Perhaps the most telling affinity is found in the right-hand panel, where Clifford appears in late middle age at the time of the painting's commission. Two visually privileged books rest beneath her right hand (Figure 1.4). The lower book is a bible; the upper, on which her hand lightly rests, is 'Charon's Booke of wisdom translated out of French into English'—or rather, Pierre Charron's *Of Wisdome*, published in several editions by Blount in collaboration with William Aspley.[131]

Another of the Folio's poems—Leonard Digges' 'TO THE MEMORIE of the deceased Authour'—also seems to emerge directly from Blount's publishing circle, in that the stationer had financed each of Digges' previous appearances in print. James Mabbe, too, whose poem 'To the memorie of M. W. *Shake-speare*' consolidates the image of Shakespeare as a man of the theatre, a working actor who has now passed 'From the Worlds-Stage, to the Graves-Tyring-roome', had also only appeared in print under Blount's imprint. The vision of Shakespeare presented by these poems owes its conception to the 'publishing circle' around Blount in the early 1620s. The bookseller's social and professional relations are an inextricable

---

[130] For a list of forty-nine of the books see Leah Knight, 'Lady Anne Clifford' in *Private Libraries in Renaissance England*, vol. 9, ed. Joseph L. Black (Tempe, AZ: ACMRS, 2017), pp. 348–63. The volumes associated with Blount include some that he published (Michel de Montaigne's *Essayes*; Epictetus his *Manual*; Cervantes' *Don Quixote*); some where he published part of the work (Samuel Daniel's *Works*; Guillaume du Bartas' *Weekes and Workes*); one that he co-published with William Aspley (Pierre Charron's *Of Wisdome*) and one that he entered into the Stationers' Register but appears not to have published (a translation of Seneca's *Works*, entered by Blount in April 1600 [Arber III.159] and eventually published by William Stansby in 1614). On Clifford's wider 'bookscape' see Leah Knight 'Reading Proof: Or, Problems and Possibilities in the Text Life of Anne Clifford' in Leah Knight, Micheline White, and Elizabeth Sauer eds, *Women's Bookscapes in Early Modern Britain: Reading, Ownership, Circulation* (Ann Arbor, MI: University of Michigan Press, 2018), pp. 253–73. Jessica Malay has recently updated what we know of Clifford's reading: 'Reassessing Anne Clifford's Books: The Discovery of a New Manuscript Inventory' in *The Papers of the Bibliographical Society of America* 115.1 (2021): 1–41.

[131] Clifford read French (labels on three other books in the painting confirm they are 'in French'), making her choice of Blount's English edition rather than one of the dozens of French editions published in the early seventeenth century seem purposeful.

Figure 1.4 Lady Anne Clifford's hand, resting on a copy of 'Charon's Booke of wisdom translated out of French into English'. Detail of Jan van Belcamp, 'The Great Picture' (1646, triptych right-hand panel). Image courtesy of Abbot Hall, Lakeland Arts Trust, England.

part of the founding rhetoric on which the posthumous identity of Shakespeare was constructed.

What does it mean that the personalities who do so much to construct Shakespeare's literary reputation have these links to Blount and his work? One way to consider this question is to repeat a central challenge of *Shakespeare's Syndicate*, which involves rethinking how the Folio was 'made'. Just as it was the journeymen printers working in William Jaggard's printing house whose fingerprints are still sometimes found on pages of the Folio, or just as users of the *Early English Books Online* database occasionally have their reading interrupted by the surprising appearance of a curator's thumb, so too do the Folio's preliminary pages remind us in other ways of the wider social and professional community of the book's publication. We could think of the Folio as another instantiation of a long-running programme to establish influence and control in the emergent field of early modern vernacular writing by the individuals clustered around Blount and his bookshop. A significant part of the initial impetus of Shakespeare's work, then—that is, the ways in which it secured interest and validated its presence in the most tenuous and vital early stages of its reception—emerged from the relations that Blount cultivated across his career.

Conclusion

We tend to think about Shakespeare's Folio today as if its literariness was predetermined; as if the status and value with which the book is imbued when we encounter it in a museum or a rare books library in fact lay immanent within the dispersed manuscripts that predated the book, and drew them inexorably into a collection with special magnetism. But aspects of those same qualities of worth and value were conferred upon the Folio during its creation by virtue of the involvement of its publishers, and in particular by Edward Blount. Importantly for Shakespeare's legacy, the Folio was published towards the end of Blount's career. By this point, having accumulated around thirty years of what Bourdieu would call 'symbolic capital', and having not yet suffered the collapse that would shortly follow because of his financial problems, Blount could be thought of as being at the zenith of his ability to sponsor a book.[132]

This chapter has suggested some ways to think about stationers as active participants in the creation of literariness, quite regardless of the category of authorship. Booksellers not only identified writerly excellence but also could amplify and even create forms of value through the strategies and practices they developed over their careers. In exploring some of these strategies in Blount's work, and by thinking about him in relation to his peers, my goal has been to complicate the location of literariness in our conceptual thinking about both early modern literature in general and about Shakespeare's Folio in particular. Blount barely features in modern copies of Shakespeare's works; if the imprint appears at all it will usually be on a facsimile of the title page.[133] Yet his name was a critical part of that book's early reception. In some ways, he continues to guarantee the literariness of Shakespeare's writing because his judgement associates the Folio with a canon of Western authors whose collective relations reciprocally endorse and constitute each other's worth. It is Blount who connects Shakespeare to Montaigne, Marlowe, John Lyly, and Samuel Daniel, among other of the authors published from the Black Bear.

Ultimately, it was Blount's vision for the Folio, as revealed in the wording of his advert for the Frankfurt Book Fair, that shaped the ways in which the first editors of Shakespeare conceived of their work. Over the seventeenth century there were three further editions of Shakespeare's Folio, and each of them replicated the wording used on the original title page of 'M^r. William Shakespeares Comedies, Histories, & Tragedies'. However, a change occurred in the eighteenth century with the arrival of Nicholas Rowe and the first recognizably edited version of

---

[132] Bourdieu, *Field of Cultural Production*, pp. 76–82.
[133] Though Blount's modern successors—the major publishing institutions that produce today's editions of Shakespeare—influence both the ways in which the playwright is read and also the careers of the academics invited to edit.

Shakespeare's writing. Rowe, making a case for a new version of Shakespeare that included the playwright's first biography, ignored the title page of the Fourth Folio on which he depended for his texts, and rebranded the collection as 'The Works of Mr. *William Shakespear*'.[134] His decision set a paradigm that was followed by the editions of Alexander Pope (1723–5), Lewis Theobald (1733), Thomas Hanmer (1744), and William Warburton (1747). It was not till Samuel Johnson's edition of 1765, by which time Shakespeare's status had been newly consolidated for the eighteenth century, that Shakespeare's writings were once again described as 'plays' on their title page. The language of 'works', having been instituted for Shakespeare by Blount in 1624, suggests one of the ways in which these editors shared with this remarkable stationer a joint ambition to establish the reputation of Shakespeare for new audiences.

---

[134] William Shakespeare, *The works of Mr William Shakespear; in six volumes*, edited by Nicholas Rowe (1709).

2

'Prudentia'

The Jaggard Publishing House

Of the many entrances and exits staged by Shakespeare's First Folio, one of most curious and least commented upon is that of its printer and publisher, William Jaggard. For one thing, the order in which we might expect these actions to take place is reversed. Jaggard's name first appears at the end of the book in the colophon, where he is listed among the publishers at whose 'charges' the book appeared. But it is the imprint on the title page that registers his departure. That imprint, as the introduction explored, attributes the Folio not to William but to his son, Isaac Jaggard, in collaboration with Edward Blount. The likely reason that father and son switch places between the colophon and imprint is the death of William Jaggard. Aged about fifty-six, and having been blind for around ten years, William lived to oversee the printing of *Cymbeline*, but he died before the title page was finished. The sequence of a book's assembly could run counter to the progress of a human life and the Folio's title page, along with the rest of the preliminaries, was the last part of the book to be printed.[1] Several documents confirm William's death in around October of 1623: Isaac took over his father's post as the official printer to the City of London on 4 November (the note which records that Isaac was given this post describes William as 'his late father deceased'), and William's will was 'proved', meaning it was ratified by a court, on the 16 November.[2] Amid many other dramas, then, the Folio also quietly stages the death of its maker, and the book embodies, in its variant Jaggards, another version of the succession narrative that characterizes Shakespeare's history plays: the son takes control of his father's empire. However, because the normal order in which we read the Folio reverses the way in which it was made, the book in fact concludes with William Jaggard's Lazarus-like revival. Given that it was Shakespeare's Folio which guaranteed Jaggard's critical afterlife, the book's colophon fittingly provides both an end and a new beginning for this most well-known of Shakespeare's stationers.

---

[1] The exception to this timeline is *Troilus and Cressida*, which, once finally acquired, was probably printed after the preliminaries. For an overview see Blayney, *First Folio* 1991, pp. 17–24.
[2] The note recording Isaac Jaggard's inheritance of the City Printer's office can be found in: *Court of Aldermen Repertory Book 1623–4*, LMA COL/CA/01/01/042, f. 1v, with a fair copy in *Letter Book II*, LMA COL/AD/01/034. William's will is also in the London Metropolitan Archives: DL/AL/C/003/MS09052/005. There is an associated probate act at: LMA DL/AL/C/001/MS09050/005, fol. 170v.

The imprint and colophon of the Folio capture the two different roles that the Jaggards played in the production of Shakespeare's book. This chapter attends to the differences between those two roles and challenges what we know about Jaggard's relationship to Shakespeare's texts and the Folio in particular. Uniquely among the syndicate of Folio publishers, the Jaggards also owned a printing house, an establishment that William Jaggard took over from the printer James Roberts in about 1606. The imprint reminds us of the physical processes of printing when it states that the book was 'printed by' the Jaggards—even if the terminology here is vague in ways discussed in the introduction. Nevertheless, it was in the Jaggard printing house that compositors, journeymen, and apprentices laboured to make the Folio, inking formes, and printing sheets that were sometimes marked up for proofing changes (several of these proofed sheets were later recycled into copies of the Folio, where they are still occasionally found today).[3] The colophon, though, confirms that as well as being the book's printer William Jaggard was also one of the publishing consortium responsible for sharing the book's 'charges'.

Over the twentieth century critics attended to William Jaggard as a printer of Shakespeare—as someone who printed books 'for' someone else, usually a bookselling publisher. Bibliographers including Edwin Willoughby, Charlton Hinman, and Peter Blayney have recovered the working practices of Jaggard's printing house in the early 1620s with remarkable detail. We know the state of his typefaces, the nature of his proofreading habits, the condition of his wooden ornaments, and the kinds of paper stocks he bought.[4] We have thought less about Jaggard as a Shakespearean publisher, rather than a printer. That distinction seems slight, but this chapter argues that this small adjustment at the ground level of thinking about Jaggard enables significant new critical and interpretive work, and challenges how we think about the authority of the First Folio.

A Printer of Shakespeare

Uniquely among Shakespeare's stationers, there is a book-length study of William Jaggard's life.[5] Jaggard's biography was written by Edwin Willoughby in 1934

---

[3] Emma Smith, 'A New Corrected Proof Sheet from Shakespeare's First Folio (1623)' in *The Library*, 19.1 (2018): pp. 69–72. Examples of these proof sheets are reproduced in Appendix A of *The Norton Facsimile: The First Folio of Shakespeare*, 2nd rev. edn, edited by Charlton Hinman (New York and London: W. W. Norton & Company, 1996), pp. 909–23.

[4] Edwin Willoughby, *The Printing of the First Folio of Shakespeare* (Oxford: The Bibliographical Society, 1932); *A Printer of Shakespeare: The Books and Times of William Jaggard* (London: Philip Allan & Co, 1934); Charlton Hinman, *The Printing and Proof-Reading of the First Folio of Shakespeare*, 2 vols (Oxford: Clarendon Press, 1963); Peter Blayney, *The First Folio of Shakespeare* (Washington, DC: Folger Shakespeare Library, 1991). See also Hinman and Blayney's introductions to the second edition of Hinman ed., *The Norton Facsimile*.

[5] John Day, who belonged to an earlier generation of stationers, may be the only English printer to share this privilege with Jaggard, thanks to C. L. Oastler's *John Day: the Elizabethan Printer* (Oxford: The Bibliographical Society, 1975) and Elizabeth Evenden's *Patents, Pictures and Patronage: John Day*

under the impetus that the stationer was, as Willoughby's title makes clear, a 'Printer of Shakespeare'. For Willoughby, Jaggard's publishing activities attenuated after his move into the printing house in Barbican, a change of circumstances which prompted Jaggard's decision to 'devote himself as much as possible to printing'.[6] That is, to position himself as a stationer who was hired by other booksellers to print books, and who had less interest in financing texts. An interest in Jaggard as master of the machinery that physically printed the First Folio organizes this account of the stationer's life, which was written at the height of New Bibliographic interest in the printing-house environment and in peering through the 'veil of print', to borrow Fredson Bowers's memorable phrase.

The idea that no matter how 'large and successful a firm the Jaggards were, they were above all printers, undertaking work that had been paid for by others', is an orthodoxy in narratives about the Folio's making.[7] Their wider printing work continued alongside the Folio, so that the creation of the literary text was continually ruptured by more pragmatic concerns. The Jaggards stopped printing the comedies, somewhere around *All's Well That Ends Well*, in order to finish William Burton's *The description of Leicester shire* (1622) for the bookseller John White; they paused between *Othello* and *Cymbeline* to print a herald's notice in August 1623.[8] Sometimes the Folio bears traces of this other printing work. Two pieces of metal type, a lower-case 'n' and 'd', were damaged in a distinctive manner when they were used in the preliminary pages of a religious dictionary printed by the Jaggards in 1622. The types appear in a sentence explaining how the dictionary works ('a**nd** some places which onely have the interpretation...'). These types are next found in Mistress Quickly's breathless fiction of the suitors who tried and failed to court Mistress Ford in *Merry Wives of Windsor*, bringing 'letter after letter, gift after gift, smelling so sweetly; all Muske, and so rushli**n**g, I warrant you, in silke an**d** golde'.[9] One resolutely unliterary text is crumbled and reconstituted as a

---

and the Tudor Book Trade (Aldershot: Ashgate, 2008). Even here, though, as with Akihiro Yamada's work on the printers Thomas Creede and Peter Short, the bibliographic focus of Oastler and Evenden differs from Willoughby's interest in Jaggard as a biographical subject: *Peter Short: An Elizabethan Printer* (Tsu, Mei Prefecture: Mei University Press, 2002); *Thomas Creede, Printer to Shakespeare and his Contemporaries* (Tokyo: Meisei University Press, 1994).

[6] Willoughby, *Printer of Shakespeare*, p. 95.
[7] Peter Stallybrass, '"Little Jobs": Broadsides and the Printing Revolution' in Sabrina Alcorn Baron, Eric N. Lindquist, and Eleanor F. Shevlin eds, *Agent of Change: Print Culture Studies after Elizabeth L. Eisenstein* (Amherst, MA: University of Massachusetts Press, 2007), pp. 315–41 at p. 326. David Scott Kastan also suggests that 'The Jaggards had increasingly defined their business primarily as a printing firm,' *Shakespeare and the Book* (Cambridge: Cambridge University Press, 2001), p. 60. For an early scholarly account of trade printing see: Ronald B. McKerrow, 'Edward Allde as a Typical Trade Printer' in *The Library* 4.2 (1929): pp. 121–62.
[8] Hinman, *Printing and Proof-Reading*, I.350–1; II.320–1.
[9] Shakespeare, *Comedies, Histories & Tragedies*, sig. D5r. The religious dictionary was Thomas Wilson, *A Christian dictionary* (1622, STC 25788), sig. A4v. See Hinman, *Printing and Proof-Reading*, I.343–5; Blayney *First Folio* 1991, p. 6. Hinman's reconstruction of what was printed alongside the Folio is discussed and adjusted by Carter Hailey 'The Best Crowne Paper' in Owen Williams and Caryn Lazzuri eds, *Foliomania! Stories behind Shakespeare's Most Important Work* (Washington, DC: The Folger Shakespeare Library, 2011), pp. 8–14.

canonical one, so that, if viewed with a bibliographer's eye, Mistress Quickly's speech is haunted by the dictionary's preface. Occasional pages of the Folio also contain 'offset' ghost impressions of the Jaggards' printing work: images that were transferred by wet ink clinging to a printing press that was used for both books. In one Folio copy, the crisp lines of type in which the Duke of York relays Richard II's downfall—as the deposed king passes through London's streets, 'dust was throwne upon his Sacred head' while his face bears 'The badges of his greefe and patience'— are undercut by the murky presence of a large woodblock portrait of a resplendent king sitting in state on his throne.[10] The image is a palimpsest, a spectral reminder of a folio history of honour Jaggard was printing at the time, albeit one that forms a suggestive visual backdrop for the start of the Bolingbroke reign. It is one of several uncanny reminders within the Folio of the busy textual milieu from which the volume emerged, and of the books that we have taken to represent the Jaggards' real concern.

To view William Jaggard as mostly a trade printer is subtly to diminish his agency in the Folio's publication. There are good reasons why scholars might wish to do this. On two occasions before the Folio Jaggard was involved with versions of Shakespeare's writing that we now think of as corrupt or in some sense 'illegitimate'. Both ventures are now among the most enduringly fascinating episodes of Shakespearean print. One book that Jaggard did publish (but did not, in its first edition at least, print) is *The passionate pilgrime* (1599). This was a poetry miscellany that featured the work of multiple authors and yet was advertised by Jaggard on its title page as having been written '*By W. Shakespeare*'.[11] Scholars now believe that only five of the *Pilgrime*'s twenty poems are authentically Shakespearean, and so the edition has been interpreted as a compelling example of a stationer using Shakespeare's name to sell books.

The second venture concerns a group of playbooks that Jaggard printed in 1619, which seems to have been the first attempt to produce a collected version of Shakespeare's work, four years before the First Folio. This collection comprised ten plays, all printed in quarto format, most of which have an attribution to Shakespeare on their title page. However, the plays also feature false imprints that contain various dates and misleading statements about who published them. It is

---

[10] Shakespeare, *Comedies, Histories & Tragedies*, sig. d3v of Folger Library STC 22273 Fo.1 no. 81 (showing act five scene two of *Richard II*). See Blayney, *First Folio* 1991, p. 7.

[11] William Shakespeare and others, *The passionate pilgrime* (1599, STC 22342), sig. A2r. There are many critical accounts of the *Pilgrime*. Important work includes Colin Burrow's edition of Shakespeare's *The Complete Sonnets and Poems* (Oxford: Oxford University Press, 2008), pp. 74–81; Arthur F. Marotti, 'Shakespeare's Sonnets as Literary Property', in Elizabeth D. Harvey and Katharine Eisaman Maus eds, *Soliciting Interpretation: Literary Theory and Seventeenth-century English Poetry* (Chicago, IL: University of Chicago Press, 1990), pp. 143–73; James Bednarz, 'Canonizing Shakespeare: *The Passionate Pilgrim*, *England's Helicon*, and the Question of Authenticity' in *Shakespeare Survey* 60 (2007): pp. 252–67; Adam G. Hooks, *Selling Shakespeare: Biography, Bibliography, and the Book Trade* (Cambridge: Cambridge University Press, 2016), pp. 109–12.

now generally thought that William Jaggard worked with his friend, the bookseller Thomas Pavier, to produce this collection, though we are not certain what their exact roles might have been. Historically, Pavier has been seen as the leading figure, but the most recent scholarship argues that Jaggard was the central force. The confusion over agency for the scheme is reflected in its various names: historically known as the 'Pavier Quartos', or the '1619 Collection', more recent work has argued these books should instead be known as the 'Jaggard Quartos'.[12]

Just as they are connected to these pivotal episodes of Shakespearean print, both William and Isaac Jaggard are therefore also deeply entangled with our ideas about the legitimacy of Shakespeare's texts and the roles of stationers in constituting that legitimacy. Both the *Pilgrime* and the Jaggard Quartos implicate William Jaggard in some form of deception. As early as the nineteenth century, the bibliographer Algernon Swinburne, outraged by Jaggard's addition of Shakespeare's name to the title page of the *Pilgrime* pamphlet, described the stationer as an 'infamous pirate, liar, and thief who published a worthless little volume of stolen and mutilated poetry, patched up and padded out with dirty and dreary doggrel'.[13] When the falsities of the 1619 quarto collection were uncovered in the early twentieth century, the findings seemed to confirm the view that Jaggard was, in the language of the day, a literary 'pirate': someone willing to play fast and loose with Shakespeare's work in order to turn a profit. The morality of this critique now seems outdated and has begun to shift in recent years, but Jaggard remains a vexed figure in the history of Shakespearean print.

The falsities of the *Pilgrime* miscellany and of the Jaggard Quartos have implications for the First Folio. If Jaggard had treated Shakespeare's work carelessly in the past, why would the King's Men have collaborated with him on this important monument to their recently deceased lead dramatist? The confusion here is compounded by the fact that in both of Jaggard's previous dealings with Shakespeare there is supporting evidence that suggests a sense of personal outrage on the part of either Shakespeare or the King's Men. In relation to the *Pilgrime*, a printed letter from Thomas Heywood claimed that Shakespeare himself was 'much offended with

---

[12] As with the *Pilgrime*, there is an extensive literature on this collection. Zachary Lesser's *Ghosts, Holes, Rips and Scrapes: Shakespeare in 1619, Bibliography in the Longue Durée* (Philadelphia, PA: University of Pennsylvania Press, 2021) offers a major new intervention. Other recent work includes Hooks, *Selling Shakespeare*, pp. 112–24; Zachary Lesser and Peter Stallybrass, 'Shakespeare between Pamphlet and Book' in *Shakespeare and Textual Studies*, edited by Sonia Massai and M. J. Kidnie (Cambridge: Cambridge University Press, 2015), pp. 105–33; Jeffrey Todd Knight, *Bound to Read: Compilations, Collections and the Making of Renaissance Literature* (Philadelphia, PA: University of Pennsylvania Press, 2013), pp. 150–66. On the name of the collection as a marker of the agencies involved, see Lesser and Stallybrass 'Shakespeare between Pamphlet and Book' and Hooks, *Selling Shakespeare*, pp. 115–19. For a contrasting view that resists the idea of Jaggard's leadership, and points out that 'Pavier simply had a much greater stake in the project than anyone else', see Andrew Murphy, *Shakespeare in Print*, 2nd rev. edn (Cambridge: Cambridge University Press, 2021), p. 524 (n. 43).

[13] Algernon Charles Swinbourne, *Studies in Prose and Poetry* (London: Chatto & Windus, 1894), p. 90.

M. *Jaggard*' for making 'so bold with his name'.[14] A few years later, the printing of the 1619 quarto collection was interrupted by a peremptory letter from the Lord Chamberlain, which is presumed to have been written on behalf of the King's Men to curtail Jaggard's printing, and which warned the Stationers' Company not to print any 'playes that his Ma*jes*tyes players do play' without getting their consent.[15]

The Folio, on the other hand, offers the most important collection of Shakespeare's plays that exist. One source of its authority is a powerful personal connection between the book and its author, whereby the plays are positioned as directly connected to, and authorized by, Shakespeare and his fellow players. The authoritative status of the Folio—at least in our critical narratives about the book's making—is thus troubled by Jaggard's involvement. It seems difficult to reconcile his treatment of the *Pilgrime* and his work on the Jaggard Quartos with our investment in the Folio's integrity. The awkwardness of Jaggard's involvement in the Folio has led some scholars to argue that William and his son Isaac maintained distinct interests: where William's literary work is 'scant and unassuming', Isaac Jaggard maintained 'a strong interest in literary publications' alongside his father's work. Perhaps it was Isaac, then, and not his father, who 'first suggested the venture' to collect and print Shakespeare's plays.[16]

The two stationers may seem to have pursued separate interests, but the idea that they maintained distinct imprints within the same business breaks down amid the details of the texts they handled. For example, while it is Isaac Jaggard's name that features in the imprint of Boccaccio's *The decameron* (1620) it was William Jaggard who had entered the right to copy for this work in the Stationers' Register earlier that year. It was William, too, who registered the manuscript copy for the other few books that eventually featured Isaac Jaggard's name in their imprints, whether those books were literary—like George Chapman's *Divine poem of Musæus* (1616)—or not, like Walter Hamond's *Method of curing wounds made by gun-shot* (1617). The only exception to that pattern among the few books for which Isaac looks to have been responsible is an edition of Thomas Heywood's play, *A woman kilde with kindnesse* (1617), the imprint of which tells us it was 'printed by Isaac Jaggard' and which was never registered. But William had already published an edition of this play in 1607 without his son's involvement, meaning the later publication cannot be seen as evidence of Isaac's individual literary drive. That Isaac was responsible for the Stationers' Register entry of 8 October 1623, in which he and Edward Blount claimed the remainder of Shakespeare's

---

[14] Thomas Heywood, *An Apology for Actors* (1612, STC 13309), sig. G4r–v.
[15] William Jackson ed., *Records of the Court of the Stationers' Company: 1602–1640* (London: The Bibliographical Society, 1957), p. 110.
[16] Sonia Massai, *Shakespeare and the Rise of the Editor* (Cambridge: Cambridge University Press, 2011), pp. 117, 162. See also Peter W. M. Blayney, 'Introduction to the Second Edition' in Shakespeare, *The Norton Facsimile*, p. xxviii.

plays, is immaterial. William was either dead or close to it by this point, and Isaac had to finish the project. More striking is the fact that this was the only time that Isaac Jaggard entered copy into the Stationers' Register—a fact that is at odds with the idea of him being an ambitious and dynamic figure interested in promoting new literary forms.

It is true that the first advert for the Folio promoted the book as 'printed by *Isaack Jaggard*' rather than William. So Isaac must have taken charge of some aspects of the venture. Yet both father and son belonged to the same printing and publishing business that was ultimately controlled by William, who was the master printer in the house at Barbican until his death, as is carefully noted in State Paper documents that track the chains of ownership of London's printing houses from this time.[17] And against the evidence of Isaac's advert, Augustine Vincent's inscription (see p. 100) identifies William Jaggard as the book's printer. Our interest in separating two stationers who collaboratively ran one business despite evidence that blurs the distinction between them is a subtle but significant marker of the threat that William Jaggard poses to something vital, even ontological, about the Folio's status.

Similar anxieties about William's involvement have led scholars to describe his contribution to Shakespeare's Folio in terms of labour and practicalities. In W. W. Greg's account of how the First Folio was made, William Jaggard was 'rather mysterious, rather shady', and the King's Men looked 'unfavourably' on him, as if the book was made in spite of his involvement.[18] The awkwardness of the collaboration could, in Greg's view, be explained by the difficulty of the Folio as a printing project. He suggested that the King's Men had 'some difficulty in finding a stationer' willing to take on a job that involved as much work as the Folio, and speculated that Jaggard was a last resort.[19] Most later retellings of the Folio's making are unsettled by Jaggard's 'embarrassing participation' in similar ways, and tend to account for Jaggard's presence as a case of practical need, echoing Greg by suggesting that '[f]ew stationers would have been eager or even able to undertake a project the size of the Shakespeare folio.'[20] There is a sense throughout these narratives that if we contain William Jaggard within the materiality of metal type, confine him to the rigid boundaries of a press's forme, then we protect something essential about the texts themselves.

---

[17] The summary of master printers drawn up by Sir John Lambe in roughly autumn of 1635 notes Isaac Jaggard took over the printing house after his father's death: TNA, SP 16/307, fol. 146 (printed in Arber III.702–3). The list's dates are inaccurate, but for similar chains of succession drawn up at this time see Arber III.700 and 701.
[18] Greg, *First Folio*, p. 9.   [19] Greg, *First Folio*, p. 10.
[20] James Marino, *Owning William Shakespeare: The King's Men and their Intellectual Property* (Philadelphia, PA: University of Pennsylvania Press, 2011), p. 111.

A Publisher of Shakespeare

The First Folio was an unusually big volume but it was not unique. Books of a similar size or significantly larger were printed by other of London's stationers at the same time.[21] And neither was Jaggard exceptional among London's printers in terms of his ability to handle a large workload: in a list that records the output of all London's printing houses in the early seventeenth century, Jaggard is found two-thirds of the way down.[22] If his involvement with Shakespeare's Folio was not a case of practical necessity, then perhaps it related to his contemporary status as a printer who was also well known as an important bookselling publisher.

Why should we think about Jaggard as a publisher rather than a printer? For one thing, the earliest traces of his career involved bookselling and occasional publishing, rather than printing. His first book, a sermon from 1594, records that it was printed 'for' rather than 'by' him.[23] A few archival references from his first active years suggest that he was involved in printing to some degree, but it was not till 1604 that a book's imprint confirmed it was 'Printed by W. Jaggard'.[24] Instead, over the first decade of his career he hired other stationers to print his books. His first edition of *The passionate pilgrime*, for example, was printed by Thomas Judson and sold by the bookseller William Leake at the sign of the Greyhound in the churchyard of Paul's Cross. Jaggard chose this collaboration wisely: both of Shakespeare's popular narrative poems, *Venus and Adonis* and

---

[21] Shakespeare's Folio required about 227 'edition sheets' (the number of sheets of paper required to complete a single 'ideal' copy). The Folio was one of the largest books to be published in 1623, but by no means the largest: Pedro Mexia's *The imperiall historie* (STC 17852) came close to the Folio with 220 sheets; William Cowper's *Works* (STC 5909) required 278 sheets; John Speed's *The Historie of Great Britaine* (STC 23046.3) required 347 sheets. And the Folio does not seem to have stretched Jaggard's own capacity: his edition of Andre Favyn's *The theater of honour and knight-hood* (STC 10717), also finished in 1623, needed 296.5 sheets. Folios requiring more than 200 sheets were uncommon but not rare enough to worry several of London's printers.

[22] David L. Gants, 'A Quantitative Analysis of the London Book Trade 1614–1618' in *Studies in Bibliography* 55 (2002): pp. 185–213, at p. 194. Jaggard is placed fourteenth in a list of twenty-one printing houses (including one category for 'unattributed printing') ranked by the number of edition sheets these houses produced in this five-year period.

[23] John Dove, *A sermon preached at Pauls Crosse the 3. of November 1594* (1594, STC 7086.5). Before this, Jaggard served his apprenticeship under the printer Henry Denham. There is little evidence of Jaggard's activities during the apprenticeship, but he witnessed and signed a bond of obligation dated 19 February 1586 on behalf of his master Denham. The bond records that Denham loaned money to the stationer Thomas Charde (see item 414 in *Catalogue of Valuable Autograph Letters, Literary Manuscripts and Historical Documents*, 20–21 July 1981 [London: Sotheby's, 1981], 239. Thanks to Henry Woudhuysen for alerting me to this reference.) The apprenticeship finished in December 1591 and there was a three-year gap before Jaggard turned up as the publisher of Dove's sermon. He may have worked as a journeyman printer in that gap, but if so then it was not with Denham, who died in about 1590: Patricia Brewerton 'Denham, Henry (*fl.* 1556–1590)', *Oxford Dictionary of National Biography* (Oxford: Oxford University Press, 2004; online edn, 23 September 2004 [accessed 13 August 2020]).

[24] Richard Humfrey, *Two guides to a good life* (1604, STC 12466). The archival references include a note dated 23 October 1600 in which William Jaggard and Ralph Blower (Blore) were fined for printing a book without license: Arber II.831 and II.833. Blower had been a printer since 1597. Jaggard also tried (but failed) to secure the right to print playbills in 1602: Jackson ed., *Records of the Court*, pp. 1, 6.

Lucrece, could also be found at the Greyhound, making it a crucial site for the retailing of Shakespeare's poetry.[25]

When he took over the printing house in about 1606 (presumably buying out James Roberts, who lived till about 1618), Jaggard launched his own publishing agenda. If we separate the entries under Jaggard's name in the *Short Title Catalogue* into those items that he published and those which he printed for others, then something like a coherent publishing programme comes into focus.[26] The 246 entries (pushed to 248 by a couple of additions not in the STC) identify a wide range of pamphlets and broadsheets, playbooks and encyclopaedias. Eighty-six of these entries identify separate editions that Jaggard published himself. Yet this ambitious series of books constituted a significant majority (71 per cent) of all the surviving edition sheets with which Jaggard was involved.[27]

This basic fact that Jaggard was what Akihiro Yamada has called a 'printer-bookseller' rather than a trade printer needs some nuancing.[28] The Jaggard business was undoubtedly also interested in a separate category of printing work that for the most part has not survived. This third kind of work is that which Peter Stallybrass has called the 'little jobs' of early modern print: ephemeral documents like broadside proclamations, tickets for events, passports for vagrants and a sea of other printed matter that circulated in early modern society without ever, for the most part, reaching the STC's cataloguing team.[29] William Jaggard was well aware of the value of this kind of jobbing work. He doggedly pursued the right to print the playbills that advertised performances in London's theatres, eventually securing the monopoly in 1615, and in 1613 was slapped on the wrist by the stationers' court for printing apprenticeship indentures when the right to do so belonged to Humphrey Lownes 1.[30] He seems also to have won a royal privilege to print copies of the ten commandments for every church and chapel in England

---

[25] See Hooks, *Selling Shakespeare*, pp. 35–65.   [26] STC, vol. 3, pp. 90–1.
[27] A list of these publications is found in appendix two of this book. The count of eighty-six editions includes the eight editions (and ten plays) that make up the 'Jaggard Quartos' of 1619. To establish sheet counts for Jaggard's output I have looked at all texts attributed to Jaggard by the STC using in most cases a physical copy of the book supported by *EEBO* and *ESTC*. The two non-STC additions are ESTC S123140, a book Jaggard printed for Thomas Pavier, and ESTC S509123, a title that Jaggard printed and published (thanks to the anonymous reader who alerted me to this edition). For several reasons these figures are by no means definitive: what survives of Jaggard's work is inevitably incomplete, and for some of his books (the customs and traffic publications of Thomas Milles, for example) it is ambiguous whether he acted as printer or publisher. The figure of 71 per cent is accurate whether or not we take partnerships into account. Ignoring all partnerships for both printing and publishing, I find that Jaggard published 4,752.5 sheets and printed 1,936.5 for others. Incorporating partnerships (treated as equal shares except for those cases where the STC identifies Jaggard's printing more precisely) I find he published 4291.75 sheets and printed 1,743.5 for others.
[28] Yamada, *Thomas Creede*.
[29] Stallybrass, '"Little Jobs"'. On jobbing printing see also James Raven, 'Jobbing Printing in Late Early Modern London: Questions of Variety, Stability and Regularity' in Louisiane Ferlier and Benedicte Miyamoto eds, *Forms, Formats and the Circulation of Knowledge: British Printscape's Innovations, 1688–1832* (Leiden: Brill, 2020), 27–49.
[30] Stern, *Documents* pp. 36–62; Jackson, *Records 1602–1640*, pp. 1, 6, 57, 452; Arber III.575.

and Ireland in 1604.[31] Moreover, in December 1610 Jaggard was 'chosen and admitted to be the Printer for this Citty' by London's court of aldermen—a post that saw him print official city notices and royal proclamations.[32] The role's importance to Jaggard is demonstrated by his request to leave 'A peice of silver plate' to the Stationers' Company with 'woordes to be ingraven thereon viz The Guift of William Jaggard Printer to the honourable Citty of Lon[don]'.[33] That wording, in which Jaggard adopted the official title of City Printer, features in some of the imprints of his own publications in ways that suggest his pride and perhaps also the repute it granted him among readers: on the title page of one of Jaggard's books now in the Bodleian Library an early reader jotted beside his name in the imprint, seemingly as an epithet for the book's printer and publisher: 'Champion for the Citty or the Cittys Champion'.[34]

While a handful of Jaggard's City Printer work survives, we have none of his playbills and very little else to represent what must have been a diverse and pervasive class of printed material.[35] The ephemeral nature of this kind of print makes Jaggard's business activities unusually difficult to assess and exposes the paradox at the heart of print popularity: that the most common material from this time is also the most likely to be lost. Still, we can use some new evidence to adjust our understanding of Jaggard's little jobs and how important they were to his business. For one thing, it seems likely that he never won that lucrative privilege to print tables of the ten commandments for churches. As Willoughby reports, notice of the privilege appears in the Docquet Book found among the State Papers. Here we find an 'order that in every parish Church & Chappell a Table of the ten Comaundmentes may be set up by William Jaggard, his deputies or assignes, at the charges of the Parish'.[36] But the State Papers Docquet Book is matched by a partner entry in the records of the Signet Office, which has the same date of May 1604 and similar wording with one important difference. In the Signet Office version, a different contemporary hand has noted beside the entry that Jaggard's application was 'not sealed—staid by the L: Cecill'.[37] The 'L: Cecill'

---

[31] Willoughby, *Printer* p. 66.
[32] *Court of Aldermen Repertory Book 1610–12*: LMA COL/CA/01/01/033, fol. 36r.
[33] *Will of William Jaggard*.
[34] Bodleian Library Gough Lond. 122 (4): a copy of Anthony Munday, *The triumphes of re-united Britania* (1605, STC 18279). The book is a civic pageant for a new Lord Mayor, so it is also possible the reader had the mayor or Munday in mind, though the note's position beside Jaggard's name is suggestive.
[35] In addition to the City Printing recorded by the STC, there are two references to Jaggard's work in this capacity in the City of London archives. They record the printing of decrees for Blackwell Hall in 1612 (*Court of Aldermen Repertory Book 1610–12*, fol. 380r) and a note from 1619 asking Jaggard to begin printing passports for criminals (*Court of Aldermen Repertory Book 1618–20*, LMA COL/CA/01/01/038, fol. 91r).
[36] *State Papers Domestic, Signet Office Docquets*, TNA SP 38/7, fol. 141v.
[37] *Signet Office Docquet Book 1603–5*: TNA SO 3/2, p. 278. Thanks to Peter W. M. Blayney for alerting me to this reference. Blayney provides an explanation for the process by which privileges were awarded in *The Stationers' Company and the Printers of London 1501–1557*, 2 vols (Cambridge: Cambridge

here must be the politician Lord Robert Cecil, mastermind of James' succession after the death of Elizabeth, and so the note is telling us that Cecil intervened to block Jaggard's award before it was ever ratified with a warrant from the Privy Seal.

So Jaggard probably never secured one of those profitable jobbing privileges. And though not much of his City of London printing survives, we can also recover some sense of the scale of this work from new evidence in the city's account books. To date, scholars have relied on the scant surviving traces of this civic printing to imagine the kinds of material that might have once existed.[38] But the accounts supply itemized annual lists of what the City Printer was paid to produce. They only survive from 1632 on, so unfortunately there is nothing from the tenures of either William (1610–23) or Isaac (1623–7), but the lists pick up with Isaac's successor, the printer Robert Young, and they allow us to reconstruct a world of lost print with unusual precision. Among other things, the accounts tell us that the City Printer was paid a yearly fee of forty shillings for their work, on top of the money they earned from individual jobs.[39] The amount of actual printing work varied year on year. In 1633, Young was paid a total of £53, 6s (or 12,792 pence) for thirteen separate jobs carried out the previous year (including five proclamations and four sets of passports for vagrants); in 1634 he collected the smaller sum of £38, 14s (9,288 pence) for seven jobs (including just one proclamation and two sets of passports).[40]

What should we make of this account of Jaggard's labour? We need to treat the figures given above about his printing and publishing work with caution. It is certainly the case that Jaggard printed a great deal of material that no longer survives. At the same time, as Peter Stallybrass notes and as the city's account books confirm, this 'staggering variety' of little jobs 'did not necessarily use up many sheets of paper'.[41] Proclamations, for example, tended to be one or two sheets of paper (by necessity printed on just one side), and the accounts tell us they were commissioned in runs of 500 copies: a number we think of as being at the bottom

---

University Press, 2013 [paperback edn 2015]), vol. 2, pp. 952–9. Note particularly the diagram on p. 955: the absence of a Privy Seal Office docquet or warrant for Jaggard's privilege suggests it was never granted.

[38] See Charles Welch, 'The City Printers' in *The Library: Transactions of the Bibliographical Society* 14.1 (1917): pp. 175–242.

[39] *City of London Cash Accounts 1633–5*: LMA COL/CHD/CT/01/001. Notes of Young's forty-shilling fee are found on fol. 44v (for 1632), 136r (for 1633) and so on. The City of London Corporation also employed a separate stationer for services like repairing and binding books, and supplying paper and ink. When the accounts begin, this stationer was John Harrison 4.

[40] *City of London Cash Accounts 1633–5*, ff. 65r–v; 154v. For context, Peter W. M. Blayney puts the printing costs for a nine-sheet quarto playbook of 800 copies in the early seventeenth century at about 1,008 pence ('Publication of Playbooks', 408). If the sums paid to Jaggard were similar to those paid to Young, then the City Printer post generated (very roughly) the same amount of revenue as printing somewhere between nine and twelve pamphlets each year (c.80–100 sheets). Brief details of the proclamations in the accounts reveal the issues that vexed London's authorities: the need for 'conservacy of the river of Thames', and the importance of reforming abuses found 'in making of Beaver hatts', among others (fol. 65v).

[41] Stallybrass, '"Little Jobs"', p. 339.

end of a book's edition size.⁴² Similarly, 4,000 'Ticketts to warne men into the Orphans Court' sounds a lot, but still only required 500 sheets of paper (meaning eight tickets were printed on each sheet), and presumably involved relatively little compositorial labour.⁴³ Over the thirteen years that Jaggard worked as City Printer, there is no doubt that this office generated considerable material.⁴⁴ But even with his City Printing and other jobbing work taken into account, Jaggard's lost ephemera would not alter the fact that he was also one of the leading publishers of his day: David Gants' study of the most productive publishers in London between 1614 and 1618, which charts their output in terms of the number of edition sheets they financed, places Jaggard above all the other members of the First Folio syndicate, as well as above other prominent publishers like Arthur Johnson, Matthew Lownes, and Simon Waterson.⁴⁵

An accurate account of William Jaggard probably lies somewhere between the two perspectives I have explored. He was far from simply a trade printer, yet neither does the trade printer (29 per cent) to publisher (71 per cent) ratio given above fully capture his activities. But we do not need to establish a precise sense of how William Jaggard distributed his labour to challenge our habit of seeing him as 'only' the Folio's printer; Jaggard was clearly a significant publishing force in his own right.

One advantage Jaggard had over most other bookselling publishers, though, was that he controlled the appearance of his books to an unusual degree. Looking at those books with a sense of Jaggard's dual identity in mind—as trade printer, and as printer-publisher—suggests he used these different categories of print to represent his identity in different ways. Almost all the title pages of Jaggard's publications proudly advertise his full name. They tend also to supply the address of his bookshop (always 'his house in Barbican' or 'dwelling in Barbican', and never the 'Half Eagle and Key'), which makes sense, given that part of an imprint's purpose was to advertise the wholesale outlet from which an edition could be bought. Leaving aside the deceptive Jaggard Quartos, 93 per cent of Jaggard's publications declare they were produced by 'William Jaggard', or sometimes 'W. Jaggard', in their imprints while just one of his books supplies his initials instead.⁴⁶ These imprints

---

⁴² On print runs see Blayney 'Publication of Playbooks', pp. 396, 412, and 422n62. Blayney suggests a first edition of a playbook might be 800 copies, rising to 1,500 copies for a second edition in the event of rapid sale.

⁴³ *City of London Cash Accounts 1633–5*, fol. 65v.

⁴⁴ Jaggard was awarded the post in December of 1610.

⁴⁵ Gants, 'Quantitative Analysis', p. 203. See also 'Figure 1' on p. 196, which finds that the Jaggard business was by some distance the London printing house that self-published the most work. For reasons I am exploring here, Gants' ratio cannot help but miss much of Jaggard's ephemeral printing, which would adjust this ratio down.

⁴⁶ Seventy-one of seventy-six editions name him in this way. Setting the Jaggard Quartos aside, I find that Jaggard published seventy-eight editions (listed in appendix two). Two of these do not have title pages (STC 22341.5, 20393). Four of the remaining seventy-six editions do not mention William Jaggard at all (STC 6540 and 22975, both of which are ambiguously Jaggard publications, but I have

typically use the wording found on Shakespeare's Folio, recording that the book was 'printed by' William Jaggard. The formula which has typically directed us to think about the Jaggards as printers was actually their preferred style of attribution for those books in which they were themselves most heavily invested.

At times these title pages record a sense of Jaggard's typographical pride. On his own publications, the typeface used for Jaggard's name in the imprint could be larger than that used for the author.[47] Reading across Jaggard's title pages reveals the growth of what Joseph Loewenstein might call the 'bibliographic ego' of this publisher, which is perhaps not surprising when we remember that Jaggard also wrote books and was in other ways sensitive to his reputation.[48] Some of his larger publications leave out the name of the author or translator altogether so that the title page suggests Jaggard's sole responsibility. When Thomas Milles's printed compendium of historical information was published in 1619 as *Times Store-House*, the book's engraved title page contained no reference to Milles or to any of the several authors whose work provided the source materials for the book. Instead the book was simply signed with the familiar formulation 'Printed by William Jaggard'. Inside, a preface from 'The Printer to the Reader' advertised Jaggard's control and agency:

> Some few yeares past, I intended the whol Worke of *Pedro Mexia*, with some other Authours on the like Arguments of variety. I then published nine Bookes, with intention to have made them up fifteen, for the first Volume: but being prevented by sicknesse, I finished but the first nine Bookes; and finding the good acceptance of them, I have adventured now on ten Bookes more.[49]

Jaggard's statement associates him powerfully with the final book: he has 'adventured', 'intended', 'published', and 'finished' the work, and the address foregrounds his biography ('prevented by sicknesse') as the meaningful frame that governs his publishing schedule.

---

followed the STC's attribution; STC 22008 [probably an internal title page to 17926, which does name Jaggard]; and 21625 [which names John Jaggard as the publisher, but given that William entered the right to copy in February 1608 and printed the edition it seems likely to be a collaboration]). The one edition that gives Jaggard's initials is STC 1486.

[47] See for example the title pages of John Swynnerton, *A Christian love-letter* (1606, STC 23558); Thomas Bell, *The jesuites antepast* (1608, STC 1824); William Attersoll, *A commentarie upon the fourth booke of Moses* (1618, STC 893); *The pathway to Canaan* (1609, STC 898).

[48] On the 'bibliographic ego' see Joseph Loewenstein, 'The Script in the Marketplace,' in *Representations* 12 (1985), pp. 101–14; *Ben Jonson and Possessive Authorship* (Cambridge: Cambridge University Press, 2002). Jaggard wrote *A view of all the right honourable the Lord Mayors of this honorable city of London* (1601, STC 14343) and 'wrote' the *Catalogue of such English books…*(1618, STC 14341). He also claimed that Helkiah Crooke's *Sōmatographia anthrōpinē* (1616, STC 20782) was in fact 'By W. J. Printer' in a style that looks like an authorship claim (it is clear who the initials identify: the book's imprint explains it was 'Printed by W. Jaggard dwelling in Barbican').

[49] 'The Printer to the Reader' in Thomas Milles, *Archaio-ploutos* (1619, STC 17936.5), sig A4v.

In a variety of ways, Jaggard promoted his own identity through his publications, exploiting the rhetorical and aesthetic protocols of his books to market his brand. By contrast, Jaggard scoured his presence from those books that he printed for the trade. The style of imprints used on books at this time varied, but the fullest formula would describe a book as having been 'printed by X for Y, and to be sold by Z', where the printer, publisher, and wholesale bookseller respectively were each identified. Yet Jaggard's trade books typically only supply the name of the book's publisher or wholesaler in the imprint. Jaggard's own name appears in full on the title page of just thirteen of his trade books—just over 12 per cent—meaning that for a majority of these titles there was little to suggest his presence to an early modern reader.[50] The language of early modern imprints was far from fixed, making it difficult to discuss broad tendencies, but from what we can tell, Jaggard's reticence here seems out of kilter with the rest of the book trade: Gants' survey finds that roughly 95 per cent of printing between 1614 and 1618 identifies its printer in some way.[51]

Printing materials were also used selectively for either Jaggard's trade printing or his publishing. One of his woodblocks, which had been in use at this printing house for many years, featured an image of the Half Eagle and Key and was probably a version of the sign that John Charlewood had originally hung outside the building. This woodblock can be found on the title pages of at least six books that Jaggard printed for the trade, but never on the title page of a book Jaggard published.[52] Similarly, the woodblock known as the 'Heb Ddieu' device after the Welsh motto carved around its edge ('HEB DDIEU HEB DDIM', meaning 'without

---

[50] I have excluded from this list Jaggard's printing of non-speculative editions, such as those printed for the City of London, the Church of England, and the Stationers' Company. Removing reissues and variants, I count 103 separate pieces of trade printing. A further group of fourteen titles (13.6 per cent) include his initials. Early modern writers and readers could be sensitive to the distinction between supplying a full name and giving only initials: 'I covenant with you,' wrote the author John Beale to his printer Joshua Kirton, 'That you shall not divulge my name in print more than in theese characters JB': undated letter written c.1658, *Hartlib Papers*, 51/6A–7B. See also: Franklin B. Williams, 'An Initiation into Initials' in *Studies in Bibliography* 9 (1957): pp. 163–78.

[51] Gants, 'Quantitative Analysis', p. 195. Gants finds that '[r]oughly 5%' of printing does not list its printer in this period, though he also notes that 'over half' of that work is non-speculative printing done for the Stationers' Company, suggesting the figure for speculative publications that hide their printer would be somewhere around 2–3 per cent (compared to Jaggard's 87.4 per cent). The default position of the Stationers' Company was, as the Bishop of London reminded it in 1630, that every master printer (a cohort that included Jaggard before his death) must add 'his name to eu'y booke that he printeth': Jackson ed., *Records of the Court*, p. 220.

[52] The woodblock is no. 136 in Ronald B. McKerrow, *Printers' & Publishers' Devices in England & Scotland 1485–1640* (London: Bibliographical Society, 1949), p. 49. The books of Jaggard's on which it features are STCs 6496, 21513.5, 21366, 25635, 25639, and 19202. The woodblock also features on the 1619 edition of *A midsommer nights dreame*, printed as part of the Jaggard Quartos, which could be considered a Jaggard 'publication'. However, *Dream* has a false imprint which dates the book to 1600 and attributes it to the stationer James Roberts, the previous owner of Jaggard's printing house ('Printed by James Roberts, 1600'). Use of the Half Eagle and Key block in this case therefore seems purposefully to distance the edition from Jaggard by associating Shakespeare's book with an earlier generation of stationer.

God, without anything') was used more frequently on Jaggard's trade books than his publishing work.[53] By my count, the device was used on the title pages of at least twenty-four of Jaggard's editions. Seven of these editions are the playbooks that Jaggard printed in 1619 but which hide his presence.[54] Of the remaining seventeen editions, just three are books that Jaggard published; the remaining fourteen were various forms of his trade printing.[55] One of the three Jaggard publications that does feature the 'Heb Ddieu' woodblock is his *A catalogue of such English bookes...* (1618), a book that, as scholars have noted, was probably aimed at members of the Stationers' Company rather than being directed towards retail readerships.[56] Jaggard's use of the 'Heb Ddieu' woodblock is not as clear-cut as the Half Eagle and Key, but it does suggest that he used both blocks carefully, in particular bibliographic contexts (just as is the case with several other woodblocks that feature on the title pages of Jaggard's books).[57] To put this another way, over

---

[53] This woodblock has come under scrutiny already because it features on most of the title pages of the Jaggard Quartos: see Marino, *Owning*, pp. 108–16; Hooks, *Selling*, p. 119; Lesser, *Ghosts, Holes, Rips and Scrapes*. The 'Heb Ddieu' woodblock is device no. 283 in McKerrow, *Devices*, p. 110. For an analysis of the device's Welsh context see Geraint Evans, 'Heb Ddieu Heb Ddim: The Welsh Printer's Device on Shakespeare Quarto Title-pages' in *Studia Celtica* 44 (2010): pp. 155–64.

[54] The books on which the device appears are: STCs 6682.3, 7657, 20992, 10237, 10314.7, 10147.4, 10147.5, 10291, 10854, 17439, 21486, 13372, 18796, 14341, 22291, 22293, 22297, 22300, 22341, 6108, 6108.3, 12391, 25109, and 26101. The last STC number identifies a complicated edition of 1619 that contains both *The whole contention* and *Pericles* printed in continuous register. This edition contains two appearances of the 'Heb Ddieu' block: the first on the title page of *Contention* and the second on the internal title page of *Pericles*. As these texts were printed in continuous register, I have only counted the woodblock's appearance on the title page of *The whole contention*. However, in examining early bindings that collect the 1619 quartos, Lesser has found that these two plays 'are never found consecutively', suggesting they were treated as distinct editions and making it possible to argue that the block appears on twenty-five of Jaggard's 'editions' (*Ghosts, Holes, Rips and Scrapes*).

[55] The fourteen remaining books on which the 'Heb Ddieu' device appears include five editions of visitation articles that Jaggard printed for the Church of England (STCs 10237, 10314.7, 10147.4, 10147.5, 10291). Unusually for Jaggard's 'trade printing' work, these visitation articles did tend to feature his full name in the imprint, and so in one sense they associate him with the 'Heb Ddieu' device. However, visitation articles were not retail publications sold in London bookshops. As Kenneth Fincham explains, these pamphlets were made to order and distributed to a small, regional 'captive market' of the churchwardens of a particular diocese in advance of a visit by a bishop or archdeacon (in Jaggard's case, the dioceses of Norwich, Peterborough, and Lincoln). The 'publisher' of these books was the Church of England, rather than Jaggard—Fincham points out the clergy sometimes got in trouble for profiteering from such publications. It seems reasonable to treat these books—which were essentially bureaucratic forms—as being removed from any commercial readership, and so to suggest that the 'Heb Ddieu' woodblock's appearance on their title pages did not contribute to the visual brand of Jaggard's publishing. See Kenneth Fincham ed., *Visitation Articles and Injunctions of the Early Stuart Church, Volume 1* (Woodbridge: The Boydell Press and Church of England Record Society, 1994), pp. xiv–xv.

[56] Marino, *Owning*, p. 114. See also Oliver Willard, 'Jaggard's Catalogue of English Books' in *Stanford Studies in Language and Literature* (1941): pp. 152–72.

[57] Much of Jaggard's work shows us that his title-page woodblocks were carefully chosen. City of London pamphlets like *The lawes of the market* (1620) or *The reformation of divers abuses used in the wardmote inquest* (1617) featured a block showing the arms of the City of London; Thomas Hill's astronomy textbook *The Schoole of Skil* (1599) featured a teaching sphere; Edward Topsell's *The historie of foure-footed beastes* (1607) featured either a sea-wolf or a gorgon on the front (depending on the issue); the title page of Helkiah Crooke's *Mikrokosmographia* (1615) featured two anatomical illustrations, and so on. Jaggard was clearly sensitive to the visual branding of his title pages.

the roughly two decades in which Jaggard occupied this printing house, it seems only two of his retail publications ever featured the 'Heb Ddieu' woodblock on their title page, in comparison with fifteen appearances of the block on books that were either printed for the trade or for the Church of England. As well as, of course, the playbooks from 1619 which deliberately obscure the fact of Jaggard's involvement. Taken as a whole, Jaggard's use of the 'Heb Ddieu' woodblock suggests it visually branded books that—like the Jaggard Quartos—belonged outside his own inventory of retail publications.

Jaggard seems to have viewed his trade printing work as separate from his publishing imprint; he diminished his visible presence in the former even as he foregrounded his agency in the latter. Crucially, it was the title pages of Jaggard's own publications that provided the interpretive frame through which readers of the early seventeenth century encountered this stationer. The public version of the Jaggard publishing house which circulated in early modern culture, and which was foregrounded by Shakespeare's Folio, was very different to the version we have received from the New Bibliographers and the STC. In recovering so many items of print associated with Jaggard, we have also recovered many that Jaggard himself managed effectively to hide.

The 'Prudentia' Woodblock

What might Jaggard's identity *qua* publisher have been? A clue can be found in the way that he positioned himself towards the start of his career. When Jaggard moved into his printing premises in Barbican, one of his first acts was to commission a new woodblock device that, unlike the Half Eagle and Key block or the 'Heb Ddieu' device, did brand many of his own publications. The block appears on the title page of one of the first books he issued from his new establishment: a large folio Roman chronicle entitled *The historie of Justine*, which Jaggard both printed and published, and which was translated by George Wilkins just as the latter was turning his attention to the co-authorship of *Pericles* with Shakespeare. The woodblock (Figure 2.1) features a divine hand emerging from clouds to grip a staff, on top of which rests a portcullis draped in chains. A snake twines itself around the hand's wrist and bites on its own tail, forming a circle in which appears the Latin word *prudentia*, meaning 'prudencie', or 'wysedome in dooyng a thyng', cut into the woodbock.[58] Laurel leaves spring from the staff and curl outwards on either side.

Woodblock devices like this offered a compelling blend of visual and legible codes. They often contained clues about the identity of their owners. Folio publisher

---

[58] Thomas Elyot, *Bibliotheca Eliotæ* (1559, STC 7663), sig. 3N2v. The device is no. 355 in McKerrow, *Printers & Publishers Devices*, p. 137.

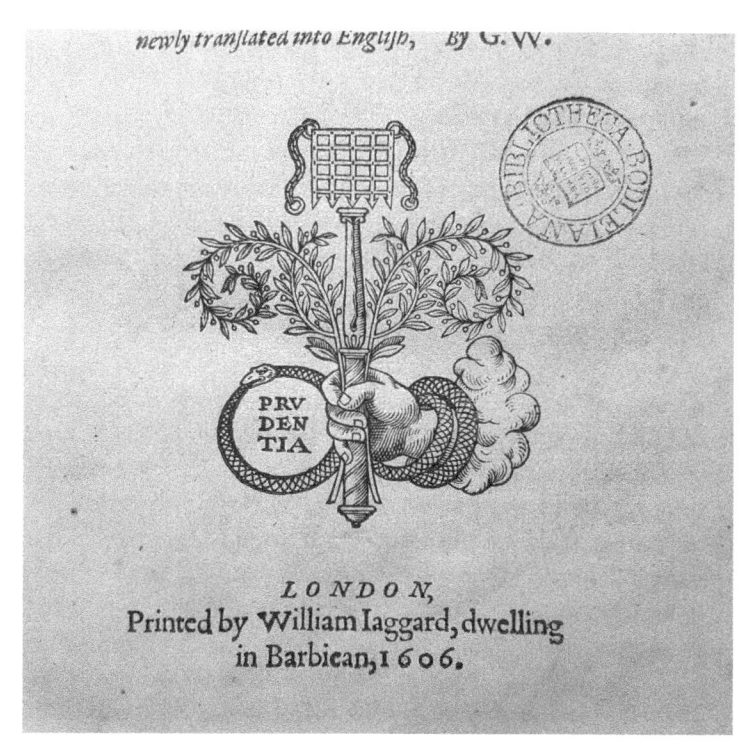

Figure 2.1 William Jaggard's 'prudentia' woodblock, taken from its first appearance on the title page (sig. A2r) of *The historie of Justine* (1606, STC 24293). Credit: Bodleian Libraries, University of Oxford, shelf-mark fol. DELTA 124. Used under Creative Commons licence CC-BY-NC 4.0.

John Smethwick, for example, used a device which features an image of the bird called a 'smew', which holds in its beak a little scroll containing the word 'wick'; Nicholas Ling, whose publication of the first and second editions of *Hamlet* is discussed in chapter four, used a device featuring the image of a 'ling' fish between his initials.[59] The author-turned-bookseller Francis Burton went further, designing a cryptogram out of the letters of his name that doubled as his own publishing device. Burton introduced the device with a short poem that issued a playful challenge to the reader to interpret, or 'untie', the image (see Figure 2.2). Burton's

---

[59] Erne, *Book Trade*, pp. 142–3; Hooks, *Selling Shakespeare*, p. 118. On the 'self-image, the beliefs and the cultural affinities' conveyed by these woodblocks, see Anja Wolkenhauer and Bernhard F. Scholz eds, *Typographorum Emblemata: The Printer's Mark in the Context of Early Modern Culture* (Berlin: Walter de Gruyter GmbH, 2018), at p. vii. For the ways in which publishing woodblocks could be 'strongly resonant with the publishing specialties of their owners' see Kirk Melnikoff, *Elizabethan Publishing and the Makings of Literary Culture*, pp. 72–6. Peter W. M. Blayney examines how the visual design of sixteenth-century woodblock capitals incorporated the initials of their owners: 'Initials within Initials,' in *The Library*, 20.4 (2019): pp. 443–61.

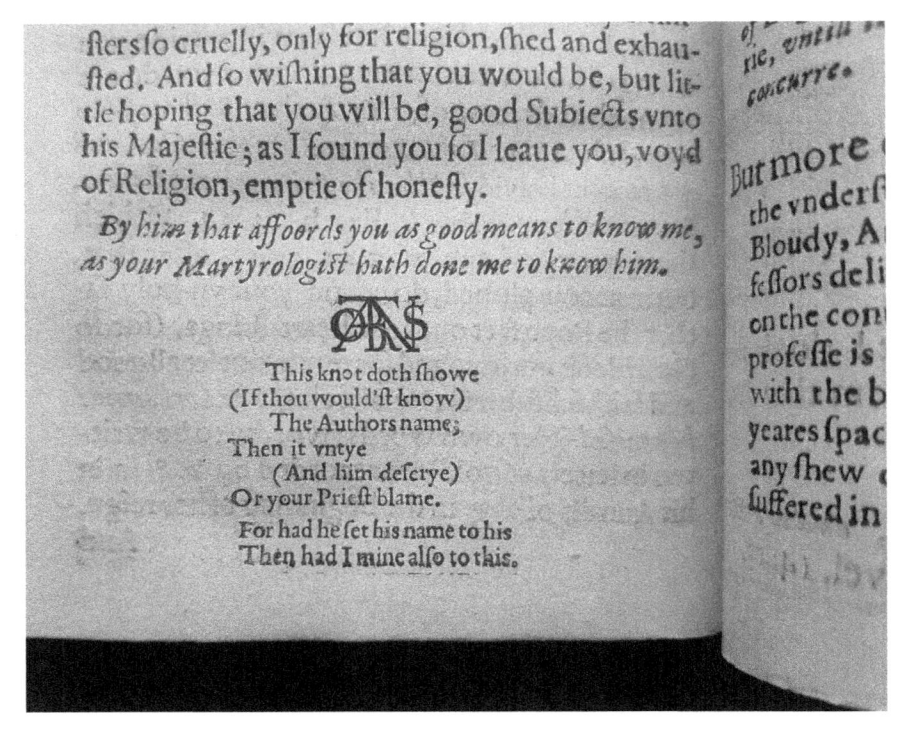

> ſters ſo cruelly, only for religion, ſhed and exhau-
> ſted. And ſo wiſhing that you would be, but lit-
> tle hoping that you will be, good Subiects vnto
> his Majeſtie; as I found you ſo I leaue you, voyd
> of Religion, emptie of honeſty.
> *By him that affoords you as good means to know me,*
> *as your Martyrologiſt hath done me to know him.*
>
> This knot doth ſhowe
> (If thou would'ſt know)
> The Authors name;
> Then it vntye
> (And him deſerye)
> Or your Prieſt blame.
> For had he ſet his name to his
> Then had I mine alſo to this.

Figure 2.2 Publishing device of Francis Burton, from *The fierie tryall of Gods saints* (1611, STC 24269), sig. F4v. In this first example the device appeared inside the book, but for the rest of his career Burton used the cryptogram on many of his title pages. Credit: Bodleian Libraries, University of Oxford, shelf-mark 4° C 110(7) Th. Used under Creative Commons licence CC-BY-NC 4.0.

cryptogram is perhaps the most literal embodiment of a wider theme in the period: that a publisher's device could be an emblem of its owner's professional identity.

The *prudentia* woodblock presented Jaggard as a judicious and authoritative merchant of information. The chained portcullis on top of the staff was a specific heraldic badge used by the College of Arms, the institution that awarded heraldic crests and underwrote the social hierarchies that structured early modern England. The portcullis therefore associated Jaggard and his books with the College, whose work he printed several times. The serpent eating its own tail—a symbol known as an 'ouroboros'—was a well-known emblem, which, as one preacher put it in 1621, 'hath of old bin made an *Hieroglyphique*' and signified the passing of time, or the 'mysticall representation of the revolution of the yeere': an appropriate symbol to include on the title page of a book about history, which became Jaggard's major publishing interest.[60] The laurel spray typically

---

[60] John Andrewes, *The Brazen Serpent* (1621, STC 591), sig. B1v.

suggests victory; its emergence from the staff, or perhaps sceptre, puts ideas of achievement in conversation with notions of authority. The snake (which 'a vertuous *Prudence*, doth expresse', according to George Wither) ties the symbols together, twining itself around both the word *prudentia* and the hand that grips the staff.[61] Taken as a whole, the motif recalls, without specifically imitating, the 'caduceus' mark made famous by large continental printing houses such as that owned by Johann Froben.

While some elements of this block may have been copied from an older device, the keyword *prudentia* was a new addition.[62] The word featured in translated form in a preface to *The history of Justine*, entitled 'the Profit of reading Histories', which stressed the importance of sceptical reading. If readers chose the wrong books, then 'by the surfet of rash and unadvised reading' a 'certaine corruptnesse of Judgement and perverse opinion is bred.'[63] Readers should instead select their books 'circumspectly and carefully' and adopt a culture of scepticism that is summed up in the original Latin text of this essay with the word *prudentia*. On Jaggard's title page the word advertised his own abilities as a discriminating bookseller. This book, both woodblock and paratext suggest, has indeed been chosen 'circumspectly and carefully' by a publisher who ratified its contents by stamping his *imprimatur* onto its title page. In selecting this word for his motto, Jaggard may also have been informed by its wider cultural purchase at the time: the character of *prudentia* was one of the four virtues that greeted King James during the pageant that marked his entry into London in 1603, symbolically depicting a key classical value that his reign was hoped to embody.[64] In the same year that *Justine* was published, the concept of *prudentia* was lauded in royal advice books as a 'mature deliberation' or an 'expert judgement'; elsewhere it was lauded as the quality of 'chosing and knowing what is to be desired or eschewed'.[65]

The sense of epistemological security embodied by this woodblock framed much of the rest of Jaggard's publishing career. Ideas about what exactly 'authority' meant within the book trade have been explored from several perspectives in recent years; Jaggard offers a different kind of authority, whereby an English

[61] George Wither, *A collection of emblemes, ancient and moderne* (1635, STC 25900d), sig. B3r.
[62] McKerrow, *Printers & Publishers Devices*, p. 137. The word occasionally featured in earlier continental printers' devices, several of which can be viewed by searching 'prudentia' on the *Consortium of European Research Libraries* (CERL) thesaurus tool: https://data.cerl.org/thesaurus/.
[63] Simon Grynaeus, 'A Preface of Simon Grineus to the Reader' in Marcus Justinus, *The Historie of Justine* (1606, STC 24293), sig. A4r–5v. On the concept of *prudentia* in this period see: Fernando Cervantes, 'Phronêsis vs Scepticism: An Early Modernist Perspective' in *New Blackfriars* 91.1036 (2010): pp. 680–94.
[64] Thomas Dekker, *The Magnificent Entertainment* (1604, STC 6510), sig. H3v.
[65] Barnabe Barnes, *Foure bookes of offices* (1606, STC 1468), sig. I1r. See also Wawrzyniec Goslicki, *The Counsellor* (1598, STC 12372), sig. H5v, and Bartholomeu Filipe, *The Counseller* (1589, STC 10753), sig. C3v–4r, where prudency and its component parts ('Prudentia Particularisis'; 'Prudentia Oeconomica', etc) are offered as the primary qualities of a statesman.

publisher positioned himself as the guarantor of information.[66] The full list of books he published is supplied in an appendix; stripped of his trade printing, these books are best described as 'proto-reference'.[67] Jaggard published a great deal of historical writing, for example, and himself contributed to this genre as an author with his *A view of all the right honourable the Lord Mayors...* (1599)—an illustrated chronicle of the city's civic leaders with short poems recording their achievements. From the Barbican premises Jaggard financed, among other books, an important history of political power entitled *Nobilitas politica vel civilis* (1608); Thomas Heywood's translation of the Roman historian Sallust (1608); a large, two-volume historical encyclopaedia entitled *The treasurie of aunciente and moderne times* (1613 and 1619); and Andre Favyn's *The theater of honour and knight-hood* (1623)—a work that claimed on its title page to be a 'compendious chronicle and historie of the whole Christian world'.[68] These were imposing, memorable books, each of which was published in folio format and often lavishly illustrated.

Natural history was another prominent category of Jaggard's work. The large folio written by Edward Topsell and published by Jaggard in 1607 as *The historie of foure-footed beastes* is now well known as the first major work on animals to be printed in English. Described on its title page as a compendium of knowledge 'necessary for all', the book included many detailed illustrations. A companion volume published in 1608 by Jaggard, *The historie of serpents*, often found bound with the first, has led to this pair of books being described as 'an exhaustive source of information about Elizabethan ideas on natural history'.[69] Jaggard's paratexts tended to frame these texts as repositories of knowledge by including a range of finding materials: Topsell's encyclopaedias included a catalogue of the authors cited, two indices of animals, and twelve lists of species names in ancient and

---

[66] Pollie Bromilow ed., *Authority in European Book Culture 1400–1600* (Abingdon: Routledge, 2016); Harry Newman, *Impressive Shakespeare: Identity, Authority and the Imprint in Shakespearean Drama* (Abingdon: Routledge, 2019); Katie Halsey and Angus Vine eds, *Shakespeare and Authority: Citations, Conceptions and Constructions* (London: Palgrave Macmillan, 2018).

[67] Ann Blair explains that 'reference books' did not emerge till the nineteenth century, though there were equivalent early modern categories: *Too Much To Know: Managing Scholarly Information before the Modern Age* (New Haven, CT: Yale University Press, 2010), pp. 118–19, and chapter 5: 'The Impact of Early Printed Reference Books'. David Gants uses the term 'information publishing' ('Quantitative Analysis' p. 209); his survey finds that the Jaggards are the fifth most productive publishers in this category behind John Legat (printer for Cambridge University); Adam Islip (who held the law book patent), Thomas Adams, and the Stationers' Company itself. Jaggard's interest in reference books has its roots in his apprenticeship. A few months after he joined the Stationers' Company in 1584, Jaggard's master Henry Denham was awarded a royal patent to print all chronicle histories and dictionaries (Arber II.438). Jaggard's training in the book trade thus involved titles like the revised edition of Raphael Holinshed's monumental *Chronicles* and the historian John Stowe's own *Chronicles of England*. It is not surprising, then, that these books have counterparts in Jaggard's own publishing career.

[68] Favyn, *Theater*, sig. A1r.

[69] David Cheney, 'Edward Topsell's The History of Four-Footed Beasts and Serpents' in *Books at Iowa* 10 (1969): pp. 31–4, at 33. On the encyclopaedic tradition in the Renaissance see Neil Kenny, *The Palace of Secrets: Béroalde de Verville and Renaissance Conceptions of Knowledge* (Oxford: Clarendon Press, 1991); Jason König and Greg Woolf eds, *Encyclopaedism from Antiquity to the Renaissance* (Cambridge: Cambridge University Press, 2013), pp. 379–502.

modern languages, all of which were cross-referenced with page numbers to help readers locate their interests. Jaggard's interest in such finding devices—which encouraged a mode of reading that relied on consultation and reference, rather than narrative experience—is typified by his publication of Edmund Bunny's *Of the head-corner-stone*. A religious book that offered a 'History of the Church from the beginning of the World unto this present Age', the title page of Bunny's work advertised its organization for the reader who wanted to dip in, rather than read continuously.[70] The book contained:

> certaine TABLES of divers sorts, for the better understanding, and use of these *Bookes*; One, of METHOD, in the beginning; and three others in the end: the first of the *Scriptures*, in two parts; the next, of other *Authors*, and their *Authorities*; the thirde, of the more speciall & principall matters, contained in the whole worke.[71]

Four tables provided a schema of authority and method, enabling readers to navigate the book through their interest in select scriptural passages, by pursuing the authors quoted, or by tracking the book's key themes, its 'speciall & principall matters'. Here and elsewhere, Jaggard's work brings to mind Peter Stallybrass's arguments about the early modern book as a 'technology of discontinuity', intended to be consulted, dipped into, read out of sequence.[72]

Despite their allure in bibliographic work, lists, as the critic Paul Tankard reminds us, make for fraught reading.[73] In lieu of piling up forms of reference published by Jaggard (the appendix shows that he also financed anatomy, lexicography, and encyclopaedias), his interest in heraldry supplies one final example. This genre comprised around one-fifth of all Jaggard's published edition sheets. It included a series of important publications that led to a well-known feud between the heralds Ralph Brooke and Augustine Vincent, in which both men quarrelled about whose work was the more accurate. Jaggard was particularly invested in this dispute, penning a lengthy response to Brooke's criticism of Jaggard's workmanship. Jaggard's reply to Brooke appeared in the front of Vincent's *A discoverie of errours* (1622), a book that energetically unearthed dozens of mistakes in Brooke's own heraldic work, and which seems to have confirmed Jaggard's place

---

[70] Edmund Bunny, *Of the Head-Corner-Stone* (1611, STC 4093), sig. A3r.
[71] Bunny, *Head-Corner-Stone*, sig ¶2r.
[72] Peter Stallybrass, 'Books and Scrolls: Navigating the Bible' in Jennifer Andersen and Elizabeth Sauer eds, *Books and Readers in Early Modern England* (Philadelphia, PA: University of Pennsylvania Press, 2002), pp. 42–79, quote from p. 73. Emma Smith has found that early owners of Shakespeare's Folio tended to read in a way that supports Stallybrass's ideas, dipping in and out of the Folio and reading locally, rather than serially: *Shakespeare's First Folio: Four Centuries of an Iconic Book* (Oxford: Oxford University Press, 2016), pp. 121–82. For another example of a finding device from within Jaggard's books, see the column of letters printed down each gutter of Justinus, *Historie of Justine*, which seems designed to aid reference-reading.
[73] Paul Tankard, 'Reading lists' in *Prose Studies* 28.3 (2006): pp. 337–60.

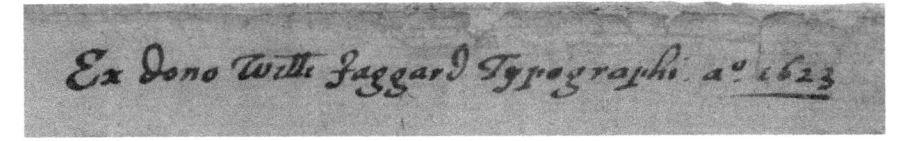

Figure 2.3 Augustine Vincent's inscription on his copy of the First Folio. Detail from Folger Library STC 22273 Fo.1 no.01. Credit: Folger digital image collection, no. 3281. Used by permission of the Folger Shakespeare Library.

as a publisher of record. Perhaps in gratitude, Jaggard gifted Vincent a copy of Shakespeare's Folio. The little manuscript note on the title page (see Figure 2.3), in which Vincent records the gift from 'Willi Jaggard Typographi' made this particular copy 'the most precious book in the world' for its collector Henry Folger.[74]

The emphasis on authority and security found throughout Jaggard's career helps us to understand quite why Brooke's criticism prompted the longest and most combative of Jaggard's prefaces. 'I owe my selfe that justice,' Jaggard wrote, 'as not to heare my name publikely proclaimed' for faults that were not, he argued, of his making.[75] A stationer, Jaggard continued, must 'maintaine his reputation in the Art he lives by'. For this publisher, who built an imprint that was powerfully associated with ideas of accuracy and completion, the reputation he lived by was something like the opposite of the 'infamous pirate, liar, and thief' reviled by the New Bibliographers.

The Passionate Pilgrime

How does this reappraisal of Jaggard extend to Shakespeare's books? The stationer's first Shakespearean venture was *The passionate pilgrime* (1599). This well-known miscellany of poems contained, as scholars since Edmond Malone have understood, five poems by Shakespeare together with fifteen more by a variety of early modern authors including Walter Raleigh and Christopher Marlowe. Despite the various authors involved, the earliest surviving title page (the first edition survives only in fragments which do not include a title page) claims the contents are 'By W. Shakespeare'. The *Pilgrime* is, as Patrick Cheney notes, a collaborative production that Jaggard presented as a single-author work.[76]

---

[74] Andrea E. Mays, *The Millionaire and the Bard: Henry Folger's Obsessive Hunt for Shakespeare's First Folio* (New York: Simon and Schuster, 2015), p. 225. See also Smith, *Four Centuries of an Iconic Book*, pp. 54–7. The copy is now 'First Folio 1' in the Folger Shakespeare Library.

[75] 'The Printer' in Augustine Vincent, *A discoverie of errours in the first edition of the catalogue of nobility* (1622, STC 24756), sig. ¶5r.

[76] Patrick Cheney, *Shakespeare: National Poet-Playwright* (Cambridge: Cambridge University Press, 2004), pp. 151–72, quote at p. 151. The fragments of the earlier edition were first identified by Joseph

Inevitably, much of the commentary on the *Pilgrime* has focused on the morality of Jaggard's actions. Was he 'outrageously piratical and misleading', as Katherine Duncan-Jones puts it, by adding the Shakespeare attribution to the book's title page?[77] Or, to take the alternative view that has gained momentum in recent years, was Jaggard's title page 'perfectly allowable' and within the 'normative practices of his trade'?[78] The responses to these questions expose our own evolving views about stationers and early modern authorship in recent decades. Rather than continuing the debate about the ethics of Jaggard's actions, I want instead to re-evaluate the importance of this book to Jaggard's involvement in the First Folio.[79] A post-Romantic investment in Shakespeare's authorship has kept the narrative of possible piracy at the centre of our thinking about both this book and Jaggard's career. The added fascination of Heywood's epistle, in which the author claimed Shakespeare himself was 'much offended with M. *Jaggard*', makes it likely the *Pilgrime* will remain an enduringly compelling case study.[80] But there is a mismatch here between the edition's continuing modern intrigue and its likely significance to readers at the time.

Jaggard first published this pamphlet of just a few sheets length in 1599, before he had settled into his Barbican printing house and publishing shop, and before his commission of the *prudentia* woodblock. Fresh archival evidence shows his circumstances were unstable at this point: in 1597, a property that Jaggard had leased on Fleet Street, probably while selling books from his first shop in St Dunstan's Churchyard, was taken from him unexpectedly: the freeholder repossessed it, arguing that it had not been kept in good enough repair.[81] None of the titles Jaggard published around the *Pilgrime* between 1598 and 1604 supply an address for him—instead he used the bookshops of other stationers for his wholesale distribution or his imprints give no address at all. This sense of instability is reflected in the variety of genres and forms of books that Jaggard published alongside the *Pilgrime*: a book of herbal remedies, a religious poem, a book of

---

Quincy Adams in his facsimile edition: *The Passionate Pilgrim by William Shakespeare* (New York and London: Charles Scribner's Sons, 1939), pp. xxi–xxxi.

[77] Katherine Duncan-Jones ed., *Shakespeare's Sonnets*, 2nd rev. edn (London: Methuen, 2010), p. 334. For summaries of the relevant material see Bednarz, 'Canonizing Shakespeare', and Marotti, 'Shakespeare's Sonnets as Literary Property'.

[78] Hooks, *Selling Shakespeare*, pp. 123 (referring both to the Jaggard Quartos and the *Pilgrime*), 111. See also Max W. Thomas, 'Eschewing Credit: Heywood, Shakespeare, and Plagiarism before Copyright' in *New Literary History* 31.2 (2000): pp. 277–93. Thomas uses the *Pilgrime* to argue that we misunderstand what is at stake in the idea of early modern plagiarism.

[79] For contributions that consider the ethics of Jaggard's work, see: Colin Burrow ed., *Complete Sonnets and Poems*, pp. 76–9; Hooks, *Selling Shakespeare*, pp. 109–12; Sasha Roberts, *Reading Shakespeare's Poems in Early Modern England* (Basingstoke: Palgrave Macmillan, 2003), pp. 153–8.

[80] Thomas Heywood, 'To my approved good Friend, M^r. Nicholas Okes' in *An Apology for Actors* (1612, STC 13309), sig. G4v.

[81] *Button v Whitfield*: TNA C 2/JasI/B40/22. Jaggard's renewal of the lease of this property, which took place in 1618, is discussed by Willoughby, *Printer*, pp. 122–4. The document Willoughby describes is now: *Conveyance of Land to William Jaggard*: LMA CLA/023/DW/01/294, item 14.

needlework patterns. Some of these works were entered in the Stationers' Register; others, like the *Pilgrime*, were not. There is nothing strange about any of this, but collectively the evidence of Jaggard's work at the time he published the first two editions of the *Pilgrime* (1599) suggests a stationer who had not yet found a set of stable professional habits and who sought to establish himself by seeking cheap, readily profitable ventures.[82] In other words, it seems unlikely that Jaggard himself saw the *Pilgrime* as a particularly important book.

The third edition of the *Pilgrime* (1612) is a little different. By this time, Jaggard's printing and publishing business was well established and his other books from around 1612 show the *Pilgrime*'s outlying status. In 1610, he published Thomas Milles' huge *The catalogue of honor* (300.5 edition sheets), which was a history of the British nobility; in 1611 he published Edmund Bunny's digest of the Bible, *Of the head-corner-stone* (151 edition sheets). In 1612 Jaggard financed Thomas Wilson's *Christian dictionarie* (103 edition sheets) and a religious commentary by William Attersoll on St Paul (135 edition sheets). His compositors would already have been at work on Thomas Milles's encyclopaedic *Treasurie of auncient and moderne times* (1613; 239.5 edition sheets), and Jaggard may have started to think about the complex anatomical illustrations for Helkiah Crooke's *Mikrokosmographia* (1615; 257 edition sheets). These were all substantial books, mostly folios, which make the third edition of the *Pilgrime*—an eight-sheet octavo—look unassuming.

Given that it seems out of place in this publishing context, why did Jaggard publish the *Pilgrime* at all in 1612? Perhaps it was because, following a decade in which Shakespeare's stock in the book trade had gradually declined, in 1611 there was a small surge of interest in the playwright among London's booksellers. Three new editions of his plays were published together with a fourth that falsely claimed to be 'Written by W. Sh.'[83] In the same year, the stationer Matthew Lownes reissued the poetry miscellany *Loves martyr*, which featured work by Shakespeare. The third edition of the *Pilgrime* may have been prompted by Jaggard's sense of a revival in the market for Shakespeare's work, combined with the ease of reprinting a short pamphlet for which Jaggard already owned the manuscript copy.

But as is well known, Jaggard did not only reprint a new edition of the same text of the *Pilgrime*. He also added several more poems, each of which he extracted from another book that he owned and had previously published: Thomas

---

[82] As Lukas Erne and Tamsin Badcoe have shown, the market for poetry books was at its peak between 1593 and 1602. Shakespeare was 'vastly more successful' than most other poets amid this publishing boom, making it likely Jaggard saw the pamphlet as an easy commercial opportunity: 'Shakespeare and the Popularity of Poetry Books in Print, 1583–1622' in *Review of English Studies* 65 (2014): pp. 33–57, at p. 47.

[83] These editions were Q3 *Pericles* (STC 22336); Q3 *Titus Andronicus* (STC 22330); Q3 *Hamlet* (STC 22277); and Q2 *The first and second part of the troublesome raigne of John King of England* (STC 14646).

Heywood's *Troia Britanica* (1609). The inclusion of these extra verses prompted Heywood's fiery comments in which he accused Jaggard of having caused 'manifest injury' by reprinting the poems and claimed that Shakespeare himself had been offended.[84] Heywood more than once set out hostile views towards the book trade, so perhaps it is no surprise to find him complaining here—but, if it is true, then the epistle offers a tantalizing glimpse of Shakespeare's own attitude towards his work in print.

Heywood's complaint puts paid to any idea that the *Pilgrime* passed unnoticed. Clearly the book provoked interest in some circles and perhaps even from Shakespeare himself, if we take Heywood at his word. But if the *Pilgrime* attracted attention as a kind of literary *cause célèbre*, then it still seems unlikely the book was charged with anything like its modern allure; the ethical force of Heywood's accusation, pushing as it does against a 'textually unstable and inherently collaborative' culture of authorship and literary property, must have been less explosive than it seems today.[85] For one thing, such 'fraudulent' (or perhaps incomplete) attributions were not particularly remarkable. As Lukas Erne has pointed out in a different context, a 'remarkably high' number of editions were wrongly attributed to Shakespeare by various stationers between 1595 and 1622.[86] And the *Pilgrime* was a relatively flimsy book: all three of its editions collectively account for somewhere around 0.3 per cent of Jaggard's publications in edition sheets. Small texts can still create a big stir, of course (a fact of which many Twitter users are aware). But given the wider context of Jaggard's books in and around 1612, it seems anachronistic to think that the *Pilgrime* determined in any meaningful sense the ways in which readers of the early seventeenth century thought of the Jaggard publishing imprint.

If early modern readers were unlikely to view the *Pilgrime* as a characteristic 'Jaggard book', the edition nevertheless represented this stationer's first experience of the contestations that could take place over the conceptual terrain of literary authorship. Heywood's outrage over the third edition of the *Pilgrime* must have

---

[84] Thomas Heywood, 'To my approved good Friend, M[r]. *Nicholas Okes*' in *An Apology for Actors* (1612, STC 13309), sig. G4r–v. To add further intrigue, the title page of the 1612 *Pilgrime* survives in two different settings. In one of them the poems are 'By W. Shakespere'; in the other the attribution has been removed. Both are bound in a copy that was owned by Edmond Malone and is now in the Bodleian Library (shelfmark Arch. G g.1). The conventional interpretation of these title pages is that Jaggard removed the attribution in response to Heywood's complaint, but Burrow (*Complete Sonnets and Poems*, p. 79), looking at the wear of these title pages, suggests the reverse may have occurred, whereby Jaggard added the attribution. A third possibility is that both versions of the title page were deliberately issued at the same time by Jaggard as the wholesaler, meaning that he offered retail booksellers the choice of whether to market the collection as by Shakespeare. The pages are in different settings of type, though, which makes it likely they were printed at different times.

[85] Francis X. Connor, 'Shakespeare, Poetic Collaboration, and *The Passionate Pilgrim*' in *Shakespeare Survey* 67 (2014): pp. 119–30, 123.

[86] Erne, *Book Trade*, p. 56. Erne finds that seven plays (in ten editions) have title pages that wrongly ascribe them to Shakespeare. These plays were published by Thomas Creede, William Jones, Nathaniel Butter, George Eld, Thomas Pavier, John Helme, Thomas Snodham, and Thomas Dewe.

left Jaggard with a sharpened sense of literary territory, and perhaps with a corresponding sensitivity to the roles that stationers could play in observing, transgressing, and constituting the boundaries of this terrain. For Jaggard, then, perhaps the real value of the *Pilgrime*—and of Heywood's response—was that the book forced him to consider the legitimacy of the ways in which he could frame, gather, and house Shakespeare's writing.

If nothing else, the *Pilgrime* demonstrates that Jaggard was interested to some degree in Shakespeare's authorship as a commercial category that he could exploit to sell books. It was the first edition of the *Pilgrime* (1599) that introduced readers to the name 'W. Shakespeare' as an organizational label for a collection of poetry. Not till the *Sonnets* in 1609 did any other version of 'Shakespeare' frame a group of poems. In that sense, William Jaggard was responsible for two major milestones in Shakespeare's career: he published the first book to use Shakespeare's name as a rubric under which to gather multiple poems, and he was also integrally involved in the book that offers the last word on Shakespeare's definitive dramatic corpus. These two ventures—the one considered 'illegitimate', the other authoritative—bookend Jaggard's career in the book trade. Between them, one further Shakespearean project adds another layer of fascination to this stationer's life.

The Jaggard Quartos

The 'Jaggard Quartos' of 1619 also mingle genuine and fraudulent conceptions of Shakespearean authorship. Together with the bookseller Thomas Pavier, William Jaggard produced a collection of ten plays, although because of the way they were printed these ten titles technically form just eight separate editions. Eight of the plays were by Shakespeare and two were not. Despite their mixed authorship, all of the plays except one featured a clear attribution to Shakespeare on the title page. The exception was an edition of *Henry V*, from which Shakespeare's name may have been excluded because the 1619 title page mimics the two earlier quarto editions of 1600 and 1602, neither of which featured a Shakespeare attribution. In some ways, then, this collection shares with the *Pilgrime* an overt and misleading investment in Shakespeare's name as a marketing device.

But in other ways this collection is much more complicated. Its rich critical history began with its discovery by the bibliographer Alfred W. Pollard in the early twentieth century. Between 1904 and 1906 Pollard found two separate quarto 'sammelband' volumes (bindings that gather a collection of different works), each of which featured the ten plays bound together; or rather, he found one volume that was still intact and a second that had recently been broken up for individual sale.[87] The plays were bound in a different order in these volumes, but

---

[87] Alfred Pollard, 'A Literary Causerie: Shakespeare in the Remainder Market' in *The Academy* (2 June 1906): pp. 528–9. Throughout this book, I follow the Folger Shakespeare Library and the Rare

each binding contained the same editions. As Pollard commented, the chances of two such sets being separately collected was 'very remote', so he thought at first they were probably 'remainders', or leftover stock, gathered and offered for resale by a stationer in about 1622 'so as to get rid of them before the Folio appeared'.[88]

Pollard's conclusion was understandable because the plays as printed have a variety of dates on their title pages. Three plays (*Pericles*, *The Merry Wives of Windsor*, and *A Yorkshire Tragedy*) claim they were printed in 1619; two more (*Henry V* and *King Lear*) give a date of 1608; and three others (*A Midsummer Night's Dream*, *Sir John Oldcastle*, and *The Merchant of Venice*) supply a date of 1600. The final two plays of the collection were early versions of the second and third parts of *Henry VI*, printed together as the first and second parts of *The Whole Contention Between the Two Famous Houses, Lancaster and Yorke* under one title page that supplies no date at all. Moreover, as if to make all these title pages more convincing, the plays also name different booksellers in their imprints. Two state they were printed by the long-retired (though probably only recently deceased) stationer James Roberts, predecessor to William Jaggard in the Barbican printing house; five claim to be 'Printed for T. P.', or Pavier; and the final two identify Arthur Johnson and Nathaniel Butter. The name of William Jaggard appears nowhere on any of the title pages.

At first glance the plays look like a piecemeal collection of (mostly) Shakespearean quartos that were printed at various points in the early seventeenth century and were financed by several different publishers. But shortly after Pollard's initial discovery came one of New Bibliography's most electric revelations: much of the information supplied in the imprints of these plays was false. By looking carefully at the watermarks of the paper used to print the plays, W. W. Greg showed they were all printed on the same mixture of paper stock, and so had almost certainly been produced at the same time. Building on Greg's work, William Neidig used forensic photography to confirm that all the plays had indeed been printed at William Jaggard's premises in Barbican in 1619.[89]

The deception rapidly attracted tremendous interest and the playbooks remain one of the most beguiling episodes of Shakespearean print. Much of the critical debate, as with the *Pilgrime*, has concentrated on the ethics of the project together with the related question of who was responsible. As Laurie Maguire has noted, the New Bibliographers worked with the narrative techniques of the detective story: there had been a crime, discovered by rigorous and scientific scrutiny,

---

Books and Manuscripts Section of the American Library Association in opting for the anglicized 'sammelband' over the German *Sammelband* and plural *Sammelbände*: https://folgerpedia.folger.edu/Sammelbands.

[88] Pollard, 'Literary Causerie', p. 529.

[89] Walter Wilson Greg, 'On Certain False Dates in Shakespearian Quartos,' *The Library* S2.9.34 (1908): pp. 113–31; William Neidig, 'The Shakespeare Quartos of 1619,' *Modern Philology* 8.2 (1910): pp. 145–63. Other important contributions include Gerald Johnson, 'Thomas Pavier, Publisher, 1600-25,' *The Library* S6.14.1 (1992): pp. 12–50; R. Carter Hailey, 'The Shakespearian Pavier Quartos Revisited,' *Studies in Bibliography* 57 (2005/6): pp. 151–95.

which meant there must also be a culprit.[90] Historically that culprit was Thomas Pavier, whose initials feature on most of the title pages, albeit Pavier in some form of shady collaboration with Jaggard. But this perspective has recently been challenged. First James Marino, and more recently Zachary Lesser and Peter Stallybrass have argued that the Jaggards were 'the central figures in the publication'.[91] In these recent accounts, William Jaggard did not only print the books 'for' Thomas Pavier, but, given that Jaggard is the only figure who can be connected with each of the editions, he may also have masterminded the project, even if it probably required the involvement of several other stationers.[92]

Part of the revisionist argument for the scheme's agency rests on the discovery of new bibliographic evidence about how these plays were sold. Lesser and Stallybrass found that several surviving copies from the collection do not have the tell-tale holes in their gutters which reveal that a book was sold individually. When a quarto playbook was sold as a lone text, it was typically 'stab-stitched', meaning it was given a cheap binding by being stitched with thread along the fold.[93] Books that lack the holes created by this type of binding must have been sold originally as part of a collection, bound among a group of texts, rather than as an individual item. Lesser and Stallybrass found that while quarto playbooks in general usually do contain these holes, because they were typically sold as individual pamphlets, several copies of titles from the Jaggard-Pavier collection do not, and must therefore have originally been sold within a collection. But Lesser and Stallybrass also found evidence that the collection contained another play that was published and printed by Jaggard: the third edition of Thomas Heywood's *A Woman Killed with Kindness* (1617).[94]

All these complications are thoroughly examined in Lesser's new book, which builds on his earlier work with Peter Stallybrass and on work by Jeffrey Todd Knight to offer a fresh appraisal of the primary evidence. Among Lesser's key findings are that this enigmatic collection was much less uniform, less tidily Shakespearean, than New Bibliography would have us believe. To Pollard's early discovery of two sammelband volumes, Lesser adds evidence for up to seventeen more which housed the plays in a variety of ways: they contain, for the most part, 'no similarity at all' in the order of their titles.[95] The plays were intended as a

---

[90] Laurie E. Maguire, *Shakespearean Suspect Texts: The 'Bad' Quartos and their Contexts* (Cambridge: Cambridge University Press, 2009), pp. 66–8. See also Lesser, *Ghosts, Holes, Rips and Scrapes*, pp. 19, 24.

[91] Marino, *Owning*, pp. 107–33; Lesser and Stallybrass, 'Between Pamphlet and Book', p. 130.

[92] Whatever the dynamics of their collaboration in 1619, Pavier and Jaggard remained close. William Jaggard gave Pavier (described as one of Jaggard's 'very good freindes') twenty shillings in his will, and named him an overseer (*Will of William Jaggard*). Pavier is also listed beside Isaac Jaggard and William Jaggard's widow, Jane, as a surety for William's son Thomas in March 1624 (*Court of Orphans Recognizances 1590–1633*: LMA CLA/002/05/001, fol. 261v).

[93] Aaron T. Pratt, 'Stab-Stitching and the Status of Early English Playbooks as Literature' in *The Library* 16.3 (2015): pp. 304–28.

[94] Lesser and Stallybrass, 'Between Pamphlet and Book'.

[95] Lesser, *Ghosts, Holes, Rips and Scrapes*, p. 64.

collection then, but seemingly one without a clear internal structure. And if Lesser's work confirms the plays were indeed sold together, then it also makes clear that Heywood's *Woman Killed* was in several cases packaged with the collection from the start. If we want to look for a single agency behind this venture, then the inclusion of Heywood's play suggests the Jaggards were indeed the key players because only William and Isaac seem able to have added copies of *Woman Killed* to volumes that contained this collection in any kind of systematic way. The addition of Heywood's play also tells us that the category of Shakespearean authorship around which we imagined this venture to have been built is not quite as sturdy as first appeared, even if there remains a clear central focus on Shakespeare in this collection.

The idea that we should rename the collection the 'Jaggard Quartos' is supported by Adam G. Hooks, who agrees that Jaggard had more agency than has previously been suspected. Hooks argues that the name of the 'Pavier Quartos', as this collection has typically been known, is a misnomer that registers the critical desire to 'preserve the integrity of William Jaggard, who would subsequently print the Folio'.[96] In other words, for the New Bibliographers and beyond, the history of the 1619 collection has been shaped by our reluctance to see the same stationer as responsible both for this collection and for the Folio. Yet, as Hooks points out, Jaggard is the only stationer who is certainly connected to all the playbooks in this collection; he also notes the presence of the 'Heb Ddieu' woodblock device on most of their title pages. This woodblock, scholars have argued, in some sense brands the playbooks as a 'Jaggard' collection in ways that would have been evident to early modern readers, further confusing our ideas about why the King's Men would have worked with Jaggard again.[97]

However, as shown above, the 'Heb Ddieu' woodblock tended to feature on books that William Jaggard printed for the trade, and only rarely appeared on books sold under his own publishing imprint. There are just two instances of this device being used on a Jaggard publication that was offered for sale to retail customers. The first of these is an edition of the Elizabethan clergyman Edward Dering's *Briefe and necessarie catechisme* (1614), the imprint of which tells us it was 'Printed by W. Jaggard. 1614'.[98] Here the device brands what is clearly a Jaggard publication, but even in this case the association is not wholly straightforward. As the STC notes, the surviving copies of this book are usually 'found as pt. 3' of the collected edition of *M. Derings workes*, which was issued in 1614 under a general title page that presents the collection as printed by Edward Griffin for Edward Blount, and which features a different woodblock.[99] Jaggard's edition of

---

[96] Hooks, *Selling Shakespeare*, p. 119.
[97] Hooks, *Selling Shakespeare*, pp. 112–24. See also Marino, *Owning*, p. 81.
[98] Edward Dering, *Briefe and necessarie catechisme* (1614, STC 6682.3).
[99] STC vol. 1, p. 300, entry for Edward Dering, *M. Derings workes* (1614, STC 6678). The woodblock on the general title page is a compartment border, rather than a printer or publisher's device.

the catechism may also have been sold separately, of course, but it looks as though most copies were packaged within a selection of Dering's writings that was primarily marketed as an Edward Blount publication, with William Jaggard's imprint and the 'Heb Ddieu' device appearing within the volume.

The only other time the block appears on a Jaggard publication directed at readers is the edition of Heywood's *A Woman Killed* (1617), which it is now known was sold as part of the Jaggard Quartos of 1619. Against these two publishing appearances are the twenty-four examples of the woodblock being used to mark books outside Jaggard's retail publishing line: eight uses of the block found on the Jaggard Quartos; five on visitation articles printed for the Church of England; ten on books printed for other stationers; and one on Jaggard's trade publication *A catalogue of such English bookes…*(1618). The only other block used in the 1619 collection is the Half Eagle and Key device which appears on the title page of *Dream*. As mentioned above, this woodblock appears on at least six books Jaggard printed for the trade but never on a book he published. And like much of Jaggard's trade printing, those six publications elide his presence, meaning that in 1619 there was almost nothing to associate him with this device. Five of the Half Eagle and Key books do not name Jaggard at all in their imprints and were instead attributed to him by the STC's cataloguing team, while the final book—a pamphlet by George Wilkins from 1607—supplies his initials, telling us the book was 'Printed by W. J.' at a time when the bookseller William Jones 2 (active 1589–1618) and the bookseller and printer William Jones 3 (active 1601–43) also worked in London.

Does this examination of Jaggard's title pages tell us anything useful? One finding is that the two woodblocks that feature on the Jaggard Quartos do not signal Jaggard's involvement in quite the ways that we might assume. With the help of modern bibliographical resources the devices clearly signal Jaggard's presence. But the history of these blocks in the early seventeenth century suggests Jaggard used them for the books in which he was least invested—his 'least public' publications. If title-page woodblocks conveyed meaning to readers, then these blocks probably signalled either that a book had been printed by Jaggard for a different publisher or—which seems more likely—they carried no clear association with any printing and publishing business. Certainly neither was a device that Jaggard regularly used to brand his leading editions.

It is also the case that both the 'Heb Ddieu' and the Half Eagle and Key devices had circulated through several different owners and businesses in their time. The 'Heb Ddieu' block appears at least as early as 1592, when the printer Richard Jones used it on the title page of Thomas Nashe's popular satire *Pierce Penilesse*.

The collection contained three parts: *Certaine letters*; *XXVII Lectures*; and the *Briefe catechisme*. The first two parts were both printed by Edward Griffin 1 for Edward Blount and may, like the *Briefe catechisme*, have also been sold separately.

The Half Eagle and Key device can be found as far back as 1562.[100] In other words, both blocks had featured on the title pages of plenty of books since before Jaggard was active in the book trade, meaning there was nothing suspicious about their appearance on a quarto that was seemingly dated from 1600 or 1608 or which lacked any date at all. The blocks we have taken to be a confusing marker of Jaggard's presence in the collection, given that in other ways he works hard to hide his involvement, turn out to be the perfect choices to grant him plausible deniability.

At the same time, the 'Heb Ddieu' device also appeared on the title page of *Woman Killed*, which, we now know, was also included in at least some versions of the collection. Here the block appeared above an imprint which plainly states that *Woman Killed* was 'Printed by Isaac Jaggard, 1617'. The device tells readers and stationers alike that the Jaggards both printed and published this edition, so it may also have suggested who printed the three other plays that were dated 1619. The presence of this device and imprint amid a collection that in other ways strives to efface the Jaggards is one of several features of this collection that remain baffling. Presumably the fact that *Woman Killed* was printed two years earlier, in circumstances that required no deception, explains the relative clarity of this title page.

Even here the connection between the 'Heb Ddieu' device and the Jaggard printing house may not be as secure as the title page of *Woman Killed* suggests. The surviving copies of the Jaggard Quartos include one copy of *Henry V* which is now individually bound in the Huntington Library. This copy bears a 'ghost' trace of the title page of *Woman Killed*, meaning an offset image created by transferred ink. The image appears on the final verso of *Henry V*, and so it reveals that this copy of *Henry V* was once bound beside a copy of *Woman Killed*. Over time, before the two titles were separated, a faint impression of the *Woman Killed* title page transferred onto the *Henry V* verso. But the same process has left a date of '1608' visible in the space of the *Woman Killed* imprint.[101] How can we explain this? As Lesser points out, we cannot be looking at a lost third edition of *Woman Killed* with an alternative date: in other respects the ghostly image exactly matches the 1617 title page. Instead, Lesser suggests we are looking at a cancel slip: a scrap of paper on which was printed a correction or adjustment of some kind, which was then pasted over the original text. On at least one copy of *Woman Killed*, then—the only title of this collection that links the 'Heb Ddieu' device to the Jaggard house—it looks as though the Jaggards tampered with the imprint.

---

[100] Thomas Nashe, *Pierce Penilesse his supplication to the divell* (1592, STC 18371); *The lawes and statutes of Geneva* (1562, STC 11725).

[101] I am here summarizing Lesser's work in *Ghosts, Holes, Rips and Scrapes*. The *Henry V* ghost image on this copy was first noticed by Jeffrey Todd Knight: *Bound to Read*, pp. 151–5, 177–9.

110   SHAKESPEARE'S SYNDICATE

It is still not entirely clear who Jaggard sought to deceive here, unless all his tactics were designed to circumvent the Lord Chamberlain's letter of May 1619 and so to avoid reprisal from the King's Men. Given the variety of strategies involved, though, there is no reason to think that early modern readers at large, both within the playhouse and beyond, saw through the jumble of misleading woodblocks, dates, and attributions found on the title pages of this collection. It was probably only certain stationers that knew the truth. After all, no evidence has been found to suggest that the falsities of this collection were known before the New Bibliographers, and more latterly the ingenuity of Jeffrey Todd Knight, Peter Stallybrass, and Zachary Lesser.

If Jaggard successfully masked the extent of his involvement with this enigmatic collection then his 'embarrassing participation' in the First Folio a few years later need not have troubled the King's Men. Heminge and Condell, together with other early modern readers, would have known Jaggard as a publisher defined by values of judgement, authority, and completion—even if he was clearly also capable of sharper practice. All of this leaves the Jaggard Quartos in an enduringly strange place in Jaggard's career. The venture's appeal clearly won out over its risks, yet at the same time the collection was carefully distanced from Jaggard's main inventory of publications. Perhaps, as several scholars have speculated, even in 1619 Jaggard was aware of the prospect of a more complete Shakespearean collection that would better suit his publishing identity, and which could provide a corrective to the version he had already produced.[102]

The First Folio

Jaggard's interactions with Shakespeare reveal him to have been alive to the commercial possibilities of the playwright, but equally sensitive to the brand he had forged for himself as a publisher. The Jaggard Quartos of 1619 show that, while this stationer saw the commercial value both of printed drama and of authorship as a marketing tool, he distanced this collection from his public identity. That attitude towards Shakespeare changed in 1623 with the arrival of the First Folio, which, in both its imprint and colophon, was unequivocally a 'Jaggard book'. How should we interpret Jaggard's involvement as a Folio publisher? Many of Jaggard's books trafficked in ideas of permanence and stability, and so rather than viewing Jaggard's earlier history with Shakespeare as a problematic feature of the Folio's making, it is more likely that Shakespeare's early readers and the King's Men

---

[102] Sonia Massai suggests the Pavier Quartos 'functioned as pre-publicity for the First Folio' (*Rise of the Editor*, p. 121); Lesser wonders whether 'plans for the Folio were already underway' (*Ghosts, Holes, Rips and Scrapes*, p. 144); Andrew Murphy considers the same possibility (*Shakespeare in Print*, 2nd rev. edn, p. 524–5, n. 43).

would have associated the Jaggard publishing house with books that were destined for libraries: encyclopaedic in scope and authoritative in content; books that 'stored up' texts 'for future Ages to delight in' as one of Jaggard's prefaces puts it.[103]

One way these ideas about Jaggard's publishing interact with the Folio concerns the book's claims to offer readers the definitive versions of Shakespeare's plays. This rhetoric begins on the Folio's title page, which, as mentioned in the introduction, presents the plays as having being 'Published according to the True Originall Copies'.[104] Similar claims are scattered throughout the Folio's preliminary pages. Early modern books often boasted of their merits in this way, though when they did so they usually drew on ideas of augmentation, correction, and revision, rather than (as the Folio does) advertising a return to textual origins. Yet in Shakespeare's Folio, these claims for the quality of the texts were brought into particular focus because half of the plays the book contained had already been printed (mindful of asking readers to 'pay twice for the same Booke', the publisher Humphrey Moseley explained that he left out all the Beaumont and Fletcher plays 'heretofore Printed' when he published their folio collection in 1647; doing so enabled Moseley to boast that 'not one' text in his book 'was ever printed before').[105] To differentiate their material from that which had already been printed, the actors John Heminge and Henry Condell promoted 'the perfection' of the Folio's contents.[106] The idea that the plays appear in their 'perfect' forms also features powerfully in the preliminary address to 'the great Variety of Readers'. A famous passage tells readers that before the Folio they were:

> abus'd with diverse stolne, and surreptitious copies, maimed, and deformed by the frauds and stealthes of injurious imposters, that expos'd them: even those, are now offer'd to your view cur'd, and perfect of their limbes; and all the rest, absolute in their numbers, as he conceived the*m*.[107]

The passage highlights several features of the Folio plays. It emphasises the quality of the texts (previously 'maimed' versions are now 'cur'd' and made 'perfect') and their status as a complete collection (the plays are 'absolute in their numbers').[108]

---

[103] 'To the most Noble and Twin-like paire, of truly Honourable and compleat perfection' in Thomas Milles ed., *Archaio-ploutos* (1619, STC 17936.5), sig. A3v.

[104] Shakespeare, *Comedies, Histories, & Tragedies* (1623), sig. πA1r.

[105] 'The Stationer to the Readers' in Francis Beaumont and John Fletcher, *Comedies and tragedies* (1647, Wing B1581), sig. A4r–v.

[106] John Heminge and Henry Condell, 'To the Most Noble and Incomparable Paire of Brethren' in Shakespeare, *Comedies, Histories, & Tragedies* (1623), sig. πA2v.

[107] John Heminge and Henry Condell, 'To the great Variety of Readers' in Shakespeare, *Comedies, Histories, & Tragedies* (1623), sig. πA3r. For discussion of this passage see David Scott Kastan, *Shakespeare and the Book* (Cambridge: Cambridge University Press, 2001), pp. 73–8; Erne, *Literary Dramatist*, 2nd edn, pp. 280–3.

[108] On the possibility that 'numbers' in this sentence might refer to versification see Valerie Wayne, 'The First Folio's Arrangement and its Finale' in *Shakespeare Quarterly* 66.4 (2015): pp. 389–408, at

The ultimate authority for both claims is Shakespeare himself; the plays are perfect and complete because they appear 'as he conceived the*m*'.

Similar rhetoric appears on the page that contains the 'Names of the Principall Actors' a little further in the preliminaries, although here the language of textual quality contains ideas that are subtly in conflict with one another. The page begins with a claim that the plays are 'Truely set forth, according to their first ORIGINALL'.[109] This line supports the version of literary value established by Heminge and Condell. Both the line and the earlier preface suggest that the 'first' and 'original' version of a text is somehow the 'best—a model that contradicts what we know about Shakespeare's habits of revision, and more broadly feels out of place in an era of literary composition that also gave us authors like Francis Bacon or Robert Burton, who obsessively revised their writing in a manner that locates authority in progression, rather than inception. By praising the texts as 'first' and 'original' the page seems also to reject the technologies of the theatre, and any sense that a work might develop over time, in favour of promoting the author as the beginning and end of creative labour. But at the same time, listed beneath this claim are the names of the actors, including Shakespeare himself. So this page tries to have it both ways, asserting the individual genius of Shakespeare even as it reminds us of the theatrical process. Nevertheless, the contentions made throughout the preliminaries about the permanence, perfection, and complete status of the Folio's texts take on new strength when situated within the ambitious publishing series Jaggard had developed alongside his work as a printer. The Folio's authority—and thus its commercial appeal—both drew on and contributed to Jaggard's other work, reverberating along the stationer's inventory through the cultural force of his imprint.

Some local features of the Folio seem also to resonate in new ways when contextualized within Jaggard's publishing interests. The Folio's contents page describes the list of plays it introduces as a 'catalogue' of the 'severall Comedies, Histories, and Tragedies'.[110] The term 'catalogue' works in a few different ways here. Its primary meaning is a 'complete enumeration' of the plays, and here the Folio's contents page supports other rhetoric in the preliminaries to promote the titles as a complete corpus of Shakespearean drama.[111] That word 'catalogue' is not found in the preliminary matter of any book published by the other Folio publishers, but it appears frequently in Jaggard's work, where it registers his interest in material that strives for organization and completion. It features in the title of Thomas Milles's *The catalogue of honor* (1610), for example, and in Jaggard's

---

p. 398. For Edward Blount's usage of the term 'cure' as a way of preparing a text for publication see letter five in appendix one.

[109] Shakespeare, *Comedies, Histories, & Tragedies* (1623), sig. πA7r.

[110] Shakespeare, *Comedies, Histories, & Tragedies* (1623), sig. A8r. On this page, see Wayne, 'Arrangement'.

[111] 'catalogue, n.' OED meaning 1a.

own *A catalogue of such English bookes* (1618). It can also be found in his paratexts: Edward Topsell's *The historie of foure-footed beastes* (1607) begins with a 'Catalogue of the Authors which have wrote of Beasts'; a preliminary leaf of Jaggard's edition of the *Historie of Justine* (1606) contains a 'Catalogue' of the material covered in the following text.[112]

A secondary meaning of 'catalogue', one less present today, was 'a register of names', carrying a particular sense of dynasty and genealogy. This is why, in Robert Cawdry's *A table alphabeticall* (1604) the first definition offered for the word catalogue is that of a 'bead-roll', meaning a pedigree or line of descent.[113] It is this meaning that explains Sir Charles Mountford's concern, in Heywood's *Woman Killed*, that if forced to sell his lands he will be 'Rac'd from the bed-roll of Gentility'.[114] This secondary meaning also explains why the word featured so prominently in the several books of heraldry with which Jaggard was preoccupied alongside his work on Shakespeare's Folio. Ralph Brooke's *A catalogue and succession of the kings* (1619), which provides the reader with the genealogy of English nobility, introduces each of the families it discusses with a separate internal 'catalogue' of their family line. The herald Augustine Vincent copied this structure in his *A discoverie of errours* (1622)—again, each of the aristocratic families Vincent examined is given an individual 'catalogue', and both books conclude with a 'Table of the Catalogues'. Comparable uses of the term are also found earlier in Jaggard's career when he published *A catalogue of the kings of Scotland* (1610).

This genealogical sense of the word, brought into focus through Jaggard's imprint, offers a new way to think about the Folio's presentation of Shakespeare's plays as his progeny. The Folio's 'catalogue' leaf supports a central metaphor of the preliminary pages, which is that Shakespeare 'fathered' his plays. Heminge and Condell describe the plays as Shakespeare's 'Orphanes' in their address to Philip and William Herbert, and Ben Jonson records his astonishment at how 'the fathers face | Lives in his issue'.[115] The metaphor consolidates the connection between Shakespeare and the 'first original' texts presented by the Folio. The same metaphor of progeny is extended by Hugh Holland, whose poem puns on the idea of Shakespeare's familial 'line': although the author's 'line of life' has now ended, Holland tells us, 'The life yet of his lines' lives on.[116] Understood in this way, the Folio's contents page offers a textual biography of Shakespeare just as Jaggard's books of heraldry strive for an accurate record of the lives of the aristocracy.

---

[112] Edward Topsell, *The historie of foure-footed beastes* (1607, STC 24123), sig. 2¶5r–8r; Justinus, *Historie of Justine*, sig. A7v (the order of the preliminaries varies in some copies).
[113] Robert Cawdry, *A table alphabeticall* (1604, STC 4884), sig. C2r.
[114] Thomas Heywood, *A woman kilde with kindnesse* (1617, STC 13372), sig. D2v.
[115] Ben Jonson, 'To the memory of my beloved, The Author Mr. William Shakespeare' in Shakespeare, *Comedies, Histories, & Tragedies*, sig. πA4v.
[116] Hugh Holland, 'Upon the Lines and Life of the Famous Scenicke Poet, Master William Shakespeare' in Shakespeare, *Comedies, Histories, & Tragedies*, sig. πA5r.

Embedded within the 'catalogue' page, then, are ideas of pedigree and status that situate Shakespeare's writing within a tradition of social class.

The Folio also insists on its status as a theatrical book, which invites us to return to a feature of Jaggard's work that falls outside his publishing. As mentioned above, Jaggard tried several times to secure the right to print the theatrical playbills which advertised the latest performances at London's professional theatres, finally succeeding in 1615.[117] None of Jaggard's playbills survive, but, unlike most of his trade printing, these bills may have carried Jaggard's imprint and thus his brand. The surviving broadsheet notices and proclamations that Jaggard printed for the City of London and for the state do tend to feature his imprint in a prominent position at the bottom of the bill.[118] Apart from his own pride in the role, there was a good reason for Jaggard to foreground his name on this class of material. The City Printer's imprint was a marker of official status; it lifted the printed sheet out of the tide of commercial material that clamoured for readerly attention and transformed the sheet on which it featured into a statement of civic import, something like a public service announcement.

When the Folio roots itself in London's theatrical culture, then, it rhetorically invokes an environment in which Jaggard's name is likely to have featured as a matter of daily course among the advertisements for new performances. In their address to readers, Heminge and Condell call on those regular theatregoers who 'sit on the Stage at *Black-Friers*, or the *Cock-pit*, to arraigne Playes dailie'.[119] Hugh Holland plays on the name of Shakespeare's own theatre when he remembers how the Folio's plays 'made the Globe of heav'n and earth to ring'. Holland conjures the spaces of an early modern playhouse when he describes Shakespeare's grave as 'Deaths publique tyring-house' (the 'tyring house' was a backstage area). The metaphor is repeated a few pages on by James Mabbe, who envisages the book as a theatrical event, complete with 'applause' from 'Spectators'. Ben Jonson laments that he can no longer hear Shakespeare's boots 'tread, and Shake a stage'.[120] The Folio's preliminaries consistently remind readers of the early modern stage. Meanwhile, later in the seventeenth century, Robert Heath's plea to his bookseller not to advertise his book by pinning its title page up 'on each wall | And corner poast close underneath the Play | That must be acted at Black-Friers that day', not only describes the playbills that Jaggard printed but also provides us with a sense of their jostling proximity to other items of print, such as the title pages of new

---

[117] See Jackson, *Records 1602–1640*, pp. 1, 6; Arber III.575; Stern, *Documents* pp. 36–62.
[118] Examples of Jaggard's civic printing from 1620 to 1623 which feature his imprint include: STC 16727.7, 16727.9, 16728.3, 16728.5, 16728.7, and 16728.9.
[119] Heminge and Condell, 'To the great Variety of Readers' in Shakespeare, *Comedies, Histories, & Tragedies* (1623), sig. πA3r.
[120] Holland, 'Upon the Lines and Life' (πA5r), I. M., 'To the memorie of M. W. Shake-speare' (πA6r), Jonson, 'To the memory of my beloved' (πA4r) in Shakespeare, *Comedies, Histories, & Tragedies* (1623). For an account of the First Folio as a 'theatrical folio' see Francis X. Connor, 'Shakespeare's Theatrical Folio' in *Philological Quarterly* 91.2 (2012): pp. 221–45.

Figure 2.4 Public notices and title pages pinned up outside a shop in the Royal Exchange in the mid-seventeenth century. Detail of 'The Royal Exchange of London' (R. White, 1671). Credit: Bodleian Libraries, University of Oxford, Gough Maps vol. 19, fol. 21. Used under Creative Commons licence CC-BY-NC 4.0.

books (see Figure 2.4).[121] If the Folio was advertised via its title page, in London's playhouses and elsewhere around the city, it may well have found itself close by, even competing for attention with, Jaggard's playbills. By recalling London's theatrical culture, then, the Folio situated its readers in a milieu that relied on Jaggard's signature to ratify its promotional material. In other words, rather than troubling the Folio, as we have traditionally thought, Jaggard's involvement probably reinforced the sense that this book was fully endorsed by both the theatre and the book trade.

'Stolne' and 'Perfect'

I have explored ways in which we might understand Shakespeare's Folio differently if we think of William Jaggard as an important publisher. This chapter concludes by returning to the fraught version of Jaggard with which it began: the figure whose involvement with the First Folio troubled the New Bibliographers.

Much of the anxiety surrounding Jaggard is fuelled by the Folio's preface, and its famous description of 'diverse stolne, and surreptitious copies, maimed, and deformed'. The preface complains these earlier works were published 'by the

---

[121] Robert Heath, 'To my Book-seller' in *Clarastella* (1650, Wing H1340A), sig. F11v–12r.

frauds and stealthes of injurious imposters'.[122] But we do not know which Shakespeare editions are 'maimed' or 'stolne'. So when it asserts its own 'perfection', the Folio solves a problem of textual legitimacy, but it also creates that problem in the first place. The fact that this language creates—or at least consolidates—a category of illegitimacy *at all* is critically important. Amid the many sources of evidence that tell us things about how early modern texts could be thought of as transgressive, these Folio comments have, probably more than anything else, guided our thinking about the textual status of Shakespeare's books. Cued by these words, many critics have considered how surviving editions of the plays or poems might variously be 'stolne' or 'deformed'. It was specifically this passage, for example, that pushed Alfred Pollard to develop his influential theories about 'good' and 'bad' quartos—Pollard sought to discover which texts the 'editors in their preface were publicly casting stones at'.[123]

As this chapter has discussed, William Jaggard's Shakespeare books—both his earlier editions of *The Passionate Pilgrime* and the later collection of Jaggard Quartos—have consistently seemed to fit the bill of being 'stolne' and/or 'maimed'.[124] While the *Pilgrime* has not (to my knowledge) been suggested as one of the editions Heminge and Condell had in mind—after all, the passage describes plays, not poems—the broader ambit of corruption and theft set out by the Folio has long governed our thinking about this lyric miscellany. The fact that Jaggard published multiple versions of 'Shakespeare', some of which were 'stolne' and one of which was 'perfect', returns us to the duality with which this chapter began, and to the 'rather mysterious, rather shady' figure who somehow printed—but also published—the First Folio.[125] How should we now think about these different strands of his career?

Biographical subjects are complicated, of course, and William Jaggard may simply have changed his mind about how best to handle Shakespeare's writing at different points in his career. But this kind of adaptation need not be limited to Jaggard. Ideas about the legitimacy of Shakespeare's books were themselves unstable. They emerged over time, not in tidy categories but spilling into one another in overlapping waves. For ten years, before the arrival of the *Sonnets*, the

---

[122] Heminge and Condell, 'To the great Variety of Readers' in Shakespeare, *Comedies, Histories, & Tragedies*, sig. A3r.
[123] Alfred Pollard, *Shakespeare Folios and Quartos: A Study in the Bibliography of Shakespeare's Plays 1594–1685* (London: Methuen and Company, 1909), pp. 64–80, 80. Pollard is one of many who have sought to interpret this passage. For example, Leo Kirschbaum's *Shakespeare and the Stationers* (Columbus, OH: Ohio State University Press, 1955) is explicit that 'the purpose of the present study is the explanation of Heminge and Condell's words' in this section of the Folio address (p. 3).
[124] Lukas Erne suggests that Heminge and Condell had the 1619 collection of playbooks in mind, arguing that the collection presented 'an illegitimate threat' to sales of the First Folio: *Shakespeare as Literary Dramatist*, 2nd edn (Cambridge: Cambridge University Press, 2013), pp. 280–3. For an alternative reading that stresses the commercial context of the Folio preface see David Scott Kastan, *Shakespeare after Theory* (New York: Routledge, 1999), pp. 78–82.
[125] Greg, *First Folio*, p. 9.

Pilgrime was the only collection of Shakespeare's poetry available in print; it was thus both the 'best' and the 'worst' of its kind. Though today we rarely read the *Pilgrime* as a serious literary concern on its own terms, the book nevertheless 'for near a century and a half passed for Shakspeare's', as the editor Edmond Malone noted in 1785.[126] What are we to make of the Shakespeare who lived in the minds of those early readers who bought a collection of the Jaggard Quartos? Shortly to be superseded by the First Folio, this version of 'Shakespeare in collection' was nevertheless known to numerous readers, as Zachary Lesser has shown, and so has an interpretive life of its own that existed prior to and alongside the larger and more prestigious collection. In the history of the Shakespearean text, we have tended to sweep these alternative Shakespeares into the 'stolne' category established by the First Folio, as if the vision of Shakespeare's texts set out by this important book in 1623 was always already understood.

Perhaps we have accepted the Folio's vision too readily. The First Folio is clearly the most important and complete collection of Shakespeare's work that exists. At the same time, modern scholars have never had a clearer sense that the Folio is flawed in ways that we might productively—if provocatively—compare with Jaggard's earlier work to reinvigorate our ideas about textual authority. The Folio lacks *Pericles* and *Two Noble Kinsmen*, as well as the sonnets and the narrative poems of course, but it is only now that we are starting to see the Folio's patchiness in other areas: its gaps and errors, its own 'fraudulences'. Much of this new way of thinking about the Folio has been enabled by developments in technology and scholarly method, and by easy access to a greater textual corpus. We read the Folio differently now, because of the tools and knowledge at our disposal. In the past, similar shifts in ways of looking at Shakespeare's texts were brought about simply through the discovery of new texts. It was Richard Farmer's 1767 discovery of Thomas Heywood's epistle, for example, which changed the status of the *Pilgrime* forever, as Edmond Malone noted.[127] Yet as the textual record has been mapped in greater detail, new discoveries emerge less from finding new titles than from looking more deeply *at* and *through* the texts we already have, by mistrusting their surfaces. Watermarks and forensic photography transformed a group of remaindered plays into the Pavier Quartos; staring at ghosts and imprints has remade them again as the Jaggard Quartos. Each shift generates new ways to think about Shakespeare in print.

Over the past twenty years, scholars of editing, revision, and authorship working with their own technological advancements have placed the claims made by

---

[126] Note dated 22 October 1785 on flyleaf of Malone's copy of *The passionate pilgrime* (1612, STC 22343) Bodleian Library shelfmark Arch. G g.1.

[127] Richard Farmer, *An essay on the learning of Shakespeare* (Cambridge, 1767), pp. 69–70. Farmer only glanced at the literary theft; his real interest was whether Shakespeare had translated Ovid. Malone notes that it was 'my friend Dr Farmer' who discovered the misattribution: *Pilgrime* (1612), note on Bodleian Library shelfmark Arch. G g.1.

the Folio about the 'perfection' and complete status of its contents under unprecedented scrutiny. We know now that the Folio silently removes Shakespeare's collaborators, and that its rhetorical insistence on the individual author, on the sovereignty of '*Shakespeares* minde', is misleading.[128] Some of the book's other invisible writerly presences have now been given the status of co-authors by the New Oxford Shakespeare with varying degrees of certainty. The same plays now feature a much busier set of attributions: *Titus Andronicus* is 'by Shakespeare and [George] Peele, with an added scene by [Thomas] Middleton (?)'; *Measure for Measure* is 'by Shakespeare; posthumously adapted by Middleton'; *1 Henry VI* is 'by Marlowe, Nashe, and Anonymous; adapted by Shakespeare'; *Macbeth* is 'by Shakespeare; adapted by Middleton'; *Henry VIII* is 'by [John] Fletcher and Shakespeare', and so on.[129] Some of the claims made by the New Oxford edition have proved tendentious and are by no means uniformly accepted. But as Joseph Rudman notes in his review, it would be very difficult to find a Shakespearean who rejects collaboration wholesale.[130]

Just as the First Folio filters out all traces of other writers (or, more pointedly, it claims that Shakespeare wrote lines that he did not), it also now seems likely that some non-Folio playbooks elided Shakespeare's presence in turn: *Edward III*, for example, printed in two quarto editions in 1596 and 1599 without naming any author, is now generally thought to include Shakespeare's work; the fourth edition of *The Spanish Tragedy* features additions that were probably by Shakespeare; *Arden of Faversham* is repositioned as a genuine collaboration by the New Oxford Shakespeare.[131] In other words, because of the way in which scholars read these plays at this point in time, the version of 'Shakespeare' presented by the First Folio is under pressure from both within (as included plays are reconceived as collaborations) and without (as Shakespeare's presence is discovered in non-Folio works).

---

[128] Jonson, 'To the memory of my beloved' in Shakespeare, *Comedies, Histories, & Tragedies* (1623), sig. πA4v.

[129] William Shakespeare, *The New Oxford Shakespeare: The Complete Works, Critical Reference Edition*, edited by Gary Taylor, John Jowett, Terri Bourus, and Gabriel Egan, 2 vols (Oxford: Oxford University Press, 2017), vol. 1, pp. vii–ix. For a critique of the edition see: Lars Engle and Eric Rasmussen, 'Review of *The New Oxford Shakespeare*' in *Review of English Studies* 69.289 (2018): pp. 356–412.

[130] Joseph Rudman, 'Review of *The New Oxford Shakespeare Authorship Companion*' in *Digital Scholarship in the Humanities* 34.3 (2019): pp. 703–5, at p. 704. See also MacDonald P. Jackson, 'Authorship Attribution and *The New Oxford Shakespeare*: Some Facts and Misconceptions' in *ANQ: A Quarterly Journal of Short Articles, Notes and Reviews* 33.2–3 (2020): pp. 148–55; and in the same volume, David Benjamin Auerbach, 'Review of *The New Oxford Shakespeare Authorship Companion*', pp. 236–41. Important contributions to the authorship debate include: Brian Vickers, *Shakespeare, Co-Author: A History of the Study of the Five Collaborative Plays* (Oxford: Oxford University Press, 2002); MacDonald P. Jackson, *Determining the Shakespeare Canon: Arden of Faversham and a Lover's Complaint* (Oxford: Oxford University Press, 2014); William Shakespeare and others, *Collaborative Plays*, edited by Jonathan Bate and Eric Rasmussen (Basingstoke: Palgrave Macmillan, 2013).

[131] Two of these plays are included in the *New Oxford Shakespeare*; the possibly Shakespearean additions to *The Spanish Tragedy* are included without the rest of the play. For discussion of these attributions see Gary Taylor and Gabriel Egan eds, *The New Oxford Shakespeare: Authorship Companion* (Oxford: Oxford University Press, 2017).

'PRUDENTIA': THE JAGGARD PUBLISHING HOUSE 119

All this to say that the authority of the First Folio is changing; both its 'perfection' and its complete status seem newly up for debate. This in turn makes the divisions we maintain between the Folio and Jaggard's earlier versions of 'Shakespeare' look more fragile, seem closer in some ways to differences of scale, rather than category. An important feature of the falsities of the *Pilgrime* and the Jaggard Quartos is that both ventures include texts that Jaggard either knew or probably knew were not Shakespearean, and that is a tactic which, as far as we know, never occurs in the Folio. But if we are willing to reframe the object of study in each case as not a series of individual *texts* but as a single *collection*—which is how each of these three ventures market themselves—then we arrive at a similarly vexed sense of quite who was responsible for what. One critical difference is that the 'deceptions' of the earlier ventures have been visible for some time and can be laid squarely at Jaggard's door. The omissions and elisions of the First Folio are only now coming into focus and they implicate a far larger cast of characters than a single stationer and perhaps even belong to the creative process itself.

External evidence condemns the *Pilgrime*, which was subject to Heywood's claim that Shakespeare had been 'much offended' by the misattribution. Yet forty years later, there is an echo of Heywood's complaint in the poet Abraham Cowley's opinion that the '*Works*' of '*Shakespear, Fletcher, Johnson*, and many others' had been 'stuffed out, either with *counterfeit pieces*, like *false Money* put in to fill up the *Bag*' or with material that was partly genuine but which these writers 'would have called in themselves' because of the 'baseness of the *Alloy*'.[132] Cowley's complaint lacks the compelling personal connection to Shakespeare found in Heywood's address, but addresses the same underlying issues. He knew that books were sometimes filled with material that was either completely '*counterfeit*' or that had been altered beyond recognition, transforming a 'little *Tomb* of *Marble*' intended to commemorate an author into 'a vast *heap* of Stones or Rubbish'. In naming Shakespeare's Folio as his first example, Cowley displays none of the veneration that today we direct at this important book, nor does he particularly seem to feel that it would reflect Shakespeare's own sense of his literary legacy.[133]

No work—certainly not *The Passionate Pilgrime* nor the Jaggard Quartos—will supplant the First Folio as the central document in the history of the Shakespearean text. But it is partly to the First Folio that we owe the idea that this history *needs a centre at all*—that is, that textual authority should be conceived of as hierarchical and exclusionary, rather than distributed. 'I have endeavour'd,' wrote Nicholas

---

[132] Abraham Cowley, 'The Preface' in *Poems* (1656, Wing C6683), sig. a1v–2r, quoted and discussed by Francis X. Connor, *Literary Folios and Ideas of the Book in Early Modern England* (Basingstoke: Palgrave Macmillan, 2014), pp. 121–4.
[133] On the likelihood that Cowley was thinking of the First Folio rather than John Benson's edition of Shakespeare's *Poems* (1640, STC 22344), see Taylor, 'Bookselling in Early Modern London' in Shakespeare, *The New Oxford Shakespeare, Critical Reference Edition*, vol. 2, p. liii. Note also Taylor's discussion of John Milton's comment of 1630 that the First Folio was an 'unvalued book'.

Rowe in the first edited collection of Shakespeare's writings—a collection he modelled on the Folio—'to compare the several Editions, and give the true Reading.'[134] Must any one version of a play be 'true', or 'perfect'? And if not, must the alternatives be 'stolne' or somehow invalid? The language we have inherited and still use to discuss textual status is unhelpfully reductive.

The question mark we retain over William Jaggard's status demonstrates our continual investment in a way of thinking about Shakespeare's books: on the one hand, the *Pilgrime* and the Jaggard Quartos and by extension any 'illegitimate' or 'corrupt' version of Shakespeare; on the other, the First Folio. Perhaps now is the time to let go of the 'stolne'/'perfect' paradigm. That is, instead of seeing William Jaggard as a vexed figure who complicates the Folio's textual authority, perhaps we should reassess our own habits of thought about the value and 'legitimacy' of Shakespeare's writing. There remain obvious and significant differences between the Folio and any other version of Shakespeare's texts. But if we can dispel the idea that the Folio was somehow without its own strategies and guile, then those differences might emerge in fresh, more precise, ways.

What would it look like to imagine 'Shakespeare' if the First Folio was not the default source of literary authority? For a starting point we might look to the riveting recent discovery of John Milton's copy of the First Folio in the Free Library of Philadelphia. This book, as Claire Bourne and Jason Scott-Warren have shown, contains hundreds of marks and notes made by Milton during his reading.[135] Several plays, including *Hamlet* and *Romeo and Juliet*, are heavily marked up with reference to quarto editions. At times Milton's emendations straightforwardly correct the Folio where its text seems awry. In Benvolio's telling of the fatal fight between Mercutio and Tybalt, it seems strange to find Folio-Romeo's 'aged arme' beating down the swords of the duelling pair, and so Milton corrects this moment to 'agil arme'.[136] But in other places where the Folio text is sound Milton introduced alternatives that were often drawn (in the case of *Romeo and Juliet* and *Hamlet*) from the fifth quartos of each play, both of which were published by John Smethwick in 1637. There is nothing obviously wrong with Juliet's line 'Proud can I never be of what I have' when she rejects the idea that she should feel delighted about her betrothal to Paris, but Milton still altered the line to Q5's 'Proud can I

---

[134] William Shakespeare, *The works of Mr. William Shakespear: in six volumes*, ed. Nicholas Rowe (1709), vol. 1, sig. A2v.

[135] Claire M. L. Bourne, 'Vide Supplementum: Early Modern Collation as Play-reading in the First Folio', in Katherine Acheson ed., *Early Modern English Marginalia* (New York: Routledge, 2018), pp. 195–233; Jason Scott-Warren, 'Milton's Shakespeare?' on the *Centre for Material Texts* website (https://www.english.cam.uk/cmt/), entry of 9 September 2019. Milton's copy of the First Folio is mounted online at: https://libwww.freelibrary.org/digital/feature/first-folio.

[136] Shakespeare, *Comedies, Histories, & Tragedies*, sig. ff3r of copy owned by Free Library of Philadelphia; discussed by Bourne, 'Vide Supplementum', p. 209. Romeo's arm is 'agill' in Q1, Q4, and Q5.

never be of what I hate'.[137] That word 'hate' foregrounds the character's emotive response to marriage with Paris, meaning that a forceful and impassioned Juliet from the quarto tradition flickers into view. She exists alongside the Folio's more rueful figure, who reflects on her current situation ('what I have') without giving way to the tumult of feelings beneath. The way Milton used his page space— tucking additions into margins, using carets to signal insertions—means that some annotations in this copy do not cancel or supplant the Folio text but instead complement or augment it. The Folio remains central, but that centrality seems in some ways as much about material bulk as textual quality: the book's pages become a resource in which to gather and move between alternative versions of Juliet, Hamlet, and so of Shakespeare. Reading becomes slower here, and against the forward momentum of plot emerges a kind of pleasurable dilation, involving constant sideways excursions into possible worlds and characters, and ever-present reminders of the play's vibrant life beyond the limits of any one edition. This is a way of reading that revels in textual variety, rather than suppressing it.

The ongoing anxiety about William Jaggard's involvement in the First Folio preserves ways of thinking about textual authority that seem increasingly dated. As scholarly methods evolve, changing what we see in the books we read, the Folio looks less like an insurmountable totem of literary authority and increasingly like one of a series of more or less imperfect gestures that all, in some way or other, frame 'Shakespeare' for new readers.

---

[137] Shakespeare, *Comedies, Histories, & Tragedies*, sig. ff5r of copy owned by Free Library of Philadelphia; Bourne, 'Vide Supplementum', pp. 210–11. The word 'hate' is present through Q1–5.

PART 2
'J. SMITHWEEKE, AND W. ASPLEY, 1623.'

3

A Minor Shakespearean

William Aspley at the Parrot

'Wrytten by m^r Shakespere'
— Stationers' Register Entry for August 1600

The bookseller William Aspley's first encounter with Shakespeare came in August of 1600. This was a year in which Shakespeare's literary career was in some senses at its peak. The playwright's name had first appeared on the title page of a printed book a few years earlier, when editions of *Richard II*, *Richard III*, and *Love's Labour's Lost* printed in 1598 each featured a title page that explained the text had been written 'By William Shake-speare'.[1] In the year 1600 ten editions of Shakespeare's work were published by seven different stationers. His writing also featured in printed compilations of popular quotations, such as *Englands Parnassus* and *Belvedere*; beyond London's printing houses, readers gathered extracts of Shakespeare's writing in manuscript collections. The law student William Scott referenced the 'very well-penned tragedy' of *Richard II* in his hand-written treatise on poetics; Edmund Pudsey mined *Romeo and Juliet* and *Hamlet*, among other plays, as he filled out his commonplace book.[2] As Lukas Erne has shown, 1600 was 'an extraordinary year for Shakespeare, with more publications than in any other year during his life'.[3]

Another way in which Shakespeare's growing fame impressed itself onto the documentary record in 1600 is that in August, when William Aspley registered the rights for two of Shakespeare's plays together with his partner, the bookseller Andrew Wise, the clerk of the Stationers' Company included an authorial attribution. The brief note that both *Much Ado About Nothing* and *2 Henry IV*

---

[1] The attribution is found on the title pages (in each case A1r) of *The tragedie of King Richard the second* (1598, STC 22308 and 22309); *The tragedie of King Richard the third* (1598, STC 22315), and *A pleasant conceited comedie called, Loves labors lost* (1598, STC 22294).
[2] William Scott, *The Model of Poesy*, edited by Gavin Alexander (Cambridge: Cambridge University Press, 2013), p. 45. Edmund Pudsey's commonplace book is in the Bodleian Library: MS. Eng. poet. d. 3. A cross-section of readerly interest in Shakespeare at the turn of the century can be found at the online database *Shakespeare Documented*: https://shakespearedocumented.folger.edu/.
[3] Lukas Erne, *Shakespeare and the Book Trade* (Cambridge: Cambridge University Press, 2015), p. 27. Erne notes that writings by Shakespeare account for a full 5 per cent of everything the London book trade produced in 1600. See also Erne's chapter on 'The Making of "Shakespeare"' in his *Shakespeare as Literary Dramatist*, 2nd edn (Cambridge: Cambridge University Press, 2013), pp. 80–101.

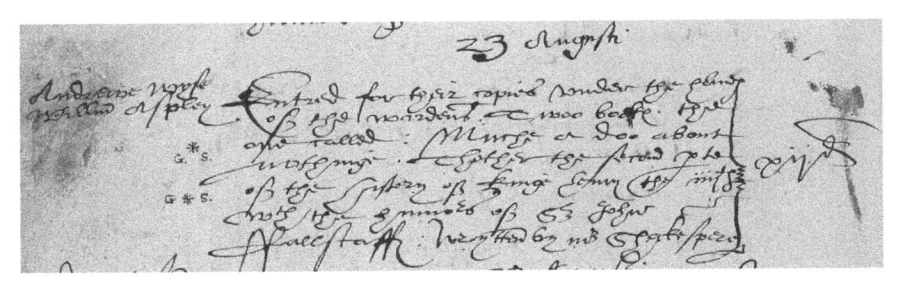

Figure 3.1 The registration by William Aspley and Andrew Wise of *Much Ado About Nothing* and *2 Henry IV* in August 1600. The starred initials beside the entry are those of George Steevens, the eighteenth-century editor who combed these manuscripts for material, leaving his mark wherever he found Shakespeare. Image of SCA *Register C*, fol. 63v. Credit: The Stationers' Company Archive.

were 'Wrytten by m^r Shakespere', cramped into the bottom of the entry (Figure 3.1) is the first time the playwright's name appears in the records of the organization that controlled book production in England: a small but significant institutional response to the marketability of Shakespeare's name.[4]

For Aspley, this record became significant in other ways, too. When his partner Andrew Wise died in 1603, Aspley took sole ownership of both these plays through an accident of biography.[5] He seems to have forgotten them for the next two decades, and with the exception of a brief foray into drama at the start of his career, Aspley focused his business on books of religious politics which supported reforms instituted by King James. Twenty years later, though, when negotiations began to collect Shakespeare's writings for the First Folio, these two plays became newly relevant for Aspley, drawing him back into a literary world he had long left behind.

The critical view of Aspley is that he was a minor Shakespearean publisher.[6] This bookseller seems to hover around the emergent Shakespeare canon in an

---

[4] SCA, *Register C*, fol. 63v; Arber III.170.

[5] Wise transferred his three other Shakespeare plays to the stationer Matthew Law on 25 June 1603 (*Richard II*, *Richard III*, and *1 Henry IV*; see Arber III.239; SCA, *Register C*, fol. 98r). For more on Wise as leading the vanguard of Shakespearean playbook publishing before his death—or at least, his disappearance from the documentary record—see Amy Lidster, 'At the Sign of the Angel: The Influence of Andrew Wise on Shakespeare in Print' in *Shakespeare Survey* 71 (2018): pp. 242-54, and Adam G. Hooks, *Selling Shakespeare: Biography, Bibliography, and the Book Trade* (Cambridge: Cambridge University Press, 2016), pp. 66–98.

[6] W. W. Greg, *The Shakespeare First Folio: Its Bibliographical and Textual History* (Oxford: Clarendon Press, 1955), p. 5. Both Aspley and his fellow Folio publisher, John Smethwick, the subject of chapter four, are typically dismissed as minor figures in the history of Shakespearean print. In addition to Greg, see: David Scott Kastan, *Shakespeare and the Book* (Cambridge: Cambridge University Press, 2001), p. 61; Andrew Murphy, *Shakespeare in Print: A History and Chronology of Shakespeare Publishing* (Cambridge: Cambridge University Press, 2003), p. 43; Eric Rasmussen, 'Publishing the First Folio' in Emma Smith ed., *The Cambridge Companion to Shakespeare's First Folio* (Cambridge: Cambridge University Press, 2016), p. 24.

ambivalent fashion. He was clearly interested in Shakespeare to some degree. Having registered the titles to *Much Ado* and *2 Henry IV*, Aspley and Wise jointly published both plays in quarto editions a few months later. They participated in the broader trend of marketing Shakespeare's name by placing it on the title pages of both editions. A few years later, Aspley was also one of two booksellers whose shop (for Aspley, the Sign of the Parrot, in Paul's Churchyard) was the wholesale outlet for the first edition of *Shake-speares Sonnets* (1609), which again foregrounded Shakespeare's name as a selling point. So while most of Shakespeare's publishers tended to be interested in either his poetry or his drama, Aspley was involved to some degree with both forms of Shakespeare's writing—as well as, of course, with both the first and second editions of Shakespeare's Folio.

But at each stage, Aspley's interest in Shakespeare came about through another, seemingly more committed Shakespearean stationer. Aspley himself had only a passing interest in the playwright, one that probably grew out of his habit of forming many partnerships (the table on p. 50 shows that Aspley formed more publishing collaborations in the first decade of his career than any other stationer who owned the right to copy for a Shakespeare play in 1623). From what we can tell, he was not a driving force in the publication of the Folio. His presence along with John Smethwick in the book's colophon—and not in the imprint—suggests a secondary role in the book's publication, and is the only evidence of his involvement. His two-play stake, out of the total of thirty-six, is the smallest owned by any of the Folio syndicate, even if the plays themselves were important and popular. The *Sonnets* was another collaborative production in which Aspley's role seems, at least on the surface, to have been minor: the book was published by the bookseller Thomas Thorpe and sold in two variant issues. One of these named Aspley in its imprint while the other named the bookseller John Wright, who worked from a shop a little north of Paul's Cross Churchyard. Thorpe and Aspley partnered several times in their careers, and it is possible Aspley was more involved in the publication of the *Sonnets* than its imprint reveals, but what evidence we have tells us he was one of two wholesale booksellers for the edition, nothing more.[7]

Equally, critical appraisal of the quarto editions of *Much Ado* and *2 Henry IV* has focused on Andrew Wise, who is consistently seen as one of the most influential publishers of Shakespeare's early printed works.[8] In contrast to Wise's steady promotion of Shakespeare through his publication of several history plays in the

---

[7] For examples of their collaborations see Arber III.37, 266, 268, 300. STC 7459 is another example in which Aspley registered the manuscript (Arber III.239) and the imprint then named Thorpe as publisher and Aspley as wholesale bookseller.

[8] In addition to Lidster and Hooks, see Sonia Massai, *Shakespeare and the Rise of the Editor* (Cambridge: Cambridge University Press, 2007), esp. chapter three, 'The Wise Quartos (1597–1602)', pp. 91–105; Tara L. Lyons, 'Serials, Spinoffs, and Histories: Selling "Shakespeare" in Collection before the Folio' in *Philological Quarterly* 91.2 (2012): pp. 185–220.

late 1590s, Aspley was indifferent about the commercial possibilities of his Shakespearean titles. After the first editions of *Much Ado* and *2 Henry IV* appeared (and once Andrew Wise had disappeared) Aspley never published them again as single editions, despite the fact that both were popular plays, as a poem from the time tells us:

> let but *Falstaffe* come,
> Hall, *Peines*, the rest you scarce shall have a roome
> All is so pester'd: let but *Beatrice*
> And *Benedicke* be seene, loe in a trice
> The Cockpit Galleries, Boxes, are all full.[9]

These lines from the opening pages of the 1640 edition of Shakespeare's *Poems* relate to both of Aspley's plays. They tell us that characters from the *Henry IV* plays—Prince Hal, Falstaff, and Ned Poins (or 'Peines')—could fill theatres ('you scarce shall have a roome'). Similarly, Beatrice and Benedick, the sparring lovers from *Much Ado*, also had playgoers swarming to fill up the 'Cockpit Galleries, Boxes'—a commendation that is supported by other contemporary references to the early popularity of this play.[10] Against this evidence of success in performance, though, Aspley ignored his Shakespeare titles and in doing so he created an altogether different story about the popularity of these plays in print, one which views the sequel to *Henry IV* as an uninspired failure relative to the first part, and which creates a confusing disjunct between the 'perennially popular' stage life of *Much Ado* and the absence of any printed editions.[11] Later publishers followed Aspley's lead, so that both *Much Ado* and *2 Henry IV* are in a select group of Shakespeare's works that were never republished as individual editions till the eighteenth century.[12] Aspley's publishing tendencies complicate the ways in which

---

[9] Leonard Digges 'Upon Master William Shakespeare', in William Shakespeare, *Poems: written by Wil. Shake-speare. Gent* (1640, STC 22344), sig. *4r.

[10] *Much Ado* was performed twice for royalty in 1613: *Stanhope's Royal Accounts*, Bodleian Library MS Rawlinson A 239, fol. 47v. The prose author Robert Burton, writing on 'Love Melancholy', assumed that readers were familiar with '*Benedict* and *Betteris* in the Comedie'. Burton was thinking about lovers who are at first sight 'offended with each others carriage' but 'begin at last to dote insensibly one upon another': *The Anatomy of Melancholy* (1628, STC 4161), sig. 3L2r. The popularity of these characters also led Charles I to add a note beside *Much Ado* on the catalogue leaf of his copy of Shakespeare's Second Folio (1632) in which he retitled the play 'Bennedik & Betrice'. The copy is now in the Royal Library in Windsor Castle, shelfmark: RCIN 1080415.

[11] James C. Bulman describes *2 Henry IV* as having 'long lived in the shadow of the more popular Part One': William Shakespeare, *King Henry IV Part 2*, ed. James C. Bulman (London: Bloomsbury Arden Shakespeare, 2016), p. 1. William Shakespeare, *Much Ado About Nothing*, rev. edn, ed. Claire McEachern (London: Bloomsbury Arden Shakespeare, 2015), p. 153.

[12] Heated rivalry between the Shakespearean publishers Jacob Tonson and Robert Walker—each seeking new plays with which to outsell the other—eventually led to a second single edition of *Much Ado* in 1734. The second individual edition of *2 Henry IV* appeared in 1720 in an octavo version published by William Chetwood. Of all Shakespeare's plays that were published before the First Folio, only these two and *Troilus and Cressida* were never republished individually in the seventeenth century.

we think about the popularity of plays. The strongest evidence for popularity remains the number of editions that were published, but this metric struggles to accommodate the idea that, through the vagaries of the book trade, a stationer might end up in charge of titles that he simply did not care much about.

That Shakespeare was not Aspley's central interest was further underscored at his death. Before he died in December 1640, Aspley made a will. It survives today, folded within a unique copy of a single-sheet almanac from 1632. In the top right corner of the printed sheet is a woodcut of the figure of Time; the scythe and hourglass which he brandishes are given fresh relevancy by the document's repurposed status as the wrapper of a testament. The will itself tells us which manuscript titles Aspley deemed his most valuable. 'I have certaine Coppies, or bookes the sole printinge thereof belongeinge unto me,' Aspley wrote. Of these books, he added:

> I give and bequeth these coppies ffollowing mr. d. Boys his Exposition of the Epistles throughout the whoole yeare Charron of Wisdome: d ffenton of Usurie, and the second and third parte of the pensive mans practice.[13]

No Shakespeare text features in this list of bequeathed copies for which Aspley had the 'sole printinge', meaning that he owned them entirely, rather than in shares with some of his many partners. Instead, the list began with Aspley's most important property: 'mr. d. Boys his Exposition of the Epistles throughout the whole yeare'. This entry identifies a series of once-popular but now forgotten books written by the clergyman John Boys (1571–1625). The list goes on to name the moral philosophical work *Of Wisdome* by the Frenchman Pierre Charron, translated into English in 1608 and published by Aspley in five editions (at least three of which were co-published with Edward Blount); the preacher Roger Fenton's *Treatise of Usurie*; and *A Pensive Mans Practice*, a popular prayer book by the cartographer John Norden.[14] These, not Shakespeare, were the authors Aspley chose to safeguard and who occupied his interests over the course of his career.

Aspley therefore challenges us to explore the interpretive potential of a stationer who was, after all is said and done, only slightly interested in Shakespeare. His own words from 1623 reflect his refusal to accommodate our modern literary interests. An initially promising set of legal depositions, including statements by both Aspley and the Shakespearean bookseller Thomas Pavier and which make

---

[13] In the will there is a small 'x' before the list of titles, suggesting an amendment, though none survives: *Will of William Aspley*, TNA PROB 10/610. See also the associated probate act (TNA PROB 8/37) and sentence (TNA PROB 11/190/12).

[14] The first three editions of Charron's work were published collaboratively by Blount and Aspley. The fourth, published in 1630 at a time when Blount's business was struggling, retains the engraved title page claiming it was printed for both booksellers, but the colophon at the end of the book names just Aspley as the edition's wholesale bookseller (STC 5054, sig. 2R8v). Aspley and Blount's publishing partnerships are listed in the introduction on p. 16.

reference to 'M*aste*r Jaggard', turn out to have little to do with Aspley's own bookselling interests. Aged '48. yeares or thereaboutes' in June of 1623, Aspley was preoccupied not with Shakespeare but with a legal fight between the Stationers' Company and the printer Bonham Norton over a valuable Latin printing privilege.[15]

At the same time, Aspley adopted a far more committed approach to the work of John Boys, the preacher named first in Aspley's bequests. The stationer established an unusual *de facto* monopoly over the writings of the clergyman by registering and publishing everything he wrote, controlling his large corpus to a degree that seems strikingly unusual within the context of the early modern book trade. This chapter explores these varyingly minor and major attitudes that Aspley displayed towards Shakespeare and Boys, which neatly invert our critical estimation of these authors. The chapter argues that Aspley's status as one of many minor Shakespearean publishers who took a passing interest in the playwright's work despite mostly concentrating on other authors was a profoundly important feature of the Folio's creation. Aspley, and other 'minor Shakespearean' publishers like him, might individually be less arresting than Andrew Wise, but collectively these figures form a category with the potential to change how we think of the playwright's work.

A Two-play Stake: Aspley's Share of Shakespeare

Aspley worked for forty years in the English book trade, publishing over one hundred books and eventually rising to become a warden and ultimately master of the Stationers' Company.[16] During this career, Aspley developed what became perhaps the most clear brand of publishing specialism of all the Folio syndicate. As discussed below, he financed a remarkably popular series of books by John Boys, a preacher whose writings on behalf of King James and the Church of England earned the clergyman both a reputation as 'a worthy and famous *Divine*', and also career advancement, including the deanery at Canterbury Cathedral.[17] The extent to which Aspley valued Boys and his theological agenda is suggested

---

[15] The depositions concern the patent for the right to print the *Accidence* and *Grammar* from the schoolmaster William Lily's popular Latin grammar: *Stationers' Company v. Bonham Norton* C 24/501/81 (Part 1). Neither Aspley nor Pavier's statement tells us anything about their particular businesses in 1623. The bookseller Edmund Weaver's statement in the same bundle discusses how he and 'M*aste*r Jaggard' organized the initial arrangement with Norton.

[16] Aspley was made a warden of the Stationers' Company, with responsibility for licensing titles for print, in 1633. He was elected master in July 1640 and died a few months later: Arber IV.281, 516.

[17] R. P. 'A Briefe View of the life, and vertues of the Authour' in John Boys, *Remaines of that reverend and famous postiller, John Boys* (1631, STC 3468), sig. A2v, A3r. For Boys's biography (not to be confused with the John Bois/Boys who helped translate the King James Bible), see William Richardson, 'Boys, John (*bap.* 1571, *d.* 1625), dean of Canterbury.' *Oxford Dictionary of National Biography* (Oxford: Oxford University Press, 2004; online edn, 23 September 2004 [accessed 16 August 2019]).

by William Jaggard's *Catalogue of such English Bookes, as lately have bene, and now are in Printing for Publication* (1618). In the *Catalogue*, Aspley's entry begins with Boys's work before offering four other religious titles, all of which complement the preacher's writing in ways that are explored in this chapter. Like many publishers, though, Aspley grew into this specialist area over the first decade of his career, and when he first opened a bookshop in 1599 the stationer began tentatively. His publishing work was characterized less by an interest in any one form or genre of writing, and more by a consistent habit of collaborating with different book-trade figures. These partnerships brought financial advantages through sharing the risks of publication and perhaps also enabled Aspley to test the water with a range of different kinds of writing.

It was this early milieu of collaborative exploration that led Aspley to Andrew Wise and to his two Shakespeare titles, which were among the first books that Aspley published. Just as is the case with William Jaggard, in this first stage of his career Aspley experimented with an assortment of genres: in 1599 he published a travel report of a recent sea voyage; a pamphlet offering the final words of Philip II of Spain, who had died a few months earlier; and his first playbook, *A warning for Faire Women*, which had recently been performed by Shakespeare's theatre company, the Lord Chamberlain's men. The titles that appeared in this year are mostly topical works of a kind that Aspley later abandoned, though the playbook curiously foreshadows both the publication of *Hamlet* a few years later and the structure of Shakespeare's Folio. *A warning* opens with the allegorical figures of Comedy, History, and Tragedy battling for control of the stage: 'all three met at once?' exclaims Comedy, 'What wonder's towards that we are got togither?'[18] Tragedy and Comedy go back and forth, mocking features of their narratives that have become tired generic tropes, including, as Comedy archly observes, 'a filthie whining ghost', who totters onstage in 'some fowle sheete' and 'cries *Vindicta*, revenge, revenge'. The play thus supplies us with one of several references confirming the popularity of the Hamlet story in the 1590s—whether or not the reference specifically recalls Shakespeare's version. In the end it is History who notices that 'The stage is hung with blacke' and so realizes that both History and Comedy must give way: the audience is 'preparde for Tragedie'.[19] The onstage tussle animates the three generic categories into which Shakespeare's plays were later organized (the Folio's 'Catalogue' page of comedies, histories, and tragedies is explored on pp. 112–14), and demonstrates that Shakespeare's theatre company was already thinking within these three dominant genres.

The registration and then publication of *Much Ado* and *2 Henry IV* is usually interpreted as a continuation of Andrew Wise's established interests. As Adam G. Hooks has shown, 'in the late 1590s, no one was selling more Shakespeare than

---

[18] Anon, *A warning for Faire Women* (1599, STC 25089), sig. A2v.
[19] Anon, *A warning*, sig A2v, A3r.

Andrew Wise'; the stationer was a major figure in the playwright's early career in print.[20] It is unsurprising, then, that *2 Henry IV* was clearly marketed as the sequel to *1 Henry IV*, a play that Wise had published the previous year. Its title page described the edition as 'The Second part of Henrie the fourth'. In other ways, too, Aspley and Wise's collaborative Shakespeare quartos share continuities with Wise's earlier work: both *Much Ado* and *2 Henry IV* were printed by Valentine Simmes, a printer Wise had already employed for editions of *Richard II* and *Richard III*.

Yet if Wise's consistent investment in Shakespearean print makes him the more clearly arresting figure, then Aspley's occasional interest reveals something no less important: Shakespeare's plays appealed to a range of stationers who did not specialize in publishing drama, but who were nevertheless tempted into financing playbooks. The start of the seventeenth century was, as scholars have shown, a boom period for the publication of playbooks.[21] Many stationers saw drama as a profitable and relatively cheap product in which to invest, meaning it could sit well alongside a range of other publication interests. At first that seems a less compelling narrative than that which surrounds stationers like Wise, or later Thomas Pavier, whose commitment to Shakespeare resonates with our own sense of the playwright's worth. But this cohort of semi-Shakespeareans form a large majority of those who published Shakespeare's books. In this sense, Aspley was far more typical of the trends by which Shakespeare's work was published than was his partner, Wise; these texts were 'push'd on by many hands', to borrow John Dryden's thought about the forward momentum of significant works, not just by a few standout stationers.[22]

We can recover some of these patterns of ownership and investment for Shakespeare's work by looking at the Stationers' Register. Before the First Folio was published there were forty-six occasions in the Stationers' Register where a text by Shakespeare was either registered or traded hands (see Table 3.1).[23] These entries begin in 1593 when the Stratford printer Richard Field registered his ownership of 'a booke intitled Venus and Adonis' and continue to (but in my list do not include) the entry of 8 November 1623 that was one of the final acts in the Folio's printing.

---

[20] Hooks, *Selling Shakespeare*, p. 66.
[21] Alan B. Farmer and Zachary Lesser, 'The Popularity of Playbooks Revisited' in *Shakespeare Quarterly* 56.1 (2005): pp. 1–32. The period 1598–1613 saw a 'boom followed by sustained high production' of plays (p. 7).
[22] John Dryden, *Of dramatick poesie: an essay* (1668, Wing D2327), sig. C1r.
[23] To answer the complicated question of what counts as a Shakespeare work I have been led by Lukas Erne's model in *Shakespeare and the Book Trade* (Cambridge: Cambridge University Press, 2013), pp. 11–19. Following recent scholarship on the play's authorship, Erne includes *Edward III* but he excludes *Love's Martyr* (1601) on the grounds that Shakespeare's writing comprises only a small portion of the text.

Table 3.1 Entry of William Shakespeare's work into the Stationers' Register, 1593–1622, ordered by chronology

Year	Date of Entry	Title	Stationer
1593	18 April 1593	Venus and Adonis	Richard Field
1594	6 February 1594	Titus Andronicus	John Danter
	12 March 1594	1 Contention (2 Henry VI)	Thomas Millington
	2 May 1594	The Taming of a Shrew	Peter Short
	9 May 1594	The Rape of Lucrece	John Harrison 1
	25 June 1594	Venus and Adonis	John Harrison 1
1595	1 December 1595	Edward III	Cuthbert Burby
1596	25 June 1596	Venus and Adonis	William Leake
1597	29 August 1597	Richard II	Andrew Wise
	20 October 1597	Richard III	Andrew Wise
1598	25 February 1598	1 Henry IV	Andrew Wise
	22 July 1598	The Merchant of Venice	James Roberts
1600	14 August 1600	Henry V	Thomas Pavier
	23 August 1600	2 Henry IV	William Aspley & Andrew Wise
	23 August 1600	Much Ado About Nothing	William Aspley & Andrew Wise
	8 October 1600	A Midsummer Night's Dream	Thomas Fisher
	28 October 1600	The Merchant of Venice	Thomas Hayes
1602	18 January 1602	Merry Wives of Windsor	John Busby 1
	18 January 1602	Merry Wives of Windsor	Arthur Johnson
	19 April 1602	Titus Andronicus	Thomas Pavier
	19 April 1602	1 Contention (2 Henry VI)	Thomas Pavier
	19 April 1602	2 Contention (3 Henry VI)	Thomas Pavier
	26 July 1602	Hamlet	James Roberts
1603	7 February 1603	Troilus and Cressida	James Roberts
	25 June 1603	Richard II	Matthew Law
	25 June 1603	Richard III	Matthew Law
	25 June 1603	1 Henry IV	Matthew Law
1607	22 January 1607	The Taming of a Shrew	Nicholas Ling
	22 January 1607	Romeo and Juliet	Nicholas Ling
	22 January 1607	Love's Labour's Lost	Nicholas Ling
	19 November 1607	The Taming of a Shrew	John Smethwick
	19 November 1607	Romeo and Juliet	John Smethwick
	19 November 1607	Love's Labour's Lost	John Smethwick
	19 November 1607	Hamlet	John Smethwick
	26 November 1607	King Lear	John Busby & Nathaniel Butter
1608	20 May 1608	Pericles	Edward Blount
	20 May 1608	Antony and Cleopatra	Edward Blount
1609	28 January 1609	Troilus and Cressida	Richard Bonian & Henry Walley
	20 May 1609	Sonnets	Thomas Thorpe
	16 October 1609	Edward III	William Welby
1614	1 March 1614	The Rape of Lucrece	Roger Jackson
1617	16 February 1617	Venus and Adonis	William Barrett
1618	2 March 1618	Edward III	Thomas Snodham
1619	8 July 1619	The Merchant of Venice	Lawrence Hayes
1620	8 March 1620	Venus and Adonis	John Parker
1621	6 October 1621	Othello	Thomas Walkley

Source: DEEP.

What does gathering these entries reveal? At one level, their distribution provides a timeline of Shakespearean activity, with hotspots in the early months of 1594 (five separate entries covering five titles) and the autumn of 1600 (four distinct entries covering five titles). The entries supply an unusual kind of early reception history, a repetitive list that affords occasional glints of intrigue in the pre-print life of these texts. If they are mostly formulaic, supplying the name of the stationer who registered the title and the fee paid, they also sometimes contain intriguing interpretive interest. The poem we know today as *The Rape of Lucrece* was first entered in 1594 as the 'Ravyshement of Lucrece', for instance, prompting us to wonder whether the subsequent title change (the poem was simply *Lucrece* for its first few editions) was authorial or whether it was instigated by John Harrison, publisher of the first edition.[24] When Andrew Wise registered the right to copy for *Richard II* on 29 August 1597, what other manuscript did he hold, which led to the adjacent but abruptly curtailed note: "Entred the same daye at the hall before the m*aste*r and wardens a booke intituled–'?[25]

If we now read bindings and bookshops as units of interpretive possibility, do the massed entries of copy among which Shakespeare's work features offer similar promise? Sometimes a work was entered among a group of clearly associated texts, such as John Danter's joint entry of the play of *Titus Andronicus* alongside 'the ballad thereof', or Matthew Law's joint entry of *Richard II*, *Richard III*, and *1 Henry IV* ('all kinges', as the clerk laconically observed in a side note).[26] On other occasions the affinities of these groupings seem more oblique. Is there anything to be made of the fact that John Harrison claimed *Venus and Adonis* alongside the courtly poem *Orchestra or A poeme of dauncing*, by Sir John Davies?[27] What larger strategy prompted Cuthbert Burby to register *Edward III* (a play in which an English monarch liberates 'diseased, sick, and lame' French citizens from a period of unjust rule) alongside a pamphlet on curing ulcers?[28] We still do not know quite why, in August of 1600, four plays (*As You Like It*, *Henry V*, *Much Ado*, and Ben Jonson's *Every Man In His Humour*) were jotted on a flyleaf of the volume we now call 'Register C' under the title 'my lord chamberlens mens plaies Entred', but were then also bracketed with a note explaining these titles were 'to be staied'.[29] As if to caution us against assuming that either the First or Second Folio cemented Shakespeare's fame, another of these notes, this time one that

---

[24] Entry for 9 May 1594: SCA, *Liber B*, fol. 306v; Arber II.648. On the evolution of the poem's title see Ben Higgins, '*Judith* and *Lucrece*: Reading Shakespeare between Copy and Work' in *English Literary Renaissance* 52.1 (2022): pp. 34–71.

[25] 29 August 1597: SCA, *Register C*, fol. 23r; Arber III.89.

[26] 6 February 1594: SCA, *Liber B*, fol. 304v; Arber II.644. 25 June 1603, SCA, *Register C*, fol. 98r; Arber III.239.

[27] 25 June 1594: SCA, *Liber B*, fol. 310r; Arber II.655.

[28] Richard Proudfoot and Nicola Bennett eds, *King Edward III* (London and New York: Bloomsbury Arden Shakespeare, 2017), p. 288. Entry on 1 December 1595: SCA, *Register C*, fol. 6r; Arber III.55.

[29] Given their ambiguous status, I have not included the 'to be staied' entries in the table of registrations below.

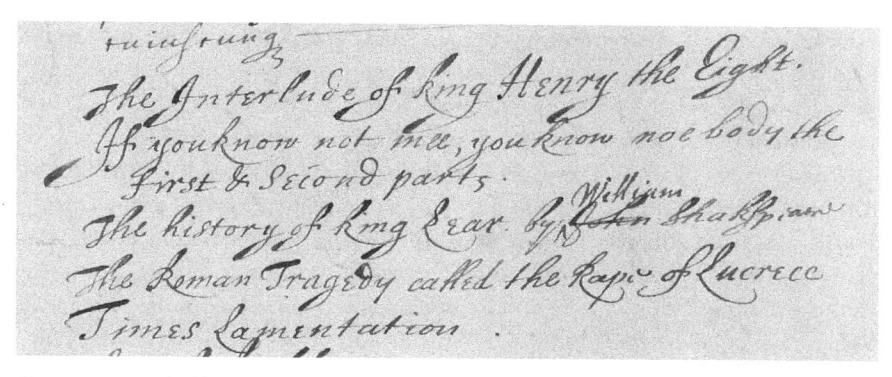

A MINOR SHAKESPEAREAN: WILLIAM ASPLEY AT THE PARROT 135

Figure 3.2 A clerk's slip in the 1639 register entry that transfers the right to print *King Lear*. Image of SCA, *Register D*, p. 440. Credit: The Stationers' Company Archive.

dates from after the Folio's publication and which records the transfer of the title to *King Lear*, contains a striking error in Shakespeare's own name (Figure 3.2). For a clerk in 1639, the 'history of King Lear' was a play that was: 'by \William/ ~~John~~ Shakspeaere'.[30] The error is a striking reminder that in the first half of the seventeenth century the name 'Shakespeare' did not necessarily require the forename 'William'; the pairing had not quite settled into one of Virginia Woolf's 'famous marriages' of linked words, even when discussing *King Lear*.[31]

When looked at collectively, though, one of the clearest impressions these entries convey is the lack of any committed or exclusive relationships between Shakespeare, the King's Men, and the stationers involved. This absence of control enabled thirty different stationers to acquire some part of Shakespeare's literary estate before the First Folio was published (thirty-one, if we include Isaac Jaggard and the entry of 8 November 1623). Even if an author or theatre company had preferred to deal with one particular stationer, perhaps angling for the '40. Shillings and an odde pottle of wine' fee offered by the fictionalized version of the printer John Danter to his prospective author in the second part of the *Returne from Pernassus* plays, there is plenty of evidence to show that it was particularly difficult to control the circulation of dramatic texts.[32] Plays might be acquired by any one of a number of unofficial means, such as through the memorial reconstruction of an actor, for example, in which case the text might end up 'corrupt and mangled' as Thomas Heywood complained darkly in 1608.[33] Or a play might reach a stationer via an audience member using the shorthand noting methods

---

[30] SCA, *Register D*, p. 440. The mistake was silently removed by Arber: IV.466.
[31] Virginia Woolf, 'Craftsmanship' in *Selected Essays* (Oxford: Oxford University Press, 2008), p. 88.
[32] *The returne from Pernassus: or The scourge of simony* (1606, STC 19310), sig. B3v. In the play Danter seems to give in, offering his author 'whatsoever it cost' for the manuscript, but the figure of forty shillings crops up elsewhere as the going rate for a short text.
[33] 'To the Reader' in Thomas Heywood, *The rape of Lucrece* (1608, STC 13360), sig. A2r.

reported as 'newly discovered' by George Buck in 1615, by which one could 'readily take a Sermon, Oration, Play, or any long speech, as they are spoken'.[34] Having been repeatedly 'published' to large theatrical audiences, the text of a play had constant potential to escape its origins and take on mutable new life.

A small group of the Shakespearean publishers listed here could be thought of as central figures, in that they owned several Shakespeare texts and seem actively to have sought out the playwright's work (see Table 3.2). Wise, who gathered the rights to print five Shakespeare titles (even if two of them were with Aspley) is the leading example of this approach; close behind are Thomas Pavier, the bookseller discussed in chapter two who owned four titles, and the stationer Nicholas Ling, who also owned four (Ling published *Hamlet*, but did not register his ownership of the right to copy in the Stationers' Register, which is why he has just three titles in Table 3.2). The elderly printer James Roberts, predecessor to William Jaggard in the printing house at Barbican, acquired three Shakespeare plays and is also associated with the 'to be staied' entries mentioned above. These are all familiar names; they are the biographical presences around which we shape our critical narratives about the early production of Shakespeare's books. Yet a much larger majority of these stationers—twenty in all—could be thought of as marginal in that they acquired only one Shakespeare title and often did little with it. How might this collective have influenced our sense of Shakespearean publication? The bookseller Thomas Fisher, for example, registered his ownership of *A Midsummer Night's Dream* in 1600 and published a quarto edition of the play in the same year, yet published nothing else by Shakespeare in his brief career. Another bookseller, Thomas Hayes, acquired the manuscript title to *The Merchant of Venice* from James Roberts also in 1600. Again, Hayes financed a single quarto edition, but had nothing more to do with Shakespeare other than enabling Hayes's son to claim the right to print *Merchant* years later in 1619. These moderate Shakespeareans rode the larger wave of interest in dramatic publication at the turn of the century before they established careers that led them in other directions.

To call Aspley a minor Shakespearean places him in a group of stationers whose individual significance is far outweighed by their collective influence. More

---

[34] George Buck, 'The Third Universitie of England' in John Stow, *The annales, or a generall chronicle of England* (1615, STC 23338), sig. 4O1v. See also Heywood's similar complaint about those who 'by Stenography, drew | The Plot: put it in print, scarce one word true': 'The Prologue' in *If you know not mee, you know no body* (1639, STC 13335), sig. A2r. On the movement of dramatic manuscripts see John Jowett, who offers the term 'exit manuscript' for a text that 'leaves the environs of the theatre' and 'migrates from the theatre to the printing house': 'Exit Manuscripts: The Archive of Theatre and the Archive of Print' in *Shakespeare Survey* 70 (2017): pp. 113–22, quote at p. 119. Tiffany Stern suggests that 'foul papers', or rough drafts of plays, may have been saved because of the value of the paper on which they were written, and so may subsequently have been acquired by a printer or publisher more easily in *Making Shakespeare: From Stage to Page* (London: Routledge, 2004), p. 146; Peter Blayney considers it likely that theatre companies sold their manuscripts to any willing stationer as an aid to publicity: 'The Publication of Playbooks', in John Cox and David Scott Kastan eds, *A New History of Early English Drama* (New York: Columbia University Press, 1997), pp. 383–422, at pp. 386–7.

Table 3.2 Entry of William Shakespeare's work into the Stationers' Register, 1593–1622, organized by stationer

Stationer	Title	Date Registered
Andrew Wise	Richard II	29 August 1597
	Richard III	20 October 1597
	1 Henry IV	25 February 1598
Andrew Wise & William Aspley	2 Henry IV	23 August 1600
Andrew Wise & William Aspley	Much Ado About Nothing	23 August 1600
Thomas Pavier	Henry V	14 August 1600
	Titus Andronicus	19 April 1602
	1 Contention (2 Henry VI)	19 April 1602
	2 Contention (3 Henry VI)	19 April 1602
John Smethwick	The Taming of a Shrew	19 November 1607
	Romeo and Juliet	19 November 1607
	Love's Labour's Lost	19 November 1607
	Hamlet	19 November 1607
Matthew Law	Richard II	25 June 1603
	Richard III	25 June 1603
	1 Henry IV	25 June 1603
Nicholas Ling	The Taming of a Shrew	22 January 1607
	Romeo and Juliet	22 January 1607
	Love's Labour's Lost	22 January 1607
James Roberts	The Merchant of Venice	22 July 1598
	Hamlet	26 July 1602
	Troilus and Cressida	7 February 1603
Edward Blount	Pericles	20 May 1608
	Antony and Cleopatra	20 May 1608
John Busby 1	Merry Wives of Windsor	18 January 1602
John Busby 1 & Nathaniel Butter	King Lear	26 November 1607
John Harrison 1	The Rape of Lucrece	9 May 1594
	Venus and Adonis	25 June 1594
William Barrett	Venus and Adonis	16 February 1617
Richard Bonian & Henry Walley	Troilus and Cressida	28 January 1609
Cuthbert Burby	Edward III	1 December 1595
John Danter	Titus Andronicus	6 February 1594
Richard Field	Venus and Adonis	18 April 1593
Thomas Fisher	A Midsummer Night's Dream	8 October 1600
Thomas Hayes	The Merchant of Venice	28 October 1600
Lawrence Hayes	The Merchant of Venice	8 July 1619
Roger Jackson	The Rape of Lucrece	1 March 1614
Arthur Johnson	Merry Wives of Windsor	18 January 1602
William Leake	Venus and Adonis	25 June 1596
Thomas Millington	I Contention (2 Henry VI)	12 March 1594
John Parker	Venus and Adonis	8 March 1620
Peter Short	The Taming of a Shrew	2 May 1594
Thomas Snodham	Edward III	2 March 1618
Thomas Thorpe	Sonnets	20 May 1609
Thomas Walkley	Othello	6 October 1621
William Welby	Edward III	16 October 1609

Source: DEEP.

so than any individual, it was this broad community of stationers who fostered the dynamism of the market for these books, creating an ecosystem of competition and collaboration which shaped the vibrant history of Shakespearean literary identity.

Place of much dissimulation: the Church
(the Church)
()

— *The Malcontent* (1604)

After a decade of explorative publishing, Aspley began to change his habits. Once established he was free to pursue his own interests beyond Shakespeare or early modern drama. From about 1608, his strategy of collaborating with stationers on a variety of genres faded away as he found the rhythm that would define his career. This change of heart, which moved him away from Shakespeare and towards religious publishing, may also have been prompted by Aspley's pursuit of topical texts, several of which fell foul of censors in ways that the stationer perhaps felt were unsustainable. The scattering of plays Aspley published at the start of his career illustrates his misadventures. The quarto edition of *2 Henry IV*, for example, survives in two different issues, only one of which includes what is now Act 3 Scene 1. This scene focuses on two speeches by King Henry, in both of which he frets over the rebellion gripping his kingdom and recalls the usurpation of Richard II. '[Y]ou perceive the body of our kingdom', the king tells his noblemen, 'How foul it is, what rank diseases grow.'[35] The political nature of the scene, and in particular its focus on a moment of usurpation and succession—sensitive issues at the end of Queen Elizabeth's reign—have led some scholars to suggest that censorship lies behind these changes. There are similar issues with Aspley's next play, Thomas Dekker's *Old Fortunatas* (1600), many copies of which have had an offending leaf removed from the middle of the book.[36]

---

[35] Shakespeare, *King Henry IV Part 2*, ed. Bulman, p. 287. The two issues of the quarto—known as Qa and Qb—are described at pp. 430–48. Bulman discusses censorship and the difficulties with that theory on pp. 445–8. Richard Dutton believes that censorship 'may have played its part' but, looking at the relationship between Qa, Qb, and the slightly expanded First Folio text of the play, he argues the changes may be revisions made by Shakespeare to prepare the play for performance at court: *Shakespeare, Court Dramatist* (Oxford: Oxford University Press, 2016), pp. 263–6, quote at p. 265. Giorgio Melchiori offers a different view, suggesting that Shakespeare decided to insert a manuscript leaf late in the production process: *The Second Part of King Henry IV* (Cambridge: Cambridge University Press, 2007), pp. 226–8.

[36] Leaf E2 was cancelled, most likely because of a speech that describes how courtly ambition can progress to treachery. The play's protagonist, the beggar Fortunatas, describes how 'In some Courts shall you see ambition Sit', which will 'melt against the Sunne of majestie' so that 'downe they tumble to destruction': Thomas Dekker, *The Pleasant Comedie of Old Fortunatus* (1600, STC 6517), sig E2r in some copies. The play's discussion of overreaching ambition seems to have been problematic by 1601

Likewise the copies of John Marston's play *The Malcontent*, which Aspley published in 1604, are 'particularly tangled' by a series of crude and panicky alterations.[37] Not least of these are the changes made to an offending line in Act 1 Scene 3 in which the scheming character Malevole described 'the publike place of much dissimulation, (the Church)'.[38] The line survives in at least three states. The most immediate and jarring alteration saw the offending noun 'Church' neatly sliced out of the page—probably by Aspley or at his direction, given that the same cuts feature in multiple copies—with a number of disorientating consequences. The cuts were made on the verso side of the leaf, which means that a reader first encounters them on the previous recto, where they emerge beside a stage direction for the entrance of several characters. The arrival of Duke Pietro, Ferrardo, and Count Equato is therefore troubled by the uneasy possibility of a further excised presence. Turn the page, though, and in some states the hole allows text from the play's induction to jump into a new frame of meaning within the play. The first few sorts of type from a line spoken by the character Sinklow (a fictionalized version of the real Shakespearean actor John Sinklo), about 'Great Alexander when he came to the toombe of Achilles' reappear through the hole, so that the reader is confronted by a confusing new line: 'From the publike place of much dissimulation, (the Great Ale.)' (Figure 3.3).[39] In other copies the effect is less legible: the cut-out hole in the Boston Public Library copy mostly shows the space between lines, but thin slices of words intrude into the top and bottom of the hole. Printed characters are briefly transformed into alienating stutters of ink, severed from signifying form.[40] A further copy in the Bodleian Library lacks the induction, and so the hole provides a window only to a modern endpaper.[41] Elsewhere, removing the problematic word only invited readers to supply their own contentious ideas. An early reader of a copy now in the Victoria and Albert museum, for example, decided the missing word was 'court', before a later reader restored the correct word 'Church' using a manuscript paste-in that carefully imitates printed type.[42] The same annotation ('court') is also found in a Folger copy (Figure 3.4). In these examples, Aspley's efforts to appease censors by removing

---

after the rebellion of the Queen's favourite Robert Devereux, the Earl of Essex. See Fredson Bowers, 'Essex's Rebellion and Dekker's *Old Fortunatus*' in *Review of English Studies* 3.12 (1952): pp. 365–6. Paul Frazer finds that Dekker's play critiques Essex in various passages: 'Performing Places in Thomas Dekker's *Old Fortunatus*' in *Philological Quarterly* 89.4 (2010): pp. 457–80.

[37] John Marston, *The Malcontent*, ed. George K. Hunter (London: Methuen, 1975), p. xxiii. *The Malcontent* survives in three distinct quarto states from 1604, but the relationship of these quartos to one another—whether each is a separate edition, and in which order they were printed, for example—is not always clear. Hunter explains the complexities: *Malcontent*, pp. xxiii–xxxviii.

[38] John Marston, *The Malcontent* (1604, STC 17480), sig. B1v.
[39] Bodleian Library, Malone 252 (4), sig. B1v.
[40] Boston Public Library shelfmark G.3977.50, sig. B1v.
[41] Bodleian Library shelfmark Malone 195 (5).
[42] Victoria and Albert Museum Library shelfmark Dyce 26 Box 28/2.

> *Enter* Malevole *after the Song.*
> See: he comes: now shall you heare the extreamitie of a Male-
> content:he is as free as ayre:he blowes ouer euery man. And sir,
> whence come you now?
>   *Mal:* From the publike place of much dissimulation, (the
> great Ale.)
>   *Pie:* What didst there?
>   *Mal:* Talke with a Vsurer: take vp at interest.
>   *Pie:* I wonder what religion thou art of.
>   *Mal:* Of a souldiers religion.
>   *Pie:* And what doost thinke makes most infidells now?
>   *Mal:* Sects, sects, I haue seene seeming *Pietie* change her
> roabe so oft, that sure none but some arch-diuell can shape her
> a Petticote.

Figure 3.3 Detail from act one scene two of *The Malcontent* (1604, STC 17481), sig. B1v. Credit: Bodleian Libraries, University of Oxford, Malone 252 (4). Used under Creative Commons licence CC-BY-NC 4.0

contention were themselves generative of more private, local acts of speculative heresy.

Any remaining interest Aspley had in topical playbooks may have evaporated after *Eastward Hoe*, a play that he published in three editions in 1605 after registering the manuscript jointly with Thomas Thorpe. Three editions in a year means this playbook was a commercial success, but that popularity may have been helped by a notorious scandal surrounding the play. Two of the authors of *Eastward Hoe*, George Chapman and Ben Jonson, were imprisoned when the play was first staged in around July or August of 1605. Sections of the play mocked the sudden influx of Scottish courtiers who had followed King James down to London in 1603; the text also took aim at the king's habit of distributing knighthoods in exchange for money and offered a dangerous mimicry of James's Scottish accent. 'I ken the man weel' drawls a Gentleman in one such moment, 'hee's one of my thirty pound Knights.'[43] The play's third co-author, John Marston, seems to have eluded the authorities, as did Aspley—at least, nothing in the archives of the state or the Stationers' Company suggests that either he or Thorpe were censured. According to Jonson, though, both he and Chapman narrowly escaped having 'their ears cut and noses'.[44] The uproar led Aspley to wield the knife once again: two internal leaves (E3 and E4) were sliced out of the first edition of this play;

---

[43] George Chapman, Ben Jonson, and John Marston, *Eastward Hoe* (1605, STC 4970), sig. F4r.

[44] Ben Jonson, 'Informations to William Drummond of Hawthornden (1619)', edited by Ian Donaldson, in Ben Jonson, *The Cambridge Edition of the Works of Ben Jonson*, 7 vols, edited by David Bevington, Martin Butler, and Ian Donaldson (Cambridge: Cambridge University Press, 2012), vol. 5,

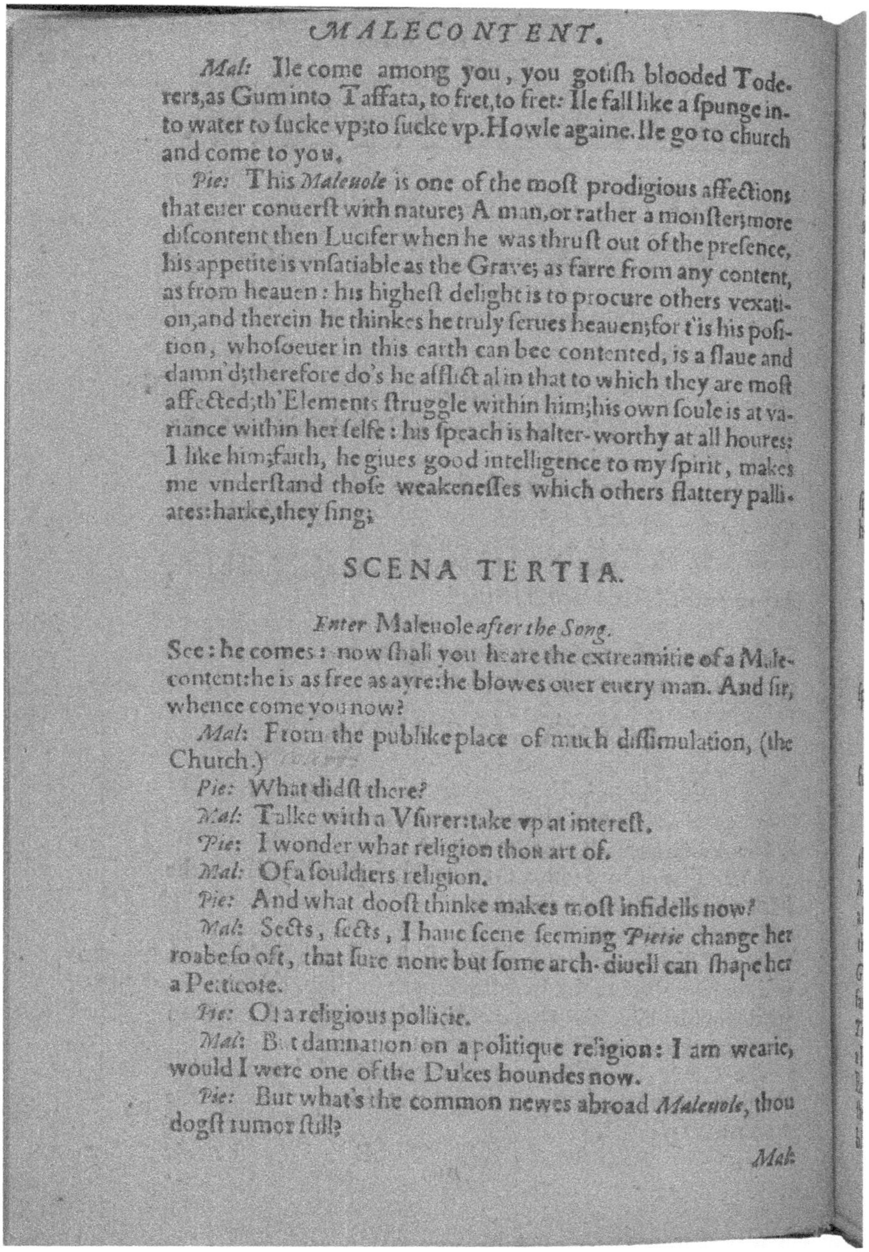

MALECONTENT.

Mal: Ile come among you, you gotiſh blooded Toderers, as Gum into Taffata, to fret, to fret: Ile fall like a ſpunge into water to ſucke vp; to ſucke vp. Howle againe. Ile go to church and come to you.

Pie: This *Maleuole* is one of the moſt prodigious affections that euer conuerſt with nature; A man, or rather a monſter; more diſcontent then Lucifer when he was thruſt out of the preſence, his appetite is vnſatiable as the Graue; as farre from any content, as from heauen: his higheſt delight is to procure others vexation, and therein he thinkes he truly ſerues heauen; for t'is his poſition, whoſoeuer in this earth can bee contented, is a ſlaue and damn'd; therefore do's he afflict al in that to which they are moſt affected; th'Elements ſtruggle within him; his own ſoule is at variance within her ſelfe: his ſpeach is halter-worthy at all houres: I like him; faith, he giues good intelligence to my ſpirit, makes me vnderſtand thoſe weakeneſſes which others flattery palliates: harke, they ſing;

SCENA TERTIA.

Enter Maleuole *after the Song.*

See: he comes: now ſhall you heare the extreamitie of a Malecontent: he is as free as ayre: he blowes ouer euery man. And ſir, whence come you now?

Mal: From the publike place of much diſſimulation, (the Church.)

Pie: What didſt there?

Mal: Talke with a Vſurer: take vp at intereſt.

Pie: I wonder what religion thou art of.

Mal: Of a ſouldiers religion.

Pie: And what dooſt thinke makes moſt infidells now?

Mal: Sects, ſects, I haue ſeene ſeeming *Pietie* change her roabe ſo oft, that ſure none but ſome arch-diuell can ſhape her a Petticote.

Pie: O! a religious pollicie.

Mal: But damnation on a politique religion: I am wearie, would I were one of the Dukes houndes now.

Pie: But what's the common newes abroad *Maleuole*, thou dogſt rumor ſtill?

Mal:

Figure 3.4 Another copy of the same edition of *The Malcontent* (1604, STC 17481), this time one that escaped censorship. An early reader has suggested 'courts' instead of 'Church'. The same annotation is found on a cut copy now in the Victoria and Albert museum. Detail of Folger Library STC 17481 copy 1. Credit: Folger digital image collection 166,669. Used by permission of the Folger Shakespeare Library.

their ragged stubs jut through the gutter of some copies, reminding us of the edition's maimed status.[45]

Publishing John Boys

Aspley and John Boys may have first encountered one another in February of 1601. The preacher stood in Paul's Cross Churchyard and delivered a public sermon at the same time—at 'the very same houre', he later recalled—that Robert Devereux, the Earl of Essex, stormed through London in the heat of his rebellion.[46] Aspley's first bookshop was wedged between two of the cathedral buttresses opposite the pulpit where Boys stood. To Aspley's left was the bookshop of Edward Blount, who was also present on that day. While Boys stood at the pulpit and expounded a happily appropriate verse from Matthew ('no man can serve two masters'), Blount offered shelter to several passers-by when the Queen's forces stormed through the churchyard.[47] If Aspley did see the preacher's sermon then he was impressed enough to publish it in 1613. In fact, Aspley invested more heavily in Boys than any other author, registering and publishing each of the eleven separate titles that Boys wrote. Many of these titles earned second and third editions, so that between 1609, when Boys's first book appeared, and 1617, when his final quarto was published, Aspley financed twenty-seven editions (and at least two re-issues) of the author's work.[48] The surprising popularity of these quartos, most of which examined and defended another part of the Book of Common Prayer, led Aspley to repackage them all as a large folio volume shortly before Shakespeare's own Folio was published. This much lesser-known Aspley folio, *The Workes of John Boys Doctor in Divinitie* (1622), sold well enough to earn a second edition in 1630 and a third in 1638. At the height of Aspley's career,

---

p. 373. See Donaldson's account in *Ben Jonson: A Life* (Oxford: Oxford University Press, 2011), pp. 205–13.

[45] The offending sections were altered for a second issue of the first edition and the text was probably also tampered with at C1v–C2r: George Chapman, Ben Jonson, and John Marston, *Eastward Ho*, edited by R. W. Van Fossen (Manchester: Manchester University Press, 1999), pp. 45–51.

[46] John Boys, *The Autumne Parte* (1613, STC 3460.6), sig. F6r.

[47] In 1601 Blount was working opposite the Great North Door of Paul's Cross Church, probably at a shop known by the sign of the Bishop's Head: Peter W. M. Blayney, *The Bookshops in Paul's Cross Churchyard* (London: The Bibliographical Society, 1990), p. 17. That Blount was present in the churchyard that day is confirmed by one Arthur Bromfeilde, who later reported that amid the hue and cry 'he withdrew into Bluntes howse a bookebynder where he found beside the master of the howse master Duckett and master Lawley and one Stanes, who intreated him not to goe forth againe but he saide he would see what should become of them': Folger Library MS V. b. 187, fol. 5v. My thanks to Peter W. M. Blayney for pointing me towards this manuscript.

[48] There is at least one issue of a Boys quarto that is not listed in the second edition of the *STC*. Bodleian Library Vet. A2 e.353 (5) is an uncatalogued issue of *The Autumne Part* (1612, STC 3460.5). The imprint of the known state of this 1612 edition includes Aspley's address ('imprinted by Felix Kyngston for VVilliam Aspley, and are to be sold at his shop in Pauls Church-yard, at the signe of the Parrot, 1612'), while the imprint of the Bodleian copy ends at 'for VVilliam Aspley. 1612.'

between 1609 and 1622, the books of John Boys were the central product of his bookshop: they account for about 65 per cent of all surviving edition sheets the stationer published during this time.

Given Aspley's biography, perhaps his interest in Boys and religious publishing is not surprising. The stationer's father, also William Aspley, had been a chaplain to Queen Elizabeth.[49] After leaving home, the younger William Aspley served as an apprentice to the powerful stationer George Bishop, deputy printer to Queen Elizabeth and owner of a monopoly on printing English Bibles.[50] It is probably not a coincidence that Bishop published the books which are the closest antecedents to the work of John Boys: the popular 'postils', or religious commentaries, of the two Lutherans Niels Hemmingsen and David Chytraeus. Their books provided expository commentary on the sections of the Bible 'that are usually red in the churches of God, upon the Sundayes and feast dayes'—in other words, they covered very similar ground to Boys's own careful elucidation of the Stuart Book of Common Prayer.[51] The progression from Bishop's investment in Hemmingsen and Chyraeus to Aspley's investment in Boys offers a textual counterpart to their book-trade genealogy. Here, as with Edward Blount's inheritance of links to the Herbert family from his master William Ponsonby, and William Jaggard's continuation of his master Henry Denham's interest in history and reference books, lines of continuity emerge within generations of the book trade.

With hindsight, Aspley's interest in religious and political conformism was present to some degree from the start of his career. Like many stationers, Aspley capitalized on the arrival of King James in London in 1603 by publishing unionist works that heralded James as the first king 'to unite these two mighty and warlike nations', or in another case marvelled at how 'the nations of the Ilands of *Brittanie*,

---

[49] Anthony à Wood, *Fasti Oxonienses: or, Annals of the University of Oxford*, continued by Philip Bliss (London: Printed for F. C. and J. Rivington, 1815), vol. I, p. 62. William Aspley senior studied at All Soul's College in Oxford as a Bible clerk and was given a vicarage in Royston in 1567. He is recorded as a scholar in the University of Oxford's Faculty of Arts on 10 November 1561 (*Supplication Roll*: Oxford University Archives NEP/supra/Reg I, fol. 198r), and admitted to the degree of BA (as Apsley) on 19 November 1561 (*Supplication* Roll, fol. 200v). My thanks to Simon Bailey, Keeper of the Archives at the University of Oxford, for this information. See also: Joseph Foster, *Alumni Oxonienses: the members of the University of Oxford, 1500–1714*, 4 vols (Oxford: Parker & Co, 1891–2), vol. I, p. 29. See also: *Certificates of Clergy Appointments*: TNA E 331/London/1, piece 7; Hertfordshire Archives: *Alphabetical List of Parochial Incumbents of the County of Hertford from Lists Compiled by Rev. GL Hennessy* (manuscript on open shelf with no shelfmark or foliation, entry for William Aspley); *Clergy of the Church of England Database* (CCEd), Record ID 165614. Aspley senior's death in 1574 is noted in a Bishop's Register: LMA DL/A/A/006/MS09531/013/001, entry for 19 July 1574.

[50] Aspley's apprenticeship is recorded at Arber II.150; his freedom in 1597 is recorded at Arber II.718. For Bishop, see Anders Ingram, 'Bishop, George (*b.* in or before 1538, *d.* 1610/11), bookseller.' *Oxford Dictionary of National Biography* (Oxford: Oxford University Press, 2004; online edn, 30 May 2013 [accessed 16 Aug 2019]).

[51] Niels Hemmingsen, *A postill, or exposition of the Gospels* (1569, STC 13061), sig. A1r. Hemmingsen's work was published in five editions between 1569 and 1585. Chytraeus's *Postil or orderly disposing of certeine epistles usually red in the Church of God, upon the Sundayes and holydayes* (1570, STC 5263) offered similar material.

were united in hart and affection' under new rule.[52] More valuable than these succession pamphlets, Aspley also secured the right to publish King James's own book *Daemonologie* (1603)—a popular philosophical account of sorcery and witchcraft. Yet this early proximity to church and state was renewed by Aspley's registration of the first Boys title in October of 1609.[53] Over the following decade or so, Aspley's books intervened in some key religious disputes, including the furore over the revisions to the Book of Common Prayer and the Oath of Allegiance crisis. Nearly all his books espoused a consistent ideological position that endorsed the *via media* religious policy of King James. In the early seventeenth century, James faced a querulous religious population, riven by the two aggressive minorities of Puritan and papist among other factions.[54] Aspley's bookshop at the Sign of the Parrot became a key site for the production and distribution of a rhetoric of conformity.

The central role Boys played in this larger publishing strategy is suggested by the sheer number of times his work was reprinted. That twenty-seven quartos of Boys's work were published in nine years could seem surprising to us today; apart from anything else, and unlike the sermons of contemporary preachers such as John Donne, Launcelot Andrewes, or Thomas Playfere, Boys's writings were never feted for their literary qualities. Though Boys was himself interested in literary and theatrical culture (there is a possible allusion to *Hamlet* in one of his sermons, and his incredulous comment that 'the very *playes* of a modern Poet, are called in print his *workes*', is among the earliest responses to Ben Jonson's collected *Workes*), but his contemporary appeal was not based on literary style.[55] One modern appraisal describes his work as 'humdrum' and 'a hefty thousand pages of middlebrow theology'.[56] Another way to think about his writing, though,

---

[52] Francis Bacon, *A briefe discourse, touching the happie vnion of the kingdomes of England, and Scotland* (1603, STC 1117), sig. A7r; John Gordon, *England and Scotlands happinesse: in being reduced to unitie of religion, under our invincible monarke King James* (1604, STC 12062.3), sig. B2v. See also Richard Martin's *A speech deliuered to the Kings most excellent Maiestie* (1603, STC 17510), also published by Aspley, which congratulates and welcomes James on behalf of the sheriffs and magistrates of London and Middlesex.

[53] Arber III.423; SCA, *Register C*, fol. 190r.

[54] For an overview see Kenneth Fincham and Peter Lake, 'The Ecclesiastical Policy of James I' in *Journal of British Studies* 24.2 (1985): pp. 169–207.

[55] Boys's comment on Jonson's *Workes* (1616) appeared in *An Exposition of the Proper Psalmes used in our English Lyturgie…The second part* (1617, STC 3467), sig. I1v. Frederick James Furnival cautiously suggests Boys alluded to *Hamlet* a few years earlier, when the preacher wrote in a sermon that 'Of all the herbes in the garden (as one wittily) Rew is the herbe of grace'. The 'one wittily' may either refer to Shakespeare or Ophelia, who amid her breakdown calls rue the 'herbe of Grace a Sondaies'. Boys's quote can be found in: *An exposition of the dominical Epistles and Gospels…The winter part* (1610, STC 3458), sig. Y2r; Ophelia's line appears in: William Shakespeare, *The tragicall historie of Hamlet, Prince of Denmarke* (1604, STC 22276), sig. L2r; the allusion is documented in *The Shakspere Allusion-Book: A Collection of Allusions to Shakspere From 1591 to 1700*, 2 vols (London: Oxford University Press, 1932), vol. 1, p. 258.

[56] Patrick Collinson, 'The Protestant Cathedral, 1541–1660' in Patrick Collinson, Nigel Ramsay, and Margaret Sparks eds, *A History of Canterbury Cathedral* (Oxford: Oxford University Press, 1995), pp. 154–203, at p. 178.

is that it was resolutely accessible. His books discuss complex and politically sensitive topics with 'blithe disregard' for the usual erudite conventions of philology or humanist reasoning which generally characterize theology of this period.[57] Instead, the preacher stuck to a doggedly everyday register in his prose, which opened his work up to a wide range of literate readers invested in the religious disputes of the day. In its avoidance of any literary or scholarly extreme, Boys's writing thus embodied his pitch to be the 'exemplar' of the period's 'theological via media'.[58]

Boys was therefore a valuable defender of King James's position amid the religious and political tensions of the early seventeenth century. Events such as the Millenary Petition—in which disenchanted Puritan ministers complained about the vestiges of Catholicism rumbling within the English Church—and the subsequent Hampton Court Conference of 1604, where King James and his bishops met with the Puritans to debate the state of the church, placed great focus on the Book of Common Prayer. Officially, King James dismissed the Puritan appeals to alter the wording of the prayer book, finding 'no cause why any Change' should be made. But at the same time, new editions of the Book of Common Prayer in 1604 and 1605 did in fact alter key phrases, leading to what Daniel Swift describes as a spirit of 'passionately contested revision' and 'manic sensitivity to a verb or turn of phrase'.[59] The grounds for these religious and political debates were often literary-critical, resting on the interpretation of phrases and words that preachers and their congregations were ordered to recite. Boys's sermons thus offered an interpretively secure path through one of the most contentious yet central texts of the time. His expositions defended the liturgy against accusations of either popery or of Godly puritanism, clearing a middle way through difficult terrain in down-to-earth prose. The need for such guidance was underscored by King James himself, whose *Directions for preachers* (1622) warned the clergy that they must rely on the Book of Common Prayer while at all costs avoiding contentious readings.

The success of both Boys and Aspley is suggested by contemporary evidence of Boys being read and circulated. Copies were sent from London in 1621 for sale in an Oxford bookshop amid a bundle of other popular texts such as *Riders dictionarie* and sheet almanacs.[60] His books found their way into the studies of students

---

[57] Beth Quitslund, '"A Second Bible": Liturgy and Interpretation in the *Expositions* of John Boys' in *Reformation* 23.1 (2018): pp. 79–99, at p. 79.

[58] Quitslund, '"Second Bible"', p. 81.

[59] Daniel Swift, *Shakespeare's Common Prayers: The Book of Common Prayer and the Elizabethan Age* (Oxford: Oxford University Press, 2013), p. 22. On the Book of Common Prayer, see also Brian Cummings's introduction in his edition: *The Book of Common Prayer: The Texts of 1549, 1559, and 1662* (Oxford: Oxford University Press, 2011), pp. ix–lii.

[60] Christopher Meredith to Thomas Huggins, 3 January 3 1621, manuscript bookseller's bill tucked in the binding of Gervase Babington, *The works of the Right Reverend Father in God, Gervase Babington* (1637, STC 1080), Huntington Library shelfmark 28116.

at the inns of court, where the lawyer Justinian Pagitt noted reading Boys in his diary of life at the Middle Temple.[61] Boys titles appear with relative frequency in the inventories of private libraries from the period.[62] The preacher's public standing reached a point that at least one other clergyman dedicated a book to him, and a biography written shortly after his death praised 'that sweet booke of his *Postills*', and tells us that Boys was widely known to readers '(though not in his person) yet in his workes'—meaning, presumably, that he was better known for his writings than for his public preaching.[63] Alongside this authorial popularity, Boys's relationship with his publisher seems to have flourished. When in 1618 Boys was awarded a new church living in Kent, William Aspley was a guarantor who vouched that Boys would pay the tax required on his new benefice.[64] That Aspley would make himself financially vulnerable on Boys's behalf suggests a level of trust and friendship that extended beyond a purely professional relationship.

For a brief period at the start of the seventeenth century, then, this now obscure preacher was in fact a bestselling author. And William Aspley was responsible for the creation and promotion of this authorial fame to a degree which may be unrivalled within the early modern English book trade. I have found no other example of an author–publisher relationship from this time period to match this pair.[65] With Boys as the central product of his bookshop, Aspley developed a wider specialism in books that supported King James's vision for the Protestant church. The bookseller can be connected, for example, with several of the authors who in 1610 founded the 'Chelsea College' school of polemicists who were tasked

---

[61] *Diary of Justinian Pagitt*, BL Harley MS 1026, fol. 75v.

[62] The *Private Libraries in Renaissance England* project (https://plre.folger.edu/) records copies of one or more Boys books in seven of its libraries.

[63] R. P., 'A briefe view of the life, and vertues of *the Authour*' in John Boys, *Remaines of that reverend and famous postiller, John Boys* (1631, STC 3468), sig. A2r–b2v. The preacher James Wats dedicated his *The controversie debated about the reverend gesture of kneeling* to Boys in 1621 (STC 25109). After the Restoration, Boys was described as 'famous to posterity' and 'the best postiller in England'. See Thomas Fuller, *The History of the Worthies of England* (1662, Wing F2440), sig. 2M2v; David Lloyd, *Memoires of the lives, actions, sufferings & deaths of those noble, reverend, and excellent personages* (1668, Wing L2642), sig. 4T1v.

[64] *Office of First Fruits 1614–18*, TNA E 334/15, fol. 104v. Aspley did the same thing for the clergyman and press licenser Richard Mockett in 1611: *Office of First Fruits 1604–13*, TNA E 334/14, fol. 187r.

[65] Possible comparisons include the partnership between the poet Samuel Daniel and the bookseller Simon Waterson. Even here, though, Waterson did not control all of Daniel's work. Edward Blount, for instance, registered and published some of Daniel's writing, as did the stationer Francis Constable. The bookseller John Marriot owned a great deal of the poet Francis Quarles's work, but again, not all of it: stationers including Richard Moore, Thomas Dewe, and Nicholas Alsop also registered Quarles's manuscripts. Discussing an earlier generation of stationer, David Carlson discusses a 'thorough-going, long-lived collaboration' between Alexander Barclay and the printer Richard Pynson: 'Alexander Barclay and Richard Pynson: A Tudor Printer and his Writer' in *Anglia* 113 (1995): pp. 283–302, quote at p. 290.

by James with responding to Catholic attacks and winning over public opinion.[66] Boys was a founder member of this college under the leadership of Matthew Sutcliffe, whose own book *The supplication of certaine masse-priests* Aspley published in three editions. Boys also praised the college in a sermon that was published by Aspley in 1613: musing on recent developments in London, Boys noted that 'there have bin many new play-houses, and one faire Burse lately built', before commending 'that ever zealous, reverend, learned Deane' (Sutcliffe) for 'founding a Colledge for a society of writers against the superstitious Idolatries of the Romane Synagogue'.[67] It was loyalty to Sutcliffe that led Boys to dedicate a book to him in 1615; another of Boys's books was dedicated to the Dean of Paul's Cross Church, John Overall, also a founder member of Chelsea College. Aspley and his bookshop connect a network of religious authors whose work shared an ideological commitment to James's policies.

These links between Aspley and the monarchy were strengthened through the stationer's publication of several books by royal command. The preacher Robert Wilkinson's two sermons *'preacht to a paire of peereles and succeeding princes'* (1614), were both dedicated to Prince Charles and published 'because your Highnesse had so commanded it'.[68] The scholar Isaac Casaubon's *The answere of Master Isaac Casaubon to the epistle of the most reverend Cardinall Peron* (1612) was a polemical tract, written on behalf of King James, in which Casaubon argued that the Church of England could legitimately call itself 'Catholic'; the book was 'an official production sponsored and underwritten by the King'.[69] Both books suggest Aspley's loyalty to the state, as do the several interventions the publisher made into the 'pamphlet warfare' brought about by the notorious Oath of Allegiance controversy.[70] One such intervention was a title by Richard Sheldon, whose book *Certain general reasons, proving the lawfulnesse of the Oath of*

---

[66] For Chelsea College, see D. E. Kennedy, 'King James's College of Controversial Divinity at Chelsea' in D. E. Kennedy, Diana Robertson, and Alexandra Walsham eds, *Grounds of Controversy: Three Studies in Late 16th and Early 17th Century English Polemics* (Parkville, Australia: University of Melbourne Press, 1989), pp. 97–119; and Jesse M. Lander, *Inventing Polemic: Religion, Print, and Literary Culture in Early Modern England* (Cambridge: Cambridge University Press, 2006), pp. 201–21.

[67] John Boys, *An exposition of the last psalme* (1613, STC 3464), sig. B4r–v.

[68] Robert Wilkinson, 'To the High and Mightie Prince Charles' in *A paire of sermons*…(1614, STC 25661), sig. A2v.

[69] Nicholas Hardy, *Criticism and Confession: The Bible in the Seventeenth Century Republic of Letters* (Oxford: Oxford University Press, 2017), p. 87.

[70] Fincham and Lake, 'Ecclesiastical Policy', p. 187. The Oath of Allegiance was King James's attempt, in the fallout from the Gunpowder Plot of 1605, to control recusancy with an oath that unequivocally acknowledged that James was the rightful king over the authority of the Pope. Edward Blount briefly references this oath in letter three in appendix one. On the oath, see Michael C. Questier, 'Loyalty, Religion and State Power in Early Modern England: English Romanism and the Jacobean Oath of Allegiance' in *The Historical Journal* 40.2 (1997): pp. 311–29; and Marcy L. North, 'Anonymity's Subject: James I and the Debate over the Oath of Allegiance' in *New Literary History* 33.2 (2002): pp. 215–32. For the impact of the oath on the literature of the period, see Andrew Hadfield, *Lying in Early Modern English Culture: From the Oath of Supremacy to the Oath of Allegiance* (Oxford: Oxford University Press, 2017), esp. pp. 69–114.

allegiance (1611), provided valuable ammunition for King James. Sheldon was a Catholic priest, on the brink of a public conversion to Protestantism, who took James's oath. In *Certain general reasons* Sheldon urged other Catholics to follow his lead: 'the Oath may, and ought in a just sense to be taken,' he wrote.[71] In what may be the only preliminary address written by Aspley (the address is unsigned, making it impossible to say for sure), the bookseller offered his book to those who were 'weake in their owne judgements', and liable to be 'il and undutifully affected to his Majestie and the State'. These dissenters, Aspley wrote, should now understand 'the justnesse of the Oath of Allegiance in England'.[72] In early bindings Sheldon's book is often found bound with another Aspley publication which triumphantly told the story of another prominent apostate: the author Theophilus Higgons, who had converted to Roman Catholicism in about 1608, but publicly recanted in a sermon preached from Paul's Cross in 1610. The text of that sermon was published by Aspley 'in testimony of his heartie reunion with *the Church of England*', and was seemingly often packaged with Sheldon's book.[73] This pair of religious success stories form a dual propaganda effort to champion the state's achievements.

One curious scrap suggests that Aspley's retailing of state wares extended beyond his own publications. A copy of *The whole volume of statutes at large*, published in 1587 by Christopher Barker, 'Printer *to the Queenes most excellent Majestie*' as the title page records, was resold second-hand by Aspley. On a flyleaf is a note written and signed by the bookseller (Figure 3.5), which records that the copy was 'Bought this 13 of feb. 1617[/18] for one pound thirteene shillings' and that 'If anie statutes in whoole or part be wantinge or anie misplased I promisse to make it good'.[74] The little guarantee of the book's condition confirms Aspley was one of several London booksellers who sold second-hand volumes at this time. The fact that the volume concerned was a collection of 'all the statutes of England, reduced into one volume' suggests it would not have been out of place beside his own publications.[75]

If Aspley's publishing interests were well established by 1623, then they are also difficult to reconcile with Shakespeare's Folio. Does it matter that when

---

[71] Richard Sheldon, *Certain general reasons, proving the lawfulnesse of the Oath of allegiance* (1611, STC 22393), sig. K1v.

[72] 'An Advertisement' in Sheldon, *Certain general reasons*, sig. ¶1v (missing from some copies).

[73] Theophilus Higgons, *A sermon preached at Pauls Crosse the third of March, 1610* (1611, STC 13455.7), sig. A1r.

[74] Note on flyleaf of *The whole volume of statutes at large* (1587, STC 9305.3), copy in private ownership. My thanks to Mark Byford for drawing my attention to this copy. For a comparison of Aspley's hand and signature see the original copy of his will: *Will of William Aspley*, PROB 10/610. For a similar manuscript guarantee by Francis Smethwick, the stationer son of John Smethwick, see Folger X. d. 254.

[75] *The whole volume of statutes at large*, sig. 3K1v. On the second-hand book trade see H. R. Woudhuysen, 'From Duck Lane to Lazarus Seaman: Buying and Selling Old Books in England during the Sixteenth and Seventeenth Centuries' in Adam Smyth ed., *The Oxford Handbook of the History of the Book in Early Modern England* (Oxford: Oxford University Press, forthcoming 2022).

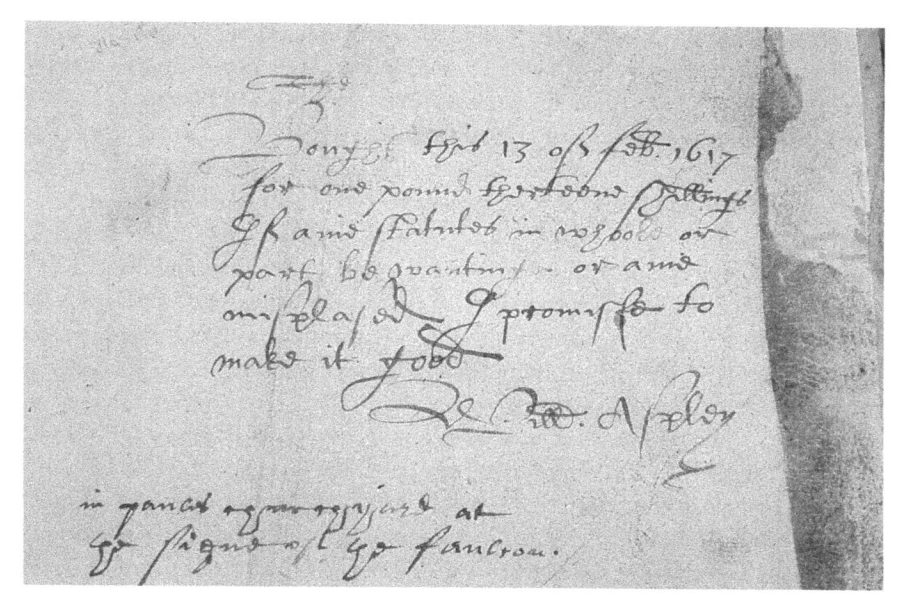

Figure 3.5 A bookseller's guarantee written by William Aspley onto the flyleaf of a copy of *The whole volume of statutes at large* (1587, STC 9305.3). Copy in private ownership; image by kind permission of Mark Byford.

Shakespeare's Folio went on sale, one of its four publishers had for years promoted the religious policies of the state and in particular the work of John Boys? Though Aspley had not published any Shakespeare work for two decades and had established a brand far removed from playbooks, he had nevertheless invested heavily in authorship as a commercial strategy. The publication of the folio *Workes of John Boys* (1622) gave him first-hand experience of repackaging an author's work within a new folio collection. If we sought a context for Aspley's involvement in the Folio syndicate, we might find it in the bibliographical model he established with Boys: the collection of many quartos into a large folio. It is unlikely that Aspley was involved in planning the First Folio from an early stage, but if we want to understand why he joined the syndicate as a shareholder in favour of selling his titles, then his successful investment in authorship as a commercial category, together with his prior relationship with Edward Blount, may have been the deciding factors.

What might be the interpretive consequences of Aspley's decision to join the syndicate? At a simple level, Aspley's involvement brought John Boys into contact with Shakespeare in unexpected ways. After 1623 these authors shared a publisher and their respective folios vied for readerly attention as the leading commodities of the same bookshop. This was one feature of books which, like the Folio, were co-published: they allowed stationers to step outside the parameters of their individual brands and join a new set of temporary colleagues. This mingling of publishing identities may have helped to reshuffle readerly expectations about the relationships between literary forms and genres. Sermons and playbooks tend to be treated separately in modern critical work, but there is evidence of more than one reader treating Boys and Shakespeare as compatible reading matter. The account books of Sir Edward Dering provide us with the first known record of the purchase of a Shakespeare Folio (two copies, in fact); they also record the purchase of 'Dr Boys his expositions on the english' for thirteen shillings shortly before he bought his Shakespeare.[76] Similarly the clergyman James Marsh, who took over from John Donne as the vicar of St Dunstan in the West parish, kept a copy of 'Boyses Autum parte' in his study alongside his Folio of 'Shacespeers playes'.[77] Perhaps one of Aspley's functions within the Folio is to remind us of an 'unfamiliar conception of the literary field', as Adam G. Hooks has put it while thinking through similar equivalencies between Shakespeare's plays and the sermons of the preacher Thomas Playfere.[78] The stationer exposes the disjunct between our reading habits and those of the past, and suggests that Shakespeare's work did not necessarily belong in its own rarefied literary category but could also be found beside a host of unexpected authors like Boys. To push this levelling impulse a little further, we might wonder if we have the question the right way around. Perhaps, in Aspley's bookshop at least, the more appropriate question is: how did the presence of Shakespeare's books influence the reception of Boys?

One consequence of this unexpected affinity between Shakespeare and Boys may have been to promote the institutionalization of Shakespeare as an author. Aspley's ardent promulgation of religio-political orthodoxy invites us to consider Shakespeare's work as a cultural and political force, brought into alignment with the ideologies of established power. If one way in which texts make their way into the safe haven of the literary canon is with the blessing of the socio-political elite, then Aspley's work on behalf of the state represented the interests of this elite to an influential degree.

Shakespeare and Boys: A Tale of Two Folios

Rather than lingering on Aspley's investment in Boys and conformism, I want to finish by exploring a differently meaningful aspect of the bookseller's involvement

---

[76] Dering's manuscript *Booke of Expenses* (Kent County Archives U350/E4) has been transcribed by Laetitia Yeandle: *Sir Edward Dering, 1st bart., of Surrenden Dering and his 'Booke of Expences' 1617-1628*, Kent Archaeological Society Papers, no. 20. Web. http://www.kentarchaeology.ac/authors/020.pdf. For more on Dering and his Shakespeare Folios, see Emma Smith, *Shakespeare's First Folio: Four Centuries of an Iconic Book* (Oxford: Oxford University Press, 2016), pp. 1–24.

[77] Ben Higgins, 'The Library of James Marsh, DD. (1593–?1645), with "Shackspeers playes" and "Donnes Poem"' in *The Library* 22.1 (2021): pp. 33–56.

[78] Hooks, *Selling Shakespeare*, p. 69.

with Shakespeare's Folio. Aspley's pro-establishment attitude invites us to think about Shakespeare within a bookshop that was in some ways a propaganda house for church and state. But the stationer's inclusion in the Folio was above all a throwback to a previous era of his life, when Aspley was one of the many booksellers who had bought one or two manuscript titles of Shakespeare's writing. One of the most compelling features of Aspley's involvement in the Folio is the contrast between Shakespeare's collected volume and the *Workes* of John Boys. These two authors worked in different genres, yet their writings followed a similar bibliographic journey. First published in a variety of single editions, the work of both authors was subsequently gathered and repackaged in a folio collection. For both authors their folio editions formed the basis of their future reputations. Just as Ben Jonson described Shakespeare in the preliminary pages of the Folio, as a 'Moniment, without a tombe' who was 'alive still, while thy Booke doth live', so Boys's own *Workes* was described soon after its publication as 'a monument of his fame, which Time cannot deface'.[79]

Yet the creation of these two 'monumental' books was underpinned by very different structures of literary ownership. While Aspley enjoyed unusual control over the writings of John Boys, Shakespeare's Folio was formed from a bibliographically amorphous and disaggregated array of texts that were published without any thought to their being gathered at some possible future moment for an authorial collection. That the manuscripts of John Boys were centralized within one bookshop brings into sharp relief the dispersal of Shakespeare's literary estate and I want to finish by arguing that these different textual scenarios had profound consequences for the collected works of these two authors.

We might start with the contents of the books. For Aspley, the creation of John Boys's *Workes* was a simple matter of reprinting copy that he already owned. Nothing that had been published was omitted; nothing relied upon a relationship with another book-trade figure.[80] By contrast, the content of Shakespeare's Folio was contingent upon some frantic attempts to dash around the various stationers involved and negotiate for the necessary texts. The Folio consortium—probably primarily Edward Blount and the Jaggards—were forced to reach terms with many minor Shakespeareans. As discussed in the introduction, their efforts did not always work: the 'cash-strapped' publisher Matthew Law held on to his valuable history plays for an awkwardly long time, tangling their printing in the Folio.[81] Tracking down reliable manuscript copy for *Twelfth Night*, *The Winter's*

---

[79] Ben Jonson, 'To the memory of my beloved, the Author Mr. William Shakespeare' in Shakespeare, *Comedies, Histories, & Tragedies* (1623, STC 22273), sig. πA4r; R. P., 'A Briefe View of the life, and vertues of the Authour' in John Boys, *Remaines*, sig. A3r–v.

[80] Aspley did register a Latin manuscript of Boys's work in 1615 (Arber III.572; SCA, *Register C*, fol. 263v), but it was never published. The stationers Felix Kingston and William Welby registered a Boys title in 1611 (Arber III.457; SCA, *Register C*, fol. 207r), but Aspley bought Kingston out in 1612 (Arber III.489; SCA, *Register C*, fol. 222r) and Welby looks to have died in 1618.

[81] Hooks, *Selling Shakespeare*, p. 99.

Tale, and *Henry VIII* also caused problems, and *Timon of Athens* may only have been included as a last-minute substitute when negotiations for *Troilus and Cressida* broke down.[82]

We know little about how these negotiations took place, but similar projects provide a sense of what may have been at stake as the Folio syndicate went from bookshop to bookshop hunting Shakespeare titles. Perhaps it was with wry recognition that both Aspley and John Smethwick sat in a meeting of the stationers' court in 1634 to hear the printer Robert Young complain that another stationer 'had begun to imprint his part of Mr Hieron'.[83] The book at stake here was a folio collection of the writings of another popular deceased author, the preacher Samuel Hieron (d. 1617). The resulting edition was published as *The workes of Mr. Sam. Hieron* (1634) after the individual titles which had been 'dispersed in the world' were gathered 'into one whole and entire Volume' by another Jaggard-like figure (in that he was also both a printer and a publishing bookseller) named William Stansby, who hoped that the book would form a 'monument of so worthy' an author.[84] Despite having tracked down several of the shareholders, Stansby had neglected to deal with Young before starting to print. When Young caught wind of the venture, he summoned Stansby 'vnto the Co^{rt}. & Complay[ned]', creating turbulence for Stansby's printing schedule in ways that were probably similar to the disruption caused by the bookseller Henry Walley when he learned that the first few pages of *Troilus and Cressida* had been printed as part of the First Folio without his permission.[85]

The records do not show how Stansby and Young resolved their dispute, but a similar wrangle in 1614 does show us how the Stationers' Company dealt with the same kind of argument over the printing of another theological folio collection. This time, the case concerned the works of the clergyman Joseph Hall. The bookseller Arthur Johnson was ordered to deliver twenty copies of 'halles workes whole' to the stationer Laurence Lisle for printing 'wthout consent of the said Lile' some of Hall's work to which Lisle owned the copy.[86] Twenty copies of a large book was a stiff financial penalty which for the Shakespeare syndicate would have equated to around ten pounds at wholesale prices, or between fifteen and twenty

---

[82] Hinman, *Printing and Proof-Reading*, vol. 2, pp. 521, 523. See also Emma Smith, *The Making of Shakespeare's First Folio* (Oxford: Bodleian Library Publishing, 2015), pp. 140–3; Blayney, 'First Folio' pp. 21–4. For a summary of issues facing the Folio syndicate in their making of the volume see Rasmussen 'Publishing the First Folio', pp. 23–8.

[83] William A. Jackson ed., *Records of the Court of the Stationers' Company 1602 to 1640* (London: The Bibliographical Society, 1957), p. 258.

[84] W. S., 'To the Right Reverend Father in God, John, Lord Bishop of Chester' in Samuel Hieron, *The workes of Mr. Sam. Hieron* (1634, STC 13384.7), sig. ¶3r–v.

[85] Jackson ed., *Records of the Court*, p. 258.

[86] Jackson ed., *Records of the Court*, p. 68. See also p. 62, for an entry of 11 October 1613, when William Welby was ordered to give another stationer finished copies of *The workes* of the clergyman Richard Greenham (1612, STC 12318) for 'having printed among Grehames workes a part of a coppie heretofore entered'.

pounds at retail (as much as £5,000 in today's money).[87] The sense we get from these examples is that booksellers guarded the texts they owned and were ready to enforce their rights. It was with this kind of censure in mind that Blount and the Jaggards assembled their volume. And in the case of Hall's folio, there may have been other consequences to Arthur Johnson's infraction. The edition was eventually finished in 1615 and it survives in two states. In one of these states Lisle's name was added to the imprint on the engraved frontispiece, suggesting that, regardless of his twenty copies, Lisle may have used whatever leverage the dispute gave him to become a named publisher of the book. Perhaps it was with this earlier experience in mind that Johnson negotiated the price for his title to *The Merry Wives of Windsor* in the early 1620s.

Most prominently, the Folio contains none of Shakespeare's poetry. This may have been a conscious decision. After all, the Folio promotes Shakespeare's connections to performance and the theatre, and Isaac Jaggard's initial Frankfurt notice (discussed in chapter one) advertised a book of 'Playes' collected 'all in one volume'. But if the syndicate was unable to secure the poetry then it may not have had a choice about which version of Shakespeare their book would present; it has been suggested that Shakespeare's popular narrative poems, *Venus and Adonis* and *The Rape of Lucrece*, were too 'difficult and expensive' for the syndicate to acquire.[88] The version of Shakespeare 'monumentalized' by the Folio was contingent in all kinds of ways upon the many figures who owned some part of the Shakespeare literary estate.

There were other consequences to the different models of literary ownership at stake in these two folios. Most of Boys's earlier quarto editions have a bibliographical coherency that could only be achieved with one publisher in charge. Aspley hired three different printers to work on various Boys titles over nine years, and yet the title page of each quarto offers a uniform *mise-en-page*: a formulaic title, a clear authorial attribution, a scriptural quote, and a woodblock above the imprint (Figures 3.6 and 3.7). Within each book, the text flows consistently, printed with the same number of lines on each page in an identical pica typeface. These features grant the books a sense of aesthetic consistency and presented the texts as a uniform series organized by their authorship.

As well styling the books as a series to readers, the bibliographical coherency of the Boys quartos may also have influenced their author's writing style, in that Boys adopted equivalent serial strategies in his compositional habits. Scattered among the printed marginal notes are many that direct a reader back to earlier printed editions of Boys's writing. These notes sometimes supply specific page

---

[87] Joseph Hall, *A recollection of such treatises as have bene heretofore severally published*...(1615, STC 12706 and 12706a). Historical calculation derived from the Bank of England's inflation calculator: https://www.bankofengland.co.uk/monetary-policy/inflation/inflation-calculator.

[88] Colin Burrow ed., *Complete Sonnets and Poems*, p. 8. See also Patrick Cheney, *Shakespeare, National Poet-Playwright* (Cambridge: Cambridge University Press, 2004), pp. 67–73.

AN EXPOSITION

OF THE DOMINICAL EPISTLES AND GOSPELS,

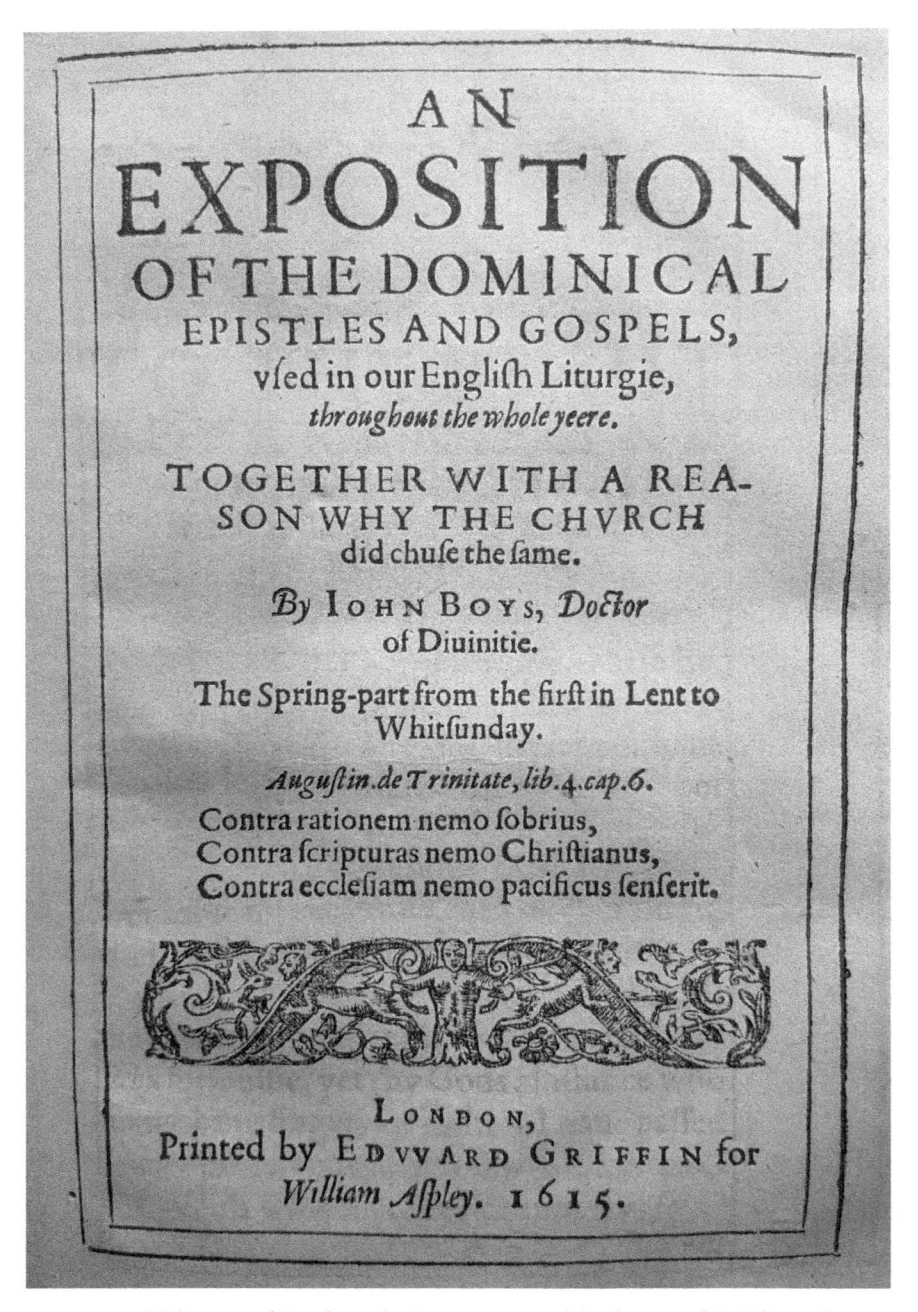

vſed in our Engliſh Liturgie,

throughout the whole yeere.

TOGETHER WITH A REA-SON WHY THE CHVRCH

did chuſe the ſame.

By IOHN BOYS, *Doctor* of Diuinitie.

The Spring-part from the firſt in Lent to Whitſunday.

Auguſtin. de Trinitate, lib. 4. cap. 6.

Contra rationem nemo ſobrius,
Contra ſcripturas nemo Chriſtianus,
Contra eccleſiam nemo pacificus ſenſerit.

LONDON,
Printed by EDVVARD GRIFFIN for *William Aſpley.* 1615.

Figure 3.6 Title page of Boys's work, *An exposition of the dominical Epistles and Gospels...the Spring-part* (1615, STC 3459.7), sig. A1r, printed by Edward Griffin. Credit: Bodleian Libraries, University of Oxford, Antiq.e.E.1615.2 (2). Used under Creative Commons licence CC-BY-NC 4.0.

AN EXPOSITION

OF THE FESTIVALL EPISTLES AND GOS-
pels, vsed in our English *Liturgie.*

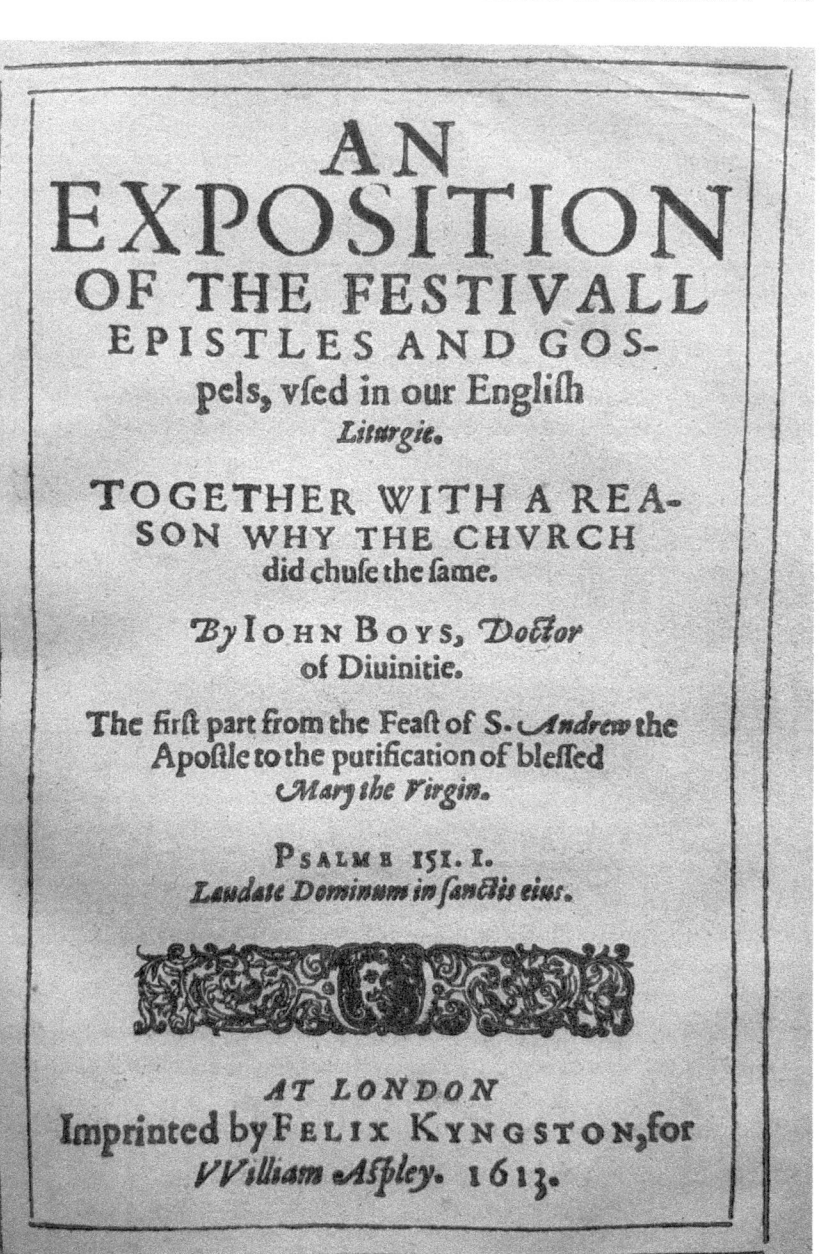

TOGETHER WITH A REA-SON WHY THE CHVRCH
did chuse the same.

By IOHN BOYS, *Doctor* of Diuinitie.

The first part from the Feast of S. *Andrew* the Apostle to the purification of blessed *Mary the Virgin.*

PSALME 151. 1.
Laudate Dominum in sanctis eius.

AT LONDON
Imprinted by FELIX KYNGSTON, for *VVilliam Aspley.* 1613.

Figure 3.7 Title page of an earlier Boys work: *An exposition of the festivall Epistles and Gospels…the first part* (1613, STC 3462), sig. A1r. This title page was printed by Felix Kingston but follows the Boys house style. Credit: Bodleian Libraries, University of Oxford, Vet. A2 e.473 (6). Used under Creative Commons licence CC-BY-NC 4.0.

numbers, suggesting that Boys wrote with copies of his own printed titles at his elbow. In his *Exposition of the proper Psalmes...* (1617), for example, a note on Ascension Day prayers invites a reader to 'See notes upon this in the former part, pag. 38: 39. 40.'[89] The note directs readers to a separate title that was published the previous year. In other words, Boys's sense of his own authorial identity looks to have been forged through a reciprocal relationship with his own printed work. In another edition, it was probably Boys who added a note to an errata which announced that 'I forbeare prefaces and Indices untill the whole be finished.'[90] Here again the note created the impression that a series of books was underway. When an index did eventually appear in 1615, it covered all of Boys's previous editions, using notation to direct readers to the other titles: 'In this Table,' the index explains, '(l) is placed for the notes upon our Liturgie: (w.) for the Winter part of the Postill: (sp.) for the Spring', and so on.[91] We might think this serial mode of publication was just a corollary of Boys's continued interest in the Book of Common Prayer, rather than a bibliographical innovation, but not all his titles fit within that larger project. Some, like his *Exposition of the last psalme* (1615), were simply standalone editions of successful sermons, but Aspley's marketing of this sermon pressed it into conformity with the rest of the series, marketing it under the same bibliographical formula that both created and relied upon the authorship of John Boys.

For Aspley, there were clear commercial benefits to this model of publishing an author's work. The uniform appeal of each of the Boys quartos generates a sense in which each text pulls gently towards the others and towards a larger sense of belonging.[92] By reminding the reader that it is only one 'part' of the whole ('*the first part*'; '*the summer-part*'; '*the winter part*', etc.), each new Boys book stimulated readerly interest in completion, and acted as a little envoy for, and fresh advertisement of, both old and future stock. The books offer a consolidated bibliographic persona which makes Boys himself the product just as much as his writing.

In contrast to the order and coherency of Boys's books, the early editions of Shakespeare's work which appeared before the Folio look cluttered and various. Again, the muddled nature of these early Shakespeare editions is a result of the involvement of so many different stationers, each of whom envisaged dramatic or

---

[89] John Boys, *An exposition of the proper Psalmes...the second part* (1617, STC 3467), sig. F4r. There are similar references within the main text itself (rather than appearing as printed marginal references) where Boys breaks off his exposition to reference a section of an earlier title. For one example from another edition see: *An exposition of the dominical Epistles and Gospels...the summer-part* (1611, STC 3460), sig. E4r.

[90] John Boys, *An exposition of...the winter part* (1610, STC 3458), sig. 2Q3v.

[91] John Boys, *An exposition of the last psalme* (1615, STC 3465.4), sig. C1r.

[92] The bookseller Humphrey Moseley did something similar with his serial publication of octavo playbooks in the 1650s: Paulina Kewes, '"Give Me the Sociable Pocket-books...": Humphrey Moseley's Serial Publication of Octavo Play Collections' in *Publishing History* 38 (1995): pp. 5–21.

literary authorship in different ways, and turned to their own networks of paper merchants, printers, and compositors to realize those ideas. For example, the format of Shakespeare's early books—either quarto or octavo—varies across the form of writing, but not uniformly. While most of the playbooks are in quarto, one (the first edition of *3 Henry VI* (1595)) is an octavo; while much of the poetry was printed in octavo, the *Sonnets* arrived in quarto. The first two editions of *Venus and Adonis* and the first edition of *Lucrece* were printed in quarto, but both then evolved into octavo for most of the seventeenth century, except for three subsequent editions of *Venus* that were printed in sextodecimo. Early modern libraries typically relied on the format of a book as an important guide to where that book should be stored, meaning that the different formats of Shakespeare's titles probably sent them to different physical spaces within any collections in which they were housed. Their title pages contain common elements but few consistent bibliographical conventions. As a group, these title pages occasionally include an authorial attribution in some form, or (for the plays) a statement of recent performance; they feature different stationers and numerous woodblocks; they sometimes highlight details of plot, genre, or character. Though title pages could remain relatively stable if a play was reprinted, it was also possible for any and all of these identifying markers to change between editions, particularly so if the ownership of the right to copy had changed hands. Within the text itself some early Shakespeare editions contain prologues, epilogues, or a list of 'The Actors Names'; some contain an address to the reader from a stationer, an 'argument' of the poem, or, for just two titles, an epistle from Shakespeare.[93] Ornaments erratically launch the text or conclude it; conventions change around features like verse and prose, or stage directions; an edition of *Othello* (1622) made the lonely choice to introduce pagination.

The mobility and variety of these various elements—the bibliographic noise that surrounds these books when looked at in aggregate—reflects the many different agents who conceived of Shakespeare in print. These stationers imagined Shakespeare's work in different ways, so that their books offer contradictory versions of what a 'Shakespeare book' actually is. For the booksellers Richard Bonian and Henry Walley, for example, the non-theatrical status of their edition of *Troilus and Cressida* (1609) was a particular selling point: this was a play, their preface tells us in one issue of the edition, that was 'never stal'd with the Stage, never clapper-clawd with the palmes of the vulger'.[94] Meanwhile, the alternative issue of the same edition markets the play as having been '*acted by the Kings Majesties servants at the Globe*', just as the printer-bookseller John Danter marketed his

---

[93] A list of actors' names was added to Q3 of *The most excellent historie of the merchant of Venice* (1637, STC 22298), sig. A1v. For the bibliographic and paratextual make-up of Shakespeare's books, see Erne, *Book Trade*, pp. 90–129.

[94] 'A never writer, to an ever reader. Newes.' in William Shakespeare, *The famous historie of Troylus and Cresseid* (1609, STC 22332), sig. ¶2r.

edition of *Romeo and Juliet* (1597) with a title page that claimed the play had been 'often (with great applause) plaid publiquely'.[95] Equally, Nicholas Ling and John Trundle could stress that their edition of *Hamlet* (1603) was acted 'in the two Universities of Cambridge and Oxford'.[96] Some of these inflections changed over time as a conception of what it meant to market Shakespeare gradually coalesced into being and stationers realized the value and the contours of the playwright's bibliographic identity. After 1598, for example, it became increasingly common (though not uniform) to add Shakespeare's name to a title page. This kind of diachronic reimagining of an authorial identity—one that was in close dialogue with customer behaviour as well as with the actions of other members of the book trade—was never present in the John Boys quartos, where the author's unitary presentation seems to have arrived in Aspley's mind fully formed in ways that gave the preacher a clear and consistent identity, but which also meant this identity was unable to adapt.

If we step back, the sense created by the early Shakespeare editions published before the Folio is of the playwright's presence being constructed by many hands in ways that obscure any central authorial identity. In place of the more coherent, if staid, presence of John Boys, we find a dispersal that spreads the constitution of Shakespearean authorship over increasingly various terrain. Our perception of Shakespeare's biography has been powerfully shaped by, and imagined through, this absence of any central or authorial control over the printed forms of his own work—even if that post-Romantic narrative has recently been challenged by Lukas Erne.[97] Yet it is hard to know whether authorial absence led to this dynamic marketplace of Shakespearean print, or whether the sheer number of stationers involved in publishing and printing the texts of Shakespeare's work frustrated any attempt to regulate the appearance of his texts.

If the two different authorial identities explored here seem well suited to their respective interests—while Boys hacked away through sections of the Book of Common Prayer, applying the same methods towards the same aims, Shakespeare's work ranged over poetry and drama, drew on a range of sources and genres, was peopled with diverse characters and set in various eras and places—then they also reflect the different circumstances of the composition of these texts. Shakespeare's plays emerged from the theatre, which seems a fundamentally more porous textual environment than the closeted study of John Boys, whose writing desk in his private library is depicted in his tomb in Canterbury Cathedral. Boys is also

---

[95] William Shakespeare, *The famous historie of Troylus and Cresseid* (1609, STC 22331), A1r; *An excellent conceited tragedie of Romeo and Juliet* (1597, STC 22322), sig. A2r.
[96] William Shakespeare, *The tragicall historie of Hamlet Prince of Denmarke* (1603, STC 22275), sig. A2r.
[97] Lukas Erne, *Shakespeare as Literary Dramatist*, 2nd edn (Cambridge: Cambridge University Press, 2013). See also Erne's *Shakespeare and the Book Trade* (Cambridge: Cambridge University Press, 2013).

A MINOR SHAKESPEAREAN: WILLIAM ASPLEY AT THE PARROT 159

Figure 3.8 John Boys in his writing study, as depicted on the title page of his *Workes* (1630, STC 3453). The Latin phrase 'Scriba doctus in regno coelorum' ('*a scribe instructed in the kingdom of heaven*') is from the book of Matthew in the Vulgate Bible. Credit: Bodleian Libraries, University of Oxford, Vet. A2 d.2. Used under Creative Commons licence CC-BY-NC 4.0.

shown mid-composition on the engraved title page to his printed *Workes* (Figure 3.8). In this image, the preacher sits alone at his desk, quill in hand, with a row of little quartos (his own?) on a shelf above him. The image is likely generic, rather than a genuine attempt to capture Boys at work, but on the title page it is positioned opposite a second vignette of the preacher reading in a study. Ranged about him as he reads are shelves that contain a mass of books of various formats and rolled-up prints, as well as signs of a more comfortable environment: a cloth over the table, a decorated floor. Against this image of reading as repose, the act of literary composition is depicted within a confined, strikingly bare space dominated by writing tools. The only ornament is a clock on the wall, granting a sense of urgency to his writerly mission. If this resembles in any way the space within which Boys wrote, then it affords a very different sense of what writing involved from that which is found in the *Thomas More* manuscript, our sole direct source of Shakespearean composition, which features the vibrantly collaborative handwriting of six different authors.[98] That sense of creative collaboration continued after the plays were written: in performance the plays relied upon a company of actors who contributed their own improvisations and personalities. The plurality of this creative endeavour seems materially embodied in the diversity of its printed forms.

There are other ways in which the different models of ownership behind Boys and Shakespeare influenced their authorial reception. The uniformity of the Boys quartos helped Aspley to sell many of Boys's titles as sammelband volumes rather than individual quartos.[99] Most Boys quartos that survive in their early bindings are found in volumes that gather up to ten of his titles.[100] These compendiums were sometimes offered for sale pre-bound by stationers. The London bookseller John Piper sent a copy of 'Boyse whole bound' to the Oxford bookseller Thomas Huggins in 1621 at the price of twelve shillings and eight pence.[101] Early prices on the first title pages of some Boys volumes also suggest they were sold in ready-prepared form: four shillings on a volume now in the Folger Library that houses six Boys titles; four shillings and sixpence on a volume in Cambridge featuring four titles; five shillings on a volume in the Parker Library of Corpus Christi College that contains five titles; eight shillings on a single edition of Boys's first book, removed from its original context and now in a buckram binding in the Huntington Library.[102] At the same time, the fact that readers must also have been able to assemble their own combinations, and yet seem overwhelmingly to have done so in ways that did not look beyond Boys's authorship, is a further tribute to Aspley's success in coding Boys's written work as a commercial package. That an individual edition by Boys, catalogued for an inventory in 1614, was described as 'A piece of Boys', is further acknowledgement that a single Boys book was only a fragment of a larger corpus.[103]

The main difference between the sale of Boys's early quarto editions and those of Shakespeare, then, is the shaping influence of authorship as a commercial category. And this has implications for how Shakespeare and Boys were read. The

---

[98] Boys's autograph manuscripts of the texts that Aspley printed are now in the Parker Library of Corpus Christi College, Cambridge: *John Boys Postils*, MS 215 and 216.

[99] Throughout this book I follow the Folger Shakespeare Library and the Rare Books and Manuscripts Section of the American Library Association in opting for the anglicized 'sammelband' over the German *Sammelband* and plural *Sammelbände*: https://folgerpedia.folger.edu/Sammelbands.

[100] The first Boys title to be published was necessarily sold individually, of course, and there are surviving examples of this title in its own single early binding (Folger Library STC 3455; British Library 1219. D. 50). But in contrast to the relative scarcity of individual John Boys books, the university and college libraries of Oxford and Cambridge collectively contain nineteen Boys-only sammelband volumes which house a variety of combinations of his titles.

[101] *John Pyper to Thomas Huggins, 3 January 1621*, Huntington Library 28116. See also Aspley's entry in William Jaggard's *Catalogue of such English bookes* in which Aspley lists a collection of Boys's work covering the liturgy 'throughout the whol yeare' (1618, STC 14341), sig. A2r.

[102] These copies are respectively Folger Library STC 3456.3; Cambridge University Library Syn. 7. 61. 39; Corpus Christi College, Cambridge, Parker Library A.11.9; Huntington Library 230343.

[103] *Probate Inventory of Edward Homer, d. 1614*: PLRE, record no: 160.15.

1610 booklists of Sir John Harington, for example, record his ownership of plenty of Shakespeare quartos distributed among various volumes in his playbook collection. These include one volume that contains seven plays we could organize under a loose heading of Shakespearean authorship (five certainly; two questionably). The volume as a whole, though, contains thirteen plays which also include titles by Ben Jonson, George Chapman, and John Marston, and so genre, rather than authorship, is the key organizing feature of this collection. The same basic idea that Shakespeare quartos belonged shuffled in among the work of other dramatists is also found in Henry Oxinden's list of his play collection drawn up in his 1647 commonplace book.[104] It seems clear that certain literary authors—the prose writer Robert Greene was one—had an appeal that shaped customer habits ('Can'st helpe mee to all *Greenes* Bookes in one Volume?' says the gentleman reader to the apprentice bookseller in a 1602 dialogue, 'But I will have them every one, not any wanting.'),[105] but the evidence of Harington and Oxinden supports Roger Chartier and Peter Stallybrass's point that titles of early modern drama tended to be bound in miscellanies rather than as authorial collections.[106]

The situation looks similar for Shakespeare's poetry. The interventions of generations of collectors and curators since the eighteenth century make it particularly difficult to assemble a clear picture of the context in which the early editions of Shakespeare's work were read (here the relative canonicity of Boys and Shakespeare has shaped the evidence of their reception. Our lack of literary interest in Boys has protected him from a modernizing drive towards order found in the treatment of Shakespeare's books, meaning that Boys books tend to survive as time capsules from the early seventeenth century. Our ambivalence towards Boys in one field—literary studies—makes him particularly valuable to another—the history of reading). But from what we can tell, early readers readily bought single editions of Shakespeare's poems and bound them with the work of other authors.[107] The habit of early modern readers of situating their Shakespeare in

---

[104] W. W. Greg, *A Bibliography of the English Printed Drama to the Restoration*, 4 vols (London: The Bibliographical Society, 1939–59), vol. 3, pp. 1306–16.

[105] 'A Conference betweene a Gentleman and a Prentice' in Samuel Rowlands, *Tis merrie when gossips meete* (1602, STC 21409), sig. A3r.

[106] Roger Chartier and Peter Stallybrass, 'Reading and Authorship: The Circulation of Shakespeare 1590-1619' in Andrew Murphy ed., *A Concise Companion to Shakespeare and the Text* (Chichester: Wiley-Blackwell, 2010), pp. 35–56, at pp. 41–2. For a possible counter-example from the Countess of Bridgewater's 1627 library catalogue of a quarto volume of 'Diuers Playes by Shakespeare 1602' see Heidi Brayman Hackel, *Reading Material in Early Modern England: Print, Gender, and Literacy* (Cambridge: Cambridge University Press, 2005), p. 266. For a wide-ranging survey of the ways in which early editions of Shakespeare were read see Jean-Christophe Mayer, *Shakespeare's Early Readers: A Cultural History from 1590 to 1800* (Cambridge: Cambridge University Press, 2018).

[107] The *Shakespeare Census* tells us, for example, that there are fifty-five surviving copies of *The Rape of Lucrece* from the early modern period (that is, all editions printed before 1700). Of these, just six survive in sammelband volumes from the seventeenth century, and all of these volumes feature work by at least one other author. The seventeenth-century *Lucrece* sammelbands are Shakespeare Census (SC) numbers 1155, 1156, 1165, 1173, 1175, and 1178. One further copy of *Lucrece* now in the Bodleian Library (shelfmark Arch. Gg. 4; SC 1157) is bound only with a copy of *Venus and Adonis*, and

new bibliographic contexts generated fresh interpretive connections between titles that scholars have recently begun to recover, challenging us to think about the attachments formed between texts in physical proximity.[108] The obvious exception here is the collection of Jaggard Quartos of 1619, which clearly demonstrates an interest in using Shakespeare's name to market a group of titles and which seems also to have been sold in ready-bound form. Even here, though, the most recent work (discussed in chapter two) has shown this version of 'Shakespeare' was not quite as Shakespearean as we have thought: in addition to the two apocryphal plays (*A Yorkshire Tragedy* and *Sir John Oldcastle*), the collection sometimes also included Thomas Heywood's play *A Woman Killed with Kindness*.[109] Tara Lyons has similarly argued that Shakespeare's authorship was just 'one of many possible organisational frameworks' at stake in the 1619 collection, alongside ideas of historicity and seriality.[110] In general, then, the more protean textual genealogy of Shakespeare was open to the buying habits and organizational interests of individual readers, which in turn created units of reading that were inherently porous and intertextual. By contrast, it is unusual to find a Boys volume that features the work of any other author. His authorial personality seems to have been somehow sealed off from other textual traffic, less open to the material appropriations and idiosyncrasies that characterized early modern reading.

What might have been the consequences of this Boys-only experience for the readers who acquired a volume? There are several rich examples of this, such as the volume owned by Leonard Staveley, a vicar and poet in Suffolk who died in 1620. Staveley, who looks to have acquired his Boys sammelband in late 1617 and who used a mirrored hand to write his name across the first title page (perhaps a sign that he was left-handed), marked up passages to use in his own sermons. He tracked across five separate Boys editions published between 1610 and 1612, and in around fifty places added the date at which he gave the resultant sermon, transforming his Boys volume into a diary of both his reading and his preaching, and enabling us to follow his continuous progress through the titles between 1617 and

---

so it looks like an authorial sammelband, albeit one of the smallest kind. But the current binding looks like the work of Edmond Malone, who was given both titles by Richard Farmer. Malone certainly rebacked the volume and probably also added the marbled endpapers and the various other paper scraps and repairs. Whether these two titles were originally bound together is difficult to say. See the *Shakespeare Census*, edited by Adam G. Hooks and Zachary Lesser. Created 2018. Accessed 21 May 2020. http://www.shakespearecensus.org.

[108] On the interpretive potential of sammelband volumes see Jeffrey Todd Knight, *Bound to Read: Compilations, Collections, and the Making of Renaissance Literature* (Philadelphia, PA: University of Pennsylvania Press, 2013). Other relevant work includes Alexandra Gillespie, *Print Culture and the Medieval Author: Chaucer, Lydgate, and their Books 1473-1557* (Oxford: Oxford University Press, 2006); Tara L. Lyons, 'Serials, Spinoffs, and Histories: Selling "Shakespeare" in Collection before the Folio' in *Philological Quarterly* 91.2 (2012): pp. 185–220; Higgins, '*Judith* and *Lucrece*'.

[109] Zachary Lesser, *Ghosts, Holes, Rips and Scrapes: Shakespeare in 1619, Bibliography in the Longue Durée* (Philadelphia, PA: University of Pennsylvania Press, 2021).

[110] Tara Lyons, 'Serials, Spinoffs, and Histories', p. 202.

1620.[111] Similar examples can be found in several other Boys volumes, such as that owned by an early reader—perhaps the Oxford poet William Strode—who created manuscript indices that covered all seven titles in his binding.[112] Another Boys sammelband held in the library of Attingham Park, Shropshire, gathers six editions published between 1610 and 1617, and shows that the reader carefully struck out the various printed pagination sequences and instead created a single continuous manuscript run of page numbers.[113] Here the technologies of reading transformed a volume of quarto editions into, in effect, a single collected works.

This kind of serial reading attention, and the prolonged engagement with an authorial voice that such readings might foster, was again partly a product of Aspley's controlled promotion of Boys's authorial brand: the stationer determined the frame within which readers engaged with Boys's work. One more example: in the middle of the seventeenth century, a Welsh vicar named Richard Lloyd, working through his own Boys volume that contained four of the preacher's titles, took offence at Boys's description of alehouse carousing as a 'welsh sermon'. Lloyd neatly underlined the word 'welsh' (Figure 3.9) and added a marginal note which exchanged it for 'Kentish', redirecting the jibe back to the author's own home county (Boys was born in Kent and became a dean of Canterbury Cathedral).[114]

What can we make of this moment of readerly pique? On a simple level the note tells us that this reader knew something of the biography of his author. But the undeniably personal quality of Lloyd's response suggests a powerful link between the printed text he held and his awareness of Boys's identity. This is a particular way of reading: one where the meanings retrieved from the text as the reader's eye travels along the line are informed by their sense of the life behind the words. Perhaps it was a similar impulse that led one reader to treat their copy of Boys's folio *Workes* as a kind of biographical scrapbook, or autograph book, into which the reader pasted examples of the signatures of the preacher and his family.[115] This sense that to hold a Boys book was also in some measure to conjure the

---

[111] I am grateful to Mark Byford, who owns this Boys volume in his private collection, for drawing my attention to Staveley's fascinating reading practices.

[112] Canterbury Cathedral Library W2/N-11-5. Strode, who wrote his name at the start of his index, used blank leaves between the Boys editions to create a running index of his interests. Similar annotations indicating sustained reading activity in Boys sammelband books can be found in Bodleian Library Vet. A2 e.353 and Vet. A2 e.171 (the latter annotated in Welsh); British Library C. 118. BB. 10 (also in Welsh); Folger Library STC 3456.3; and Cambridge University Library Syn. 7. 61. 39.

[113] Library of Attingham Park, Shropshire, shelfmark NT005719.

[114] Bodleian Library shelfmark Vet. A2 e.171 (4). Ownership information in the volume identifies Lloyd as the vicar of Llanynys in Denbighshire. Elsewhere a witness of his ownership to the book is dated 1659.

[115] Bodleian Library shelfmark Vet. A2 d.2, a copy of Boys's *Workes* (1630, STC 3453), into which has been pasted a leaf containing the signatures of John Boys together with those of Dorothy Boys and Anthony Boys. The three may have been siblings (Boys was one of ten children). Despite the clear intention to transform the volume into an autograph book, it is also possible that these signatures belong to a different branch of the sizeable Boys family. It is not clear when they were added, though an auction note on the flyleaf records that they were present in 1858 at least.

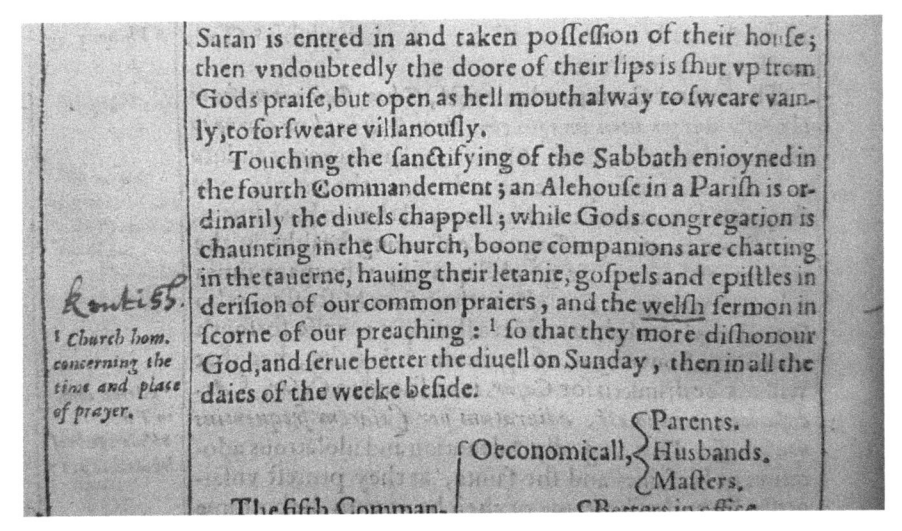

> Satan is entred in and taken poſſeſſion of their houſe; then vndoubtedly the doore of their lips is ſhut vp from Gods praiſe, but open as hell mouth alway to ſweare vainly, to forſweare villanouſly.
> Touching the ſanctifying of the Sabbath enioyned in the fourth Commandement; an Alehouſe in a Pariſh is ordinarily the diuels chappell; while Gods congregation is chaunting in the Church, boone companions are chatting in the tauerne, hauing their letanie, goſpels and epiſtles in deriſion of our common praiers, and the welſh ſermon in ſcorne of our preaching : [1] ſo that they more diſhonour God, and ſerue better the diuell on Sunday, then in all the daies of the weeke beſide.
>
> [marginalia: *Church hom. concerning the time and place of prayer.*]

Figure 3.9 Richard Lloyd's note on his copy of John Boys, *The autumne part from the twelfth Sundy after Trinitie* (1613, STC 3460.6), sig. L3v. Image: Bodleian Libraries, University of Oxford, Vet. A2 e.171 (4). Used under Creative Commons licence CC-BY-NC 4.0.

author's presence, his 'corpus' in both a literary and physical sense, was prompted into being at least partly by Aspley's grip on the Boys estate.

Aspley no doubt enjoyed the control he had over the appearance of Boys's writing in print, and his will, quoted at the start of this chapter, suggests the commercial benefits of his monopoly. Yet there were other advantages to the dispersed model of ownership represented by Shakespeare's plays. If readerships grew partly around the social currency of the names of booksellers and writers, then a co-published book like Shakespeare's Folio combined readerships which might not otherwise have crossed paths. The Folio brought together the readerships established by the four publishing businesses who were directly involved with the book's production, but it might also appeal to anyone interested in Shakespeare's name as it had featured on an edition published by any other of those minor Shakespearean publishers listed by the tables earlier in this chapter. The edition of *Lucrece*, for example, published in 1624 by Roger Jackson—a stationer with no history of collaboration with any of the Folio publishers—and which advertised on its title page that it was 'By Mr William Shakespeare', might helpfully stimulate readerly interest in the Folio. By contrast, a book which, like the folio *Workes* of John Boys, had been controlled by one stationer—not only in the publication of the collection but also in all the prior quarto editions which the collection gathered—presumably had to work harder to reach fresh social and cultural networks. If the variety and contingency of the early single editions of Shakespeare's work extended their bibliographic reach, this seems likely to have translated into an equivalent variety of readerly interest in the Folio. We could think about this reach in terms of simple topography: as is discussed in more detail in the following chapter, Shakespeare's books were advertised for wholesale from bookshops all over London, from Cornhill in the east to Westminster and the Strand in the west. Aspley, on the other hand, remained in his bookshop at the Sign of the Parrot on the north side of Paul's Churchyard from 1608 till his death in 1640. The Boys books would have been sold in other retail bookshops, too, of course, but their wholesale distribution point was always Aspley's bookshop, suggesting that Boys was at some level confined to Aspley's network of professional relationships.

The two respective models of publication and literary ownership described here are extremes in the early modern English book trade. Shakespeare's work was highly prized at the start of the seventeenth century, as has recently been shown, and thus ownership of his manuscripts was probably unusually contested; Boys and Aspley were no less unusual for the exclusivity of their relationship and the strength of their collaboration.[116] Perhaps the single most important consequence of these differences was that Aspley's investment in and control over the writings of John Boys ensured that the author's texts were never in competition with one another. As described above, each Boys title was designed and marketed towards a shared goal of being sold by William Aspley. The ways in which each title was framed reflected that goal. By contrast, the printed editions of Shakespeare's work competed with and jousted against one another for a reader's attention and money. The books enacted a proxy war for the commercial competition between the owners of those manuscript titles.

The fact that Shakespeare's work was published within a vibrant and competitive literary field had profound consequences for the future of his texts. For one thing, in their eagerness to be sold, the editions of Shakespeare's work invoked a language of revision, augmentation, and correction. The texts emerged into the world packaged in competitive rhetoric that served the dual function of making a commercial appeal while also encouraging certain ways of thinking about textual status. One play is described as 'Newly corrected by *W. Shake-speare*'; another is 'enlarged to almost as much againe as it was, according to the true and perfect Coppie'; another has 'new additions of the Parliament scaene' or has been 'plaid before the Kings Maiesty at Whitehall'.[117] Part of the appeal of the *Sonnets* is that they were 'Never before Imprinted', as their title page tells us (here, rather than any one particular text, it is the corpus of Shakespeare's writing which is being

---

[116] The popularity of Shakespeare's work is charted by Lukas Erne, *Book Trade*, pp. 25–55.
[117] William Shakespeare, *The history of Henrie the Fourth* (1599, STC 22281); *The tragicall historie of Hamlet, Prince of Denmarke* (1604, STC 22276); *The tragedie of King Richard the Second* (1608, STC 22311); *M. William Shake-speare, his true chronicle history of the life and death of King Lear* (1608 [i.e. 1619], STC 22293).

augmented).[118] The eager language of Shakespeare's title pages established a model of literary authority that is entirely absent from the work of an author like Boys, whose books never had to fight with one another for attention and so remained outside the discourses of novelty and amplification that characterize so much of Shakespeare's early work in print. We might assume that such title-page marketing language was commonplace, but as Alan B. Farmer has shown, there was something 'truly unusual' about the extent to which Shakespeare's books featured these editorial pledges.[119] Part of what generated this language was the sheer number of stationers who were involved in Shakespearean production. The collective impression of Shakespeare's title pages is of his books thickening as they move through time, accreting revisions and additions as stationers competed with one another to offer the latest and most vendible Shakespearean product. It was of course this sense of amplification that enabled the Folio to assert its own powerful and corrective claim to clear away the clutter and return to the 'True Originall Copies'. There could be no equivalent sense of these frictional contestations and positionings among the quarto editions of John Boys.

The model of literary authority established for Shakespeare's writing in its earliest stages was therefore enabled by the very lack of centralized control over his manuscripts that led to minor Shakespearean stationers like William Aspley owning just one or two plays alongside their other interests. The climate of interest created by a competitive market presumably also drove some stationers to seek out more Shakespeare, or to try their luck at attributing a text to him. To an extent, then, book-trade competition of this kind underpins the shady penumbra of works at the edge of the accepted canon of Shakespeare's writing. The two authors also end up with quite different evidence for their popularity: in contrast to the steady release of new Boys books by William Aspley, who had only to glance at his stock pile to judge when the time was right for a new edition, the many agents involved in judging the market for a fresh Shakespeare book leave us with a more haphazard and variable account of supply and demand.

We need to think more about the isolated, glancing book-trade figures who participated in the construction of Shakespeare's corpus. Our dismissal of Aspley and Smethwick, among others, is probably a symptom of our reluctance to conceive of Shakespeare as someone who was unimportant, as a footnote to a career that was profitably focused elsewhere. Yet what these figures help us to see is the ways in which the dispersal of Shakespeare's manuscripts underpinned the creation of the author's bibliographic character, which in turn shapes our own

---

[118] William Shakespeare, *Shake-speares sonnets* (1609, STC 22353).
[119] Alan B. Farmer, 'Shakespeare as Leading Playwright in Print, 1598–1608/9' in Margaret Jane Kidnie and Sonia Massai eds, *Shakespeare and Textual Studies* (Cambridge: Cambridge University Press, 2015), pp. 87–104, quote at p. 98. See also Sonia Massai, 'Editorial Pledges in Early Modern Dramatic Paratexts' in Helen Smith and Louise Wilson eds, *Renaissance Paratexts* (Cambridge: Cambridge University Press, 2011), pp. 91–106.

engagement with the playwright and his work in unexpected ways. We tend to invoke Shakespeare's aloof attitude towards print as the main reason for the widespread dispersal of his work, but perhaps we could consider the ways in which certain forms of literary production are inherently more porous than others, more disposed to reproduction and circulation in their pre-print life. In contrast to the theatrical environment in which Shakespeare's plays were first created and published, Boys's manuscripts seem to have moved within a closed channel from his study to Aspley's bookshop.[120] These contrasting scenarios mean that, while Boys's folio *Workes* was the product of a relatively narrow publishing agenda, the Shakespeare Folio could be thought of as having coalesced out of a more dispersed popular consciousness. The decision to publish the Folio was made within a climate of cultural interest in Shakespeare's work that had been created by a plurality of agents of the book trade—something that seems inherently more healthy, less vulnerable, than the single cabinet packed full of Boys manuscripts at the Sign of the Parrot.

At the same time, it is worth noting that the two folios met with different success. Though the two books were comparable in length (Boys was 254.5 edition sheets to Shakespeare's 227) and in price (two copies of Boys's folio feature early prices of fourteen shillings; another gives fifteen shillings, matching the price of an unbound Shakespeare Folio), there was a period of time in which Boys seems comfortably to have outsold the playwright.[121] This was not the case at first: the two authors took roughly the same amount of time to reach the point where those involved decided to finance a second edition (eight years for Boys; nine for Shakespeare). However, for Boys, the second edition of his folio sold enough copies to warrant a third edition after eight years, whereas for Shakespeare, it would be a full thirty-one years after the publication of the Second Folio before the stationer Philip Chetwind published the third edition of the *Comedies, Histories, and Tragedies* (1663/4).

Conclusion

When William Aspley died in 1640, the will discussed at the start of this chapter left all of the rights to Boys's titles to two figures that Aspley described as his kinsmen, 'freamen of the Stationers, and booth capable': William Page and Robert

---

[120] Boys's texts were probably originally delivered as sermons but were significantly revised to create a coherent project that defends the liturgy. The result is less a record of sermons preached than a series of linked 'commentaries of quite various lengths', as Quitslund puts it: 'A Second Bible', p. 81.

[121] Prices for Boys folios are found on Bodleian Library shelfmarks Vet. A2 d.25 and Antiq.d.E.1638.5, and Folger Library shelfmark STC 3454 Copy 2 (on which the earlier but legible '15ˢ' has been overwritten for a later sale as '10ˢ'). Of course, without knowing the number of copies printed for each edition, comparing sales of Boys and Shakespeare can only be speculative.

Lunn. Regardless of Aspley's professional esteem, both figures disappeared within a few years without publishing any books by Boys, and it seems neither stationer sold or bequeathed the Boys rights they had inherited. Without a publisher to sponsor his books, interest in the preacher's writings faded, and no further editions of Boys's work were printed in England. The preacher's moment had passed, the arc of his popularity tethered to Aspley's own biography.[122] By contrast, the bibliographic multiplicity of Shakespeare's books is part of their continual life within editorial and textual scholarship. That is to say, a large part of the richness of scholarly debate about the status and meaning of Shakespeare's texts can be traced back to the distribution of his literary property, and to the complicated dynamic of competition and collaboration which underpinned its acquisition. Considered in this way, the same feature of the Boys quartos which gave them such appeal in the early seventeenth century—their designed uniformity and tidy textual stability—renders them relatively unresponsive to questions about their textual status. On one level they are an editor's dream; on another, their consistency and accuracy leaves Boys with the kind of glassily perfect textual record that cannot sustain the kinds of questions, intrigue, and scholarly methods enabled by Shakespeare's work.

The fact that so many stationers like Aspley owned small fragments of the Shakespeare estate makes them individually less compelling than figures such as Edward Blount or Andrew Wise. But as this chapter has shown, in other ways these stationers were no less critical. Aspley's importance is precisely that he was not particularly interested in Shakespeare's writing for most of his career. This freed him to invest heavily in other areas, as we have seen, enabling Shakespeare's work to mingle with a range of publishing identities and textual specialisms. Aspley thus reminds us to lift our gaze up and consider the interpretive potential of groups and networks of booksellers involved in literary production, rather than attending solely to the individual agent.

There are of course many reasons why the folio collections of Shakespeare and Boys have experienced very different trajectories in their reception, and most of them have to do with the content of what these authors wrote rather than the ways in which their books were marketed. But this chapter has uncovered some of the ways in which the content of an author's book—particularly a collected works—was inextricably shaped by the bibliographic forms and publishing practices underpinning its production. Faced with many different versions of Shakespearean identity in print, created by numerous minor Shakespeareans, the

---

[122] Boys was not helped by the arrival of William Laud to the office of Archbishop of Canterbury in 1633: Quitslund 'A Second Bible', p. 99. No more of Boys's books were produced in England after Aspley's death, but some were printed in Germany in the 1680s: *Stern und Kern aller Episteln und Evangelien durchs gantze Jahr* (Brunswick, 1683 and 1685); *Der fünffte Theil Ist eine Erklärung aller gewöhnlichen Fest- und Apostel-Tags-Episteln* (Brunswick, 1683); *Johann Boys SS. Theol. Doct. und Decan. Zu Canterburie* (Brunswick, 1685).

publishers of the First Folio had to decide how to position their own work. One final way to think about the result of their decisions concerns the difference between reproduction and invention. Boys's folio *Workes* was content simply to reproduce its author. After all, if the *Workes* is not quite a facsimile of Boys's prior quarto editions then it does little more than reorganize their page layout. On the other hand, Shakespeare's *Comedies, Histories, & Tragedies* invented its author in ways that continue to shape our reading today.

4
'Under the Diall'
John Smethwick in St Dunstan's Churchyard

John Smethwick's relationship to Shakespeare's Folio seems to be summed up by the presentation of his name in the book's colophon. The variant printed there—'J. Smithweeke'—is found in none other of the hundred or so books published over his lengthy forty-year career. The unusual orthography suggests his absence from the venture, as if to confirm he was not on hand to intervene as the final page of *Cymbeline* came through the press. Elsewhere in the imprints of those books which he published himself, this stationer was most often John 'Smethwicke', though variants of 'Smethicke' and 'Smithicke' occasionally appear. Other than the Folio's colophon, I know of only one place where this spelling of his surname was repeated, in an entry that records a different kind of absence: the brief manuscript notice of his burial, which took place in July 1641, and for which event the churchwarden of St Dunstan in the West, on Fleet Street, charged thirteen shillings and four pence for 'the ground in St Anne's Chapell for M*aster* John Smithweeke'.[1]

That burial took place in the same building in which John Smethwick had been baptized: the medieval church of St Dunstan in the West, which jutted half-in and half-out of Fleet Street, and was wedged in among the various inns of court buildings that still characterize this area of London (Figure 4.1). Smethwick's family had deep roots in this parish. His father, a successful draper named Richard Smethwick, had married his wife Johan in St Dunstan's in 1560 and served several parish offices.[2] The couple christened at least ten children there. John Smethwick and his siblings were probably educated in the grammar school annexed to the church, established by Queen Elizabeth in 1562.[3] The archives of this parish contain the documentary residue of the lives of both the stationer and his father, such

---

[1] *Churchwarden's Accounts of St Dunstan in the West 1628–1644*, LMA P69/DUN2/B/011/MS02968/003, fol. 611v.

[2] *Percival Boyd's Register Roll*, Draper's Company Archives, no shelfmark, unfoliated entry under 'Smethwick'. My thanks to Penny Fussell, archivist of the Draper's Company, for help with this roll. For Richard Smethwick's parish offices: *Wardmote Inquest Book of St Dunstan in the West*: LMA CLC/W/JB/044/MS03018/001, fol. 31r, 33r. Richard died in late 1577 or early 1578; his will, in which he bequeathed to John a property—'white ffriars gate in London', in Fleet Street opposite St Dunstan's—is: TNA PROB 11/60/368.

[3] *Appointment of Governors to Free School of St Dunstan in the West*, LMA P69/DUN2/E/001/MS03793.

Shakespeare's Syndicate: The First Folio, its Publishers, and the Early Modern Book Trade. Ben Higgins, Oxford University Press. © Ben Higgins 2022. DOI: 10.1093/oso/9780192848840.003.0005

Figure 4.1 Detail of the south side of the church of St Dunstan in the West, with Fleet Street in the foreground. The image is an engraving from 1737 which shows the church before it was rebuilt in the nineteenth century. The church clock on the left was added in 1671 and perhaps replaced the 'dial' by which Smethwick identified his shop. Detail from 'The South East Prospect of the Church of St. Dunstan in the West' (Robert West, 1737). Credit: Bodleian Libraries, University of Oxford, Gough Maps vol. 20, fol. 29b. Used under Creative Commons licence CC-BY-NC 4.0.

as the births and occasional deaths of their children, or their civic service, including John's stint as a street constable alongside the publisher John Jaggard (brother of William). John Smethwick also served as a parish churchwarden, including under the vicarage of John Donne, during which time Smethwick paid ten shillings to the clergyman for an Easter sermon preached in 1628.[4] When he died, the bookseller left forty shillings of bread to the parish poor. Among other bequests, his bookshop 'and all my books thearin, and Also all my Bookes in Quieres at home or else wheare' went to his son, Francis Smethwick.[5]

I have stressed the connections between John Smethwick and the area of London in which he lived and worked because his address at St Dunstan's affords

---

[4] Smethwick family baptisms and burials recorded in: *Parish Register of St Dunstan in the West*, LMA P69/DUN2/A/001/MS10342, fol. 44v, 53v, 58v, 62r, etc. For John Smethwick's parish offices see: *Wardmote Inquest Book*, fol. 95v, 96v, 101r, 102v, 104r, 114v. Further offices are recorded in: *Vestry Minute Book of St Dunstan in the West*, LMA P69/DUN2/B/001/MS03016/001, p. 43, 74, 90, 118, 123, 139, etc. The payment to John Donne is recorded in *Chuchwarden's Accounts*, fol. 338v. See also R. C. Bald, 'Dr. Donne and the Booksellers' in *Studies in Bibliography* 18 (1965): pp. 69–80.

[5] *Will of John Smethwick*, TNA PROB 10/619. The proven copy is TNA PROB 11/186/520.

one way to think about the distinctive nature of his presence within the Folio syndicate. The legacy gifted to his son Francis included John Smethwick's ownership of four plays by Shakespeare.[6] It was these plays which involved John Smethwick in the publication of the Folio: two of Shakespeare's best-known tragedies, *Romeo and Juliet* and *Hamlet*, and two comedies, *Love's Labour's Lost* and *The Taming of the Shrew*, all of them acquired in a transfer dated 1607.[7] Holding these four plays made Smethwick the most significant stakeholder with whom the Folio syndicate had to negotiate when it came to assembling the volume in the early 1620s in terms of the number of titles he owned, and perhaps also for the value of his tragedies, given the popularity of *Hamlet* and *Romeo and Juliet*.[8] Presumably Smethwick parlayed his four titles into membership of the Folio syndicate, though we know nothing about that process. Like William Aspley, Smethwick was a marginal figure within the Folio's publication who appears only in the Folio's colophon at the end of the book. In this chapter I suggest an alternative way to recuperate Smethwick into our thinking about the Folio by attending to the address of his bookshop.

If we plot the wholesale locations of those who financed the Folio, we find that the book owes its immediate origins to three different areas of early modern London. Each of these sites was a primary outlet for both the trade and retail distribution of Shakespeare's Folio. One of these locations was the printing house and occasional bookshop run by William Jaggard in Barbican explored in chapter two. Another, in the case of William Aspley and Edward Blount, was Paul's Cross Churchyard—exactly where we would expect to find the Folio on sale. The churchyard at Paul's Cross was the home of the London book trade and a vibrant 'Exchange of all Authors', as Thomas Nashe observed in the 1590s.[9] In the early 1620s Aspley and Blount occupied neighbouring shops on the north side of the churchyard, so through their addresses they enjoyed an equivalency that is

---

[6] The plays are not specifically mentioned in John's will but were transferred to Francis shortly after the death of 'his late father', as recorded in a Stationers' Company entry of 24 August 1642: George E. B. Eyre, H. R. Plomer, and Charles R. Rivington eds, *A Transcript of the Registers of the Worshipful Company of Stationers; From 1640–1708*, 3 vols (London: privately printed, 1913–14), vol. 1, p. 50.

[7] SCA, *Register C*, fol. 161r; Arber III.365. Smethwick's entry was for 'The taminge of A Shrewe' (rather than 'the' shrew) and so it probably identified an earlier, non-Shakespearean play by that title. However the nature of literary property at this time meant that Smethwick's entry probably also extended to Shakespeare's version, as is suggested by the fact that Smethwick went on to publish the first quarto of Shakespeare's *The Shrew* in 1631. For a summary of the relationship between these two plays, see William Shakespeare, *The Taming of the Shrew*, edited by Barbara Hodgdon (London: Methuen, 2010), pp. 7–18.

[8] Only Thomas Pavier, who owned at least two history plays (perhaps three, depending on how we interpret the complicated ownership of *3 Henry VI*) as well as *Titus Andronicus* owned as much Shakespeare in the early 1620s. The plays' collective ownership is explored in chapter three.

[9] Thomas Nashe, *Strange newes, of the intercepting certaine letters* (1592, STC 18377), sig. D3r. See also Roze Hentschell, *St Paul's Cathedral Precinct in Early Modern Literature and Culture* (Oxford: Oxford University Press, 2020), pp. 104–43.

generally denied them in histories of the Folio's making.[10] Unlike Jaggard, Blount, and Aspley, though, John Smethwick spent his career working just under a mile or so to the west, outside the walls of the City of London in an alternative and much smaller hub of book production in the churchyard of St Dunstan—a 'little St. Paul's', as John Donne's biographer R. C. Bald put it when he described 'the concentration of stationers' shops' found in the area.[11] It was here that Smethwick served his apprenticeship in the book trade under the stationer Thomas Newman.[12] And it was here, within a community of stationers with a distinct set of concerns, removed from the main marketplace of print, that Smethwick published and sold his own books from a shop that was found 'under the diall', or timepiece, of the church, as many of his imprints document.

If the Folio owes its immediate origins to these three locations, then it also drew in a different sense on the various other addresses from which Shakespeare's books had previously been published: Cornhill, the Royal Exchange, and Holborn, among other pockets of London touched by the diaspora of Shakespeare in print. There were, in the early seventeenth century, conventional locations at which one might buy a new Shakespeare title. However the First Folio unsettled this established geography by tilting the focus of Shakespeare publishing away from Paul's Cross and towards Smethwick and his fellow booksellers in St Dunstan's. The publication of the Folio seems to have been a critical moment, after which Shakespeare's books began a ragged march westwards across the city, where those titles that continued to be published despite Shakespeare's diminishing popularity found their resting place in and around this alternative churchyard. The imprints and colophons of the First and Second editions of the Folio capture this shift in geographic emphasis. While John Smethwick was the only First Folio stationer based to the west of the city walls, the book's second edition, published nine years later in 1632, emerged from a different set of publishing coordinates. It was financed by two stationers who worked from Paul's Cross (William Aspley and Robert Allott, who by this point had taken over the bookshop and the Shakespearean titles owned by Edward Blount), and three from the St Dunstan's community: Richard Hawkins, Richard Meighen, and of course, John Smethwick.[13]

---

[10] Peter W. M. Blayney, *The Bookshops in Paul's Cross Churchyard* (London: The Bibliographical Society, 1990), pp. 23 and 26.

[11] Bald, 'Dr. Donne', p. 69. Though St Dunstan's was outside the city walls, it was still within the City of London proper. The western limit of the city was Temple Bar, a large gateway that separated Fleet Street from the Strand.

[12] On Newman, see Henry Woudhuysen, *Sir Philip Sidney and the Circulation of Manuscripts 1558–1640* (Oxford: Clarendon Press, 1996), pp. 365–84; Robert Steele, 'Printers and Books in Chancery' in *The Library* S2, 10.37 (1909): pp. 101–6, at pp. 103–4.

[13] Richard Meighen owned two bookshops, one of which neighboured Smethwick in the churchyard, the other was opposite St Dunstan's in Middle Temple gate. Richard Hawkins worked on Chancery Lane beside Serjeants' Inn, adjacent to St Dunstan's. On the Second Folio's imprints and

What can we make of this peculiarly Shakespearean map of the London book trade? Building on the 'spatial turn' of recent scholarship on the history of the book, this chapter uses the final member of the Folio syndicate as a cue to attend to the places from which Shakespeare's books were made, and in particular to the influence of St Dunstan in the West and its environs on the playwright's legacy.[14] The chapter first establishes the broader geography of Shakespeare publishing before looking in more detail at Smethwick's address and the movement of Shakespeare's books around London. The chapter finishes by considering the place of the Folio within this authorial topography, and by asking to what extent it matters that the printed life of author might begin in one part of London but finish elsewhere.

The Geography of Shakespeare's Books

Where were Shakespeare's books published? If we wade into the muddle of nouns—green dragons and pied bulls, conduits and gates—by which the playwright's books located themselves in their imprints, what can we learn about how interest in Shakespeare's work was dispersed around the city? I focus here on the time between the appearance of Shakespeare's first book in 1593 (an edition of the narrative poem *Venus and Adonis*, sold at 'the white Greyhound in Paules Church-yard') and 1640, the year in which the stationer John Benson published his heavy-handed edition of Shakespeare's *Poems* from his bookshop 'in S^t. *Dunstans* Church-yard', beside John Smethwick.[15] These two editions bookend an alternative version of Shakespeare's life: not one defined by his birth and death but rather the earliest continuous span of time in which his work was being regu-

---

colophon see: William B. Todd, 'The Issues and States of the Second Folio and Milton's Epitaph on Shakespeare' in *Studies in Bibliography* 5 (1952): pp. 81–108.

[14] Miles Ogborn and Charles W. J. Withers survey work on the 'geography of the book' in the introduction to their edited work, *Geographies of the Book* (Farnham: Ashgate, 2010), pp. 1–28. Important work on the spaces of the early modern book trade in London includes Robin Myers, Michael Harris, and Giles Mandelbrote, eds, *The London Book Trade: Topographies of Print in the Metropolis from the Sixteenth Century* (London: British Library, 2003); James Raven, *Bookscape: Geographies of Printing and Publishing in London before 1800* (London: British Library, 2014). Helen Smith's chapter '"Certaine women brokers and peddlers": Beyond the London Book Trades' offers a valuable analysis of how women who sold books navigated the spaces of retail in London and beyond: '*Grossly Material Things': Women and Book Production in Early Modern England* (Oxford: Oxford University Press, 2012), pp. 135–73. Tye Landels-Gruenewald offers a helpful overview in three blog posts: 'Georeferencing the Early Modern London Book Trade: 1. Theory without Practice' in Janelle Jenstad ed., *The Map of Early Modern London*, University of Victoria, 20 June 2018: https://mapoflondon.uvic.ca/BLOG16.htm. See also the 'Shakeosphere' project run from the University of Iowa: https://shakeosphere.lib.uiowa.edu/, and the brief summary of recent work on space in book history in Daniel Bellingradt, Paul Nelles, and Jeroen Salman eds, *Books in Motion in Early Modern Europe: Beyond Production, Circulation and Consumption* (Basingstoke: Palgrave Macmillan, 2017), pp. 8–10.

[15] William Shakespeare, *Venus and Adonis* (1593, STC 22354), sig. [A]2r; *Poems: written by Wil. Shake-speare. Gent* (1640, STC 22344), sig. *1r.

larly printed. A quick pass over these forty-seven years shows they began with an intense decade or so of productivity, in which many of Shakespeare's books were published from a few key locations. As the writer's popularity began to fade, ownership of the rights to copy for his work began to disperse throughout the city.[16] There were occasionally later local flurries of Shakespearean interest until Benson's edition of the *Poems* in 1640, after which the playwright's work ceased to be regularly published by London's booksellers.[17] Following the 1640 *Poems*, it was fifteen years before another Shakespeare book was published, and although a third edition of the Folio appeared in 1663/4, no further individual editions of plays or poems were financed till after the Great Fire of 1666 had razed many of London's bookshops to the ground, destroying much of London's commercial topography in the process.[18]

Where is a book 'made'? Placing any of Shakespeare's books on a map is a complicated task: beneath the promising fixity of name, place, and date contained in imprints, early modern books consistently evade the kind of singularity required by a map. Most obviously, the printing houses which carried out the physical work of making Shakespeare's books were generally not the same sites that financed publication; neither were the printing houses typically the places where those books ended up being sold. William Jaggard, who both printed and published the Folio as well as selling copies from his premises in Barbican, is an exception. More generally, Peter W. M. Blayney explains that 'hardly any' of the bookshops in Paul's Churchyard 'ever housed a press'.[19] Early modern books come apart the more closely we look at them and those parts belong to different places. Even within a single printing business a book was in continual motion as it was assembled. In the sixteenth-century offices preserved at the Plantin-Moretus museum in Antwerp it is possible to move through rooms ranged around an

---

[16] For an account of the first phase of Shakespeare publishing that explores the spaces 'both linguistic and literal' of these editions see Helen Smith, '"To London all"? Mapping Shakespeare in Print, 1593–1598' in Margaret Kidnie and Sonia Massai eds, *Shakespeare and Textual Studies* (Cambridge: Cambridge University Press, 2015), pp. 69–86, at p. 69.

[17] On Benson's edition see Faith Acker, *First Readers of Shakespeare's Sonnets, 1590–1790* (Abingdon: Routledge Press, 2021); 'John Benson's 1640 Poems and its Literary Precedents' in Emma Depledge and Peter Kirwan eds, *Canonising Shakespeare: Stationers and the Book Trade, 1640–1740* (Cambridge: Cambridge University Press, 2017), pp. 89–106. Emma Depledge's chapter in the same work ('Shakespeare for Sale, 1640–1740', pp. 17–25) offers an overview of Shakespeare's work after the date where this chapter's focus ends.

[18] I am here not counting the reissued state of *The Merchant of Venice*, which repackaged the edition of 1637 under a new title page dated 1652 and which advertised the book for sale by William Leake at the Crown 'in *Fleetstreet*, between the two Temple Gates': *The most excellent historie of the merchant of Venice* (1652, Wing S2938). In 1655 three new editions of Shakespeare's work were published: Jane Bell's edition of *King Lear*, published beside Christ Church hospital; William Leake's *Othello*, published from Fleet Street between the gates of the Inner and Middle Temples; and an edition of *The Rape of Lucrece*, published jointly by John Stafford beside Fleet Bridge, and Will Gilbertson in Giltspur Street. Taken as a whole, this group broadly supports my argument in this chapter about the gradual westwards drift of Shakespeare publishing.

[19] Peter W. M. Blayney, *The Stationers' Company and the Printers of London 1501–1557*, 2 vols (Cambridge: Cambridge University Press, 2013), vol. 1, p. 70.

expansive courtyard and to imagine a book gradually becoming itself as it travelled from the typesetters' station to the corrector's room, then to the printing room, storehouse, and finally to the shop for sale.[20]

If a book's production was dispersed, so too was its distribution and sale. Publishers tend to be thought of as the 'prime movers' of an edition but they also sometimes turned to other booksellers to act as wholesalers. The first edition of the *Sonnets* (1609), for example, was published by Thomas Thorpe, who hired the printer George Eld to make the book, and then advertised the bookshops of William Aspley (in Paul's Churchyard) and John Wright (beside Newgate market) as the points of sale. An accurate account of the origins of most early modern books would describe journeys between points, whereby the book would accrete material and meaning as it moved between agents and then enjoy a period of stability and use before coming undone again as printed waste. Instead of any definitive map, then, there are many richly different cartographies of the Shakespearean book trade which depend on the interests of those who navigate them.

Yet if each early modern book was the sum of a variety of geographically disparate labour, then the finished product for most part elided that dispersal by printing what was usually just a single address on the title page: the book's wholesale distribution point.[21] In most cases this was the address of the bookseller who had published the edition; for a minority of Shakespeare's books (as with the *Sonnets*) this address belonged to an extra agent. For this chapter I have prioritized these wholesale locations that are advertised by the books themselves. In the few cases where the imprint contains no address I have used the location of the stationer who acted as the edition's wholesale bookseller. The result is a map which treats imprints not as facts of a book's making but as rhetorical statements that schematically ordered the spaces of the city for the readers who encountered Shakespeare's title pages.[22]

---

[20] On a less grand scale, the 1667 inventory of the London printer Robert Ibbitson records cases of type, galleys, and chases 'In the Composing Roome' and, in a separate 'printing Roome', three printing presses, a book press, and waste paper: *Inventory of Robert Ibbitson*, TNA PROB 4/2828.

[21] Imprints can be unreliable of course, or simply difficult to interpret. The imprint of the first edition of Shakespeare's *Titus Andronicus* (1594, STC 22328) states the book was: 'Printed by John Danter, and are to be sold by *Edward White & Thomas Millington*, at the little North doore of Paules at the signe of the Gunne' (A2r). This seems to mean the edition was published by the printer John Danter, who registered the manuscript of *Titus* in 1594, and so who presumably owned the play when it was first printed, but other interpretations are possible. Lukas Erne has argued that Danter transferred his rights in the manuscript to Edward White and Thomas Millington 'after entering it but before the play was published', pointing to Danter's similar treatment of Robert Greene's *Orlando Furioso* at the same time: *Shakespeare and the Book Trade* (Cambridge: Cambridge University Press, 2013), pp. 139–41. The way in which we read an imprint can change depending on our knowledge of the stationers involved.

[22] On the rhetorical—rather than straightforwardly factual—status of imprints, and how they relate to the cityscape around them, see: Helen Smith, '"Imprinted by Simeon such a signe": Reading Early Modern Imprints' in Helen Smith and Louise Wilson eds, *Renaissance Paratexts* (Cambridge: Cambridge University Press, 2011), pp. 17–33; see also pp. 35–7 of the introduction above.

In what ways might these addresses be meaningful? The location from which an edition launched itself into the world by no means circumscribed its reach. After all, books were bought within the trade by other stationers and then offered for retail in any number of other locations. It is with this sense of geographic reach in mind that the anonymous author of *The cobler of Canterburie* (1608) finished his preliminary epistle by bidding his readers 'Farewell from Shop wheresoever it be': the epistle imagines being read in a bookshop, but seems deliberately careless of the exact location.[23] Just occasionally, the trade transactions by which books circulated between stationers survive: in 1604, two copies of Shakespeare's poem *The Rape of Lucrece* (published and sold wholesale from Paternoster Row) were sent from London in a bundle that also contained copies of the plays *The Spanish Tragedy* and *The Malcontent*, to 'Master Crosly at Oxforde booke sellers', perhaps in response to student interest in these popular works.[24] In another example from 1600, John Smethwick—then aged 'twenty Seaven yeares or there aboutes'—recollected a reader who called into his shop for a music book that was not one of Smethwick's own editions. The stationer simply hurried over to a neighbouring bookseller and acquired a few copies to place on his own shelves (according to an irritated Smethwick, the reader in fact never returned, and he gave the books back).[25] Books could infiltrate playhouses and fairs; they were smuggled around the country in pedlars' packs, and hawked by the chapmen and colporteurs who 'cryeth and selleth pamphlets up and down the city' and beyond.[26]

The diffuse paths of early modern textual retail, though, were distinct from the topographies framed by a book's title page. Wherever a book might end up, it was in some way always tethered to the peculiarly specific area of London from which it had emerged—marked, via its imprint, as the product of a particular time and place, and as the commodity of a particular business. Just as a passport confirms its owner's origins wherever they travel, the title pages of most early modern books carried this information with them to the point of destruction. Adrian Johns has discussed how early modern readers used the address advertised in a book's imprint to help them evaluate the meanings of the text. Johns describes how an imprint provided practical information to both readers and stationers

---

[23] 'The Coblers Epistle to the Gentlemen Readers' in *The cobler of Canterburie* (1608, STC 4580), sig. A4r.
[24] John Crosley ran a bookshop on Oxford's High Street. His bill, dated 22 August 1604, is in the Bodleian Library: MS Top. Oxon. d. 238, fol. 49r. It lists two copies of 'Lucretia' at a cost of 6d for both. It is possible the title identifies copies of Thomas Middleton's poem *The ghost of Lucrece* (1600, STC 17885.5), though, given the popularity of *The Rape of Lucrece* (four editions by this point), the balance of probability suggests Shakespeare.
[25] *Eastland v. East*: TNA REQ 2/203/4, ff. 4r–5r. See also Margaret Dowling, 'The Printing of John Dowland's *Second booke of songs or ayres*' in *The Library* Series 4, vol 12.4 (1932): pp. 365–80.
[26] George Ruggle, *Ignoramus* (1662, Wing R2212), sig F3v. On such itinerant figures see Margaret Spufford, *Small Books and Pleasant Histories: Popular Fiction and its Readership in Seventeenth-century England* (London: Methuen, 1981), pp. 111–28; Smith, *Grossly Material Things*, pp. 135–73.

about a book's distribution, but also informed their understanding of its 'perceived epistemic status'.[27]

Shakespeare's London was, as is commonly noted, a far smaller city than its modern counterpart. Its neighbourhoods and communities were distinct: 'there are so many little worlds in Her,' wrote Donald Lupton of London in 1632, 'I am almost affraide to meddle.'[28] Lupton did meddle, writing a guidebook that distinguished many of these urban worlds and made clear that the different streets and parishes were associated with different kinds of social, civic, and intellectual identities.[29] In 1633, one anonymous urban *flaneur* needed only to walk 'Through Pauls, Ludgate, & Fleet-street' and on to 'Temple, Strand, and new Exchange' in order to be struck by the 'fashions rare and strange' of London's western locales.[30] Shakespeare's books were conceived within, and marked as belonging to, these different localities of stationers and readers—what we might think of (remembering the critic Stanley Fish and historians of reading such as Roger Chartier and Kevin Sharpe) as little 'bibliographic communities' nested within the city.[31] These locales and their significations are perhaps more clearly visible in the much later literature of the early eighteenth century. So the prolific author Thomas Brown, reflecting on prosperity in 1711, observed how 'contemptibly' a '*Paul's Churchyard* Bookseller' would look upon a colleague who 'sells second-hand Books under the Trees in *Morefields*', where the location of each figure signified their status.[32] John Macky, in his 1714 guide to London markets, felt able to specify that readers looking for '*Divinity* and *Classics*' should head to 'the *North* side of St. *Paul's* Cathedral', while those seeking '*Law*, *History*, and *Plays*' should search 'about *Temple-bar*'.[33] But given the growth of London over the seventeenth century,

---

[27] Adrian Johns, *The Nature of the Book: Print and Knowledge in the Making* (Chicago, IL: University of Chicago Press, 1998), esp. chapter two: 'Literary Life: The Culture and Credibility of the Printed Book in Early Modern London', pp. 58–186 at p. 73. Imprints, in this way of thinking, participate in the 'fictions of settlement' described by Lawrence Manley, whereby representations of early modern London were 'not merely mimetic, but socially functional, tied to the task of producing and reproducing the socio-economic relationships essential to urbanization': *Literature and Culture in Early Modern London* (Cambridge: Cambridge University Press, 1995), pp. 126–7.

[28] Donald Lupton, *London and the countrey* (1632, STC 16944), sig. B1r.

[29] See Smith, '"Simeon such a signe"', pp. 23–5; Johns, *Nature of the Book*, pp. 67–74; Julie Sanders, *The Cultural Geography of Early Modern Drama, 1620–1650* (Cambridge: Cambridge University Press, 2011), pp. 178–212.

[30] *There's nothing to be had without money* (1633, STC 18699).

[31] Stanley Fish's idea of the 'interpretive community'—the notion that groups of readers can share values and conventions—was first set out in his essay 'Interpreting the *Variorum*', in *Critical Inquiry* 2.3 (1976): pp. 465–85. See also: *Is There a Text in This Class? The Authority of Interpretive Communities* (Cambridge, MA: Harvard University Press, 1980). Fish's ideas were developed by Roger Chartier, *The Order of Books: Readers, Authors, and Libraries in Europe between the Fourteenth and Eighteenth Centuries*, trans. by Lydia G. Cochrane (Stanford, CA: Stanford University Press, 1994); and Kevin Sharpe, *Reading Revolutions: The Politics of Reading in Early Modern England* (London: Yale University Press, 2000).

[32] Thomas Brown, *The fourth volume of the works…* (1711), sig. B5v.

[33] John Macky, *A journey through England* (1714), sig. O7r. Macky also specifies that 'Antient Books' belong to '*Little-Britain* and *Pater Noster-Row*' and that '*French-Booksellers*' are found 'in the *Strand*'.

we might expect its bookselling spaces to convey just as much if not more meaning in the more knowable urban environment of Shakespeare's time.

Beyond their imprints, early modern books acknowledge and deploy these communities in various ways, including by connecting urban spaces to distinct cultures of literacy. In a poem that begins a translation of Aesop's fables published in 1577, the book—from its vantage point amid a display in 'Paules Churchyarde'— begs a passing reader to rewrite its text in verse, rather than the prose it currently contains. 'I am not for your tourne,' the reader tells the crestfallen book, 'ye must repayre unto | The Innes of Court and Chauncery, | where learned have to do.'[34] The suggestion is that the book must hurry west down Fleet Street to the fashionable inns of court environment to find an able penman ready to transform prose into poetry. In 'A Continued Inquisition against *Paper-Persecutors*' (1625), the poet A. H. worries about pamphlets and ballads filling 'Not only *Little* but *Great Britaine*' and glares at the 'abortive Broods of Barbican' who produce such matter.[35] Here, rather than modish verse, it is the effusion of cheap print that is associated with certain areas of London, and probably in particular with the well-known ballad publisher John Trundle and his Barbican bookshop. Similarly, here is Robert Armin, the mordant 'fool' who became the leading comic performer in Shakespeare's theatre company, and who is himself listed among the First Folio's 'Principall Actors', tracing a path for his books through the layout of the city:

> I thanke all men of my minde, gently to judge, not rashly to revile, Well, when my Bookes are in Paules Church-yarde, if they passe through Paules I care not, for in Fleet-streete I have friendes that will take Lud-gate to defende me.[36]

Armin is concerned with the fate of his books. He hopes that his work will be gently judged, not rashly reviled, and he knows that the geography of the city's bookselling trade offers the potential for differing responses. In his telling, Armin's books are mobile, embarking on a journey that suggests both their failure in one area and their possible redemption in new markets. The books begin in Paul's Cross Churchyard, where if not bought they will 'passe through', and move west on to 'Fleet-streete', where they may be saved. Perhaps one variable at stake in the movement of a book, then, is its novelty: first Paul's Cross, then on to other areas. Different corners of the city here become metonyms for distinct communities of stationers and readers with their own value judgements about what to

---

[34] 'The argument betweene Esope and the Translatour' in Aesop, *The fabulous tales of Esope the Phrygian* (1577, STC 186.5), sig. ¶3r.

[35] The poem appears as a continuation of John Davies, *A scourge for paper-persecutors* (1625, STC 6340), sig. [2]A1r–[2]A4r, quotes at [2]A1v and [2]A3r.

[36] Clunnico Snuffe [Armin's pseudonym], 'To the Right Worthy Sir Timothie Trunchion' in Robert Armin, *Quips upon questions* (1600, STC 775.5), sig. A2v. Armin's quote begins, 'I thinke all men of my minde', but the vowel seems likely to be a compositor's slip, which I have here corrected.

read.[37] Parts of the city seem almost to rise up against one another (Armin's friends 'will take Lud-gate to defende me') as they battle for control of an author's work. Urban infrastructure is repurposed, so that the imposing stone of Ludgate, which stood between Fleet Street on one side and the road that led into Paul's Churchyard on the other, marks other kinds of division.

Just as these addresses might influence reception, so too does the geography of imprints enable us to follow a kind of topographical drama that is bound up with when and where London's publishers themselves 'read' Shakespeare as an appealing product. These different locations could sometimes shape a book: the prose work *Essayes and characters* (1618) by Geffray Minshull, for example, seems particularly sensitive to the environment of its publication and wholesale. Minshull was a legal student known to posterity only for this book, written while he was in prison for debt. Two editions were published in the same year. The first was financed by the bookseller William Jones 'dwelling in Red-crosse streete'—an area north of the City of London and close to William Jaggard's bookshop. The second was published by Matthew Walbancke, and sold 'at his shops at the new and old Gate of Grayes-Inne'.[38] Gray's Inn, one of the four inns of court, was west of the city, a little north of St Dunstan's Churchyard. Whereas the first edition was published anonymously, the second identified Minshull and his membership of Gray's Inn on its title page. This latter edition also included a new dedication to the 'worthy young Gentlemen' of 'Grayes-Inne', in which Minshull described his work as a 'paper Bullet' that he had 'shot up and downe Fleetestreet', perhaps suggesting that he had made arrangements with local booksellers to stock copies. He goes on to explain that he added his name to the book because he knew that he 'could not lye hidden' to his 'noble Friends' who lived nearby.[39] Minshull's *Essayes* seems in an unusually clear way to envisage its audience as geographically constituted. That need not in reality have been true, of course, but readers who encountered the text far from Walbancke's bookshop were still confronted by a book that loudly advertised its local affinities. The text was enshrined in the neighbourhood of its publication and wholesale.

Armin and Minshull both name specific places in their addresses—Fleet Street, Ludgate, Gray's Inn, Paul's Cross—but it seems misguided to pin down the boundaries of the communities and readerships these toponyms represent. Cities

---

[37] David Fallon makes a similar point for a later era in his reading of the Piccadilly bookshops under the Tory–Whig rivalry of the late eighteenth and early nineteenth centuries. The address, Fallon notes, became well known for catering to 'politicised constituencies of readers' looking for a 'Conservative literary culture': 'Piccadilly Booksellers and Conservative Sociability' in Kevin Gilmartin ed., *Sociable Places: Locating Culture in Romantic-period Britain* (Cambridge: Cambridge University Press, 2017), pp. 70–94, quotes at pp. 72 and 87.

[38] Geffray Minshull, *Certaine characters and essayes of prison and prisoners* (1618, STC 18318), sig. A1v; *Essayes and characters of a prison and prisoners* (1618, STC 18319), sig. A1v.

[39] G. M., 'To the Most Worthy young Gentlemen (my noble Visitants) of Grayes-Inne' in *Essayes and characters of a prison and prisoners* (1618, STC 18319), sig. A2r–v.

are porous realms that rely on their inhabitants being able to roam freely. Those who belong to particular spaces 'flow' between and connect many other sites, to borrow an important term from cultural geography.[40] Readers also constantly 'poach' across borders that are intellectual and imaginative as well as literal and material, as Michel de Certeau reminds us.[41] Still, as in Robert Frost's poem about the risks of moving a peach tree out of its natural climate, the fact that there was 'no fixed line' around these areas of London does not change that there were nevertheless 'roughly zones' with their attendant conditions and possibilities.[42] In what zones were Shakespeare's books produced? The following map (Figure 4.2) shows the locations advertised by all Shakespeare editions between 1593 and 1640 inclusive. To convey a sense of Shakespeare's popularity, the size of each circle is in proportion to the number of editions it represents. The only exception to this scale is Paul's Cross, which housed so many editions that an accurate mark would engulf the entire map.[43]

One of the striking things to emerge is how small the total footprint of the Shakespearean book trade was. With the exception of three editions—one of *Othello* (1622), published from Westminster, one of *Venus and Adonis* (1627) from Edinburgh, and one of *1 Henry IV* (1639), which was published by John Norton 2 and advertised for wholesale by the bookseller Hugh Perry in the Strand—the map captures every pre-1641 Shakespeare book. London's dominance of the book trade at large is here starkly presented through one author's work. Within this small but vibrant terrain, there were roughly four main areas of London from which Shakespeare's books were published and sold, though these areas were active at different times. In the east, the enclave around Cornhill and the Royal Exchange (a bustling centre of trade that opened in 1571) hosted several editions of Shakespeare's playbooks in the 1590s and early 1600s. To the north, William Jaggard accounts for his own (somewhat contentious) zone around Barbican. The central area around Paul's Cross (which here includes Paternoster Row) housed a large majority of Shakespeare's printed work. Finally, to the west was John Smethwick's home of St Dunstan's churchyard and its environs: Chancery Lane beside Serjeants' Inn, and the Middle Temple (which here also includes Middle Temple Gate). The locations are approximate, but nevertheless

---

[40] On 'flow theory' see Sanders, *Cultural Geography*, pp. 10–13.
[41] Michel de Certeau, 'Reading as Poaching' in *The Practice of Everyday Life*, trans. Steven F. Rendall (Berkeley and Los Angeles, CA: University of California Press, 1988), pp. 165–76. Bellingradt and Salman distinguish between 'place' as a geographical location and 'space'—something to be understood as 'socially constructed, relational, and dynamic': *Books in Motion*, p. 8.
[42] Robert Frost 'There Are Roughly Zones' in *The Poetry of Robert Frost: The Collected Poems*, ed. Edward Connery Lathem (New York: Henry Holt and Company, 1969), p. 305.
[43] The circle centred on Paul's Cross is presented at half its actual size. The information on which this map is based is included in appendix three. I have followed Lukas Erne's rationale for defining what is and is not a Shakespeare edition, resulting in, among other things, the inclusion of *Edward III* (1596 and 1599) but the exclusion of *Loves Martyr* (1601): Erne, *Book Trade*, pp. 11–19.

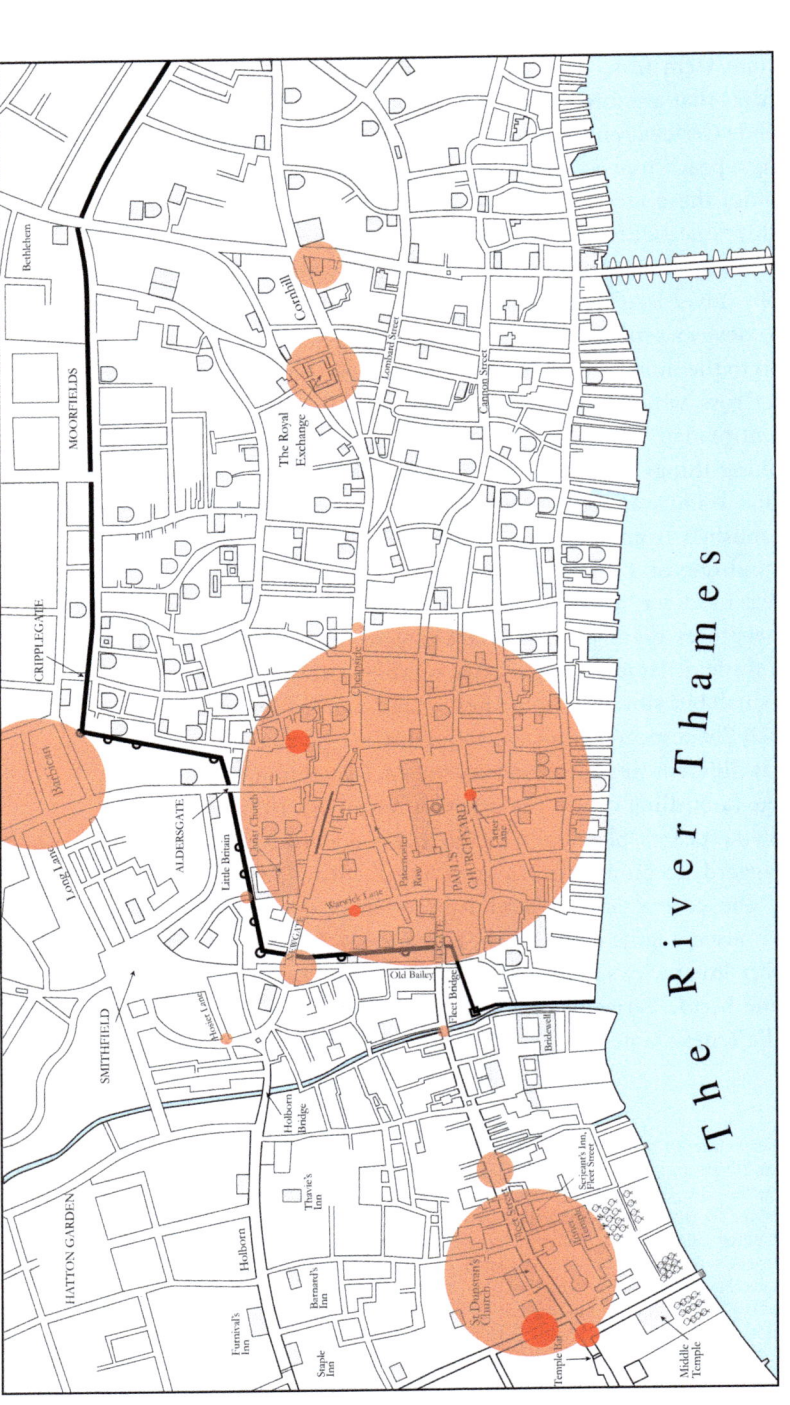

Figure 4.2 The sites from which Shakespeare's books were offered for wholesale between 1593 and 1640 inclusive. The locations are: Paul's Cross, including Paternoster Row (57 editions, shown half-size); St Dunstan in the West (14 editions); Barbican (11 editions); the Royal Exchange (6 editions); St Peter's Church in Cornhill (4 editions); Fleet Street (3 editions); Chancery Lane near Serjeants' Inn (3 editions); Old Bailey without Newgate (3 editions); Foster Lane (2 editions); Middle Temple Gate (2 editions); Fleet Bridge (1 edition); Hosier Lane (1 edition); Christ Church Gate (1 edition); Warwick Lane (1 edition); Carter Lane (1 edition); Cheapside (1 edition). Three editions are missing: *Othello* (1622) published by Thomas Walkley from Britain's Burse in Westminster; *Venus and Adonis* (1627) published in Edinburgh, and *1 Henry IV* (1639) published at Ivy Bridge in the Strand, further west than the map shows. The Jaggard Quartos are recorded in Barbican; another possible location (not shown here) would be Ivy Lane, the address of Thomas Pavier's bookshop in 1619. The map is based on that used in *STC*, vol. 3, insert between pp. 246–7 ('London in December 1666').

show the popular areas of London from which Shakespeare's work emerged, giving us a kind of heat map for the playwright's popularity in print.

It might seem that this map doubles as a record of general book trade activity in the period, but that is not quite correct. Less obvious on the map are the many areas of London that were active in the book trade but which seem never to have been interested in, or were never able to publish, Shakespeare's books: Snow Hill, Little Britain, and Pope's Head Alley, among others. The area around Blackfriars, for example, hosted plenty of bookselling activity during this period and moreover featured the Blackfriars theatre—home of Shakespeare and the King's Men from 1608. That none of Shakespeare's books were published or offered for wholesale from beside his theatres (either here at Blackfriars or over the river in Southwark beside the Globe) suggests there were distinct topographies of print and of performance, and that any collaboration between these two industries did not rely on physical proximity. When the First Folio labours to bring the theatre into the printed book, through its many references to the particularities and personalities of the London stage and its contributions from John Heminge and Henry Condell, it bridges this geographic separation to create a volume charged with the significance of both trades.

Just as the map establishes common areas of Shakespeare publishing, it also highlights the eccentricity of those single editions that were financed from locations scattered around and between these popular zones. Sometimes these lonely editions, which are the spatial equivalent of the 'minor Shakespearean' stationers explored in chapter three, are less isolated than they appear. The single Shakespeare book that was distributed wholesale from John Wright's bookshop at Christ Church Gate was the *Sonnets* (1609). Wright's shop initially seems an unusual choice of outlet, given that all of Shakespeare's poetry had by that point been sold from either Paul's Churchyard or Paternoster Row. However, this edition was divided between two states, the second of which had a title page that advertised William Aspley's shop in Paul's Churchyard as its wholesale outlet, meaning that the *Sonnets* belonged to both parts of London. Other of these outlying editions invite us to wonder how meaningful it was that some of Shakespeare's books belonged in some way to spaces that were outside the central areas of the trade. Did early modern readers notice that a handful of Shakespeare's books lacked strategies of habitation on their title pages that were conventional to the rest?

The falsely dated collection of Shakespeare quartos published by William Jaggard and Thomas Pavier in 1619 offers a particularly muddled set of coordinates in space and time. In this exceptional case we know that the imprints are false. In the map above (Figure 4.2), these quartos are placed in Barbican, based on the most recent research that argues William Jaggard was the central agent involved in their publication.[44] During the six years between 1613 and 1618, only

---

[44] These arguments are explored in chapter two on pp. 104–10.

four editions of Shakespeare's work were published: editions of *1 Henry IV* (1613), *Richard II* (1615), and *Venus and Adonis* (1617) from Paul's Churchyard, and an edition of *The Rape of Lucrece* (1616) from Fleet Street. Against this slow drip-feed of new editions, the mass of Shakespeare books which emerged from the Barbican in 1619 is tangible evidence of the oddity of this collection, and how it disrupted the wider rhythms of Shakespearean print. Then again, if we take the false imprints of this collection at their word and plot them at the locations they claim then the plays emerge as problematic in other ways. One of the titles—an edition of *Henry V*—has an imprint that falsely states it was published in 1608 for Thomas Pavier. In 1608, Pavier's bookshop and publishing business was located in Cornhill.[45] This area of London did briefly host the publication of several Shakespearean editions in the late 1590s, and so the topography of this imprint seems superficially plausible. However, the last legitimate Shakespeare book to be published from Cornhill appeared in 1600: Thomas Millington's edition of *Richard Duke of Yorke* (an early version of *3 Henry VI*). No further Shakespeare editions were published and sold from here before the Restoration, meaning that while the individual elements of the *Henry V* imprint are perfectly credible, the combination of date and place seems jarring, and suggests the falsities that were uncovered in other ways by New Bibliography.

As the 1619 collection shows, thinking about geography and the places of Shakespeare publishing also requires thinking about time, a more challenging variable to map. The image above (Figure 4.2) flattens nearly fifty years of publishing rhythms into a single layer. But London's interest in Shakespeare rose and fell in different quarters of the city at different times, like a restless pulse. The flurry of interest in Shakespeare to the east of Paul's Cross, beside the Royal Exchange and St Peter's Church in Cornhill, was as brief as it was productive. The booksellers Thomas Millington, Cuthbert Burby, and Thomas Pavier, each of whom worked from this area of London at the start of their careers, were at the cutting edge of Shakespeare publishing when they produced ten editions of Shakespeare's plays from these two neighbouring locations between 1594 and 1602. In this first boom phase of the playwright's popularity, if the White Greyhound in Paul's Churchyard gained a reputation for financing Shakespeare's poetry then the Royal Exchange and St Peter's in Cornhill were key sites for the distribution of his history plays.[46] These neighbouring locations hosted multiple editions of the second and third parts of *Henry VI*, originally published in Cornhill as *The First part of the Contention*

---

[45] See for example *The hystorie of Hamblet* (1608, STC 12734.5), published by Pavier 'at his shop in Corne-hill, neere to the Royall Exchange'. See also Gerald Johnson, 'Thomas Pavier, Publisher, 1600–25' in *The Library* Series 6, vol. 14.1 (1992): pp. 12–50 at pp. 15–16.

[46] On the White Greyhound as 'a crucial site for and representative of the continued circulation of Shakespeare's poetry' see Adam G. Hooks, 'Shakespeare at the White Greyhound,' in *Shakespeare Survey* 64 (2011): pp. 260–75, at p. 272. Tara Lyons discusses the serial publication of many of these early history plays by Millington and Pavier in 'Serials, Spinoffs, and Histories: Selling "Shakespeare" in Collection before the Folio,' in *Philological Quarterly* 91.2 (2012): pp. 185–220.

betwixt the two famous Houses of Yorke and Lancaster, as well as *The true Tragedie of Richard Duke of Yorke*, and two editions of *Edward III*, now generally accepted as part of Shakespeare's canon. From 1602, though, this area's interest in Shakespeare ended, despite the fact that booksellers continued to thrive at both locations. In this case, the movement of these plays to a new area of London was entangled with the biography of their publishers. When Millington died in 1603, his Shakespearean titles were acquired by Pavier, who then moved his business to Paul's Churchyard (or rather, to Ivy Lane, just beside the churchyard). In 1602 Burby also closed his bookshop in the Royal Exchange and took over a premises in Paul's Churchyard. Here the journey of these stationers—and so the movement of one cluster of Shakespearean publication—from the east of the city towards the centre of the book trade looks optimistic. The same tastes and publishing intuitions that had led these stationers to acquire Shakespeare's work had presumably enabled wider success, enough to propel stationers who began their careers in a secondary area of book-trade commerce towards the centre.

Shakespeare in St Dunstan's Churchyard

How did Shakespeare's books arrive at St Dunstan's? This alternative churchyard has tended to be passed over by scholars of the book trade in favour of its much larger relative at Paul's Cross, yet has its own rich history of making books. The legal printer Richard Pynson, who can be placed beside the church from 1502, may have been the first to produce books from this location; he was followed by many others.[47] Despite this lineage, the market for books in and around St Dunstan's was on an entirely different scale to that found to the east in Paul's Cross churchyard. Over the course of the sixteenth century there were rarely more than one or two stationers active beside the church in any given year.[48] There simply was not enough space here to host the kind of community found at St Paul's, where booksellers lined the edges of the churchyard and wedged in between the buttresses of the cathedral itself. Furthermore, the St Dunstan's shops tended to host printers, or printer-publishers like Pynson and his successor Richard Tottell, rather than the publishing booksellers of Paul's. Having grown up in the parish and finished his apprenticeship in 1597, John Smethwick appeared in the churchyard from the turn of the century. An imprint of 1600 records that he briefly ran a bookshop 'within Temple Barre'—the large gateway that marked the western end of Fleet Street—but by 1602 he was set up within the churchyard

---

[47] Pynson began his printing career on the Strand in 1491 but had moved onto Fleet Street beside St Dunstan's by 1502: Blayney, *Stationers' Company and the Printers of London*, vol. 1, pp. 47–9, 70. See also Blayney's maps of Fleet Street in vol. 2, pp. 983–9.
[48] See Index 3E 'London Addresses' in STC vol. 3, p. 257.

itself, where he worked alongside Matthew Lownes and Nicholas Ling. In what follows, I move forwards from this trio of stationers to chart the arrival of Shakespeare's books at this location, suggesting ways that we might read their publication from this address as meaningful, before finishing with the First Folio.

1603: Q1 *Hamlet*

The first Shakespeare title to be financed from St Dunstan's was *Hamlet*, probably in the form of the first edition of 1603. In the context of Shakespeare's career this was relatively late; the playwright had passed the peak of his printed popularity. Around forty editions of Shakespeare's work had already been published, almost all from Paul's Cross, the Royal Exchange, and Cornhill. Just one of those earlier editions, *A Midsummer Night's Dream* (1600), had been published from somewhere along Fleet Street (the title's briefly active bookseller, Thomas Fisher, gave a sign for his shop—the White Hart—but did not specify its location more precisely). Why then did *Hamlet* make its way across to St Dunstan's at this juncture? The short answer is that it was brought here by Nicholas Ling—a canny elderly bookseller who, nearing the end of his career, moved his business from Paul's Churchyard to a new premises beside the bookshops owned by Smethwick and Lownes in 1602.[49] Ling published the first quarto of *Hamlet* in collaboration with the bookseller John Trundle, who was based in Barbican. The edition thus belonged to both locations, although it was more powerfully linked with Ling, whose elaborate woodblock device featured on the title page. Trundle did not often advertise his own premises as a retail bookshop, and the following year Ling worked alone to finance the second and much enlarged version of *Hamlet*, sold from his shop 'under Saint Dunstons Church in Fleetstreet'.[50] Despite Trundle's early involvement, the story of *Hamlet* was a well-judged text with which to introduce Shakespeare to the churchyard at St Dunstan's. To understand why this might be involves looking more closely at the character of this bibliographic community.

If the St Dunstan's location carried any particular connotations to early modern readers then it was likely to have been associated with the inns of court:

---

[49] Ling worked in various shops in Paul's Churchyard till 1601. He was 'in Fleetstreete, neere Saint Dunstones Church' by 1602: Michael Drayton, *Englands heroicall epistles* (1602, STC 7197), sig. A1r. Gerald D. Johnson notes that he had made an earlier foray into this parish in 1598 before moving his entire business: 'Nicholas Ling, Publisher 1580–1607' in *Studies in Bibliography* 38 (1985): pp. 203–14, at pp. 212–14.

[50] William Shakespeare, *The tragicall historie of Hamlet* (1604/5, STC 22276-a), sig. [A]1r. Zachary Lesser sums up theories surrounding the publication of this play's first quartos: *Hamlet after Q1: An Uncanny History of the Shakespearean Text* (Philadelphia, PA: University of Pennsylvania Press, 2015), pp. 60–71.

the institutions that provided young scholars with a legal education.[51] Ranged around the church were the four major houses: the Inner and Middle Temples; Lincoln's Inn on Chancery Lane; Gray's Inn at the north end of Chancery Lane. Scattered among these larger inns were several smaller inns of chancery which housed a range of associated members and students. Two of these, Clifford's Inn and Serjeants' Inn, huddled up against the St Dunstan's churchyard itself, separated only by a brick wall and a narrow passageway respectively. One effect of this crowded urban infrastructure was to make the church a focal point for students and lawyers.[52] Members of the book trade who worked beside the church thus catered for the needs of this community, supplying the materials essential to an education at the inns and life as a legal professional. Such activities would by no means have fully occupied the stationers who worked here, but archival traces confirm there were relationships between the legal community and the local book trade. In 1597, for example, Gray's Inn allowed a petitioner to build two new shops beside its entrance as long as the lease of these shops should go to 'none but a bookeseller'.[53] Smethwick himself provided 'one half the new books' when the Temple Church—based on the south side of Fleet Street, across from St Dunstan's—decided to restock its titles in 1620.[54] In 1630 the stationer Richard Meighen, who ran a bookshop that neighboured Smethwick's own shop in St Dunstan's churchyard, decided to open a second bookshop beside the gate to the Middle Temple itself. Members of the inn agreed the lease, but explicitly reminded him that he should 'sell books for students of the law'.[55] It was from this shop that Meighen went on to publish both a quarto edition of Shakespeare's *The Merry Wives of Windsor* in 1630 and the second edition of Shakespeare's Folio in 1632.

Given the proximity of St Dunstan's to the various inns of court and chancery, it is tempting to think that Ling's early editions of *Hamlet* were informed by the neighbourhood of his bookshop. His premises in St Dunstan's was ideally situated to appeal to the local 'Universitie, as it were, of students', as John Stow put it in his 1603 *Survay of London*, many of whom had recently completed an undergraduate degree at Oxford or Cambridge and had now graduated to the final stage of

---

[51] For an introduction to the educational and cultural life of the inns, see J. H. Baker, 'The Third University 1450–1550: Law School or Finishing School?' in Jayne Elisabeth Archer, Elizabeth Goldring, and Sarah Knight eds, *The Intellectual and Cultural World of the Early Modern Inns of Court* (Manchester: Manchester University Press, 2013), pp. 8–24.

[52] St Dunstan's reserved a chapel on its north side for members of Clifford's Inn: *Vestry Minute Book*, LMA P69/DUN2/B/001/MS03016/001, p. 104.

[53] Reginald Fletcher ed., *The Pension Book of Gray's Inn: 1569–1669* (London: Gray's Inn, 1901), p. 133.

[54] F. A. Inderwick ed., *A Calendar of the Inner Temple Records, Volume 2: 1603–1660* (London: The Inner Temple, 1898), pp. 126–7. See also the Inner Temple's 1635 decree that 'there should be no shops in the House but those for selling books, parchment, and the like' (p. 22), and the Middle Temple's protection of shops that were occupied by 'tradesmen proper and useful to the Society, such as stationers, booksellers': Charles Martin ed., *Minutes of the Parliament of the Middle Temple, Volume II: 1603–1649* (London: Middle Temple, 1904), p. 1435.

[55] Martin ed., *Minutes of the Parliament*, p. 766.

their educations.[56] In Stow's words, the inns were 'replenished partly with young studentes, and partly with graduates and practisers of the law'; the inns of chancery were mostly filled with attorneys and solicitors, 'and yet there want not some other being young students' who had again arrived 'from one of the Universities'.[57] During the legal terms this community would swell into a thriving population: in 1602, the lawyer Sir Edward Coke judged there were about a thousand members in the four main inns combined, not including the inns of chancery.[58] Perhaps unsurprisingly, then, the inns could be envisaged as a possible readership. The clergyman and natural philosopher John Beale, urging his publisher to finance 1,000 copies of his latest book in about 1640, made his case for the relatively large edition size by claiming that he knew 'it wilbe well recomended' to 'the Innes of Courts, & to both Universityes'.[59]

The right to copy for *Hamlet* was first registered by the printer James Roberts in 1602. Ling never entered his ownership of the copy in the Stationers' Register, but he must have acquired it legitimately because it was one of the titles that John Smethwick acquired from Ling's estate in 1607. Another of Ling's entries in the Stationers' Register suggests that he did envisage Shakespeare's work cohering with material that was more clearly directed towards an inns of court clientele. In January of 1607, Ling entered three other Shakespeare plays: *Romeo and Juliet*, *Love's Labour's Lost*, and *The Taming of a* [/*the*] *Shrew*. On the same day he also entered one other work: the scholar Sir Thomas Smith's *The common-wealth of England* (Ling produced a note to show he acquired Smith's title 'by bergaine & assignement' from the bookseller Gregory Seton, investing the acquisition with a sense of purpose).[60] Ling died before he was able to publish an edition of Smith's book, but it became a bestselling title for Smethwick, who published six editions between 1609 and 1640. While nothing limits the appeal of Smith's work to lawyers or to students, it was clearly relevant to an inns of court education. Smith was regius professor of civil law at Cambridge before he died in 1577 and his book, which supplied a forensic analysis of England's structures of legal governance,

---

[56] John Stow, *A survey of London* (1603, STC 23343), sig. F7r. See also Sir George Buck's description of 'the Colledges, and collegiate houses founded in this Cittie, for the professors of the Municipall, or common Law' as part of a 'Third Universitie of England' in John Stow, *The annales* (1615, STC 23338), sig. 4M1r.

[57] Stow, *A survay*, sig. F7v. See also Donald Lupton's description of the inns of court: 'here are Students and Professors; here are Students that will not be Professors; here are Professors & Students: here are Professors yet not Students; & here bee some that are neyther Students nor Professors', *London and the countrey* (1632, STC 16944), sig. C8v.

[58] Wilfred R. Prest, *The Inns of Court under Elizabeth I and the Early Stuarts 1590–1640* (London: Longman, 1972), p. 8.

[59] John Beale to Josua Kirton, Hartlib Papers, 51/6A–7B. The '*Innes-of-Court-Man*' was a common character type; the quotation here is from Henry Parrot's imaginative account of a list of bookshop customers in his poem 'Trahit sua quemq*ue* Voluptas' ('each man is led by his own taste') in *The mastive* (1611, STC 19333), sig. H4v.

[60] SCA, *Register C*, fol. 147r; Arber III.337.

was intended for 'the learned in the lawes and policy'.⁶¹ The work covered broader questions that might form part of a legal education ('What is just or law in every Common-wealth'; the 'devision & definition of the lawes of this Realme'); introductions to specific courts (chapters on 'The Court of Starre-chamber'; 'The Court of Requests'), and offered helpful procedural summaries ('Of three manners and formes of tryals'; 'Of Judges in the Common law of England, the maner of tryall and pleading').⁶² If we find resonance and meaning in the togetherness of titles when they share a binding or space on a bookseller's shelf, then perhaps the affinity between Shakespeare and Smith represented by Ling's entry of 1607 suggests the stationer had in mind for both authors the same imagined readership founded on the legal institutions among which his own bookshop was situated.

Hamlet, of course, is no lawyer, but he is a university student. His identity as a scholar is central to his in-between status in the play, not to mention his introspection. The death of his father has prevented him from finishing his education and so from graduating into the world as a fully formed agent. Hamlet breaks off his studies to attend his father's funeral, and in act one both Claudius and Gertrude prevent him from going back to school in Wittenberg ('Stay here with us' urges the Queen, 'go not to *Wittenberg*').⁶³ Read with this focus on his student identity, Hamlet's anxieties about if and how and when he should act to revenge his father's murder seem related to his status as a young man who is not yet fully formed. In a curious moment early in the play, for example, we see Hamlet collapse into the guise of a student just when we might expect him to act. Having listened to the ghost of his father recount the story of his 'most unnaturall' murder 'by a brothers hand', Hamlet reels under conflicting emotions. Overcome, he vows to 'wipe away all sawes of Bookes' (a 'saw' was a sententious saying), and 'triviall fond conceites' that he has stored in 'the tables | Of my memorie'.⁶⁴ But as he wavers on the brink of action he retreats, crying out:

> Yes, yes, by heaven, a damnd pernitious villaine,
> Murderous, bawdy, smiling, damned villaine,
> (My tables) meet it is I set it downe,
> That one may smile, and smile, and be a villayne;
> At least I am sure, it may be so in *Denmarke*.
> So uncle, there you are, there you are.⁶⁵

At this critical moment of emotion, Hamlet intellectualizes his suffering and retreats into the practices of early modern pedagogy. Having first dismissed 'all

---

⁶¹ Thomas Smith, *The common-wealth of England* (1609, STC 22862), sig. A2r.
⁶² Smith, *common-wealth*, sig. A3r–4v.
⁶³ William Shakespeare, *The tragicall historie of Hamlet Prince of Denmarke* (1603, STC 22275), sig. B3v.
⁶⁴ Shakespeare, *Hamlet* (1603), sig. C4r, C4v.   ⁶⁵ Shakespeare, *Hamlet* (1603), sig. C4v–D1r.

Sawes of books', both because commonplaces cannot do justice to the depth of feeling he experiences, and also because they represent an educational practice of note taking that Hamlet associates with youth and a time of 'triviall fond conceites', he nevertheless fumbles for 'My tables', meaning his pocketbook, to write down the phrase that has struck him. Having begun by dismissing the idea that stores of language can help him here, the climax of Hamlet's speech is that his student mind finds comfort in generating and recording a (relatively common) maxim. Hamlet's concluding thought, 'So uncle, there you are, there you are', suggests that he has taken out his notebook and recorded the phrase, enacting the process he has just sworn to set aside.

Elsewhere in the play relations between students structure Hamlet's social loyalties, inform his decisions, and enable the plot to unfold. His loyal university friend and 'fellow studient' Horatio is both confidant and ally in the plot to uncover Claudius's guilt; the play's opening moments foreground Horatio's identity as a possible aid to communicating with the ghost of Hamlet's father: 'Thou art a scholler, speake to it *Horatio*'.[66] Less helpful are Hamlet's old schoolfellows Rosencrantz and Guildenstern (or 'Rossencraft' and 'Gilderstone' as they are introduced in Q1). Hamlet's initially warm greeting to this pair as his 'kinde Schoole-fellowes' rapidly dissolves into the suspicion that they 'would play upon mee' like a pipe. Eventually the pair deliver instructions for their own death following Hamlet's substitution of the letter that was originally intended for him.[67]

With this chapter's emphasis on the urban milieu of the play's publication in mind, perhaps Ling's decision to finance Q1 *Hamlet* immediately after his move west was encouraged by the narrative focus on a character whose dramatized identity as a student offered particular purchase to readers of the St Dunstan's area, many of whom cohered around the pedagogical and rhetorical practices of legal study.[68] This interpretation of the play's publication is supported by the first quarto of *Hamlet* itself, which deliberately appeals to the student market in a way that is unique among Shakespeare's early printed books by including a reference to university performance on its title page. The play was 'diverse times acted' not only in London but 'in the two universities of Cambridge and Oxford'.[69] If these performance details were, as Alan H. Nelson has suggested, a marketing device added by the publisher, rather than an accurate record of performance history,

---

[66] Shakespeare, *Hamlet* (1603), sig. B1v.
[67] Shakespeare, *Hamlet* (1603), sig. B4v, E2v, G1r. In Q1 the death of Rossencraft and Gilderstone is reported by Horatio at H2v–3r.
[68] For the ways in which early modern plays could draw on the identities and practices of London neighbourhoods see Sanders, *Cultural Geography*, pp. 178–212.
[69] Shakespeare, *Hamlet* (1603), sig. [A]2r. Smethwick also foregrounded links between St Dunstan's and the universities in a similar manner: his edition of William Lisle's *The faire Æthiopian* (1630, STC 13047.5) was sold 'at S. *Dunstans* Church-yard in Fleet-street, and by S. *Maries* in both Universities'.

then Ling's environment in St Dunstan's could explain why the publisher added this unusual tagline.[70]

Regardless of Gabriel Harvey's comment that *Hamlet* was a play for 'the wiser sort', the popularity of both this play and the wider Hamlet story was never limited to a university or inns of court readership. After all, the earliest recorded performance of Shakespeare's play may have taken place on a boat off the coast of West Africa, and many other early printed references attest to its wider popularity. Nevertheless, thinking about Ling's arrival in a new bibliographic community at St Dunstan's, and his sense of when and how to establish both himself and Shakespeare in a fresh part of the city, enriches our sense of how the earliest editions of *Hamlet* were conceived as publishing ventures.

1609: Q3 *Romeo and Juliet*

The next Shakespeare book to be financed from St Dunstan's was the third quarto of *Romeo and Juliet* (1609), an edition published by John Smethwick following his inheritance of Nicholas Ling's titles after the latter's death in 1607.[71] *Romeo and Juliet* was an unusually mobile text. The first three editions each appeared from a distinct area of London, none of which was the main hub of Paul's Cross (Figure 4.3). The first quarto's shortened version was printed and published by John Danter beside Smithfield in 1597; the second was published two years later by Cuthbert Burby beside the Royal Exchange in the east; Smethwick's third quarto rehoused the play to the west of the city. The play is therefore a good test case to ask: how should we read these repeated traversals of the city? To what extent did it matter that a book was published in different locations?

The fact of movement itself reveals that a text was undergoing change in some form. The most common reason books travelled between addresses was the transfer of their ownership between stationers, and so the appearance of a new address in a book's imprint registers a fluctuation within the book trade. A change like this might involve a clash of estimations. On the one side, a stationer may have considered a title to be no longer valuable and so up for sale. On the other side of such a transaction was a stationer who saw the same title differently and was willing to pay, investing an old text with positive momentum. One of these scenarios must lie behind the 1628 transferral of *Othello* from the Westminster bookseller Thomas Walkley to the St Dunstan's figure Richard Hawkins, who published an edition in 1630.[72] Walkley continued in the book trade till 1658 and remained

---

[70] Alan H. Nelson ed., *Records of Early English Drama: Cambridge*, 2 vols (Toronto, ON: University of Toronto Press, 1989), vol. 2, p. 725 and appendix 10. See also William Shakespeare, *Hamlet*, ed. Ann Thompson and Neil Taylor (London: Arden Shakespeare, 2006), pp. 55–6.

[71] SCA, *Register C*, fol. 161r; Arber III.365.   [72] SCA, *Register D*, p. 160; Arber IV.194.

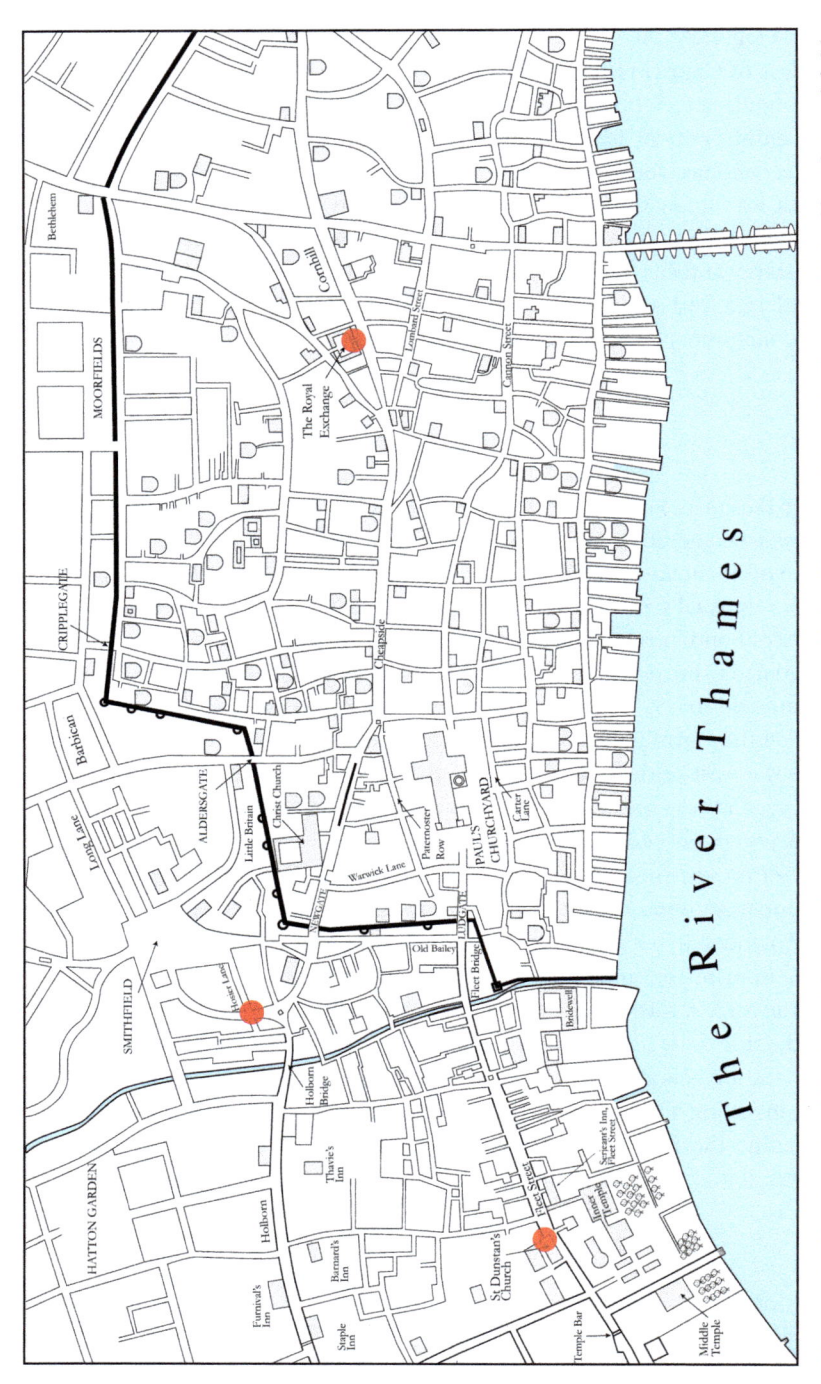

Figure 4.3 The sites of publication of the first three quartos of *Romeo and Juliet*. The first edition (1597) was published beside Smithfield (centre); the second quarto of 1599 was from the Royal Exchange (right); John Smethwick's third edition was published from St Dunstan's Churchyard on the left of this image in 1609. The map is based on that used in *STC*, vol. 3, insert between pp. 246–7 ('London in December 1666').

interested in drama: he published most of his playbooks (nineteen of twenty-five editions) after he sold *Othello*. Was Walkley simply bored of the author of whom he had boasted in 1622 that his 'name is sufficient to vent his worke'?[73] Or did Hawkins pursue this title with the Second Folio in mind? The relocation of a book was in some ways a precarious moment, when the book's cultural status teetered between ascendancy or decline.

The changes that propelled a book into motion might also be biographical. In the case of *Romeo and Juliet*, both of its first two owners died shortly after the editions they published. The different imprint addresses on the play's title pages are in a sense also little epitaphs for the play's previous owners. The play's path between its three points of publication and wholesale inscribes a map of social relations: before he died, John Danter worked with the play's next owner Cuthbert Burby several times; Burby in turn worked regularly with Nicholas Ling, who acquired Burby's titles. Here the circulation of a text looks like the cargo of friendship. The work moved along pathways that had themselves been forged over the collaborative publication of other books.

The version of a text that emerged at the end of such bookish journeys could be quite different to that found at the start. For *Othello*, Hawkins stripped the text of Walkley's address, transforming it into an example of the incomplete 'booke without an Epistle' with which Walkley's own introduction took issue.[74] Such textual transformations are particularly apparent for *Romeo and Juliet*, a play that was completely overhauled for its second edition. The differences are stark enough that we might ask what it was that actually moved between the bookshops of Danter and Burby. A copy of Danter's printed edition certainly found its way into Burby's hands and was used to set parts of the second quarto.[75] But this printed copytext was also joined by a new manuscript—perhaps theatrical or perhaps authorial, critics are undecided—which enlarged the play with around seven hundred new lines, including by developing Juliet's role and changing important features of the play's final two acts. A few scenarios are possible. Either Burby acquired the new manuscript first, in which case he had to deal with Danter in order to publish an edition. Or Burby first acquired the right to copy for the existing printed edition and then sought a new manuscript to update the text. Either way, the play's movement between Danter and Burby exposed it to—or was prompted by?—the grafting on of new material.

---

[73] Thomas Walkley, 'The Stationer to the Reader' in William Shakespeare, *The tragoedy of Othello* (1622, STC 22305), sig. A2r.
[74] Walkley, 'Stationer to the Reader' in Shakespeare, *Othello* (1622), sig. A2r.
[75] William Shakespeare, *Romeo and Juliet*, edited by René Weis (London: Bloomsbury Arden Shakespeare, 2012), p. 98; *Romeo and Juliet*, edited by Francis X. Connor in *The New Oxford Shakespeare: The Complete Works Critical Reference Edition*, 2 vols (Oxford: Oxford University Press, 2017), vol. 1, pp. 667–759, at pp. 668–70.

194   SHAKESPEARE'S SYNDICATE

The play's arrival at St Dunstan's for its third edition prompted further, if less immediately arresting, changes. Smethwick produced a carefully modified version of the previous quarto; his edition makes several intelligent textual interventions to correct dialogue. The third quarto notices and corrects, for example, the fact that two speeches by Juliet appear in succession in the previous edition. In the faulty text, when Juliet bids Romeo goodnight ('Parting is such sweete sorrow, | That I shall say good night, till it be morrow') she then answers herself: 'Sleep dwel upon thine eyes, peace in thy breast.'[76] A simple error perhaps, but one which Smethwick's edition corrected by reassigning Juliet's 'sweete sorrow' lines to Romeo, creating a reading that was retained by the Folio. We might imagine this sort of error to have been picked up by a sharp-eyed agent in the printing house: a corrector, perhaps, or one of Sonia Massai's 'annotating readers'.[77] If so, then the intervention reminds us that the labour force by which books were made and sold also changed with the stasis or motion of a text. Smethwick hired the printer John Windet based in Paul's Wharf to print the third quarto of *Romeo and Juliet*, whereas for the previous edition, Cuthbert Burby had hired Thomas Creede, who worked south of Burby's Royal Exchange bookshop. The play's movement between publishers therefore pushed it into different networks of working relationships that might affect, at the level of the printing house, habits of spelling, correction, and punctuation, and at the level of retail, the arts and relationships by which apprentices and the master bookseller promoted the book for sale.[78] Movement here introduced the play to fresh pairs of eyes and new working practices, subjecting it to a process of refinement and evolution that in the case of *Romeo and Juliet* removed obvious errors and paid increasing attention to literary qualities like metre and characterization. Perhaps our careful bibliographic scrutiny of the relations between some of Shakespeare's more editorially complex texts is a form of reading that is itself implicitly cartographic, whether or not we attend to that variable. When we record textual variance and notice alternative conventions around spellings or speech prefixes or running titles, we establish local textual habits and practices that belonged to particular workshops. To compare these differences, then, is also to move between such workshops and create a different kind of 'map' that helps us to navigate editorial possibility. It is just as conceivable,

---

[76] The moment and its correction appear on D4v of the two respective editions: William Shakespeare, *The most excellent and lamentable tragedie, of Romeo and Juliet* (1599 and 1609, STC 22323–4). Sonia Massai discusses Smethwick's handling of the text in *Shakespeare and the Rise of the Editor* (Cambridge: Cambridge University Press, 2007), pp. 173–9.
[77] Massai, *Rise of the Editor*, pp. 31–8.
[78] The pattern of textual improvement we see between Q2 and Q3 *Romeo and Juliet* continued into the fourth quarto, which was financed by Smethwick in parallel with the First Folio. Sonia Massai finds that an even 'shrewder annotator' worked on this fourth quarto, introducing changes that show 'an alert agent intent on perfecting' the play: *Rise of the Editor*, pp. 176, 177. Even if a text remained within the same publishing house, its circulation among new readers could enable change.

though, that the journey of a book could introduce fresh layers of error.[79] The movement of a text between publishers thus looks to have been replete with possibilities for both error and improvement.

If it seems far-fetched to introduce the variable of geography into a play's textual history, we should remember that Shakespeare's books invite this approach through the language on their title pages. Around one-third of his plays foreground specific geographic locations when they advertise their performance at London's theatres: the first quarto of *King Lear* draws our attention to its performance at 'the Gloabe on the Bancke-side', above its print address at Nathaniel Butter's bookshop 'at the sign of the Pide Bull neere S. *Austins* Gate'. The title page grants the two forums of publication an equivalency of status.[80] Mention of the Globe theatre is a relatively common feature of Shakespeare's title pages but is not the only performance venue: his books also foreground performance before King James 'at White-Hall', or 'at the Black-Friers'.[81] As well as attaching themselves to specific locations, successive editions of the books also offer connections to their textual predecessors, and by doing so they implicitly establish relationships to other parts of the city. Burby's Royal Exchange quarto of *Romeo and Juliet* was, its title page tells us, a 'corrected, augmented, and amended' version of the Smithfield text; Smethwick's St Dunstan's quarto was also 'Newly corrected'. Here the books stand in complicated relation to their past selves. Each new edition acknowledged the existence of its predecessor in order to disavow it. Perhaps early modern readers treated such claims with weary cynicism (though Alan B. Farmer has recently challenged this idea).[82] Yet movement to a fresh publishing location here seems one way that such rhetoric might gain credibility. The physical distance between the bookshops of Danter, Burby, and Smethwick might consolidate the textual distance each edition sought to establish from its own legacy, helping the new book to establish new horizons of expectation about what readers might encounter within.

Escaping its bibliographic locale could alter a book's status in other ways. The first five editions of Shakespeare's popular narrative poem *The Rape of Lucrece*, for

---

[79] Just as it updated Burby's text, Smethwick's 1609 edition also introduced several new accidental errors. In some copies, as the Prince sums up the 'glooming peace' of the play's conclusion, his final couplet finishes not with a full stop but a comma, creating for a brief unsettling moment—at least as this play is printed on the page—the striking effect of the character jumping out of his dramatic world to shout the 'FINIS' that ends the playbook: 'For never was a storie of more woe, | Then this of *Juliet* and her *Romeo*, | FINIS.': Shakespeare, *Romeo and Juliet* (1609, STC 22324), sig. M2r.

[80] William Shakespeare, *M. William Shak-speare: his true chronicle historie of the life and death of King Lear* (1608, STC 22292), sig. [A]2r.

[81] Shakespeare, *King Lear* (1608), sig. [A]2r; William Shakespeare, *The tragoedy of Othello* (1622, STC 22305), sig. A1r. Six editions of plays by Shakespeare name the Blackfriars Theatre; eighteen mention the Globe; three give Whitehall. These figures are from *DEEP: Database of Early English Playbooks*. Ed. Alan B. Farmer and Zachary Lesser. Created 2007. Accessed 10 April 2021. http://deep.sas.upenn.edu.

[82] Farmer, 'Shakespeare as Leading Playwright in Print, 1598–1608/9'. The marketing language of Shakespeare's title pages is examined in more detail at the end of chapter three.

example, were all published from either in or beside Paul's Cross Churchyard. But in 1614 *Lucrece* passed through Robert Armin's imaginary barrier of Ludgate when it was acquired by the bookseller Roger Jackson, who worked from a bookshop on Fleet Street. The edition that Jackson subsequently published in 1616 looks markedly different to any of the previous five. While all earlier editions of the poem carried the simple title of 'Lucrece', Jackson was the first to foreground the poem's sexual violence by offering the full title that we now use: 'The Rape of Lucrece'. He was also the first—perhaps inspired by news of the playwright's recent death—to add Shakespeare's name to the title page. Other changes included the addition of a new contents leaf to the start of the poem which divided the text into twelve sections, each of which was then identified within the poem by a marginal note.[83] One effect of Jackson's additions was to create a more easily navigable version of *Lucrece*. In another of his books published in the same year, Jackson suggested such neat organization was a deliberate response to the needs of those who browsed his bookshop on Fleet Street. He noted that his recent books had 'found generall approbation and applause', but admitted they had not been 'so orderly digested by the Penne', and went on to explain that he had 'for your greater delight in reading, and ease in finding [...] Methodically reduced' the book—a miscellany of quotations entitled *The rich cabinet*—into new headings.[84] Despite being the sixth edition of the poem, Jackson's version of *Lucrece* is thus significant in that he reconceived the text within the cultures and mores—what Pierre Bourdieu might describe as the *habitus*—of his publishing business in Fleet Street. Changes such as those that Jackson introduced, which came to define how *Lucrece* was read in the seventeenth century, reflect the predilections and concerns of publishers embedded in different environments. Part of the richness of the textual history of Shakespeare's books is therefore indebted to their continued circulation among the city's different bibliographic communities.

1611: Q3 *Hamlet*

The final Shakespeare book to be published from St Dunstan's before the arrival of the First Folio was the third edition of *Hamlet*, published by Smethwick in 1611. The text itself was a reprint of the previous edition with several corrections and alterations (including neatening the generic status of the play from a 'tragicall historie' to simply 'The tragedy of Hamlet'). Though textually unremarkable, this edition nevertheless marks the moment at which interest in Shakespeare took

---

[83] William Shakespeare, *The Rape of Lucrece* (1616, STC 22350), sig. A3v. On the poem's editorial history see Sasha Roberts, *Reading Shakespeare's Poems in Early Modern England* (Basingstoke: Palgrave Macmillan, 2003), pp. 102–42; Ben Higgins, '*Judith* and *Lucrece*: Reading Shakespeare between Copy and Work' in *English Literary Renaissance* 52.1 (2022), pp. 34–71.

[84] R. J., 'The Printer To the courteous Readers' in T. G., *The rich cabinet* (1616, STC 11522), sig. A2r–v.

root in St Dunstan's. Alongside Q3 *Hamlet*, the bookseller John Helme, a new arrival to this churchyard, financed his own 'Shakespearean' offering: the second quarto of the first and second parts of the anonymously authored play *The troublesome Raigne of John King of England*.[85] The play was not in fact by Shakespeare, but Helme's attribution on the title page ('Written by W. Sh.') seems designed to trick readers into thinking they were buying a copy of Shakespeare's play, *The life and death of King John*, unpublished before the First Folio.[86] Not a genuine Shakespeare offering, then, but Helme's cunning attribution nevertheless registered his awareness of the commercial value of Shakespeare's name. Shortly afterwards, another new arrival to St Dunstan's—the bookseller Richard Moore—signalled further interest in Shakespeare's work when he financed a second edition of the important poetry miscellany *Englands Helicon* (1614), which mingled Shakespeare's verse with writings by other contemporary poets.[87]

This fresh interest in Shakespeare's work from the booksellers of St Dunstan's was partly driven by a surge of new arrivals. In 1605, the church's parishioners (Smethwick among them) clubbed together to buy land on the adjacent Fetter Lane for the specific purpose of expanding St Dunstan's churchyard—a move that seems to have paved the way for new booksellers to arrive over the next few years, bringing fresh and acquisitive eyes.[88] This sense of the churchyard becoming a dynamic bookselling environment is captured by a survey of 1629. Walking around the yard, the surveyor recorded seven shops, six of which were owned by bookselling publishers:

>William Washington a Shop
>Richard Meighen a Shopp
>John Smithwick a shoppe
>John Mariott a Shopp
>Richard Moore a Shopp
>\Thomas Jones a shopp/
>John Stemp a Shopp
>\Edward Marshall/
>Francis Grigge a Shopp[89]

---

[85] *The First and second Part of the troublesome Raigne of John King of England* (1611, STC 14646). The first part begins on A2r, the second on G4r. The first imprint to place Helme in the churchyard dates from 1608.

[86] Lukas Erne, *Shakespeare and the Book Trade* (Cambridge: Cambridge University Press, 2013), p. 81; see also J. W. Sider ed., *The Troublesome Reign of John, King of England* (New York: Garland, 1979), pp. xiv–xv.

[87] *Englands Helicon* (1614, STC 3192), sig. E5r for the Shakespearean sonnet.

[88] *Churchwarden's Accounts for St Dunstan in the West*, LMA P69/DUN2/B/011/MS02968/001, fol. 499r–500v. The publisher William Holme 3 arrived in 1606; John Busby 2, Richard Moore, and John Helme joined in 1608; Roger Barnes joined in 1610.

[89] *Scavengers' Rate Assessments*, LMA P69/DUN2/C/001/MS03783, fol. 10v. The odd one out here was Edward Marshall, a maker of funerary monuments, who took over Grigge's workshop.

The fact that the bookseller John Stempe and the tomb sculptor Francis Grigge were struck through and replaced in the time it took to complete the survey suggests their shops did not lie empty for long. The same process of erasure and replacement features in a second survey made the following year, which confirms the layout of the churchyard shops and provides the only known glimpse of Smethwick's son George, here presumably expanding his father's publishing and bookselling business to a second premises:

> \george Smithwick/
> ~~William Washinton~~ a shopp
> Richard Meighen a shopp
> John Smithwicke a shopp
> John Mariott a shopp
> Richard more a shopp
> Thomas Jones a shopp
> Edward Marshall a shopp[90]

The third editions of both *Hamlet* and of *Romeo and Juliet* thus mark a stage of growth and consolidation within this bibliographic community. The generative nature of this newly crowded environment can be seen in various forms of collaboration. It was a consortium of four exclusively St Dunstan's booksellers who financed Michael Drayton's topographical poem *Poly-Olbion* (1612), a large and expensive folio with engraved maps.[91] Four publishers working from within this churchyard were collectively responsible for each of the twenty-two editions of the poet Francis Quarles's work that were published between 1620 and 1635, suggesting these stationers nurtured certain authors in ways that overran the boundaries of any one of their bookshops and instead formed a kind of neighbourhood specialism.[92] In another example of the relationship between literary production and geographic proximity, the bookseller John Benson borrowed three of the titles used in his *Poems: written by Wil. Shake-speare. Gent* (1640) from a book

---

[90] *Scavengers' Rate Assessments*, LMA P69/DUN2/C/001/MS03783, fol. B9r. It was to a different son, Francis, that Smethwick eventually left his bookselling business (see p. 171 above, with reference to Smethwick's will). Francis left little trace of his activities, beyond his publication of two editions of Thomas Lodge's *Euphues golden legacie* (1634, STC 16673.5 and 1642, Wing L2810) and an intriguing single folio leaf, now in the Folger Library, on which is recorded a manuscript guarantee, similar to that shown in Figure 3.5 on p. 149, that the unknown volume from which the leaf was detached was originally 'Bought of Francis Smethwicke the 6th of Feburary 1639 and he doeth warent it to be perfit or to make it perfit or to give hime his mony againe': Folger. X. d. 254.

[91] Michael Drayton, *Poly-Olbion by Michaell Drayton Esqr* (1612, STC 7226). This alternative syndicate, which included the stationers Matthew Lownes, John Browne, John Helme, and John Busby 2, may have been inspired by the fact that Smethwick had already published several editions of Drayton's *Poems* from the churchyard (in 1608 and 1610 for example).

[92] These publishers were: Richard Moore (three editions), Thomas Dewe (two editions), George Winder (one edition), and John Marriot (sixteen editions).

that was published by his churchyard neighbour Thomas Jones.[93] That Benson lifted these titles from sheets of his neighbour's book suggests a kind of textual porousness among this community. Strikingly, none of these booksellers used individual signs to identify their shops; instead they preferred to identify themselves simply by their collective address in the churchyard. It was not till after the Folio was published that any more of Shakespeare's works came to this locale, but the local expansion that began at about the time that Smethwick financed Q3 *Hamlet* would eventually sustain the final years of Shakespeare publishing in the first half of the seventeenth century.

1623: the First Folio

'[B]eleeve this,' wrote the booksellers Richard Bonian and Henry Walley, musing darkly on Shakespeare's death in their preface to *Troilus and Cressida* (1609), 'when hee is gone, and his Commedies out of sale, you will scramble for them.'[94] There was no immediate scramble for new editions of Shakespeare's work after 1616, but the following years saw the publication of the Jaggard Quartos of 1619 and ultimately the First Folio in 1623. After the Folio, though, interest in Shakespeare dwindled in every area of London except in the community around St Dunstan's church (Figures 4.4 and 4.5). The bookshops of Paul's Cross acted as the wholesale outlets of just three further individual editions of a Shakespeare play before the Restoration. The elderly bookseller Matthew Law, by now reaching the end of his life, acted as the wholesaler for the seventh edition of *Richard III* (1629). The printer John Norton, recognizing that the market for Shakespeare's books teetered between two churchyards, published an edition of *1 Henry IV* (1632) which advertised two wholesale outlets: one beside St Dunstan's church, and one at William Sheare's bookshop 'at the great south doore of Saint Pauls-Church'.[95] And the only other Shakespearean playbook that was published after the Folio and marked as belonging to Paul's Churchyard had its own claim to

---

[93] These three titles, which in Benson's edition frame sonnets sixty-one, sixty-two, and seventy, originally appeared in Jones's edition of Henry Parrot's *Cures for the itch* (1626, STC 19328). Jones published this title from a bookshop in the Strand; by 1627 he was collaborating with the St Dunstan's publisher John Marriot, and by 1629 he had moved into the churchyard himself. Faith Acker suggests that unsold sheets of Jones's book were brought into St Dunstan's, where they caught John Benson's eye: *First Readers of Shakespeare's Sonnets, 1590–1790* (Abingdon: Routledge, 2020). As Margreta de Grazia has noted, the addition of these titles to Shakespeare's sonnets ('*Sat fuisse*'—'to have sufficed'; '*Patiens Armatus*'—'the sufferer in arms'; and '*Nil magnis Invidia*'—'envy is nothing to the great') is 'the result of careful, imaginative and even literary readings': 'The First Reader of *Shake-speares Sonnets*' in Leonard Barkan, Bradin Cormack, and Sean Keilen eds, *The Forms of Renaissance Thought* (London: Palgrave Macmillan, 2009), pp. 86–106, at p. 95.
[94] 'A never writer, to an ever reader. Newes' in William Shakespeare, *The famous historie of Troylus and Cresseid* (1609, STC 22332), sig. ¶2r–v.
[95] William Shakespeare, *The historie of Henry the Fourth* (1632, STC 22286), sig. A1r.

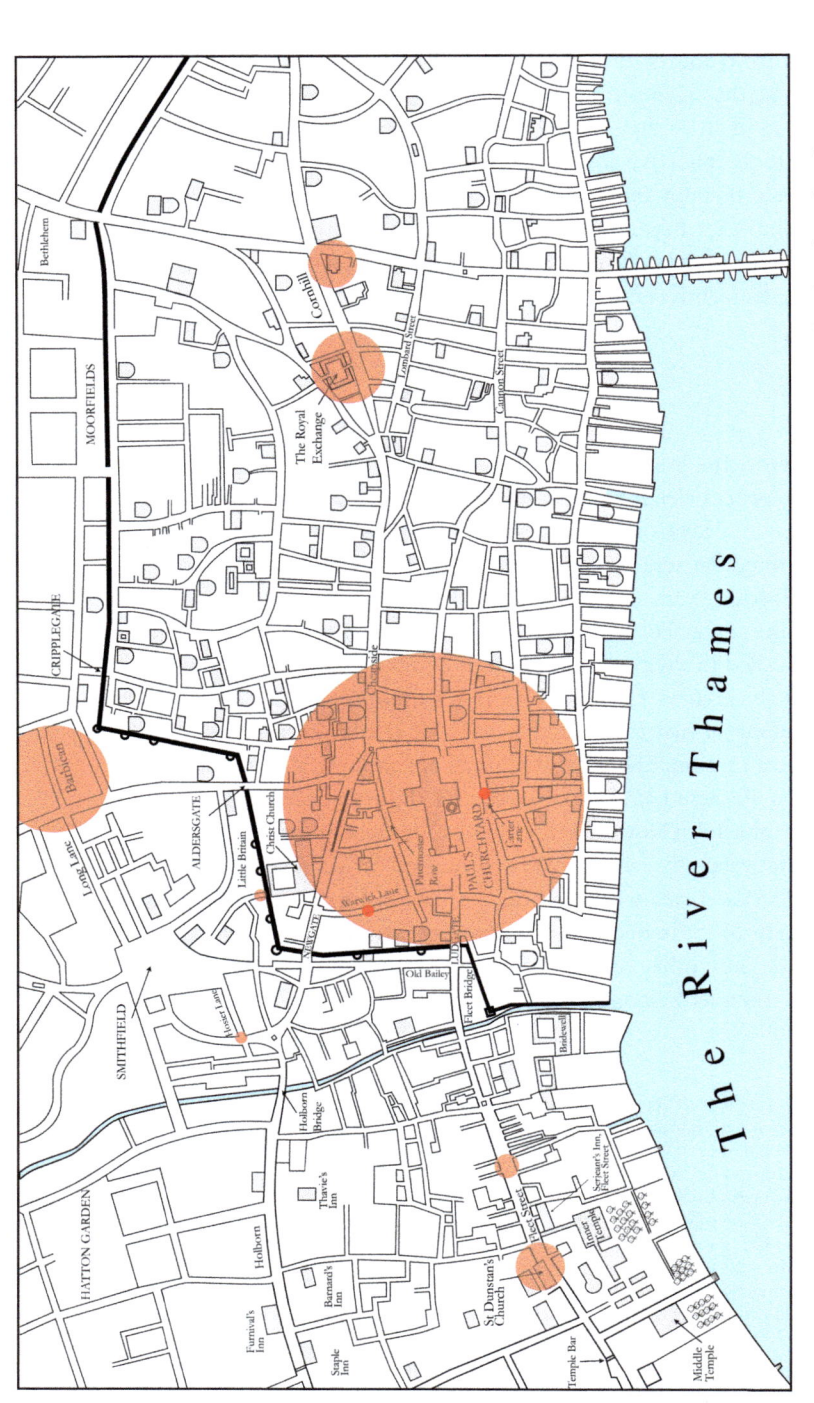

Figure 4.4 Wholesale locations of Shakespeare's books between 1593 and 1622 inclusive. The map shows Paul's Churchyard and Paternoster Row (49 editions—shown at half scale); Barbican (9 editions); the Royal Exchange (6 editions); St Peter's Church in Cornhill (4 editions); St Dunstan's Churchyard (4 editions); Fleet Street (2 editions); Carter Lane (1 edition); Hosier Lane (1 edition); Warwick Lane (1 edition); and Christ Church Gate (1 edition). The 1622 *Othello* published from Britain's Burse in Westminster is not shown. Here and elsewhere, editions with multiple wholesale locations are counted at each location. This map and the one below are based on that used in *STC*, vol. 3, insert between pp. 246–7 ('London in December 1666').

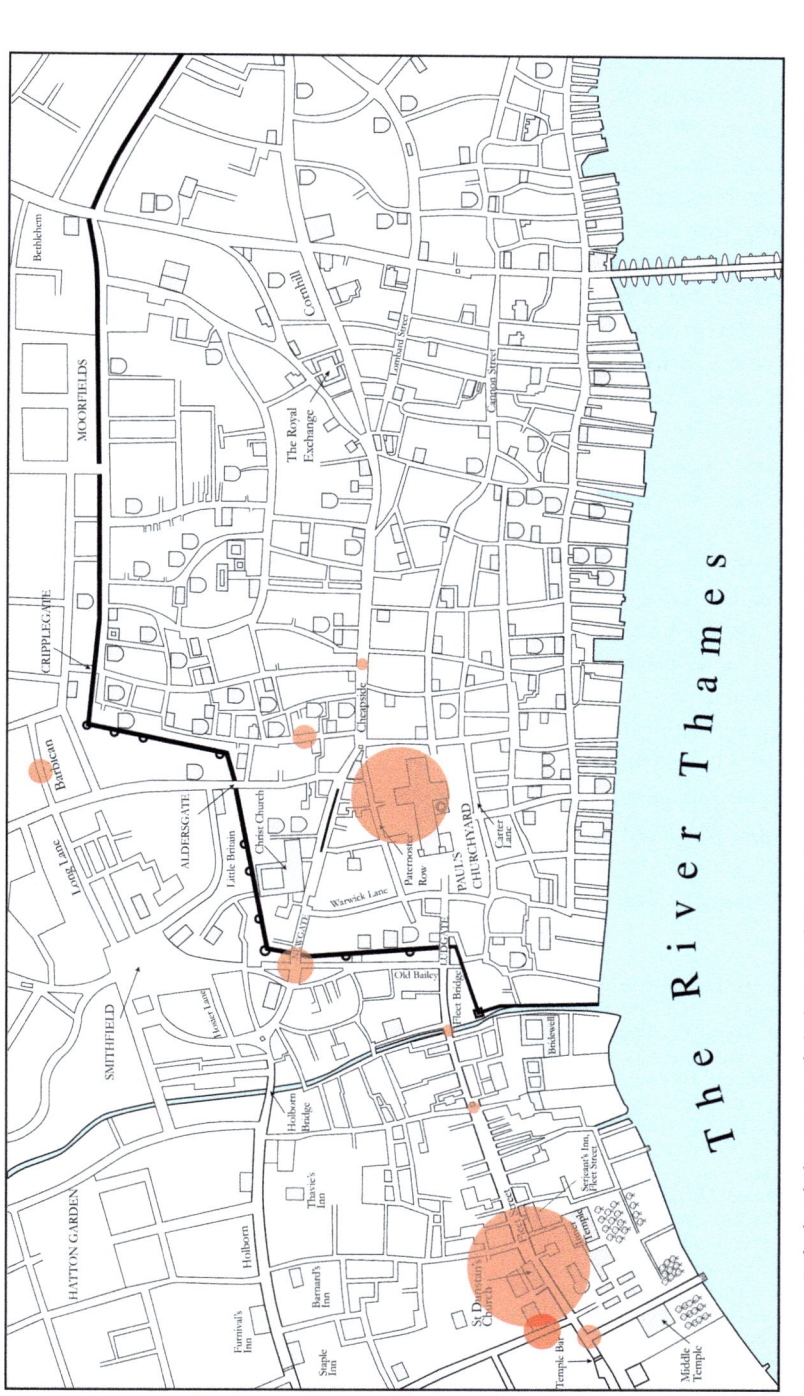

Figure 4.5 Wholesale locations of Shakespeare's books between 1623 and 1640 inclusive. The map shows St Dunstan's Churchyard (10 editions); Paul's Churchyard (8 editions—here shown at full scale); Chancery Lane by Serjeants' Inn (3 editions); Old Bailey without Newgate (3 editions); Barbican (2 editions); Middle Temple Gate (2 editions); Foster Lane (2 editions); Fleet Street (1 edition); Fleet Bridge (1 edition); Cheapside (1 edition). Two editions are not shown: the 1627 *Venus and Adonis* published in Edinburgh and the 1639 edition of *1 Henry IV* published from the Strand.

novelty. This was the first quarto of *The two noble kinsmen* (1634), published by John Waterson from his shop at the sign of the Crown with a title page that advertised the text as collaboratively written by 'the memorable Worthies of their time; M^r. *John Fletcher*, and M^r. *William Shakspeare*'.[96] Yet Waterson's edition was a failure. This is one of the rare instances in which we know at least part of the fate of an early modern playbook: twenty-six years later, the bookseller Humphrey Moseley was 'still trying to unload copies' of this sluggish and unwanted edition.[97]

As Waterson struggled to recoup his investment in his semi-Shakespearean quarto, a reduced but steady market for the playwright's work had emerged on the other side of the city, inviting us to speculate whether the fate of *Kinsmen* might have been different had its publisher been more alert to the new geography of Shakespeare's books. Smethwick alone published seven further editions of Shakespeare's work after the Folio. So confident was he that readers would buy individual editions of Shakespeare's writing alongside a Folio collection that he financed multiple editions of both *Romeo and Juliet* (1623 and 1637) and *Hamlet* (1625 and 1637).[98] Smethwick also published editions of *Love's Labour's Lost* (1631) and the first quarto of *The Taming of the Shrew* (1631) in the build-up to the Second Folio (1632). Other booksellers around him followed suit. Richard Meighen—Smethwick's bookshop neighbour on the survey above—published *The Merry Wives of Windsor* (1630); Richard Hawkins, who worked beside St Dunstan's on Chancery Lane near Serjeants Inn, bought the title to *Othello* from Thomas Walkley and published an edition in 1630. Both Meighen and Hawkins then joined the syndicate which published the Second Folio in 1632. A scattering of Shakespeare plays appeared from other locations, some of which were western (an edition of *The Merchant of Venice* (1637) from Fleet Bridge; another of *1 Henry IV* (1639) from the Strand) and some of which were not (two editions of history plays from Foster Lane; an edition of *Pericles* (1635) from Barbican). But

---

[96] John Fletcher and William Shakespeare, *The two noble kinsmen* (1634, STC 11075), sig. [π]1r. Emma Smith suggests that *Kinsmen*, along with *Pericles* (and nearly *Timon of Athens*) was excluded from the First Folio because its collaborative authorship did not fit with the First Folio's investment in Shakespeare as a solo author: *The Making of Shakespeare's First Folio* (Oxford: Bodleian Library, 2015), pp. 13–15. Lois Potter gives a different view, suggesting the omission was because Fletcher considered the play unfinished: John Fletcher and William Shakespeare, *The Two Noble Kinsmen*, edited by Lois Potter (London: Thomas Nelson and Sons, 1997), p. 13.

[97] Zachary Lesser, 'Shakespeare's Flop: John Waterson and *The Two Noble Kinsmen*' in Marta Straznicky ed., *Shakespeare's Stationers: Studies in Cultural Bibliography* (Philadelphia, PA: University of Pennsylvania Press, 2012), pp. 177–96, at p. 178. Lesser's view is also that the play was 'in the wrong shop at the wrong time' (p. 196), but for different reasons. Lesser argues that when John Waterson took over his father's bookshop at the Crown, he repositioned the business by publishing different kinds of books but failed to capture a new readership. Copies of 'The two Noble kinsmen' were advertised for sale by Moseley in Arnauld d'Andilly, *The manner of ordering fruit-trees* (1660, Wing L942A), sig. a5v. By this point Moseley had given up on promoting the Shakespeare connection: the play was listed as a collaboration between Francis Beaumont and John Fletcher.

[98] For the dates of the undated fourth quartos of *Hamlet* and *Romeo and Juliet*, see: R. Carter Hailey, 'The Dating Game: New Evidence for the Dates of Q4 *Romeo and Juliet* and Q4 *Hamlet*' in *Shakespeare Quarterly* 58.3 (2007): pp. 367–87.

the decades-long association between Shakespeare and Paul's Churchyard was broken. Finally in 1640 Benson published his edition of the *Poems*, a book that was offered for wholesale from Benson's shop 'in S^t. *Dunstans* Church-yard.'

In the early 1620s, then, when the negotiations began for the texts of the First Folio, perhaps those involved were sensitive to the geography of interest in Shakespeare's work. In some ways it seems striking that Smethwick joined the syndicate as a shareholder. There are clearer precedents for William Aspley's involvement: he had collaborated several times with his churchyard neighbour Edward Blount over the publication of some popular titles. Yet Smethwick's links to the Shakespeare syndicate are at one remove, mediated through figures like the stationer Edward Weaver, who both left his 'loving freinde' Smethwick twenty-five shillings for a gold ring on his death, and who also served several important turns for Blount over the years.[99] Perhaps Smethwick's closeness to the Jaggard family, established through shared parish duties with the bookseller John Jaggard, brother to William, became relevant (Smethwick and John Jaggard were both parish constables for St Dunstan's in 1619 and again in 1620). Or perhaps, like the bookseller Laurence Lisle discussed briefly in chapter three, Smethwick used the rights to his valuable plays to secure a place in the publishing team. But regardless of the interplay of cause and effect, one result of Smethwick's inclusion in the syndicate was to grant the Folio an established wholesale distribution point within a distinct and thriving bookselling community in ways that imbued the book with a fresh set of commercial circumstances and possibilities.

Conclusion

What might it mean that Shakespeare's printed work emerged in one part of London and gradually shuffled elsewhere? It is tempting to interpret the post-Folio westwards drift of Shakespeare publishing as the beginnings of a new kind of cultural ascendancy for the playwright. The area around St Dunstan's was, as described above, dominated by the inns of court: institutions that thrived on their own powerful literary and intellectual cultures. The inns were deeply invested in dramatic activities and Shakespeare had an established performance presence among them from an early stage in his career. The playwright's theatre company is known to have performed *The Comedy of Errors* at Gray's Inn in 1594 and *Twelfth*

---

[99] *Will of Edmund Weaver*, TNA PROB 11/177/292. Weaver acted as a surety with Edward Blount for the orphans of the stationer Richard Bankworth in 1620 and witnessed the will of Blount's son-in-law: *Court of Orphans Recognizances*, LMA CLA/002/05/001, fol. 135r; *Will of Richard Bankworth*: TNA PROB 11/138/543.

Night at the Middle Temple in 1602.[100] In 1636, though, when the poet Abraham Cowley mocked the 'Semy-gentleman of th' Innes of Court' who might easily be discovered 'in his study' puzzling away 'At *Shakespeares* Playes, instead of my L. *Cooke*', it is noticeable that the young lawyer in question is reading Shakespeare in his study rather than watching him at a playhouse. That Cowley's caricature reads a copy of Shakespeare's 'Playes' may suggest the poet had the Folio in mind for this vignette. That same term 'Playes' was used a few years earlier by the Puritan writer William Prynne to complain about the second edition of the Folio; Prynne disparaged the fact that 'Shackspeers Plaies' were printed on paper that was 'far better than most Bibles'.[101] It seems possible that the status afforded to Shakespeare through the prestige and cost of a Folio publication made his writing appeal in fresh ways to this fashionable and highly literate domain of readers and to the booksellers who worked among them.

Yet that triumphant narrative, in which the geography of bookselling might allow us to trace Shakespeare's journey into the cultural elect, could only be part of the story. Any sense of success here is undercut by the ensuing dearth of Shakespearean publication. Rather than the growth of St Dunstan's publishing heralding a new era of interest in Shakespeare's work, it was a precursor to his lapse into obscurity. After Benson's *Poems* (1640), individual editions of the plays or poems were few and far between. Paying attention to print culture suggests that Shakespeare's real cultural status did not arrive till the early eighteenth century and the interventions of editors like Nicholas Rowe, Lewis Theobald, and Alexander Pope, at which point both collected works and single editions of Shakespeare's writing became increasingly popular. In this context, the emergence of St Dunstan's as the home of Shakespeare publishing in the late 1620s and 1630s looks like the final flare of life from an author whose reputation was waning. The retirement of Shakespeare's books across the city heralded a difficult phase of their author's literary life: after the initial flush of popularity had faded but before the redemption of posterity and canonicity. Just as we think of 'late Shakespeare' as a critical category that includes plays like *The Winter's Tale*, *The Tempest*, and *Cymbeline*, so too does this final cluster of editions record a different kind of 'lateness' that marks the final years of Shakespeare's early relevancy.

What role does the First Folio play in these narratives of ascendancy and decline? One of the most powerful commercial forces in the early modern book trade was novelty. 'I have noted' scorns a preliminary address in John Webster's *The white divel* (1612) 'those ignorant asses' who visit a bookseller 'not to inquire

---

[100] Alan H. Nelson, 'The Universities and the Inns of Court' in Richard Dutton ed., *The Oxford Handbook of Early Modern Theatre* (Oxford: Oxford University Press, 2011), pp. 280–91. Nelson also suggests an inns of court connection for *Troilus and Cressida*.

[101] Abraham Cowley, *Poeticall blossomes* (1636, STC 5907), sig. E5v–6r. Prynne's comments appear in a marginal note to his *Histrio-mastix. The players scourge* (1633, STC 20464a), sig. **6v.

for good bookes, but new bookes'.[102] Those who seek novelty are fools, according to this address, but the language nevertheless suggests the prevalence of what Michael Saenger has called 'the search for newness' among readers.[103] This hunger for novelty was associated more than anywhere else with Paul's Cross Churchyard. The cathedral was a thriving social centre that hosted the latest books, gossip, and international news. Like a Habermasian 'public sphere', this was a space that structured opinion and taste.[104] In 1609, Thomas Dekker directed an imaginary companion in search of the latest reading material

> to Paules Church-yard, where planting your selfe in a Stationers shop, many instructions are to bee given you, what bookes to call for, how to censure of new bookes, how to mew at the old.[105]

One of the first instructions Dekker gives concerns the age of the books. Within his division of old and new, he makes clear that titles deserve different kinds of scrutiny: new books should be afforded genuine critique ('censure'), while the custom is that older titles should be mocked (we should 'mew' at them). Dekker satirized the behaviour and values of a certain kind of gullish reader, but it is easy to find his emphasis on novelty as an evaluative category in many other early modern sources: 'the first question at every Stationers shoppe' wrote the preacher Thomas Jackson in 1603, 'is, what new thing?' If just 'once the Calendar be chaunged' then a book is 'never enquired after'; such out of date books are then only fit to 'serve for covers' or binding waste for 'everie immodest Poeme'.[106]

As a commercial venture, Shakespeare's Folio embodied a complicated set of relations to this febrile hunger for new textual matter. Though Shakespeare himself was by this point an old commodity, the Folio offered eighteen previously unprinted plays and significantly different versions of ten others. It also foregrounded a new textual authority and sense of completion throughout. When Leonard Digges wrote in his preliminary poem that 'at length' the publishers have given 'The world thy Workes' he both suggested that the Folio was a long time coming and hinted at the public appetite for the unpublished (and so 'novel') material.[107]

At the same time, the Folio's claims about its contents irrevocably changed 'Shakespeare' as a textual product. The book's allure rested precisely on its promise to preclude any future need for the sorts of augmentations or corrections on

---

[102] 'To the Reader' in John Webster, *The white divel* (1612, STC 25178), sig. A2r–v.
[103] Michael Saenger, *The Commodification of Textual Engagements in the English Renaissance* (Abingdon: Routledge, 2016), p. 68.
[104] For the newsmongers of Paul's Churchyard see Hentschell, *St Paul's Cathedral Precinct*, pp. 23–67.
[105] Thomas Dekker, *The guls horne-booke* (1609, STC 6500), sig. F3v.
[106] Thomas Jackson, 'To the right worshipful Robert Honnywood' in *Davids pastorall poeme* (1603, STC 14299), sig. ¶5v.
[107] Leonard Digges, 'To the Memorie of the Deceased Authour Maister W. Shakespeare' in Shakespeare, *Comedies, Histories & Tragedies* (1623), sig. πA5+1r.

which booksellers thrived, and by which so many earlier editions of Shakespeare's work were justified. The First Folio is the end point of the discursive values that had thus far shaped the commodification of Shakespeare's writing; after this book, Shakespeare could never be 'new' again. Or rather, any future Shakespeare work that *was* 'new' was indelibly marked by its absence from the Folio. It may have been for this reason that John Waterson's edition of *Kinsmen* (1634), loudly foregrounds the book's collaborative status on its title page. By bracketing Fletcher and Shakespeare together as co-authors, the book seems to excuse its own absence from the Folio. It is certainly for this reason that Benson began his edition of the *Poems* by acknowledging that it 'had not the fortune' to be housed 'with the rest of his everliving Workes'.[108] A post-Folio claim of novelty for a Shakespeare text was therefore a declaration of troubled status. The obvious example of this is *Pericles*, dogged throughout its life by its omission from the Folio. When this play was eventually incorporated into the Shakespeare canon in the Third Folio of 1663, it arrived alongside six other plays we now think of as apocryphal.

If the limitations imposed upon Shakespeare publishing by the First Folio were recognized in Paul's Churchyard, they were less important west of the city centre. One reason for this may have been that time—at least in the way that it measured an author's relevancy—ran at different speeds among different book-trade communities. These varying time zones are immediately visible at distances of greater scale (between city and country, for example), but perhaps London's neighbourhoods contained other, more local temporalities. Just as the bells of London's churches were known to strike the hours at different times, so that three o'clock would ripple erratically across the urban landscape, so too could authors lose their lustre at different speeds in different spaces. The booksellers of St Dunstan's were set apart from the centre of the book trade and may have been less ruled by the need to chase the latest commodity.

Broader changes in the market for playbooks may also have influenced Shakespeare's commercial appeal. A 'second boom' in playbook publishing began after the publication of the First Folio, meaning that the period between 1628 and 1640 saw, on average, more playbooks published per year than had ever appeared before.[109] We might expect that surge to have produced more Shakespeare quartos, but one of the effects of a glut of new playbook titles might have been, to quote Franco Moretti, a 'drastic reorientation of audiences towards the present', meaning that there were simply too many new titles vying for readerly attention

---

[108] I. B., 'To the Reader' in William Shakespeare, *Poems: written by Wil. Shake-speare. Gent* (1640, STC 22344), sig. *2r.

[109] Alan B. Farmer and Zachary Lesser, 'The Popularity of Playbooks Revisited' in *Shakespeare Quarterly* 56.1 (2005): pp. 1–32, at pp. 7–13.

for customers to be interested in revisiting the past.[110] Between 1624 and 1640, dramatists like James Shirley (twenty-eight first editions of plays in that time) and Thomas Heywood (twenty-two first editions) supplied the material that fed the market's need for novelty.

Yet if the Folio conclusively ended Shakespeare's 'new' commercial appeal, it also remade him as what we might think of as a legacy product. The book lifts Shakespeare out of the discourses of fashion, haste, and ephemerality to which most authors were subject. Jonson's praise in the preliminaries, for example, reaches for ideas of permanency and stability:

> But stay, I see thee in the *Hemisphere*
> Advanc'd, and made a Constellation there!
> Shine forth, thou Starre of *Poets*, and with rage,
> Or influence, chide, or cheere the drooping Stage.[111]

Jonson suggests that Shakespeare's constancy, his fixity, will help London's theatres to navigate the vicissitudes of fashion. Here the currency of novelty is turned on its head and reimagined as flimsy and in need of regulation. That sense of a stability achieved by rising above the particularities of the changing moment seems also to have been in John Aubrey's mind in the later seventeenth century. When writing Shakespeare's biography, Aubrey judged the playwright was successful because he refused to write 'upon particular persons, and coxcombeities, that 20 yeares hence, they will not be understood'.[112] Aubrey's thought echoes—and may have been seeded by—the language of stasis and endurance found in the Folio's preliminaries, where Shakespeare was described as 'not of an age, but for all time!', as Jonson famously wrote.[113] It is an endless trope of Folio scholarship to point out that the book forges a new bibliographic identity for Shakespeare, but perhaps we need to think more about how the language of Shakespeare's canonicity was born out of the death of a different kind of commercial impetus. An alternative idiom and set of values through which to envisage Shakespeare's continuing relevancy was prompted into being by the needs of the book trade to articulate the playwright's worth once the concept of novelty could no longer apply.

Finally, there are other reasons that the geography of Shakespeare publishing was in flux when the First Folio arrived. Shakespeare's work was first published in the 1590s. Thirty years later the stationers who shaped the early reception of

---

[110] Moretti uses the phrase to discuss changes in reading habits prompted by the rise of the British novel in the late eighteenth century: *Graphs, Maps, Trees: Abstract Models for a Literary History* (London: Verso, 2005), p. 7.

[111] Ben Jonson, 'To the memory of my beloved, The Author Mr. William Shakespeare' in William Shakespeare, *Comedies, Histories & Tragedies*, sig. πA4v.

[112] John Aubrey, *Brief Lives with An Apparatus for the Lives of our English Mathematical Writers*, edited by Kate Bennett, 2 vols (Oxford: Oxford University Press, 2018), vol. 1, p. 366.

[113] Jonson, 'To the memory' in Shakespeare, *Comedies, Histories & Tragedies*, sig. πA4v.

Shakespeare's writing, many of whom have appeared throughout this book, had mostly died. Andrew Wise and Nicholas Ling were long dead; Thomas Pavier died in 1625; Matthew Law in 1629. Edward Blount, as discussed in chapter one, died in 1632 but published little after the First Folio; William Jaggard died in 1623; Isaac Jaggard in 1627.[114] These deaths signalled the end of an era of literary taste; they remind us that Shakespeare's literary life was deeply entangled with the biographies of those who published him.[115]

* * *

If the unusual spelling of John Smethwick's surname in the colophon of the First Folio symbolized his secondary status in the publication of Shakespeare's work, then that situation had changed by the time the Second Folio was published in 1632. This later edition changed the style of both the imprint and colophon. Rather than the pairing of Isaac Jaggard and Edward Blount on the title page, the Second Folio featured five different title pages that were attached to the rest of the printed sheets, creating different 'issues' from the same edition. Now, each of the Folio's publishers had a title page that suggested their individual responsibility for the book, creating a version of Shakespeare's work that hides, rather than foregrounds, its collaborative status.[116]

John Smethwick's version of the Second Folio's title page revised the spelling of his surname to the more commonly found 'John Smethwick'. Perhaps that was a quietly satisfying moment for this bookseller. He may also have enjoyed the fact that copies of the Second Folio printed for the 'minor partners' in this later

---

[114] Isaac Jaggard's brief will was made on 5 February 1626/7 and proved a few weeks later on 23 March: LMA DL/AL/C/003/MS09052/007. He left twenty pounds to his brother Thomas Jaggard, then a student at Cambridge; five pounds to the poor of his parish; and the residue of his estate to his wife, Dorothy Jaggard, who is discussed in the epilogue below.

[115] Moretti wonders whether 'a rhythm in the sequence of generations' accounts for the twenty-five to thirty-year lifespan of the literary trends he maps: *Graphs, Maps, Trees*, p. 21 (quoting Karl Mannheim).

[116] William B. Todd, 'The Issues and States of the Second Folio and Milton's Epitaph on Shakespeare' in *Studies in Bibliography* 5 (1952): pp. 81–108. The various imprints of F2 suggest that Thomas Cotes was not a member of the publishing syndicate (he printed the book 'for' its five named publishers). However Todd argues the Cotes brothers did act as publishers and that one variant of the Allott imprint may identify their copies ('Issues and States', pp. 97–8). It seems likely the Cotes brothers did have some publishing stake because by this point they owned the rights to a significant number of Shakespeare titles. In June 1627, Thomas and Richard Cotes registered ownership of the parts of 'Shackspheere playes' that had previously been owned by Isaac Jaggard (Arber IV.182; SCA *Register D*, p. 146). The entry does not list individual titles, but probably identifies half-shares in the plays that were earlier registered by Edward Blount and Isaac Jaggard on 8 November 1623. Then in November 1630, Richard Cotes further registered the rights to *Henry 5, Titus Andronicus, 2 Henry VI* (as 'Yorke and Lancaster'), *Pericles, Hamlet*, and two plays with connections to Shakespeare through suspect attributions: *Sir John Oldcastle* and *A Yorkshire Tragedy* (Arber IV.242; SCA *Register D*, p. 208). The brothers retained all these rights (which must for some of the plays still have been half-shares) because they were later transferred in a bulk assignment. On 6 August 1674, John Martin and Henry Herringman registered all these titles from the Cotes' estate: Eyre, Plomer, and Rivington eds, *Transcript of the Registers*, II.488.

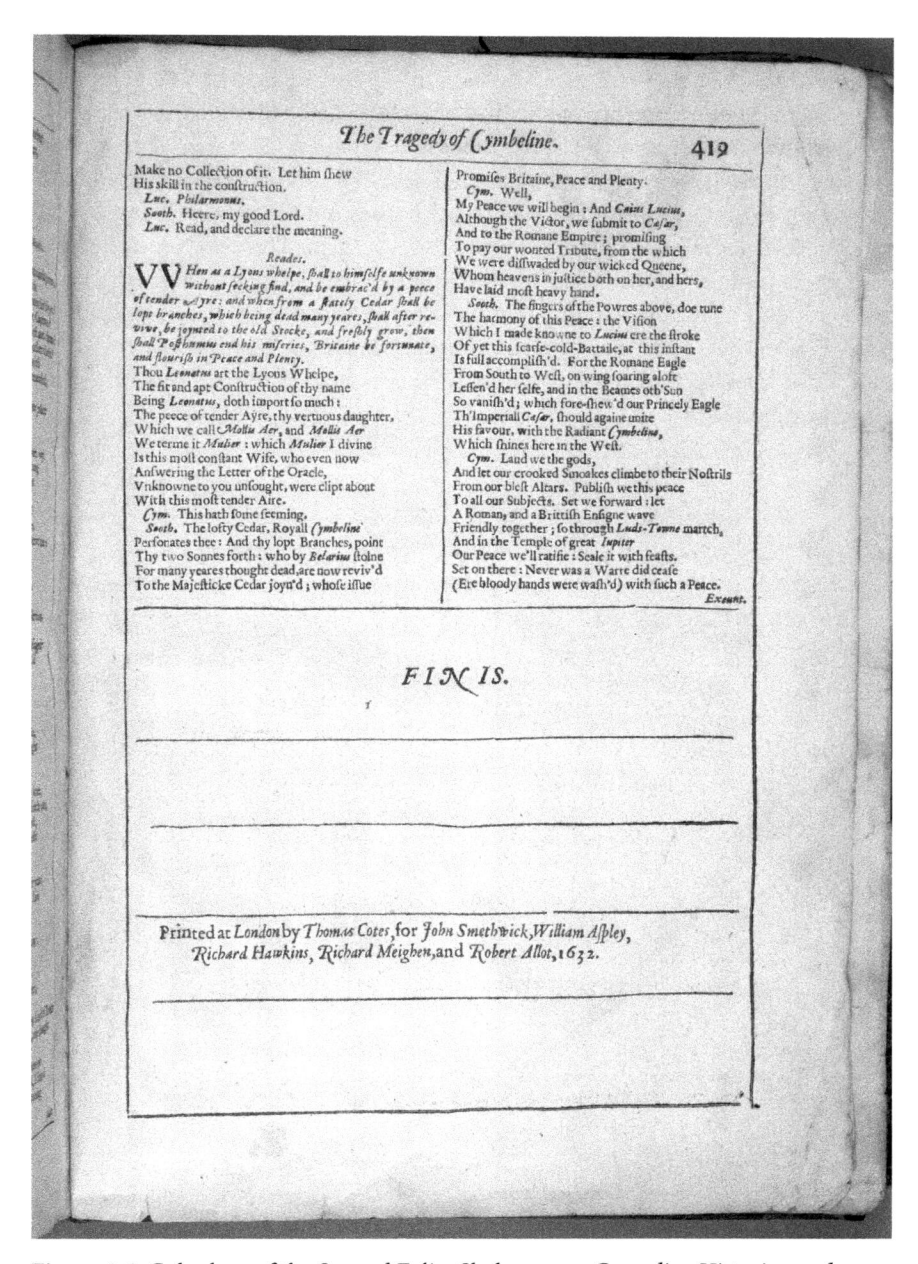

Figure 4.6 Colophon of the Second Folio: Shakespeare, *Comedies, Histories, and Tragedies* (1632, STC 22274a). Credit: Corpus Christi College, Oxford (2022) Phi.F.3.8, sig. 3d4r. This image is reproduced with kind permission of the President and Fellows of Corpus Christi College.

syndicate are sometimes highlighted at auction today as being particularly scarce; time has promoted the lesser shareholders into points of sale.[117] The colophon of the Second Folio, though, on the final printed page of the book (Figure 4.6), remained the same across each of the various issues of the edition. Here, Smethwick was named first in the list of five shareholders. This pre-eminence may reflect nothing more than compositorial whim, but it does not seem entirely by chance that Smethwick's name is followed by that of William Aspley, while the three newcomers huddle subserviently on the line beneath. Perhaps, then, his being listed first quietly acknowledges Smethwick's new seniority as the most experienced Shakespeare publisher of this second consortium, and the leader of the community around St Dunstan's that had by this point claimed the market for the playwright's legacy.

---

[117] See for example the Second Folio sold at auction by PBA Galleries in San Francisco in February 2016 for $177,500. The catalogue notes that its imprint (an Aspley copy) is 'decidedly one of the rarest' issues: 'Sale 579: Rare Books and Manuscripts', lot 99. Accessed 15 May 2021. https://www.pbagalleries.com/view-auctions/catalog/id/384/lot/119215/Mr-VVilliam-Shakespeares-Comedies-Histories-and-Tragedies-Published-according-to-the-true-originall-copies. Similarly, a Second Folio with the Smethwick imprint sold by Peter Harrington after 2015 was promoted as having 'one of the scarcest of the variant imprints': 'Shakespeare Second Folio'. Accessed 15 May 2021. https://www.peterharrington.co.uk/blog/shakespeare-second-folio-john-smethwick-imprint-1632.

Epilogue

'her *parte* in Shackspheere playes'
—SCA, *Register D*, p. 146

The bibliographic history of the First Folio is overwhelmingly male. This is true both in terms of the key figures involved at each stage of the book's production and who have featured in this book, and (with the recent and important exception of the work of Emma Smith and a few other notable scholars like Valerie Wayne) in the tradition of Anglo-American bibliography that has done so much to enrich our understanding of Shakespeare's books in the modern critical era. The women of this story, such as Dorothy Jaggard, widow to Isaac Jaggard, who transferred 'her *parte* in Shackspheere playes' to the printers Thomas and Richard Cotes in 1627, tend to be less visible. As book history seeks new ways to expand its disciplinary contours and to recuperate historically marginalized groups, what if anything can we recover about a final few figures that lie hidden at a further remove beneath the imprint and colophon of Shakespeare's Folio? I place these figures at the end of this book not to isolate them or further reinforce their archival marginality but to draw together and emphasize the scant traces of their presence that underpin each of the previous chapters. As several scholars have recently shown, the raw materials of our research elide the presence of female labour in numerous ways.[1]

Traces of these bookwomen are hard to find, and still harder to connect to Shakespeare's work except in tenuous ways. Edward Blount's debt, discussed in chapter one, came to him through his wife, Elizabeth Bankworth Blount. The Bill of Complaint relating to this debt names the pair as equal orators, and also makes clear that the early labour of recovering this huge sum was handled by 'your oratrix Elizabeth' who 'exhibited severall Inventories' at multiple courts and 'by force thereof became lawfully Interested' in the money before Edward joined its

---

[1] Kate Ozment, 'Rationale for Feminist Bibliography' in *Textual Cultures* 13.1 (2020): pp. 149–78; Valerie Wayne ed., *Women's Labour and the History of the Book in Early Modern England* (London: Arden Shakespeare, 2020); Leah Knight, Micheline White, and Elizabeth Sauer eds, *Women's Bookscapes in Early Modern Britain: Reading, Ownership, Circulation* (Ann Arbor, MI: University of Michigan Press, 2018). Further material can be found at Cait Coker and Kate Ozment eds, *Women in Book History: A Bibliography*: http://www.womensbookhistory.org/. Within the early modern period many of these efforts build on Helen Smith's 2012 monograph *'Grossly Material Things'* and the earlier work of Maureen Bell, 'Women in the Early English Book Trade 1557–1700' in *Leipziger Jahrbuch zur Buchgeschichte* 6 (1996): pp. 13–45.

pursuit.[2] The capacity of Blount's publishing business in the early 1620s, and so to some extent his ability to invest in Shakespeare, looks to have been influenced by Elizabeth's willingness to litigate. Difficult as it was for women to make their presence felt in the documentary record of book production, 'M*istress* Blount', as she is identified in the Stationers' Register, also emerges elsewhere. As far as we can tell from imprints and colophons, Elizabeth Blount never published a book herself, and so she does not feature in the list of widow publishers active in London recently compiled by Alan B. Farmer.[3] Yet, like many booksellers' widows, after her husband's death it was Elizabeth who handled parts of his estate. She signed and dated a note in July 1633 that 'surrendred into the Authors hands' a manuscript that Edward Blount had failed to publish, and acted in a similar way in 1636, presenting a note under her 'hand & seale' that transferred her shares in a title that was originally registered by Edward.[4] Given that Elizabeth (twice a book-trade widow) had ample trade knowledge and experience, and given too that the last stages of Edward's life were spent (we now know) both abroad in Paris and ultimately 'in his sicknes', it seems likely that Elizabeth was more involved in running the bookselling and publishing business at the Black Bear than the archives would suggest. Elizabeth died in February of 1644 and her will contains just one direct reference to the bookselling trade: a suggestive final instruction that she be buried in the stationers' church of St Faith under St Paul's, 'as neere my husband Banckworth as convenientlie I may'.[5] It was not Edward Blount but her first husband, the bookseller Richard Bankworth, who occupied her thoughts at the end of her life.

The wives of John Smethwick and William Aspley both predeceased their husbands, denying us the chance to see whether they would have emerged in the archives of those bookselling businesses once their husbands had died. For these two women the documentary record affords only sparing glimpses of their presence. Francis Smethwick, wife of John, was buried in Fleet Street in 1627, a year in which John's bookselling business published nothing at all.[6] William Aspley's wife was certainly living in 1619, when the bookseller Thomas Adams bequeathed mourning gowns both to Aspley 'and to his wife', but she had died by 1640, when Aspley's own testament recorded his wish that he be 'buried by my wyfe, and childe' and that 'the stone which standeth in my yeard on which my name is engraven' be 'layd upon' them all.[7] Such fleeting references do little more than confirm these two booksellers were married and without more evidence the

---

[2] *Blount vs Roydon*, TNA C 3/333/25.
[3] Alan B. Farmer, 'Widow Publishers in London, 1540–1640', in Wayne ed., *Women's Labour*, pp. 47–73.
[4] Arber IV.270 and 368; SCA *Register D*, pp. 236 and 342.
[5] *Will of Elizabeth Bankworth Blount*, TNA PROB 10/641/3.
[6] Burial entry for 20 December 1627 in *Parish Register of St Dunstan in the West*, LMA P69/DUN2/A/001/MS10342.
[7] *Will of William Aspley*, TNA PROB 10/610.

records can only invite us to take the route of 'responsible speculation' recommended by Rebecca Olsen as a strategy to counter the ideological investments of the archival record when imagining the forms of unrecorded labour these women contributed to their husband's bookselling businesses.[8] Ben Jonson's 'Epigram, to my Book-seller', places us firmly in an early modern bookshop of the era of Aspley and Smethwick listening to the comments of the clientele; the poem draws on the women of this retail environment. Jonson urges the bookseller himself to be 'my Bookes intelligencer', meaning that he should 'note | What each man sayes of it, and of what coat | His judgement is'.[9] At the same time, the bookseller's wife is also implicated in the sociality and commerce of the bookshop. Jonson divides the customers into different types: those who are 'wise, and praise' the book; those who are foolish and 'can give no Bayes', meaning are unable to recognize poetic merit or award a figurative laurel wreath; and finally those whose wit reaches 'no higher, but to spring | Thy Wife a fit of laughter'.[10] Depending on how we read this poem, we might think it displays a kind of misogynistic scorn towards bookwomen here, because socializing or flirting with the bookseller's wife seems to be what the witless customer does (the poem ends by inviting the bookseller to 'let them kisse thy Wife'). But perhaps the wife deserves particular admiration in this poem because she has to tolerate the most tedious of all the bookshop's clientele, triaging the buyer who may not even be interested in books, laughing at his jokes, maintaining the society of the bookshop. In Jonson's telling, the day-to-day labour of customer service is shared between the bookseller and his wife.

Some of the richest information about the women close to the publication of the First Folio comes from the Jaggard family, though again, much of this information relates to their deaths. The will of William Jaggard is far outstripped in detail by that of his wife, Jane, who died just two years after her husband in November 1625.[11] It was Isaac Jaggard who came into ownership of the printing and publishing business in Barbican following his father's death, but at the same time, given the nature of Jane's will, it is clear that she was involved in the family business. When Jane describes 'such stocke and debts as are oweing unto mee aswell in the Stacioners hall as elsewhear', and recalls more debt 'oweing unto me by mathew lownes Stationer' she reminds us of her own status as an active agent in the book trade economy to which both she and her husband belonged. In her gift of 'all my bookes in the Closett in my Chamber' to her son Thomas Jaggard as part of an expectation that he would 'goe to one of the universities to reape such

---

[8] Rebecca Olson, 'The Continuing Adventures of *Blanchardyn* and *Eglantine*: Responsible Speculation about Early Modern Fan Fiction' in *PMLA* 134.2 (2019): 298–314.
[9] Ben Jonson, 'Epigram, to my Book-seller', from *Underwood*, in volume three of *The workes of Benjamin Jonson* (1640 [i.e. 1641], STC 14754), sig. 2H1v.
[10] Jonson, 'Epigram, to my Book-seller', sig. 2H1v.
[11] *Will of William Jaggard*, LMA DL/AL/C/003/MS09052/005; *Will of Jane Jaggard*, LMA DL/AL/C/003/MS09052/006, item 170.

frutes of Learneing' as he was able, she both confirms her own literacy and makes provision for that quality in her children in ways that do not feature in William's testament (reading may have been particularly important to Jane, given that William had been blind since about 1612).[12]

This sense that Jane Jaggard was an active force in the printing and publishing business in Barbican is further suggested by a series of tax surveys made in the years immediately after William's death. An assessment made in 1621 places the business in the parish of St. Botolph without Aldersgate, where the household of 'William Jagger' was charged a little over four pounds as part of a tax levied by the crown.[13] By 1625, though, with William dead, two further taxes both record 'Widdowe Jaggard' as the head of the same household, before a final survey made at the end of the year shortly after Jane's death in November lists Isaac Jaggard as the new taxpayer.[14] The same neighbours crop up around the property, confirming the location remained stable. Perhaps this miniature chain of accountability tells us only that following the death of his mother Isaac Jaggard became nominally responsible for a property he already effectively ran, but if nothing else the brief presence of 'Widdowe Jaggard' in these tax records also seems like a determined rebuttal to the idea that the premises in Barbican in which the First Folio was printed was governed seamlessly by a patrilineal succession from father to son. Unlike the wills of John Smethwick and William Aspley, the testament of William Jaggard makes no specific provision for the future of his printing house and occasional bookshop. Again, that may be simply because the business was already considered to belong to Isaac Jaggard, but if we read the will on its own terms, then the printing house would fall into the 'Residue of all my goodes' bequeathed 'unto Jane my wife', leaving open the possibility that it was Jane Jaggard alongside Isaac who shepherded the Folio through the final stages of its making.[15] Following Isaac's death in 1627, it was Dorothy who, as mentioned above, distributed the rights to both the 'Bills for players' and to Shakespeare's plays, among other titles, and Dorothy too who oversaw the sale of the printing house.[16] Notes drawn up by Sir John Lambe in roughly 1635 record that Thomas Cotes, the printer of Shakespeare's Second Folio (1632), bought the Barbican premises 'of Jaggards Executrix'; here the presence of another female custodian of this business (whose temporary stewardship did not preclude her shaping its future) surfaces in the interstices between male ownership.[17]

---

[12] *Will of Jane Jaggard*. Like her husband, Jane also made provision for their apprentice, Abraham Woodfall (William let him off a year's service; Jane granted him forty shillings).

[13] *Assessment of Aldersgate Ward 1621*, TNA E 179/146/463. Perhaps this household was a separate building from the printing house, but there is no other Jaggard entry on the surveys. On printing houses existing within and alongside domestic spaces see Smith, 'Grossly Material Things', pp. 125–8.

[14] *Assessment of Aldersgate Ward 1625*, TNA E 179/147/510; E 179/147/535; *Subsidy for Aldersgate Ward 1625–6*: LMA CLC/W/FA/030/MS01503/2, fol. 5v.

[15] *Will of William Jaggard*.   [16] Arber IV.182; SCA, *Register D*, p. 146.

[17] TNA SP 16/307, fol. 145–6a; Arber III.703.

EPILOGUE 215

Oddly enough one other scrap survives in relation to Jane Jaggard: a receipt, made out by a parish clerk in exchange for 'all ffunerall duties' of 'Mistress Jaggard', who, we learn, was 'buryd in november 1625'.[18] It is symptomatic of broader methodological problems in book history that Jane Jaggard emerges in most striking detail—the cost of the candles that were burnt at her burial, the price of the perfume scattered around her grave—only at her death.

* * *

This book has supplied a response to what are probably the least-read words of Shakespeare's First Folio: the book's imprint and colophon. By taking seriously the interpretive life of these statements and the stationers they name, I hope to have offered a new account of the publication of this famous book, and to have used the Folio to organize and think through some features of early modern publication that are relevant in more expansive ways to the history of the Shakespearean text. If in one sense this study participates in the ongoing privileging not only of Shakespeare's writing but also of the First Folio, further consolidating the book's centrality in ways that have already troubled many scholars and led to a resigned sense of 'Folio Fatigue', then in other ways I hope to have demystified that dominance by exposing some of the book's own sly artifice. I aimed in this book to challenge the Folio's elevated cultural status by setting it firmly among the inventories of the figures who made it, beside the work of forgotten preachers and volumes of heraldic history. Furthermore, I sought to confront some of our entrenched ideas about textual status that can still be traced back to this famous volume. Above all I hope to have used the Folio's enduring interest to open up other lines of inquiry about early modern print.

What might those inquiries be? Throughout this book I have aimed to turn a potential methodological complication—that is, the involvement of several stationers in the Folio's publication—into the start of a discussion about the critical work we do with book-trade agents. Part of that discussion relates to the tension between the individual and the community; between the compelling case study of a single stationer and a wider view of those who made books in early modern England. Robert Darnton's appeal for scholars to remember the 'Forgotten Middlemen of Literature', made back in 1990, has inspired many rich accounts of individual bookmen and increasingly of bookwomen. An echo of Darnton's appeal was heard twenty years later in William Sherman's observation that book history remained 'curiously unpeopled'.[19] Both sentiments no longer ring quite so loudly in the ears of early modern book historians and scholars of Shakespeare's

[18] Westminster Abbey Muniments 13574.
[19] Robert Darnton, *The Kiss of Lamourette: Reflections in Cultural History* (New York & London: W. W. Norton and Company, 1990), pp. 136–53; William H. Sherman, 'The Social Life of Books' in Joad Raymond ed., *The Oxford History of Popular Print Culture, Volume One: Cheap Print in Britain and Ireland to 1660* (Oxford: Oxford University Press, 2011), pp. 164–71 at p. 165.

texts. Figures like Andrew Wise and Thomas Pavier and Edward Blount are becoming familiar presences, brought into view mostly through richly focused micro-histories. As we learn more about the individuals who made books, though, we also enable the larger narratives that can be told by joining these accounts up. Just as in other areas of early modern studies critics are thinking through the possibilities of working at different scales, so too can book historians now begin to move between the individual agent and the community of book production in order to tell new histories of making.[20] The arrival of new resources such as the *Shakespeare Census*, the *CERL Thesaurus*, and fresh databases of the wills of early modern stationers and of printing waste all offer different ways of thinking more expansively about book history, particularly when combined with existing tools like *EEBO*, *ESTC*, *DEEP*, and the *British Book Trade Index*.[21] These latter resources tend to depend in turn on an earlier generation of indispensable bibliographic scholarship, such as Greg's *Bibliography of the English Printed Drama*, and the first and subsequently second revised edition of the *STC*. A deep and important genealogy of bibliographic scholarship has brought us to a moment that is alive with possibilities for fresh critical labour.

This book has explored ways in which literary value is determined in part by the personalities of its production. Both my first two chapters connected aspects of the textual status of the First Folio to the involvement of its publishers. In chapter one, I sought new ways to historicize what we mean when we call a stationer 'literary'. I argued that by tracing a mixture of economic, cultural, and social factors in Edward Blount's work we can establish how book-trade agents were implicated in the creation of literary hierarchies. The second chapter considered William Jaggard's involvement in narratives about the legitimacy of Shakespeare's texts. I hope to have dispelled any lingering sense that Jaggard was a book trade 'pirate', as the New Bibliographers thought, and to have supplied a new account of his career that positions him as both a printer and a publisher of record—albeit one who was also willing to mask his presence. This chapter finished by suggesting that current work on early modern authorship has the potential to unsettle

---

[20] On issues of scale see Adam Smyth 'The Scale of Early Modern Studies' in *English Literary Renaissance* 50.1 (2020), pp. 145–52; in the same volume see also Zachary Lesser 'The Material Text between General and Particular, Edition and Copy', pp. 83–92. Other relevant work includes Higgins, 'Judith and Lucrece'; Jeffrey Todd Knight, 'Economies of Scale: Shakespeare and Book History' in *Literature Compass* 14.6 (2017): e12393; Claire M. L. Bourne, 'Shakespeare and "Textual Studies": Evidence, Scale, Periodization and Access' in Lukas Erne ed., *The Arden Research Handbook of Shakespeare and Textual Studies* (London: Bloomsbury Arden Shakespeare, 2021), pp. 21–49.

[21] *Shakespeare Census*. Edited by Adam G. Hooks and Zachary Lesser. Created 2018. http://www.shakespearecensus.org; *CERL Thesaurus* (http://thesaurus.cerl.org/); as of 2021, Kirk Melnikoff is creating a database of the wills of all stationers involved with printed drama; Adam Smyth, Anna Reynolds, and Megan Heffernan are currently assembling a database of early modern printed waste; *DEEP: Database of Early English Playbooks*. Edited by Alan B. Farmer and Zachary Lesser. Created 2007. Accessed 10 April 2021. http://deep.sas.upenn.edu; *British Book Trade Index*: http://bbti.bodleian.ox.ac.uk/.

our reliance on the First Folio as the dominant source of literary authority and to invest other of Shakespeare's books with a fresh sense of interpretive possibility. My account of William Jaggard thus joins a larger body of critical work that is interested less in the creaky binary of texts being either 'good' or 'bad' than in more nuanced ways of understanding textual status.

This book has also recuperated Aspley and Smethwick into narratives about the First Folio, less by making arguments about their direct influence on the Folio itself than by responding thematically to their involvement. In these chapters I aimed to model new ways of understanding what a stationer might represent— not just a traditional biographical life, but also a category of booksellers, or an address in London—and so here *Shakespeare's Syndicate* joins a variety of other work exploring what it means to engage critically with an early modern life. Examples of this include the paratactic 'paper trails' brilliantly pursued by Jason Scott-Warren in his account of Richard Stonley, the first recorded buyer of *Venus and Adonis*; or the 'bio-bibliography' assembled by Adam G. Hooks, in which Shakespeare's life emerges not through scrutiny of traditional biographical sources (the parish or legal archive, familial relations) but from the printed books that created and conveyed Shakespeare's identity throughout the seventeenth century.[22] For chapter three on William Aspley I pursued the category of the 'minor Shakespearean' and argued that the distribution of an author's literary property could have a surprising number of interpretive consequences for the future of that author's work, particularly when those titles are later gathered 'all in one volume', as Isaac Jaggard's Frankfurt advert proudly boasted of Shakespeare's Folio. In chapter four, my account of John Smethwick's relevancy to the First Folio took its cue from his address in St Dunstan's in the West. The stationer himself faded into the background, replaced by an interest in the spaces of London from which Shakespeare's books were published and sold—and in particular the churchyard on Fleet Street in which John Smethwick lived, worked, and eventually died. Using Smethwick to think about novelty, place, and the market for Shakespeare's writing revealed that the Folio was at once both the culmination of what had been and the starting point for myriad future explorations of the author's legacy.

I have argued that the Folio's publication was a richly meaningful event, and that we can 'read' this event through careful attention to its circumstances: the people involved with the project; the places from which the book was sold; its place in the diachronic progression of Shakespearean publication. The result is an account of the First Folio both 'as history' and also 'in history', to borrow a phrase from a recent collection that surveys the field of book history and materiality.[23]

---

[22] Scott-Warren, *Shakespeare's First Reader*; Hooks, *Selling Shakespeare*.

[23] Heidi Brayman, Jesse M. Lander, and Zachary Lesser eds, *The Book in History, The Book as History: New Intersections of the Material Text* (New Haven, CT: Beinecke Rare Book & Manuscript Library with Yale University Press, 2016).

The arguments I have made look both at and through the Folio's imprint and colophon, but the questions this practice has generated are relevant to the publication of any early modern work. The literary culture of the early modern period is full of examples that demonstrate the interpretive potential of the event of a text's publication across different media. Ben Jonson's memorial elegy to Vincent Corbett was first 'published' in manuscript form by being nailed to the wall of St Mary's Church in Twickenham in 1619, where it was gazed at by the congregation beside companion verses by John Selden and Richard Corbett. This was a form of site-specific display that while technically public was nevertheless rooted in Corbett's own social, religious, and parochial community. Jonson's poem alludes to its situation beside those other verses, so that when it was republished without its companions in Jonson's *Workes* (1641), the poem became an altogether knottier, even a misleading, text.[24] The Christian mystic Jane Lead (1624–1704) wrote down her visions on notecards and 'published' them in scribal form by handing them out to her close companions; the traveller Thomas Coryate did something similar (if less devout) with his printed books in the early 1600s, loading copies onto a donkey and embarking on a wandering tour of the country that saw him distribute copies to friends and noblemen.[25] Examples like this dilate the 'moment' of publication so that it seems to unfold with lazy chronology over a geography that is both spacious and at the same time socially precise. Robert Boyle distributed his *Some receipts of medicines* (1688) with similar care. After the edition was printed Boyle bought up every copy, 'without excepting those copies, that are wont to be claimd & taken by those that had to do with the presse'. He then personally distributed copies to a select readership to help him assess 'whether 'twere adviseable to retaine them in their privacy, or to let them appeare in publick'.[26]

Examples like these reach far beyond Shakespeare and the First Folio, but in their variety they suggest that publication—on a simple level, the ways in which a text could travel between realms, from private to public—could be a stranger, richer process than we might think.[27] In *Shakespeare's Syndicate*, by moving

---

[24] Beinecke Library, Osborn MS fb 230, later published in print as: Ben Jonson 'An Epitaph on Master Vincent Corbet', in *The workes of Benjamin Jonson* (1641), sig. 2B1r–v. The poem as printed has several confusing lines that depend on it being read on the vellum sheet beside Selden and Corbett.

[25] Sylvia Bowerbank, *Speaking for Nature: Women and Ecologies of Early Modern England* (Baltimore, MD: Johns Hopkins University Press, 2004), pp. 110–12; Thomas Coryate, *Coryats Crambe* (1611, STC 5807), sig. H1v (see also Coryate's record of the events of presentation in earlier sections of the book).

[26] Quoted and discussed in Michael Hunter, *Robert Boyle (1627–91): Scrupulosity and Science* (Woodbridge: The Boydell Press, 2000), p. 208.

[27] Many other examples demonstrate ways in which early modern authors exploited the publication process to introduce layers of meaning to their work and to influence the reception of their writing. The obsessive post-print slip insertions and manuscript additions of writers like Margaret Cavendish and Thomas Milles, for instance, complicate our understanding of the temporality of the 'edition' (Smyth, *Material Texts*, pp. 125–8; William Sherman and Heather Wolfe, 'The Department of Hybrid Books: Thomas Milles between Manuscript and Print' in *Journal of Medieval and Early Modern Studies* 45.3 (2015): pp. 457–85). The private testament of Dame Helen Branche (d. 1594) was

between the particularities of the lives of the Folio's makers and an expansive sense of the book's publishing circumstances, I have sought to celebrate the Folio's enduring and intrinsic interest within the canonical frameworks we have inherited from modernity, and at the same time to embrace this volume's ability, as a locus of scholarly energy, to generate new ways of thinking about early modern print.

'published' in a different way when it was ransacked and versified in print by an array of poets keen to promote her charity in order to consolidate their own patronage (Scott-Warren, *Shakespeare's First Reader*, 180–1).

APPENDIX 1

The Letters of Edward Blount

A Note on the Transcriptions and on Blount's Seals

Blount's letters provide valuable insight into the concerns of early modern booksellers. They also make visible some of the epistolary networks this figure cultivated. I have sought to make these letters accessible, and with that in mind have adopted the following conventions. Abbreviations (including the occasional use of tildes) are silently expanded and superscript letters are silently lowered. Any marks of punctuation that signal an abbreviation have been removed (yor becomes your; S^{r.} becomes Sir; m^{r.} becomes master; B. becomes Bishop; 5^{t.} becomes 5th; boñe becomes bonne). These conventions also apply to the endorsements. Exceptions to this practice of modernizing are the superscript ^{l} for *libra*, or pounds, and the superscript ^{d}, or *denarius*, for pence, which are both retained. I have modernized the i/j and u/v graphs, as well as Blount's use of the y character for thorn þ (y^t becomes that), and I have also made regular his erratic use of capital letters at the start of sentences. Original lineation is retained, together with spelling, punctuation, legible cancellations, and the odd underlining. In just a few cases where there is an obvious error or the paper is damaged I have added or completed a word in square brackets to convey the sense.

Of these eight letters, two are in the State Papers Domestic series held by The National Archives in Kew and six are in the British Library. Among the State Papers there is a further document signed by Blount: a receipt, dated June 1615 and made out to Sir Dudley Carleton for taking delivery of and cleaning some artworks, which I have not included below.[1] Five of the British Library letters were discovered by Gary Taylor, who puts them to excellent use in his work; the sixth is a new addition.[2]

The remains of three different seals can be found on Blount's letters: two that are different evolutions of the same 'merchant's mark' and one with a floral design. The merchant's mark was a widely used class of symbol that conveyed an individual's professional identity, just as a publisher's woodblock device might embody their brand. In Blount's earliest surviving letter this mark (Figure A1), which includes his initials, is approximately 12 × 14mm ('merchant's mark 1'); in its later form it is larger (roughly 16 × 21mm), and had two flowers added either side of the base ('merchant's mark 2'; Figure A2). Both of these seals may have been mounted on signet rings.[3] Blount's final surviving letter features a different seal, one that is smaller and carries a generic floral design (Figure A3). At the end of his life Blount looks to have set aside a mark that signifies a mercantile context in favour of one that less obviously implicates him in networks of trade and exchange. In the context of

---

[1] TNA, SP 14/80, fol. 183. Blount dates the receipt to 3 June 1614 but collected the payment on 15 June 1615. The receipt is endorsed 19 June 1615. It seems unlikely—though presumably possible—that Carleton kept Blount waiting a year for this payment, so perhaps the earlier date was an error.

[2] Taylor, 'Making Meaning'; 'Blount [Blunt], Edward'; '*Comedies, Histories, & Tragedies*'.

[3] For a contemporary ring with a similar design see F. A. Girling, *English Merchants' Marks: A Field Survey of Marks Made by Merchants and Tradesmen in England Between 1400 and 1700* (Warwick Sq, London: Oxford University Press, 1964), p. 23.

Figures A1, A2, and A3 Blount's personal seals, not shown to scale. The image at the top shows the first and smallest iteration of Blount's merchant's mark from a detail of TNA SP 14/80, fol. 136b; the image appears courtesy of The National Archives, Kew. The second and larger version of the same mark, with flowers added at the base, is from a detail of BL Additional MS 72361, fol. 110v. The image at the bottom of this page shows the final seal from a detail of BL Additional MS 78683, fol. 73v. Both of the latter images © The British Library Board, reproduced with permission.

Blount's gradual withdrawal from bookselling, as explored in chapter one, it is tempting to interpret this change as further evidence of a shift away from his publishing and mercantile identity (John Donne, who devised a new seal following his ordination in 1615, is perhaps the best-known example of an early modern figure manifesting a change of their identity through the apparatus of correspondence).[4]

---

[4] On Donne's seals see M. Thomas Hester, Robert Parker Sorlien, and Dennis Flynn eds, *John Donne's Marriage Letters in The Folger Shakespeare Library* (Washington, DC: The Folger Shakespeare Library, 2005), p. 33. This appendix is modelled on this excellent edition of Donne's letters.

Transcriptions

1. Edward Blount to Sir Dudley Carleton
26 April 1615
TNA, SP 14/80, fol. 136

Blount's earliest two surviving letters concern services rendered to Sir Dudley Carleton (1574–1632), an ambassador in Venice. A 'bill of exchange' was a way to transfer money around Europe without having to move cash between continents. These first two letters tell us that Blount received such a bill from Carleton which required the stationer to pay twenty-five pounds to 'master Cuttele'. The usual procedure was that on paying this sum Blount would receive a second bill of exchange from Cuttell, which could then be sent to Italy to authorize Carleton to withdraw the equivalent sum (in this case from the Guadagni merchant house). The letters records some of Blount's European connections and the non-bookselling services he offered to the right clients.

                        To the Right Honorable   [address leaf]
                            Sir Dudley Carleton
                      Knight: Lorde Ambassador
                       for his majestye of Greate
                        Brittaine: to the state
                            of Venice.

Right Honorable

I have payed to master Cuttele your bill of exchange of
25^{ll} which according to your order I have returned
by way of rechange upon your Lordship, the rate of
the exchange at this present going at 57^d and a half
amounteth to 104^d duccats and 9 grosse for the   5
sayed valew received of master fishebourne and master
Browne, which I pray your lordship to see well
payed to the Guadaigne, and so I rest your
Lordships humble servant: Ed: Blount
London this 26: Aprill: 1615.   10

Description: bifolium, trimmed and mounted. Address leaf contains red wax seal (merchant's mark 1). 223–5 × 331mm. Watermark: flag with initials 'G B'; Gravell Flag.001.1. Endorsed on the address leaf: 'Master Blunt the 26. of April. 1615:'

line 1: *bill of exchange*] A letter authorizing remittance without the need to ship bullion; also sometimes used as an instrument of credit.
line 3: *rechange*] exchanged currency.
line 5: *grosse*] Appears as 'grsse'.
line 8: *Guadaigne*] The Guadagni was a well-known Italian merchant house.

2. Edward Blount to Sir Dudley Carleton
23 June 1615
TNA, SP 14/80, fol. 186

Eight weeks later, Blount continues to work as Carleton's agent in London, following up on a problem relating to the transaction described in his previous letter. It seems the second bill of exchange, probably sent by Blount to Venice to authorize Carleton's withdrawal, was rejected, though it is not clear why. Carleton's secretary at this point was Isaac Wake (appointed in 1610); letter eight below records a probable visit from Blount to Wake in 1631, by which time Wake had become an ambassador. The connection to Carleton and his circle represented by these early letters thus endured to the end of Blount's life.

Right Honorable.
It pleased your Lordship to draw upon me by your bill of
exchange the sum of 25^l starling payable to master Cuttell. [This]
Bill I discharged by paying so muche mony to master Cut[tell]
at the tyme when it was due. And according to your ord[er]
and direction in your letter returned so muche bake [to]   5
your Lordship by bill payable to the Guadagini in ven[ice.]
The bills have bin presented & rejected and returned [in]
manner protested; wher the fault resteth or in wh[o]
I knowe not; but the marchant hath byn with me a[bout]
it but yesterday: Lett me intreate your Lordship   10
take some speedy order for the satisfying therof: [I]
rest your Lordships humble servant   Ed: Blount
London. 23 of June <u>1615</u>

Description: single leaf, trimmed, mounted, and repaired. 218-20 × 334mm. No watermark. Some loss of text at right margin.

line 2: *sum*] A tilde suggests Blount may have meant the Latin *summa*.
line 6: *Guadagini*] The well-known Italian merchant house mentioned in the previous letter.

3. Edward Blount to Sir William Trumbull
15 June 1621
BL Additional MS 72361, ff. 68–9

The first of Blount's five surviving letters to Sir William Trumbull in Brussels is a lengthy mixture of news and gossip. In much of the below Blount answers queries put to him by Trumbull in a letter which does not survive. The stationer begins by asking for the return of an unnamed manuscript he loaned to Trumbull: it was a unique copy which he expects Trumbull to either read or copy. Several familiar personalities appear: 'master Bill' is probably the bookseller John Bill; 'master Dallington' is the author Robert Dallington, whose books Blount published. The courteous and deferential tone of this letter fades away in successive correspondence as Blount's calls for the return of the manuscript grow more urgent.

Worthy Sir
        Yours of 31 May I receaved, for which
I am muche bound to you. Concerning that manuscript
I sent you, mentioned in yours; may it please you to
give your self what satisfaction you thinke fitt; for in
my love of your worthe I sent it to that end. So that when   5
you filled your desyre eyther by reading or Coppying it
you wilbe pleased to returne it by some trusty messinger
because I have not any coppye therof, and yett have
promised .2. or .3. freinds the reading; hoping you would
have returned it before. Here is a booke lately extant,   10
written by Doctor Montegue against master Seldon, whose booke
I ymagine you have. If I knewe howe to send it, I would.
Or if it please you to direct me ~~me~~ howe, I will. For the
2: postscripts or demandes you desyre to be satisfyed in;
Thus. I have sent you inclosed, a briefe of more then you   15
mention of the first scandal raysed of that Bishop. Yett it
is not all. For here is another which I partly beleeve, because
it probable and likely, though not certayne. Preston, who
had long endured ymprisonment, and had divers tymes byn
called to answere, at [length] grewe tractable and was Content to   20
yeald to and take the oathe: whereupon, most of his best
Catholick freinds and relieving benifactors gave him over &
withdrewe their supplies from him; so that he lived not in that
fulnesse as before. During the tyme of the Bishops sickness
which was long; Sir William Paddye was his Phisitian, &   25
usually visitt him twise or thrise a day, one day being
ther with the Bishop and talking of sondry businesses, Sir W
tould the Bishop what an exigent or straight Preston was

driven to, and howe poore he was nowe since the Catholiks
withheld their benevolence from him. Commending him for a
good Scholler and pittying him in his want. And withall
moved the Bishop to send him some reliefe what he
thought fitt. The Bishop of this motion and Motive, sent
him 5^{li} by Sr W but I knowe not by whome. This is
liklye thoughe not certayne. But of this you may
receave further Satisfaction hereafter.
For your second demand or postscript Concerning the private
Conference betwee our Englishe divines and ministers and
that dangerous Champion Muskett; Thus. It is true
that suche meetings ther were betweene Doctor Featly whome
I suppose you well knowe to be a worthy learned Scholler,
and the sayed Muskett, the occasion of these meetings
were well grounded and justly, but to long to relate.
Two of their meetings was att master Bills howse, wher, by the
neerenesse of freindship, I was allowed to come my self
and to bring .2. or 3. of my freinds, I carried master Dallington
for one who was desyrous to be ther. Some others I gott in
by favor. Ther were many Schollers and gentlemen of
the one syde, and many Catholick gentlemen and leard
learneder priests then Muskett on the other syde. Two priests
for scribes of Musketts syde, .2. Schollers for scribes of
Doctor Featlyss side. But not to hold you long with what is not
worthy writing, I never heard nor knewe a more simple
ignorant audacious shamelesse foole then Muskett; Such
an one as I dare undertake to finde in every Colledge
of Oxford and Cambridge, that have not yett taken degree
of master of Arts & that shall make a Asse of him; for he had
nothing in him but meere sophistry, and would never abyde
an to followe or conclud an Argument. In a word, it was
(as master Dallington sayth) the unequalest matche at Cock-
fight that ever he was at. For the muche better Scholler
had the best cause, and the poorest leanest scholler had
worst cause to defend. Well they were ashamed of their
Disputant, for the 5th day being appoynted, the place read
and Doctor Featly ther attending, the[y] refused to come, and
made exscuses forsooth, that it might turne to their great
prejudice, if it should be publickly knowne, the place
being neere the prison within .3. or 4: howses, Doctor Goad and
master Dallington went to them, and perswaded them
but they would none, they durst not abyde the test

any longer. And this, upon my honesty is the truthe
of their great Musketts Conquest. Sir I shalbe always
to doe you service if it please you to Comand me.
So I take my leave and rest at your Command

London. 15. June 1621.   Ed: Blount 75

Description: bifolium; the address leaf must have been on a separate document (Blount mentions further material 'inclosed'). 209 × 318mm. Endorsed on final verso: '15. of June. 1621. From Master Ed: Blounte.' The final two lines and signature as presented here are written in the left margin, at a right angle to the rest of the letter.

line 1: *Yours of 31 May*] The letter seemingly does not survive.
line 10: *a booke lately extant*] Richard Montagu's *Diatribæ* (1621, STC 18037), published by Matthew Lownes. The book was a response to John Selden's *Historie of tithes* (1618, STC 22172).
line 16: *the first scandal raysed of that Bishop*] John King, Bishop of London, who died a few months before this letter in March 1621 following a lengthy sickness. A rumour circulated that the bishop had converted to Roman Catholicism on his deathbed.
line 18: *Preston*] Roland Preston (1567-1647, known in religious matters as Thomas Preston), a Benedictine monk who became a prominent figure in disputes about the oath of allegiance.
line 21: *the oathe*] The oath of allegiance, James I's attempt to secure the loyalty of the nation's Catholics.
line 25: *Sir William Paddye*] Sir William Paddy (1554-1634), physician to James I.
line 34: by Sr W] Blount thought twice about confirming Paddy's identity.
lines 37-8: *the private Conference*] A religious debate between the clergyman Daniel Featley (1582-1645) and the Roman Catholic priest George Fisher (*alias* Musket; *c*.1580-1645) which took place over 21-22 April 1621. An account was printed in Daniel Featley, *The Romish Fisher . . .* (1624, STC 10738.3).
line 44: *master Bills howse*] Probably John Bill, a prominent London bookseller.
line 46: *master Dallington*] Sir Robert Dallington (1561-*c*.1636), a courtier and author whose books Blount published in 1605 and 1613. The letter shows us they remained friends after their bookish collaborations. Dallington appears again in letter seven below.
line 64: *5th day*] Perhaps a slip for '3rd day' or an unclear letterform. The printed account tells us that the conference ended in the manner Blount describes on its third day (*Romish Fisher*, sig. P4r-v).
line 68: *Doctor Goad*] Probably the theologian Thomas Goad (1576-1638).

4. Edward Blount to Sir William Trumbull
6 July 1621
BL Additional MS 72361, ff. 109–10

Blount's next letter to Trumbull follows quickly on from the first. Just three weeks have passed, and Blount's sole focus is the return of the manuscript. We learn the manuscript was first delivered by 'Thorpe', presumably the stationer Thomas Thorpe, publisher of Shakespeare's Sonnets (1609). As in other letters, this document was originally accompanied by other correspondence (Blount asks Trumbull to arrange delivery of 'this inclosed') in ways that suggest a wider network of exchange.

To the Right worshipfull
Master Trumball. Agent
for his majesty of great
Brittayne in Bruxells</div> [address leaf]

Sir
    My duety remembred, I intreate you wilbe pleased to returne that manuscript which I sent you by Thorpe for I had promised the viewe thereof to .2. or 3 of my especiall good freindes before I sent it you, and they doe Call upon me dayly for the performing of my promise.   5
Therfore if you have read it or Coppied it, you shall doe me a favour in returning the same, with your Censure. Having nothing els to write worthy your viewe, I intreat you wilbe pleased to lett one of your servants deliver this inclosed, so praying for your health and long lyfe   10
I take my leave and rest at your Command.

London 6th July   Ed: Blount
1621.

Description: bifolium; address leaf contains red wax seal (merchant's mark 2). 213 × 315mm. Endorsed on address leaf: '6. of July. 1621. From Master Edward Blounte.'

line 2: *Thorpe*] Probably the stationer Thomas Thorpe.
line 5: *Call upon me dayly*] Presumably at Blount's bookshop at the sign of the Black Bear in Paul's Cross Churchyard, here transformed into a site of textual critique.
line 7: *with your Censure*] The sense seems to be that Blount is asking for a reader's report on a title he is considering for publication.
line 10: *this inclosed*] The material does not survive with the letter.

5. Edward Blount to Sir William Trumbull
8 November 1622
BL Additional MS 72364, ff. 125–6

Over a year after their previous correspondence comes perhaps the richest of Blount's surviving letters to Trumbull. It offers a long and highly figurative discussion of two manuscripts. Some of the language is elusive, but the letter reveals the concerns early modern booksellers brought to bear on the texts they handled. Much of the letter involves Blount puzzling away at the meaning of Trumbull's own long-delayed letter. As he works through Trumbull's lines, Blount retains the proverbial imagery that was probably introduced by his correspondent to describe two texts. The 'cow' seems to be a manuscript Trumbull has had for some time without reading or copying; the 'calf' is a second text Trumbull has sent that comes with some privacy concerns. Blount is worried, because although Trumbull's letter suggests both texts have been sent to London, in fact the bookseller has only received the second (presumably less significant or unlooked for) 'calf'. Blount is confused by Trumbull's intentions for this second manuscript; he understands that just 'one payre eyes may survey it' but is uncertain whether Trumbull also desires him to 'enfranchise' it, which probably means to publish it, either in scribal form or as a printed book. It might be a foreign-language text in need of translation before publication (the text needs to be 'naturalized here with us'), which would explain why Blount assures Trumbull that 'my practice in this cure' is secure. That term 'cure' twice features in Blount's description of his handling of a text prior to publication, reminding us of the First Folio's own description of its plays as 'cur'd, and perfect of their limbes' in the preliminary address 'To the great Variety of Readers'. However by the end of the letter Blount is uncertain which manuscript Trumbull's instructions identify; he does not know whether it is 'the Cowe you keepe, or the Calfe you sent'. If the letter's tone is testy, it nevertheless finishes with a genial postscript concerning Trumbull's son. As Blount notes, the younger Trumbull was taught by James Mabbe, the translator whose work was published by Blount and who is generally accepted as the author of the Folio poem 'To the memorie of M. W. Shake-speare'. Mabbe reappears in letter seven.

                      To the Right worshipfull Master William   [address leaf]
                             Trumball, Agent for his
                            Majestye of great Brittayne
                                    in Bruxels

Worthye Sir
       3 dayes since, (by Germin,) I received your ridle.
Which with me will aske some tyme to unfould or disclose without some
directions from your self. 30. are your lynes besydes two postscripts,
the subscription, and date, the 18 of february 1621[/22]. Long on the
way and hard passage berlakins. In the two first lynes you are   5
driven to Confesse, the detaining of an enclosed prisoner too long.
A great faulte, without amendes. For ought I perceive you meane
to detaine him longer: and yett in your 3: next, you vowe to
have neither perused nor transcribed it, worse; but worst of
all, your demand in your .5. ensuing lynes, wher you conjure   10
me to gett it coppied out for you, and you will pay the charge,
thank me, reade it, and give your Censure, bothe of matter and
style. In answere of which, I say no more, nor can say lesse, lett
me intreate you, first to ~~send it~~ enfranchize it and send it to

me, and then your will shalbe accomplished: In the fowre next, 15
you tell me it is nowe comming towards me like the Parsons Cowe;
with a calf at the tale, I wishe it had beene so, and no tale. I
must nowe confesse, I received the calfe you speake of, but no
Cowe. This Calfe you say hath two imperfections, can cannot drink
of all waters, nor endure all lights: No matter: Custome and 20
Conversation are two rare Artificers, and (with Tymes helpe)
can make a creature familier with that which Nature teacheth
to avoyde: and for my practice in this cure you may be secure:
for a calf is but a creature and may be taught either to
drink or indurre any water or lyght. When, as I have knowne 25
a Cowe hath byn taught to speake to a king. So m[uc]he for
4 lynes more. Ending with Verbum Sapienti, which I right[l]y construe
Verbum Patienti. Nowe I am at a nonplus; and knowe not
what to answere to the sequell, for that I understand not your
meaning no more then you <u>can tell whether it may gett free</u> 30
Course and be naturalized here with us or not. Further, you say,
but one payre eyes may survey it, till it be exposed i[n] publik
viewe. Of the Author nothing, of the sender lesse. If it cannott
be enfranchised with us: it may passe into free provinces or
<u>try its fortune</u>. Lett me intreate your opening of these 35
lynes, whether you meane the Cowe you keepe, or the Calfe you
sent. For neither lame Thomas nor I can understand you
though it cost us .3. quartes of Canary to drinke your health
treble in the Companie of Germyne and Coale. For to tell you
seriouslye these lynes of yours put us bothe into a feare least 40
Germine had mistaken himself, and delivered the Cowe to master
secretary and brought the Calf to me. For this in my handes
assure your self it shall be carried and cured with what ~~disc~~
discretion is fitting a creature of that nature, and if it
may please you playnely to expresse your will therin, I will 45

Description: bifolium; address leaf contains blind impression of seal (merchants' mark 2) but no wax survives. 213 × 317mm. Endorsed on address leaf: '8. of november. 1622 from Master Ed: Blounte.'

line 1: *Germin*] The name of Trumbull's messenger, mentioned again below; *your ridle*] Trumbull's enigmatic letter.
line 4: *subscription*] The final clause or formula in a letter that leads into the signature; *18 of february 1621*] The date is likely old style, but even so the letter has taken nearly nine months to arrive.
line 5: *berlakins*] A mild oath; a contraction of *by our lady-kin*.
line 6: *an enclosed prisoner*] A manuscript.
line 11: *coppied out for you*] Blount was able to provide manuscript copying services, confirmed in line 15.
line 14: *enfranchize it*] Release the manuscript.
lines 16–7: *Parsons Cowe; with a calf at the tale*] Listed as proverbial but without gloss in John Ray, *A collection of English proverbs* (1678, Wing R387), sig. V1v. The sense is of something returning in increased or supplemented form. Trumbull has promised that the manuscript is on its way, accompanied by a second text (the 'calf').

Continued

not be wanting to serve you in ought you Comand, and I
able to performe. Ever resting at your Comand

London 8th: November 1622   Ed: Blount

I must needes come in with a Postscript too, and tell that your soone is
well, and a great proficient in the spanishe tongue, by   50
the meanes of master James Mabbe, of Magdalen College.
Who takes as muche delight in reading to him and other
gentlemen of that howse; as they take in that their desyre.

line 17: *and no tale*] Blount would rather have the 'cow' than the 'calf'. 'Tale' here probably plays on both 'tail' and 'story'.
line 19: *two imperfections*] Two considerations.
lines 19–20: *cannot drink of all waters, nor endure all lights*] The sense is that the manuscript cannot be made public.
line 23: *my practice in this cure*] My ability to prepare a text for wider circulation or publication.
line 26: *taught to speake to a king*] This fascinating phrase may recall a text that Blount had previously prepared for a royal audience in some way, perhaps through presentation or dedication.
line 27: *Verbum Sapienti*] A word to the wise. Shortened form of *verbum sapienti sat est* (a word is enough for a wise person).
line 28: *Verbum Patienti*] A word to the suffering or patient.
line 30: whether it may gett free] The antecedent of 'it' in this line is unclear, and Blount points out this confusion below. The underlining could supply emphasis or may mark sections where Blount quotes Trumbull's words.
line 31: *naturalized*] Perhaps suggesting the text was written in another language and required translation, or perhaps just meaning 'published' and so 'given a home in London'.
line 34: *enfranchised*] Published, and so 'freed' to a wider audience, either scribally or in print.
line 37: *lame Thomas*] Perhaps Thomas Thorpe, the stationer mentioned in letter four.
line 38: *quartes*] A quart was a quarter of a gallon; *Canary*] White wine.
line 39: *Coale*] An unknown drinking companion.
lines 41–2: *master secretary*] Perhaps George Calvert, secretary of state to James I, with whom Trumbull was in regular correspondence at this time. Again we get the sense that the Trumbull-Blount exchange was situated in a larger circle of correspondence whose members were to some extent aware of one another.
line 42: *this in my handes*] The 'calf' or secondary manuscript.
line 43: *carried and cured*] Prepared for wider circulation or publication, perhaps involving translation.
line 49: *your soone*] Trumbull's son, also William, who matriculated at Magdalen College, Oxford, in February 1623.
line 51: *James Mabbe*] The Hispanist and translator James Mabbe (1571/2–1642?), who appears again in letter seven and who contributed a poem to the preliminaries of the First Folio. Mabbe was also a correspondent of Trumbull (see fol. 90-1 in this manuscript).

APPENDIX 1   233

6. Edward Blount to Sir William Trumbull
9 May 1623
BL Additional MS 72365, ff. 130-1

Six months later comes another letter to Trumbull. The earlier issues over the two manuscripts seem to be forgotten. Blount has chosen three books 'of worth' to send to Brussels: a folio edition of Eadmer, a single sheet proclamation, and a medical pamphlet. What stands out from the letter is the role of the bookseller as a mediating filter in conveying the products of the London book trade to correspondents based elsewhere. Blount's promise to send any other texts that are 'worthye your view' is a confident assertion that the bookseller can discriminate on Trumbull's behalf.

[address leaf]

> To my worthy and muche honoured
> freind master William Trumball
> Residen for his Majestye of great
> Brittaine
> in Bruxells

Sir
    I send you by this ordinarye Eadmerus sett forthe by
Sir Robert Cotton and master Selden. A booke of muche
esteeme here and the only booke of worth come
forthe this tearme. Also a pamphlett of direction
for your health, and a proclamation for knights.   5
Which is all that is published this tearme. May it
please you to exscuse my boldness in this, and
if ought els come forthe worthye your view whe[n]
Germin cometh away, I will not fayle to send it
        Your worships at Comand   10
London 9th May. 1623   Ed: Blount

Description: bifolium. 202 × 314mm. Endorsed on address leaf: '9. of May 1623. From Master Ed: Blounte.'

line 1: *ordinarye*] A courier or messenger; *Eadmerus*] An edition of the historian Eadmer prepared by Sir Robert Cotton and John Selden: *Eadmeri monachi Cantuariensis Historiæ novorum* (1623, STC 7438), published by William Stansby.

lines 4–5: *pamphlett of direction for your health*] Perhaps Tobias Venner, *Viæ rectæ ad vitam longam* (1623, STC 24648), a pamphlet of 5.5 sheets on health that was entered into the Stationers' Register by George Winder on 9 May 1623, the same day Blount wrote his letter.

line 5: *proclamation for knights*] Probably *A proclamation for registring of knights* (1623, STC 8709), a single-sheet broadside containing a proclamation dated 25 April.

line 9: *Germin*] Trumbull's messenger, mentioned in letter five. Appears as 'Germi' but expanded.

234   APPENDIX 1

7. Edward Blount to Sir William Trumbull
30 May 1623
BL Additional MS 72365, ff. 116–17

Blount's final surviving letter to Trumbull reports the visit of a mutual friend, James Mabbe; the pair have a half-made plan for a companionable trip to Brussels later in the summer. That Mabbe relied on Blount to convey his own letter tells us that the bookseller was accustomed to acting as a courier for other correspondence. Along with Mabbe's letter, Blount also sends two more books and reports on a convivial evening spent drinking with Mabbe, together with Sir Robert Dallington, and one 'Doctor Fox'.

                      To the much honoured master   [address leaf]
                      William Trumball.
                      Agent for majestye of great
                      Brittaine to the Archeduchy
                      in Bruxells

Worthy Sir
    A strickt charge was layed upon me by my good freind
master Mabb to send this inclosed safe to you: I am bound to
observe his Comand, and serve you: yesternight he did
remember your health in a glasse of Canarrye, which
righted by Doctor Fox, master Rob: Dallington and my self. This   5
morning he is gone for Oxford. And hath made
half a promise to see Bruxells this sommer if his Gout
will give him leave. And hath prevailed with me to keepe
him companye in that Journeye. Here is litle newes
worthy your self: Only I send you by this messinger, the   10
History of Xenophon: and the Catholick moderator.
Which are all the newe bookes come forth this tearme.
Sir I take my leave and rest at your Command ever

London. 30. May 1623   Ed: Blount

Description: bifolium; address leaf contains two impressions of red wax seal (merchant's mark 2), both partially damaged. 209 × 315mm. Endorsed on address leaf: '30. of May 1623. From Master Ed: Blounte.'

line 2: *master Mabb*] The translator James Mabbe, also mentioned in letter five; *this inclosed*] Presumably a letter from Mabbe. None is collected in this manuscript (though a Mabbe letter to Trumbull can be found at BL Additional MS 72364, fol. 90–1).

line 4: *Canarrye*] White wine.

line 5: Doctor Fox] Perhaps Thomas Foxe (1592–1662), physician and fellow of Magdalen College, Oxford, alongside Mabbe. An alternative candidate is Simeon Foxe (1569–1642), uncle to Thomas, friend to John Donne, and fellow of the College of Physicians. Simeon had rooms in the college, on Paternoster Row behind Blount's bookshop; *Rob: Dallington*] Courtier and author Sir Robert Dallington (1561–c.1636), mentioned in letter three.

lines 5–6: *This morning he is gone*] Blount's bookshop occasionally doubled as a boarding house, making it possible Mabbe stayed at the Black Bear.

line 11: *History of Xenophon*] *The historie of Xenophon*, trans. John Bingham (1623, STC 26064), published by Ralph Mab (Mabbe); *Catholick moderator*] Henry Constable, *The Catholike moderator* (1623, STC 5636.2), published by Nathaniel Butter.

8. Edward Blount to Christopher Browne
15 August 1631
BL Additional MS 78683, fol. 73

This letter, the only known connection between Blount and Browne, shows the bookseller to be caught up to some degree in England's diplomatic relations with France. Blount is visiting Paris, probably to spend time with the ambassador Sir Isaac Wake, who is not named in the letter but had just arrived in Paris. Wake values Blount's presence enough to 'not lett me stirr from him', perhaps catching up on news and gossip from London. We learn that Blount planned to join a forthcoming trip to see King Louis XIII, presumably supporting Wake's embassy in some form. At this point in his life, Blount's fortunes had declined for some years; this trip prompted a final flurry of bookselling work. After returning from Paris, Blount registered four works in December 1631 and another in January 1632. Perhaps services rendered to Wake during his time abroad returned to Blount as some last form of patronage or sponsorship.

                    To the Right worshipfull   [verso]
                    master Browne at his howse
                    at Detford, these

Worthye Sir

I cannot lett this Convenient messinger passe without saluting
you and good mistress Browne: master Richard Browne is in
bonne Sanser. And we did last night at supper and this
day at dinner remember you both, I have not much to
write, be we are but newely arrived and my Lord will   5
not lett me stirr from him, yett this day I have
gotten a litle libertye to write, having left master
Rowlanson, Doctor Hodson, Verselius and Lanier with
his Lordship to talk with all. This is a great Hollyday
Sainct Lois, which keepes me within dores. The King is at   10

Description: single leaf; contains red wax seal (floral design) on verso. Address on verso. No endorsement.
headnote: *four works in December 1631 and another in January 1632*] These were Lodovico Melzo's 'Millitary Rules', first published as *Regole Militari* (Antwerp, 1611) but for which there is no extant English edition; a copy of Giorgio Basta's *The Government of Light Cavalry*, published as *Il Governo della Cavalleria Leggera* (Frankfurt and Venice, 1612) but again lacking an English edition; the Frenchman Nicolas Faret's *The honest man: or, The art to please in court* (1632, STC 10686); William Crompton's sermon *A wedding-ring* (1632, STC 6061); and Michel Baudier, *The history of the imperiall estate of the grand seigneurs* (re-entered by William Stansby in September 1633 and eventually published by Richard Meighen in 1635 as STC 1593).
superscription: *master Browne*] Christopher Browne (*d.* 1645) of Saye's Court, Deptford.
line 2: *mistress Browne*] Thomasine Gonson Browne (*b.* 1563); *Richard Browne*] Sir Richard Browne (1605–1683), diplomat and son of Christopher and Thomasine. At this point Richard Browne was twenty-six years old and was secretary to Sir Isaac Wake (1580/81–1632), the English ambassador who in 1631 moved embassy from Venice to Paris.

Continued

Monseaw, where my Lord intends to goe shortly and
with him the Doctor and my self and some others which have
nothing els to doe but see the King and Cardinall.
All the bruites of Armyes in france, I fynd to be
nothing here. Pardon my haste. I present my Service   15
to your self and the good gentle woman your wife.
And rest your servant to be Commanded

Paris. 15th and   Ed: Blount
25: August 1631

line 3: *Sanser*] Sancerre, roughly 120 miles south of Paris.
line 5: *my Lord*] Probably Wake, who was previously secretary to Sir Dudley Carleton in Venice (see letters one and two).
lines 7–8: *master Rowlanson*] Probably Thomas Rowlandson, one of Wake's secretaries.
line 8: *Doctor Hodson*] Perhaps the clergyman Phineas Hodson, whose sermon Blount had published in 1628: *The king's request* (STC 13551); *Verselius and Lanier*] These names are unclear. Blount may here switch from listing his travel companions to naming authors whose work he has left with Wake. Possible candidates for 'Verselius' would be the anatomist Andreas Vesalius (1514–1564) or perhaps the French theologian Theodore Beza, who went by the Latin name 'Theodorus Beza Vezelius'. If these names are authors then 'Lanier' could conceivably be the poet Emilia Lanier (1569–1645), whose *Salve Deus rex Judaeorum* was published in London in 1611, though this seems unlikely. Perhaps Blount simply identifies other members of the group, and if so one likely figure would be the musician and art dealer Nicholas Lanier (1588–1666), a favourite of King Charles and someone who is known to have visited Venice in the 1620s to collect artwork.
lines 9–10: *Hollyday Sainct Lois*] The feast of Saint Louis, on 25 August, celebrates the life of Louis IX.
line 10: *The King*] Louis XIII (1601–1643).
line 11: *Monseaw*] Monceaux, forty miles north of Paris.
line 13: *Cardinall*] Cardinal Richelieu (1585–1642).
line 14: *bruites*] Rumours.
lines 18–19: *15th and 25: August*] Continental Europe used the 'new style' Gregorian calendar, ten days ahead of the 'old style' Julian calendar used in England, hence Blount supplies both dates.

APPENDIX 2

The Publications of William and Isaac Jaggard

The following list supplies the speculative publishing of both William and Isaac Jaggard during William's lifetime, with the following caveats:

- The table excludes items printed for other publishers or for institutions.
- The table includes reissued titles (marked with '0 (RI)' in the 'Sheets' column), but excludes a variant state (STC 894.5) and a group of four titles, the only known copies of which are now lost but were once owned by the twentieth-century bookseller and Shakespearean scholar Captain William Jaggard.[1]
- Following recent work by William Sherman and Heather Wolfe, the table also excludes eight books written by Thomas Milles that mostly concern customs and trade issues. These books were printed by Jaggard but were probably funded by Milles himself.[2] The table also excludes STCs 1119.5 and 1120, an edition and an issue that both have false imprints.
- I have followed the STC in attributing STC 22975 (1612?) to Jaggard, though whether he published it is ambiguous.
- The only surviving copy of STC 24627a.6 (1598) is imperfect and so has a label of '1.5+' sheets.
- Finally, because I am interested in recording the public face of Jaggard's publishing profile around the quarto collection of 1619, this table does not include the ten titles (printed in eight editions) that form the Jaggard Quartos.

---

[1] These four entries (STCs 263, 19443, 24057, and 25792) were copied into the second edition of the STC from Pollard and Redgrave's first edition. Peter W. M. Blayney suspected they were damaged copies of other editions that were misdated by Captain Jaggard: 'The Numbers Game: Appraising the Revised STC' in *Papers of the Bibliographical Society of America* 88.3 (1994): pp. 353–407, at 358n19. When Captain Jaggard's library was sold at auction after his death the listings included many seventeenth-century works but none of these four titles: *A Catalogue of Books Both Old and Modern*, vol. 7, sale of 18–19 March 1948 (London: Hodgson & Co, 1948), pp. 32–8. Patrick Jaggard, descendant of Captain Jaggard, tells me in private correspondence that none of the captain's books remain in the family.
[2] Sherman and Wolfe, 'Department of Hybrid Books', p. 464.

Table 1 Jaggard publications

Year	STC #	Author	Short title	Genre	Sheets
1594	7086	John Dove	*A Sermon Preached…3 November 1594*	Religion (sermon)	4.5
	7086.5	John Dove	*A Sermon Preached…3 November 1594*	Religion (sermon)	4
1595	13973	William Hunnis	*Hunnies Recreations*	Religion (verse)	6.5
1598	24627a.6	Cesare Vecellio	*The True Perfection of Cutworks*	Needlework	1.5+
1599	13502	Thomas Hill	*The Schoole of Skil*	Astronomy	35
	264	Albertus Magnus	*The Secrets of Albertus Magnus*	Medicine	8
	22341.5	Various	*The Passionate Pilgrime*	Verse (miscellany)	3.5
	22342	Various	*The Passionate Pilgrime*	Verse (miscellany)	4
1601	14343	William Jaggard	*A View of All the Right Honourable…*	History (chronicle)	23.5
1603	12465.5	Richard Humfrey	*The Anathomie of Sinne*	Religion (treatise)	16
1604	12466	Richard Humfrey	*Two Guides to a Good Life*	Religion (treatise)	0 (RI)
1605	1486	Richard Barnfield	*Lady Pecunia*	Verse	6.5
	7606	G. Ellis	*The Lamentation of the Lost Sheepe*	Religion (verse)	7
	18279	Anthony Munday	*The Triumphes of Re-united Britania*	Civic pageant	3
	21786	Thomas Savile	*The Prisoners Conference*	Moral dialogue	7.5
1606	889	William Attersoll	*The Badges of Christianity*	Religion (treatise)	57.75
	24293	Justinius	*The Historie of Justine*	History (classical)	93
	23558	John Swynnerton	*A Christian Love-Letter*	Religion (treatise)	10.5
1607	6337	John Davies	*Yehovah Summa Totalis*	Religion (verse)	9.5
	6540	Thomas Dekker	*West-ward Hoe*	Drama	8.5
	13371	Thomas Heywood	*A Woman Kilde with Kindnesse*	Drama	8
	13967	Richard Humfrey	*The Conflict of Job*	Religion (treatise)	30.5
	24123	Edward Topsell	*The Historie of Foure-Footed Beastes*	Natural History	204
1608	1824	Thomas Bell	*The Jesuites Antipast*	Religion (treatise)	28.5
	1832	Thomas Bell	*The Tryall of the New Religion*	Religion (treatise)	7

	11922	Robert Glover	*Nobilitas Politica vel Civilis*	History (heraldry)	51
	12467	Richard Humfrey	*Two Guides to a Good Life*	Religion (treatise)	17.5
	21625	Sallust	*Two Most Worthy and Notable Histories*	History (classical)	52
	24124	Edward Topsell	*The Historie of Serpents*	Natural History	84
1609	898	William Attersoll	*The Pathway to Canaan*	Religion (treatise)	58.5
	13366	Thomas Heywood	*Troia Britanica*	History (verse)	117
1610	894	William Attersoll	*A Continuation of the Exposition…*	Religion (treatise)	89.5
	1810	Anon	*Adam Bell*	Verse	3
	11691a	Jacques Gaultier	*Rodomontados*	Prose satire	5
	17926	Thomas Milles	*The Catalogue of Honor*	History (heraldry)	300.5
	22008	Thomas Milles	*A Catalogue of the Kings of Scotland*	History (heraldry)	9
1611	4093	Edmund Bunny	*Of the Head-Corner-Stone*	Religion (treatise)	151
	4093.5	Edmund Bunny	*Of the Head-Corner-Stone*	Religion (treatise)	0 (RI)
	6718	Edward Dering	*A Short Catechisme for Housholders*	Religion (catechism)	2.5
	18263	Anthony Munday	*A Briefe Chronicle*	History (chronicle)	39.75
	18267	Anthony Munday	*Chruso-thriambos*	Civic pageant	3
	18267.5	Anthony Munday	*Chruso-thriambos*	Civic pageant	3
1612	890	William Attersoll	*A Commentarie Upon…S. Paul*	Religion (treatise)	135
	20393	W. Primroes	*A Funerall Poeme*	Verse	0.5
	22343	Various	*The Passionate Pilgrime*	Verse (miscellany)	8
	22975	G. T. (trans)	*A Briefe Discourse of the Hypostasis*	Medicine	2
	25786	Thomas Wilson	*A Christian Dictionarie*	Religion (dictionary)	103
1613	13483	Thomas Hill	*A Pleasant History*	Medicine	30
	17936	Thomas Milles (ed.)	*Treasurie of Auncient and Moderne Times*	History (encyclopaedia)	239.5
1614	889.5	William Attersoll	*The New Covenant*	Religion (treatise)	77
	6682.3	Edward Dering	*A Briefe and Necessarie Catechisme*	Religion (catechism)	25
	6719	Edward Dering	*A Short Catechism for Housholders*	Religion (catechism)	2.5
	25791	Thomas Wilson	*A Commentarie Upon…S. Paul*	Religion (treatise)	160.5
1615	107	Thomas Adams	*The Blacke Devill*	Religion (sermon)	24

Continued

Table 1 Continued

Year	STC	Author	Short title	Genre	Sheets
	6062	Helkiah Crooke	Mikrokosmographia	Medicine (anatomy)	257
	ESTC S509123	Anon	The Treasure of Gladnes	Religion (prayer)	2
1616	5811	Thomas Coryate	Thomas Coriate Traveller	Travel	8
	5812	Thomas Coryate	Thomas Coryate, Travailer	Travel	0 (RI)
	6062.2	Helkiah Crooke	Mikrokosmographia	Medicine (anatomy)	0 (RI)
	18304	Musaeus	The Divine Poem of Musaeus	Verse	2
	20782	Helkiah Crooke	Somatographia Anthropine	Medicine (anatomy)	20
	25787	Thomas Wilson	A Christian Dictionarie	Religion (dictionary)	113
1617	265	Albertus Magnus	The Secrets of Albertus Magnus	Medicine	8
	6720	Edward Dering	A Short Catechisme for Housholders	Religion (catechism)	2.5
	19191	Ambroise Paré	Method of Curing Wounds Made by Gunshot	Medicine	18
	13372	Thomas Heywood	A Woman Kilde With Kindnesse	Drama	9
	24991.5	Thomas Wallis	The Path-way to Please God	Religion (prayer)	2
	25835	Thomas Wimbledon	A Sermon No Lesse Fruitfull then Famous	Religion (sermon)	4
	25836	Thomas Wimbledon	A Sermon No Lesse Fruitefull, then Famous	Religion (sermon)	4
1618	893	William Attersoll	A Commentarie Upon....Moses	Religion (treatise)	325
	6062.4	Helkiah Crooke	Mikrokosmographia	Medicine (anatomy)	0 (RI)
	14341	William Jaggard	A Catalogue of Such English Bookes	Bibliography	1.5
1619	3832	Ralph Brooke	A Catalogue and Succession of the Kings	History (heraldry)	87
	17936.5	Thomas Milles	Archaio-ploutos	History (encyclopaedia)	251
1620	3172	Giovanni Boccaccio	The Decameron	Prose Fiction	200
	6721	Edward Dering	A Short Catechisme for Housholders	Religion (catechism)	2.5
	13859	Henry Howard	A Defensative Against the Poyson	Astrology (treatise)	80
	25796	Thomas Wilson	Saints by Calling	Religion (treatise)	54
1622	13859.5	Henry Howard	A Defensative Against the Poyson	Astrology (treatise)	0 (RI)

	24756	Augustine Vincent	*A Discoverie of Errours*	History (heraldry)	193.5
	25788	Thomas Wilson	*A Christian Dictionarie*	Religion (dictionary)	120
1623	6721.5	Edward Dering	*A Short Catechisme for Househoulders*	Religion (catechism)	2.5
	10717	André Favyn	*The Theater of Honour and Knight-hood*	History (heraldry)	296.5
	22273	William Shakespeare	*Comedies, Histories, & Tragedies*	Drama	227

APPENDIX 3

The Wholesale Locations of Shakespeare's Books, 1593–1640

This table shows the data from which the maps in chapter four have been constructed. There are a few cases where the circumstances of a book's publication and sale are not clear. I have followed Erne *Book Trade* pp. 13–17 by including an edition of *Love's Labour's Lost* in 1597 though no copy survives, and pp. 151–5 in making Robert Raworth the publisher of the 1607/8 edition of *Venus and Adonis* that has a false date of 1602 in its imprint. The following two editions of the poem (the ninth, printed in 1608/9?, and tenth, in 1610?) were also both dated 1602 in their imprints. For these latter editions I have followed Woudhuysen and Duncan Jones, *Shakespeare's Poems* p. 515, who suggest these two editions may have been published by Leake. One of the 1598 editions of *1 Henry IV* survives only in a copy that lacks a title page, hence the question marks.

The 'Locale of Bookshop' column lists the locale of the premises owned by the publisher or wholesale bookseller of each edition. The column standardizes this information. So Matthew Law's bookshop at the sign of the Fox, which is sometimes identified as being near 'St. Austin's Gate', and at other times near 'St Augustine's Gate', or without mention of a gate at all, is identified each time as 'Paul's Churchyard (near St. Augustine's Gate)'. Where an imprint names a publisher or wholesale bookseller but does not include the sign or address of their bookshop, I have supplied that information. Square brackets indicate that a bookshop sign was not named in that imprint.

Table 2 Chronological locations

Year	Short title	Publisher	Wholesale bookseller (where different)	Sign of bookshop identified by imprint	Locale of bookshop owned by publisher or wholesale bookseller
1593	*Venus and Adonis*	Richard Field	John Harrison 1	White Greyhound	Paul's Churchyard
1594	*1 Contention*	Thomas Millington		No sign	St Peter's Church, Cornhill
1594	*Titus Andronicus*	John Danter	Edward White & Thomas Millington	Gun	Paul's Churchyard (at Little North Door)
1594	*The Rape of Lucrece*	John Harrison 1		White Greyhound	Paul's Churchyard
1594	*Venus and Adonis*	Richard Field	John Harrison 1	White Greyhound	Paul's Churchyard
1595	*Richard Duke of York*	Thomas Millington		No sign	St Peter's Church, Cornhill
1595?	*Venus and Adonis*	John Harrison 1?		White Greyhound?	Paul's Churchyard?
1596	*Edward III*	Cuthbert Burby		No sign	Royal Exchange
1596	*Venus and Adonis*	John Harrison 1		[Greyhound]	Paternoster Row
1597?	*Love's Labour's Lost*	Cuthbert Burby?		No sign?	Royal Exchange?
1597	*Richard II*	Andrew Wise		Angel	Paul's Churchyard
1597	*Richard III*	Andrew Wise		Angel	Paul's Churchyard
1597	*Romeo and Juliet*	John Danter		No sign	Hosier Lane
1598	*1 Henry IV*	Andrew Wise		Angel	Paul's Churchyard
1598?	*1 Henry IV*	Andrew Wise?		Angel?	Paul's Churchyard?
1598	*Love's Labour's Lost*	Cuthbert Burby		No sign	Royal Exchange
1598	*Richard II*	Andrew Wise		Angel	Paul's Churchyard
1598	*Richard II*	Andrew Wise		Angel	Paul's Churchyard
1598	*Richard III*	Andrew Wise		Angel	Paul's Churchyard
1598	*The Rape of Lucrece*	John Harrison 1		[Greyhound]	Paternoster Row
1599	*Edward III*	Cuthbert Burby		No sign	Royal Exchange

Continued

Table 2 Continued

Year	Short title	Publisher	Wholesale bookseller (where different)	Sign of bookshop identified by imprint	Locale of bookshop owned by publisher or wholesale bookseller
1599	1 Henry IV	Andrew Wise		Angel	Paul's Churchyard
1599?	The Passionate Pilgrim	William Jaggard?	William Leake?	Greyhound?	Paul's Churchyard?
1599	The Passionate Pilgrim	William Jaggard	William Leake	Greyhound	Paul's Churchyard
1599	Romeo and Juliet	Cuthbert Burby		No sign	Royal Exchange
1599	Venus and Adonis	William Leake		Greyhound	Paul's Churchyard
1599	Venus and Adonis	William Leake		Greyhound	Paul's Churchyard
1600	1 Contention	Thomas Millington		No sign	St Peter's Church, Cornhill
1600	2 Henry IV	Andrew Wise & William Aspley		[Angel & Tiger's Head]	Paul's Churchyard
1600	Henry V	Thomas Millington & John Busby		No sign	Carter Lane (near the Paul's Head)
1600	The Merchant of Venice	Thomas Hayes		Green Dragon	Paul's Churchyard
1600	A Midsummer Night's Dream	Thomas Fisher		White Hart	Fleet Street
1600	Much Ado About Nothing	Andrew Wise & William Aspley		[Angel & Tiger's Head]	Paul's Churchyard
1600	The Rape of Lucrece	John Harrison 1		[Greyhound]	Paternoster Row
1600	The Rape of Lucrece	John Harrison 1		[Greyhound]	Paternoster Row
1600	Richard Duke of York	Thomas Millington		No sign	St Peter's Church, Cornhill
1600	Titus Andronicus	Edward White		Gun	Paul's Churchyard (at the Little North Door)
1602	Henry V	Thomas Pavier		Cat and Parrots	Royal Exchange

1602	The Merry Wives of Windsor	Arthur Johnson	Fleur de Luce and Crown	Paul's Churchyard
1602	Richard III	Andrew Wise	Angel	Paul's Churchyard
1602?	Venus and Adonis	William Leake	[Greyhound]	Paul's Churchyard
1603	Hamlet	Nicholas Ling & John Trundle	No sign	St Dunstan's Churchyard & Barbican
1604	1 Henry IV	Matthew Law	Fox	Paul's Churchyard (near St. Augustine's Gate)
1604/5	Hamlet	Nicholas Ling	No sign	St Dunstan's Churchyard
1605	Richard III	Thomas Creed & Matthew Law	Fox	Paul's Churchyard (near St. Augustine's Gate)
1607	The Rape of Lucrece	John Harrison 1	[Greyhound]	Paternoster Row
1607/8? ('1602')	Venus and Adonis	Robert Raworth 'William Leake'	Holy Ghost	Paul's Churchyard
1608	1 Henry IV	Matthew Law	Fox	Paul's Churchyard (near St. Augustine's Gate)
1608	King Lear	Nathaniel Butter	Pied Bull	Paul's Churchyard (near St. Augustine's Gate)
1608	Richard II	Matthew Law	Fox	Paul's Churchyard (near St. Augustine's Gate)
1608/9? ('1602')	Venus and Adonis	William Leake	Holy Ghost	Paul's Churchyard
1609	Pericles	Henry Gosson	Sun	Paternoster Row
1609	Pericles	Henry Gosson	Sun	Paternoster Row
1609	Romeo and Juliet	John Smethwick	No sign	St Dunstan's Churchyard (under the Dial)

Continued

Table 2 Continued

Year	Short title	Publisher	Wholesale bookseller (where different)	Sign of bookshop identified by imprint	Locale of bookshop owned by publisher or wholesale bookseller
1609	Sonnets	Thomas Thorpe	William Aspley & John Wright	[Parrot] & no sign	Paul's Churchyard & Christ Church Gate
1609	Troilus and Cressida	Richard Bonian & Henry Walley		Spread Eagle	Paul's Churchyard (over against Great North Door)
1610? ('1602')	Venus and Adonis	William Leake		Holy Ghost	Paul's Churchyard
1611	Hamlet	John Smethwick		No sign	St Dunstan's Churchyard (under the Dial)
1611	Pericles	Simon Stafford		[Bell]	Warwick Lane
1611	Titus Andronicus	Edward White		Gun	Paul's Churchyard (near Little North Door)
1612	The Passionate Pilgrim	William Jaggard		No sign	Barbican
1612	Richard III	Thomas Creed & Matthew Law	Matthew Law	Fox	Paul's Churchyard (near St. Augustine's Gate)
1613	1 Henry IV	Matthew Law		Fox	Paul's Churchyard (near St. Augustine's Gate)
1615	Richard II	Matthew Law		Fox	Paul's Churchyard (near St. Augustine's Gate)
1616	The Rape of Lucrece	Roger Jackson		No sign	Fleet Street (near conduit)
1617	Venus and Adonis	William Barrett		[Three Pigeons]	Paul's Churchyard
1619 ('1608')	Henry V	'Thomas Pavier' [i.e. William Jaggard & Thomas Pavier]		No sign & [Cat and Parrot?]	Barbican? & Ivy Lane?
1619 ('1608')	King Lear	'Nathaniel Butter' [i.e. William Jaggard & Thomas Pavier]		No sign & [Cat and Parrot?]	Barbican? & Ivy Lane?

1619 ('1600')	The Merchant of Venice	'James Roberts' [i.e. William Jaggard & Thomas Pavier]		No sign & [Cat and Parrot?]	Barbican? & Ivy Lane?
1619	The Merry Wives of Windsor	'Arthur Johnson' [i.e. William Jaggard & Thomas Pavier]		No sign & [Cat and Parrot?]	Barbican? & Ivy Lane?
1619 ('1600')	A Midsummer Night's Dream	'James Roberts' [i.e. William Jaggard & Thomas Pavier]		No sign & [Cat and Parrot?]	Barbican? & Ivy Lane?
1619	Pericles	'Thomas Pavier' [i.e. William Jaggard & Thomas Pavier]		No sign & [Cat and Parrot?]	Barbican? & Ivy Lane?
1619	The Whole Contention	'Thomas Pavier' [i.e. William Jaggard & Thomas Pavier]		No sign & [Cat and Parrot?]	Barbican? & Ivy Lane?
1620	Venus and Adonis	John Parker		[Three Pigeons]	Paul's Churchyard
1622	1 Henry IV	Thomas Purfoot & Matthew Law	Matthew Law	Fox	Paul's Churchyard (near St. Augustine's Gate)
1622	Othello	Thomas Walkley		Eagle and Child	Britain's Burse
1622	Richard III	Thomas Purfoot & Matthew Law	Matthew Law	Fox	Paul's Churchyard (near St. Augustine's Gate)
1623	Comedies, Histories, & Tragedies	Edward Blount		[Black Bear]	Paul's Churchyard
		William Jaggard		No sign	Barbican
		William Aspley		[Parrot]	Paul's Churchyard
		John Smethwick		No sign	St Dunstan's Churchyard (under the Dial)
1623?	Romeo and Juliet	John Smethwick		No sign	St Dunstan's Churchyard (under the Dial)
1624	The Rape of Lucrece	Roger Jackson		No sign	Fleet Street (near conduit)
1625?	Hamlet	John Smethwick		No sign	St Dunstan's Churchyard (under the Dial)

Continued

Table 2 Continued

Year	Short title	Publisher	Wholesale bookseller (where different)	Sign of bookshop identified by imprint	Locale of bookshop owned by publisher or wholesale bookseller
1627	Venus and Adonis	John Wreittoun		No sign	Edinburgh (beneath the Salt Throne)
1629	Richard III	John Norton & Matthew Law	Matthew Law	Fox	Paul's Churchyard (near St. Augustine's Gate)
1630	The Merry Wives of Windsor	Richard Meighen		No sign	Middle Temple Gate & St Dunstan's Churchyard
1630	Othello	Richard Hawkins		No sign	Chancery Lane (near Serjeants' Inn)
1630	Pericles	Robert Bird		[Bible]	Cheapside
1630	Venus and Adonis	John Haviland	Francis Coles	No sign	Old Bailey (without Newgate)
1630–6?	Venus and Adonis	John Haviland?	Francis Coles?	No sign?	Old Bailey? (without Newgate?)
1631	Love's Labour's Lost	John Smethwick		No sign	St Dunstan's Churchyard (under the Dial)
1631	The Taming of the Shrew	John Smethwick		No sign	St Dunstan's Churchyard (under the Dial)
1632	Comedies, Histories, & Tragedies	John Smethwick		No sign	St Dunstan's Churchyard (under the Dial)
		Richard Hawkins		No sign	Chancery Lane (near Serjeants' Inn)
		Robert Allott		Black Bear	Paul's Churchyard
		William Aspley		Parrot	Paul's Churchyard
		Richard Meighen		No sign	Middle Temple Gate
1632	1 Henry IV	John Norton 2	William Sheares	No sign	Paul's Churchyard (at Great South Door) & Chancery Lane (near Serjeants' Inn)

1632	The Rape of Lucrece	John Harrison 4	Golden Unicorn	Paternoster Row
1634	The Two Noble Kinsmen	John Waterson	Crown	Paul's Churchyard
1634	Richard II	John Norton 2	No sign	Foster Lane
1634	Richard III	John Norton 2	No sign	Foster Lane
1635	Pericles	Thomas Cotes	No sign	Barbican
1636	Venus and Adonis	John Haviland	No sign	Old Bailey (without Newgate)
		Francis Coles		
1637	Hamlet	John Smethwick	No sign	St Dunstan's Churchyard (under the Dial)
1637	The Merchant of Venice	Laurence Hayes	No sign	Fleet Bridge
1637	Romeo and Juliet	John Smethwick	No sign	St Dunstan's Churchyard (under the Dial)
1639	1 Henry IV	John Norton 2	No sign	The Strand (next to Ivy Bridge)
		Hugh Perry		
1640	Poems	John Benson	No sign	St Dunstan's Churchyard

Bibliography

Primary Works

MANUSCRIPTS

Beinecke Library
Osborn MS fb 230, *Funerary placard for Vincent Corbett*

Bodleian Library
MS Ashmole 1057, *Book fair catalogues*
MS Aubrey 2, *Papers of John Aubrey*
MS Bodleian 313, *Papers of Thomas Lydiat*
MS Eng. c. 2278, *Letters of Robert Herrick*
MS Eng. poet. d. 3, *Edmund Pudsey's commonplace book*
Gough Maps Volume 19, *Prints and drawings of London*
Gough Maps Volume 20, *Prints and drawings of London*
MS Rawlinson A 239, *Stanhope's Royal Accounts*
MS Top. Oxon. d. 238, *Bookseller's bill of John Crosley*

British Library
Additional MS 34192, *Presentation manuscript of George Silver*
Additional MS 72360, *Trumbull Papers, Vol. CXIX*
Additional MS 72361, *Trumbull Papers, Vol. CXX*
Additional MS 72364, *Trumbull Papers Vol. CXXIII*
Additional MS 72365, *Trumbull Papers, Vol. CXXIV*
Additional MS 78683, *Evelyn Papers, Vol. DXVI*
Harley MS 1026, *Diary of Justinian Pagitt*
Lansdowne MS 841, *Miscellaneous letters 1476–1763*

Drapers' Company Archives
Percival Boyd's Register Roll, no shelfmark

Durham Cathedral Library
Hunter MS 130, *Copy of John Earle's Micro-cosmographie*

Edinburgh University Library
MS H-P. Coll. 401, *Miscellany of Richard Jackson, c.1623*

Folger Library
MS V. b. 187, *Statement of Arthur Bromfeilde*
MS Y. c. 622, *Bolton Corney to John Payne Collier, 25 March 1858*
MS X. d. 254, *Single leaf book guarantee from Francis Smethwick*

Hartlib Papers

8/66A–B, *Advertisement For Music Teaching*
41/1/32A, *Ralph Austen to Samuel Hartlib, 6 June 1653*
51/6A–7B, *John Beale to Josua Kirton, undated c. 1658*

Hertfordshire Archives

Alphabetical List of Parochial Incumbents of the County of Hertford from Lists Compiled by Rev. GL Hennessy, open shelf

Huntington Library

28116, *John Pyper to Thomas Huggins 23 March 1621,* manuscript papers bound into endleaves of printed book

Kent County Archives

U350/E4, *Sir Edward Dering's Booke of Expenses*
U269/1, *John Florio to Lionel Cranfield, Lord High Treasurer, 1621*

London Metropolitan Archives

CLA/002/05/001, *Court of Orphans Recognizances 1590–1633*
CLA/023/DW/01/294, *Conveyance of Land to William Jaggard*
CLA/023/DW/01/302, *Husting Roll 303, Item 40*
CLC/W/FA/030/MS01503/2, *Subsidy for Aldersgate Ward 1625–6*
CLC/W/JB/044/MS03018/001, *Wardmote Inquest Book*
COL/AD/01/034, *Letter Book II*
COL/CA/01/01/033, *Court of Aldermen Repertory Book 1610–12*
COL/CA/01/01/038, *Court of Aldermen Repertory Book 1618–20*
COL/CA/01/01/042, *Court of Aldermen Repertory Book 1623–4*
COL/CHD/CT/01/001, *City of London Cash Accounts*
DL/A/A/006/MS09531/013/001, *Bishop's Register 1559–93/4*
DL/AL/C/001/MS09050/005, *Probate Act of William Jaggard*
DL/AL/C/003/MS09052/005, *Will of William Jaggard*
DL/AL/C/003/MS09052/006, item 170, *Will of Jane Jaggard*
DL/AL/C/003/MS09052/007, *Will of Isaac Jaggard*
P69/DUN2/A/001/MS10342, *Parish Register of St Dunstan in the West*
P69/DUN2/B/001/MS03016/001, *Vestry Minute Book*
P69/DUN2/B/011/MS02968/003, *Churchwarden's Accounts 1628–1644*
P69/DUN2/C/001/MS03783, *Scavengers' Rate Assessments*
P69/DUN2/E/001/MS03793, *Appointment of Governors to Free School*

National Library of Wales

Great Sessions 8/5, *Great Sessions Docket Rolls*

Oxford University Archives

NEP/supra/Reg I, *Supplication roll*

Parker Library, Corpus Christi College, Cambridge

MS 215–6, *Postils of John Boys*

Rosenbach Museum and Library
MS 239/18, *Miscellany*

Stationers' Company Archives
TSC/1/E/06/02, *Register C*
TSC/1/E/06/03, *Register D*
TSC/1/F/02/01, *Liber B*
TSC/1/C/01/06/01, *Call of the Livery Book Volume 1*
TSC/1/G/01/04/07, *Liber Computi Pro Pauperibus, 1608–1676*

The National Archives, Kew
C 2/JasI/B40/22, *Button v Whitfield*
C 3/333/25, *Bill of Complaint, Blount vs Roydon*
C 24/501/81 (Part 1), *Stationers' Company v. Bonham Norton*
C 33/145, *Entry Book A 1623*
C 33/147, *Entry Book A 1624*
E 179/146/463, *Assessment of Aldersgate Ward 1621*
E 179/147/510, *Assessment of Aldersgate Ward 1625*
E 179/147/535, *Assessment of Aldersgate Ward 1625*
E/190/24/4, *Port of London accounts 1620–1*
E/190/31/3, *Port of London accounts 1625–6*
E 331/London/1, *Certificates of Clergy Appointments*
E 334/14, *Office of First Fruits 1604–13*
E 334/15, *Office of First Fruits 1614–18*
E 351/2793, *Accounts of Henry, Prince of Wales*
PROB 4/2828, *Inventory of Robert Ibbitson*
PROB 8/37, *Probate Act of William Aspley*
PROB 10/641/3, *Will of Elizabeth Bankworth Blount*
PROB 10/610, *Will of William Aspley*
PROB 10/619, *Will of John Smethwick*
PROB 11/60/368, *Will of Richard Smethwick*
PROB 11/138/543, *Will of Richard Bankworth*
PROB 11/177/292, *Will of Edmund Weaver*
PROB 11/186/520, *Proven Copy of Will of John Smethwick*
PROB 11/190/12, *Sentence of the Will of William Aspley*
REQ 2/203/4, *Eastland vs East*
SO 3/2, *Signet Office Docquet Book 1603–5*
SP 14/80, *State Papers Domestic, James I*
SP 16/307, *State Papers Domestic, Charles I*
SP 38/7, *State Papers Domestic, Signet Office Docquets*

Westminster Abbey Muniments
13574, *Funeral receipt of Jane Jaggard*

COPY-SPECIFIC PRINTED BOOKS
The whole volume of statutes at large (1587, STC 9305.3)
   Copy in private ownership

Babington, Gervase. *The works of the Right Reverend Father in God, Gervase Babington* (1637, STC 1080)
    Huntington Library 28116
Boys, John. *The Autumne Part* (1612, STC 3460.5)
    Bodleian Library Vet. A2 e.353 (5)
Boys, John. *An exposition of al the principall Scriptures* (1609, STC 3455)
    British Library 1219. D. 50
    Folger Library STC 3455
Boys, John. Sammelband volumes.
    Attingham Park, Shropshire, NT005719
    Bodleian Library Vet. A2 e.171
    Bodleian Library Vet. A2 e.353
    British Library C. 118. BB. 10
    Canterbury Cathedral Library W2/N-11-5
    Cambridge University Library Syn. 7. 61. 39
    Folger Library STC 3456.3
    Huntington Library 230343
    Parker Library, Corpus Christi College, Cambridge A.11.9
Boys, John. *The workes of John Boys Doctor in Divinitie* (1630, STC 3453)
    Bodleian Library Vet. A2 d.2
Cavendish[?], William. *Horæ subseciuæ* (1620, STC 3957)
    Library of Belton House, Lincolnshire, NT 3058918
Charron, Pierre. *Of wisdome: three bookes* (1608, STC 5051)
    British Library C.82.b.13
Dallington, Robert. *Aphorismes Civill and Militarie* (1613, STC 6197)
    Folger STC 6197 Copy 1
Delamothe, G. *The French Alphabet* (1639, STC 6550)
    Bodleian Library 8° B 287 Linc
Drayton, Michael. *Poems: by Michael Drayton Esquire* (1610, STC 7220)
    Bodleian Library J-J Drayton f.12
Florio, John. *A worlde of wordes* (1598, STC 11098)
    Folger Library STC 11098 Copy 1
    York Minster Library VII.K.2
    St John's College, Cambridge G.8.9
Marlowe, Christopher. *Hero and Leander* (1613, STC 17418)
    British Library C.57.i.45
Marston, John. *The Malcontent* (1604, STC 17481)
    Bodleian Library Malone 195 (5)
    Bodleian Library Malone 252 (4)
    Boston Public Library G.3977.50
    Folger Library STC 17481 copy 1
    Victoria and Albert Library Dyce 26 Box 28/2
Montaigne, Michel de. *The essayes* (1603, STC 18041)
    Worcester College, Oxford, L. L. e. 13
Munday, Anthony. *The triumphes of re-united Britania* (1605, STC 18279)
    Bodleian Library Gough Lond. 122 (4)
de Santa María, Juan. *Christian policie* (1632, STC 14830.7)
    Huntington Library 475778
Shakespeare, William. *Mr. William Shakespeares comedies, histories, & tragedies* (1623, STC 22273)
    Bodleian Library Arch. G c.7

Folger Library STC 22273 Fo.1 no.01
Folger Library STC 22273 Fo.1 no.81
Shakespeare (and others), William. *The passionate pilgrime* (1612, STC 22343)
Bodleian Library Arch. G g.1.

PRINTED BOOKS[1]

Catalogus uniuersalis pro nundinis Francofurtensibus autumnalibus…(Frankfurt, 1622, STC 11329.8)
Catalogus universalis pronundinis Francofurtensibus vernalibus…(Frankfurt, 1624, STC 11330.2)
Catalogus universalis pro nundinis Francofurtensibus autumnalibus de anno M.DC.XXIIII (1624, no STC number)
The clergyes bill of complaint (1643, Wing C4644)
The cobler of Canterburie (1608, STC 4580)
Englands Helicon (1614, STC 3192)
The fierie tryall of Gods saints (1611, STC 24269)
The first and second part of the troublesome raigne of John King of England (1611, STC 14646)
Heir follouis. Ane compendeous buke, of Godly psalmes (Edinburgh, 1565, STC 2996.3)
The hystorie of Hamblet (1608, STC 12734.5)
The lawes and statutes of Geneva (1562, STC 11725)
There's nothing to be had without money (1633, STC 18699)
A Pleasant and Delightfull Poeme of Two Lovers, Philos and Licia (1624, STC 19886)
A proclamation for registring of knights (1623, STC 8709)
The returne from Pernassus: or The scourge of simony (1606, STC 19310)
The Troublesome Reign of John, King of England, edited by J. W. Sider (New York: Garland, 1979)
A warning for faire women (1599, STC 25089)
Acosta Jose de. *The naturall and Morall Historie of the East and West Indies* (1604, STC 94)
Aesop. *The fabulous tales of Esope the Phrygian* (1577, STC 186.5)
Aleman, Mateo. *The rogue* (1622/3, STC 288)
Alexander, William. *A Paraensis to the Prince* (1604, STC 346)
d'Andilly, Arnauld. *The manner of ordering fruit-trees* (1660, Wing L942A)
Andrewes, John. *The Brazen Serpent* (1621, STC 591)
Armin, Robert. *Quips upon questions* (1600, STC 775.5)
Attersoll, William. *A commentarie upon the fourth booke of Moses* (1618, STC 893)
Attersoll, William. *The pathway to Canaan* (1609 STC 898)
Aubrey, John. *Brief Lives with An Apparatus for the Lives of our English Mathematical Writers*, edited by Kate Bennett. 2 vols (Oxford: Oxford University Press, 2018)
Babington, Gervase. *The works of the Right Reverend Father in God, Gervase Babington* (1637, STC 1080)
Bacon, Francis. *A briefe discourse, touching the happie union of the kingdomes of England, and Scotland* (1603, STC 1117)
Bacon, Francis. *Certaine considerations touching the better pacification, and edification of the Church of England* (1621, STC 1119.5)
Barnes, Barnabe. *Foure bookes of offices* (1606, STC 1468)
Beaumont, Francis, and John Fletcher. *Comedies and tragedies written by Francis Beaumont and John Fletcher* (1647, Wing B1581)

---

[1] Early printed books were published in London unless otherwise stated.

Bell, Thomas. *The jesuites antepast* (1608, STC 1824)
Boys, John. *The Autumne Parte* (1613, STC 3460.6)
Boys, John. *An exposition of the dominical Epistles and Gospels...the summer-part* (1611, STC 3460)
Boys, John. *An exposition of the dominical Epistles and Gospels...The winter part* (1610, STC 3458)
Boys, John. *An exposition of the last psalme* (1613, STC 3464 and 1615, STC 3465.4)
Boys, John. *An Exposition of the Proper Psalmes used in our English Lyturgie...The second part* (1617, STC 3467)
Boys, John. *Der fünffte Theil Ist eine Erklärung aller gewöhnlichen Fest- und Apostel-Tags-Episteln* (Brunswick, 1683)
Boys, John. *Johann Boys SS. Theol. Doct. und Decan. Zu Canterburie* (Brunswick, 1685)
Boys, John. *Remaines of that reverend and famous postiller, John Boys* (1631, STC 3468)
Boys, John. *Stern und Kern aller Episteln und Evangelien durchs gantze Jahr* (Brunswick, 1683 and 1685)
Boys, John. *The workes of John Boys Doctor in Divinitie* (1622, STC 3452 and 1630, STC 3453)
Brathwait, Richard. *Whimzies: or, a new cast of characters* (1631, STC 3591)
Brome, Richard. *A joviall crew, or, The merry beggars* (1652, Wing B4873)
Brown, Thomas. *The fourth volume of the works of Mr. Thomas Brown* (1711)
Bryskett, Lodowick. *A discourse of civill life* (1606, STC 3959)
Bunny, Edmund. *Of the Head-Corner-Stone* (1611, STC 4093)
Buck, George. 'The Third universitie of England' in John Stow, *The annales, or a generall chronicle of England* (1615, STC 23338), sigs. 4L5r–4O3v
Buoni, Thomasso. *Problemes of beauty* (1606, STC 4103 and 1618, STC 4103.5)
Burton, Robert. *The anatomy of melancholy* (1621, STC 4159 and 1628, STC 4161)
Campion, Thomas. *Observations in the art of English poesie* (1602, STC 4543)
Caius, John. *De antiquitate Cantebrigiensis Academiæ* (1574, STC 4345)
Cavendish[?], William. *Horæ subsecivæ* (1620, STC 3957)
Cawdry, Robert. *A table alphabeticall* (1604, STC 4884)
Chapman, George (translator). *The Divine Poem of Musæus* (1616, STC 18304)
Chapman, George, Ben Jonson, and John Marston. *Eastward Hoe* (1605, STC 4970)
Chapman, George, Ben Jonson, and John Marston. *Eastward Ho*, edited by R. W. Van Fossen (Manchester: Manchester University Press, 1999)
Chaucer, Geoffrey. *The assemblie of foules* (1530, STC 5092)
Chester, Robert and others. *Loves martyr: or, Rosalins complaint* (1601, STC 5119)
Churchyard, Thomas. *The mirror of man, and manners of men* (1594, STC 5242)
Chytraeus, David. *Postil or orderly disposing of certeine epistles usually red in the Church of God, uppon the Sundayes and holydayes* (1570, STC 5263)
Cokain, Aston. *A Chain of Golden Poems* (1658, Wing C4894)
Constable, Henry. *The Catholike moderator* (1623, STC 5636.2)
Constaggio, Gerolamo. *The historie of the uniting of the kingdom of Portugall to the crowne of Castill* (1600, STC 5624)
Coryate, Thomas. *Coryats Crambe* (1611, STC 5807)
Coryate, Thomas. *Coryats crudities* (1611, STC 5808)
Cosin, John. *The Correspondence of John Cosin, D.D. Lord Bishop of Durham: Together With Other Papers Illustrative of his Life and Times*, 2 vols Edited by George Ornsby (Durham: Andrews & Co for the Surtees Society, 1869–72)
Cowley, Abraham. *Poems* (1656, Wing C6683)
Cowley, Abraham. *Poeticall blossomes* (1636, STC 5907)

Cowper, William. *The workes of Mr Willia[m] Cowper late Bishop of Galloway* (1623, STC 5909)
Crofts, Robert. *The way to happinesse on earth* (1641, Wing C7007)
Crooke, Helkiah. *Sōmatographia Anthrōpinē* (1616, STC 20782)
Daniel, Samuel. *A Panegyric Congratulatory* (1603, STC 6259)
Davies, Sir John. *A discoverie of the state of Ireland* (1613, STC 6349)
Davies, John. *A scourge for paper-persecutors* (1625, STC 6340)
Dekker, Thomas. *The guls horne-booke* (1609, STC 6500)
Dekker, Thomas. *The Magnificent Entertainment* (1604, STC 6510)
Dekker, Thomas. *The Pleasant Comedie of Old Fortunatus* (1600, STC 6517)
Dekker, Thomas. *The pleasant comodie of patient Grisill* (1603, STC 6518)
Delamothe, G. *The French alphabeth* (1592, STC 6545.5)
Dering, Edward. *Briefe and necessarie catechisme* (1614, STC 6682.3)
Dering, Edward. *M. Derings workes* (1614, STC 6678)
Dogget, Thomas. *The country-wake: a comedy* (1696, Wing D1828)
Donne, John. *Poems, by J. D.* (1633, STC 7045)
Dove, John. *A sermon preached at Pauls Crosse the 3. of November 1594* (1594, STC 7086.5)
Drayton, Michael. *Englands heroicall epistles* (1602, STC 7197)
Drayton, Michael. *Poly-Olbion by Michaell Drayton Esqr* (1612, STC 7226)
Dryden, John. *Of dramatick poesie: an essay* (1668, Wing D2327)
Eadmer. *Eadmeri monachi Cantuariensis Historiæ novorum* (1623, STC 7438)
Elyot, Thomas. *Bibliotheca Eliotæ* (1559, STC 7663)
Farewell, Christopher. *An East-India colation; or a discourse of travels* (1633, STC 10687)
Favyn, Andre. *The theater of honour and knight-hood* (1623, STC 10717)
Featley, Daniel. *The Romish Fisher...* (1624, STC 10738.3)
Filipe, Bartholomeu. *The Counseller* (1589, STC 10753)
Fletcher, John and William Shakespeare. *The two noble kinsmen* (1634, STC 11075)
Fletcher, John and William Shakespeare. *The Two Noble Kinsmen*, edited by Lois Potter (London: Thomas Nelson and Sons, 1997)
Florio, John. *John Florio: A Worlde of Wordes A Critical Edition*, edited by Hermann Haller (Toronto, ON: University of Toronto Press, 2013)
Florio, John. *A worlde of wordes* (1598, STC 11098)
Frost, Robert. *The Poetry of Robert Frost: The Collected Poems*, edited by Edward Connery Lathem (New York: Henry Holt and Company, 1969)
Fuller, Thomas. *The History of the Worthies of England* (1662, Wing F2440)
Gainsford, Thomas. *The rich cabinet* (1616, STC 11522)
Gentleman, Tobias. *Englands Way to Win Wealth* (1614, STC 11745)
Goodwin, John. *A fresh discovery of the high-Presbyterian spirit* (1655, Wing G1167)
Goodwin, John. *The saints interest in God* (1640, STC 12031)
Gordon, John. *England and Scotlands happinesse: in being reduced to unitie of religion, under our invincible monarke King James* (1604, STC 12062.3)
Goslicki, Wawrzyniec. *The Counsellor* (1598, STC 12372)
Granada, Luis de. *Of prayer and meditation* (1611, STC 16911.5)
Hall, Joseph. *A recollection of such treatises as have bene heretofore severally published...* (1615, STC 12706 and 12706a)
Hartman, G. *The family physitian* (1696, Wing H1003)
Heath, Robert. *Clarastella* (1650, Wing H1340A)
Hemmingsen, Niels. *A postill, or exposition of the Gospels* (1569, STC 13061)
Heywood, Thomas. *An Apology for Actors* (1612, STC 13309)
Heywood, Thomas. *If you know not mee, you know no body* (1639, STC 13335)

Heywood, Thomas. *The rape of Lucrece* (1608, STC 13360)
Heywood, Thomas. *A woman kilde with kindnesse* (1617, STC 13372)
Hieron, Samuel. *The workes of Mr. Sam. Hieron* (1634, STC 13384.7)
Higgons, Theophilus. *A sermon preached at Pauls Crosse the third of March, 1610* (1611, STC 13455.7)
Hobbes, Thomas. *Leviathan*, edited by David Johnston, 2nd edn (London and New York: W. W. Norton & Company, 2020)
Hodson, Phineas. *The king's request* (1628, STC 13551)
Humfrey, Richard. *Two guides to a good life* (1604, STC 12466)
Jackson, Thomas. *Davids pastorall poeme* (1603, STC 14299)
Jaggard, William. *A catalogue of such English bookes, as lately have bene, and now are in printing for publication* (1618, STC 14341)
Jaggard, William. *A view of all the right honourable the Lord Mayors of this honorable citty of London* (1601, STC 14343)
Johnson, Rob. *Essaies, or rather Imperfect offers* (1601, STC 14695)
Jonson, Ben. *Ben: Jonson's Execration Against Vulcan* (1640, STC 14771)
Jonson, Ben. 'Informations to William Drummond of Hawthornden (1619)', edited by Ian Donaldson, in vol. 5 of *The Cambridge Edition of the Works of Ben Jonson*, 7 vols, edited by David Bevington, Martin Butler, and Ian Donaldson (Cambridge: Cambridge University Press, 2012)
Jonson, Ben. 'The Staple of Newes' in *Bartholmew fayre: a comedie* (1631, STC 14753.5)
Jonson, Ben. *The Staple of News*, edited by Anthony Parr (Manchester: Manchester University Press, 1988)
Jonson, Ben. *The workes of Benjamin Jonson* (1616, STC 14752 and 1640 [i.e. 1641], STC 14754)
Justinus, Marcus. *The Historie of Justine* (1606, STC 24293)
Kirkman, Francis. *The unlucky citizen* (1678, Wing K638)
Lisle, William. *The faire Æthiopian* (1630, STC 13047.5)
Lloyd, David. *Memoires of the lives, actions, sufferings & deaths of those noble, reverend, and excellent personages, that suffered by death, sequestration, decimation, or otherwise, for the Protestant religion* (1668, Wing L2642)
Lodge, Thomas. *Euphues golden legacie* (1634, STC 16673.5 and 1642, Wing L2810)
Lucan. *Lucans first booke*, translated by Christopher Marlowe (1600, STC 16883.5)
Lupton, Donald. *London and the countrey* (1632, STC 16944)
Lydiat, Thomas. *Solis et lunae periodus* (1620, STC 17046)
Lyly, John. *Sixe court comedies* (1632, STC 17088)
Macky, John. *A journey through England* (1714)
Manning, Francis. *The generous choice* (1700, Wing M486)
Marcelline, George. *The triumphs of King James the First* (1610, STC 17309)
Marlowe, Christopher. *Hero and Leander* (1613, STC 17418)
Marston, John. *The Malcontent* (1604, STC 17480)
Marston, John. *The Malcontent*, edited by George K. Hunter (London: Methuen, 1975)
Martin, Richard. *A speach delivered to the Kings most excellent Maiestie* (1603, STC 17510)
Maxwell, James. *The golden art* (1611, STC 17700)
Mexia, Pedro. *The imperiall historie* (1623, STC 17852)
Middleton, Thomas. *The Changeling* (1668, Wing M1982)
Middleton, Thomas. *The ghost of Lucrece* (1600, STC 17885.5)
Middleton, Thomas. *The Roaring Girle* (1611, STC 17908)
Milles, Thomas. *Archaio-ploutos* (1619, STC 17936.5)
Milton, John. *Areopagitica* (1644, Wing M2092)

Minshull, Geffray. *Certaine characters and essayes of prison and prisoners. Compiled by Novus Homo* (1618, STC 18318)
Minshull, Geffray. *Essayes and characters of a prison and prisoners* (1618, STC 18319)
Montagu, Richard. *Diatribæ* (1621, STC 18037)
Montaigne, Michel de. *The essayes or morall, politike and millitarie discourses of Lo: Michaell de Montaigne* (1603, STC 18041)
Montenay, Georgette de. *A booke of armes* (1619, STC 18046)
Murrell, John. *A delightfull daily exercise for ladies and gentlewomen* (1621, STC 18302)
Nashe, Thomas. *Pierce Penilesse his supplication to the divell* (1592, STC 18371)
Nashe, Thomas. *Strange newes, of the intercepting certaine letters* (1592, STC 18377)
Nashe, Thomas. *The terrors of the night* (1594, STC 18379)
Nicolay, Nicolas de. *The navigations, peregrinations and voyages* (1585, STC 18574)
Parker, Martin. *The poet's blind mans bough* (1641, Wing P443)
Parrot, Henry. *Cures for the itch* (1626, STC 19328)
Parrot, Henry. *The mastive* (1615, STC 19333)
Payne, John. *Royall exchange* (1597, STC 19489)
Pepys, Samuel. *The Diary of Samuel Pepys*, edited by Robert Latham and William Matthews, 11 vols (London: HarperCollins, 2000 [first published 1971])
Powell, Thomas. *Humane industry* (1661, Wing P3072)
Prynne, William. *Histrio-mastix. The players scourge* (1633, STC 20464a)
Ray, John. *A collection of English proverbs* (1678, Wing R387)
Rowlands, Samuel. *Tis merrie when gossips meete* (1602, STC 21409)
Ruggle, George. *Ignoramus*, (1662, Wing R2212)
San Pedro, Diego de. *The pretie and wittie historie of Arnalt & Lucenda* (1575, STC 6758)
Scott, William. *The Model of Poesy*, edited by Gavin Alexander (Cambridge: Cambridge University Press, 2013)
Selden, John. *Historie of tithes* (1618, STC 22172)
Shakespeare, William. *As You Like It*, edited by Juliet Dusinberre (London: Arden Shakespeare, 2006)
Shakespeare, William. *The Bodleian First Folio: Digital Facsimile of the First Folio of Shakespeare's Plays*: http://firstfolio.bodleian.ox.ac.uk/
Shakespeare, William. *The Complete Sonnets and Poems*, edited by Colin Burrow (Oxford: Oxford University Press, 2008)
Shakespeare, William. *An excellent conceited tragedie of Romeo and Juliet* (1597, STC 22322 and 1599, STC 2232)
Shakespeare, William. *The famous historie of Troylus and Cresseid* (1609, STC 22331 and 22332)
Shakespeare, William. *The Norton Facsimile: The First Folio of Shakespeare*, 2nd edn, prepared by Charlton Hinman, introduced by Peter W. M. Blayney (London: W. W. Norton & Company, 1996)
Shakespeare, William. *Hamlet*, edited by Ann Thompson and Neil Taylor (London: Arden Shakespeare, 2006)
Shakespeare, William. *The history of Henrie the Fourth* (1599, STC 22281 and 1632, STC 22286)
Shakespeare, William. *King Edward III*, edited by Richard Proudfoot and Nicola Bennett (London and New York: Bloomsbury Arden Shakespeare, 2017)
Shakespeare, William. *King Henry IV Part 2*, edited by James C. Bulman (London: Bloomsbury Arden Shakespeare, 2016)
Shakespeare, William. *The most excellent and lamentable tragedie, of Romeo and Juliet* (1599, STC 22323 and 1609, STC 22324)

Shakespeare, William. *The most excellent historie of the merchant of Venice* (1637, STC 22298 and 1652, Wing S2938)

Shakespeare, William. *M. William Shake-speare, his true chronicle history of the life and death of King Lear* (1608, STC 22292 and 1608 [i.e. 1619], STC 22293)

Shakespeare, William. *Mr. William Shakespeares comedies, histories, & tragedies* (1623, STC 22273 and 1632, STC 22274)

Shakespeare, William. *Much Ado About Nothing*, rev. edn, edited by Claire McEachern (London: Bloomsbury Arden Shakespeare, 2015)

Shakespeare, William. *The New Oxford Shakespeare: The Complete Works Critical Reference Edition*, 2 vols, edited by Gary Taylor, John Jowett, Terri Borous, and Gabriel Egan (Oxford: Oxford University Press, 2017)

Shakespeare, William. *The Passionate Pilgrim by William Shakespeare*, edited by Joseph Quincy Adams (New York and London: Charles Scribner's Sons, 1939)

Shakespeare, William. *A pleasant conceited comedie called, Loves labors lost* (1598, STC 22294)

Shakespeare, William. *Poems: written by Wil. Shake-speare. Gent* (1640, STC 22344)

Shakespeare, William. *The Rape of Lucrece* (1616, STC 22350)

Shakespeare, William. *Romeo and Juliet*, edited by Francis X. Connor, in *The New Oxford Shakespeare: The Complete Works Critical Reference Edition*, 2 vols (Oxford: Oxford University Press, 2017), vol. 1, pp. 667–759

Shakespeare, William. *Romeo and Juliet*, edited by René Weis (London: Bloomsbury Arden Shakespeare, 2012)

Shakespeare, William. *The Second Part of King Henry IV*, edited by Giorgio Melchiori (Cambridge: Cambridge University Press, 2007)

Shakespeare, William. *Shakespeare's Poems*, edited by Katherine Duncan-Jones and H. R. Woudhuysen (London: The Arden Shakespeare, 2007)

Shakespeare, William. *Shake-speares sonnets* (1609, STC 22353)

Shakespeare, William. *Shakespeare's Sonnets*, edited by Katherine Duncan-Jones, 2nd rev. edn (London: Methuen, 2010)

Shakespeare, William. *The Taming of the Shrew*, edited by Barbara Hodgdon (London: Methuen Drama, 2010)

Shakespeare, William. *Titus Andronicus* (1594, STC 22328)

Shakespeare, William. *The tragicall historie of Hamlet Prince of Denmarke* (1603, STC 22275 and 1604, STC 22276)

Shakespeare, William. *The tragedie of King Richard the second* (1598, STC 22308 and 1608, STC 22311)

Shakespeare, William. *The tragedie of King Richard the third* (1598, STC 22315)

Shakespeare, William. *The tragoedy of Othello* (1622, STC 22305)

Shakespeare, William. *Venus and Adonis* (1593, STC 22354)

Shakespeare, William. *The works of Mr William Shakespear: in six volumes*, edited by Nicholas Rowe (1709)

Shakespeare, William and others. *Collaborative Plays*, edited by Jonathan Bate and Eric Rasmussen (Basingstoke: Palgrave Macmillan, 2013)

Shakespeare, William and others. *The Passionate Pilgrime. By W. Shakespeare* (1599, STC 22342)

Sheldon, Richard. *Certain general reasons, proving the lawfulnesse of the Oath of allegiance* (1611, STC 22393)

Silver, George. *Paradoxes of defence* (1599, STC 22554)

Smith, Henry. *Three Sermons by Master Henry Smith* (1616, STC 22742)
Smith, Thomas. *The common-wealth of England* (1609, STC 22862)
Speed, John. *The historie of Great Britaine* (1623, STC 23046.3)
Stow, John. *The annales, or a generall chronicle of England* (1615, STC 23338)
Stow, John. *A survay of London* (1603, STC 23343)
Stuart (King James I and VI), James. *Basilikon Doron* (1603, STC 14354)
Swynnerton, John. *A Christian love-letter* (1606 STC 23558)
Taylor John. *A common whore* (1622, STC 23742.5)
Taylor John. *Taylors water-worke* (1614, 23792)
Topsell, Edward. *The historie of foure-footed beastes* (1607, STC 24123)
Tuke, Samuel. *The adventures of five hours* (1704)
Tuvill, Daniel. *Essaies politicke, and morall* (1608, STC 24396)
Ursinus, Zacharias. *The summe of Christian religion* (1611, STC 24537)
Venner, Tobias. *Viæ rectæ ad vitam longam* (1623, STC 24648)
Vermigli, Pietro Martire. *The common places of the most famous and renowmed [sic] divine Doctor Peter Martyr* (1583, STC 24669)
Webster, John. *The white divel* (1612, STC 25178)
Vincent, Augustine. *A discoverie of errours in the first edition of the catalogue of nobility* (1622, STC 24756)
W., R. *Martine Mar-Sixtus* (1591, STC 24913)
Wats, James. *The controversie debated about the reverend gesture of kneeling* (1621, STC 25109)
Wilkinson, Robert. *A paire of sermons successively preacht to a paire of peereles and succeeding princes* (1614, STC 25661)
Wilson, Thomas. *A Christian dictionary* (1622, STC 25788)
Wither, George. *A collection of emblemes, ancient and moderne* (1635, STC 25900d)
Wither, George. *The schollers purgatory* (1624, STC 25919)
Womock, Laurence. *Beaten oyle for the lamps of the sanctuarie* (1641, Wing W3338)
Woolley, Hannah. *The Ladies Directory* (1662, Wing W3281)
Xenophon. *The historie of Xenophon* (1623, STC 26064)

Secondary Works

A Catalogue of Books Both Old and Modern, vol. 7, sale of 18–19 March 1948 (London: Hodgson & Co, 1948)
Catalogue of Distinguished Printed Books Autograph Letters and Manuscripts, the Property of the Newberry Library, Chicago Sold by Order of the Trustees consequent upon the accession of The Louis H. Silver Collection. 8–9 November 1965 (London: Sotheby & Co, 1965)
Catalogue of Valuable Autograph Letters, Literary Manuscripts and Historical Documents, 20–21 July 1981 (London: Sotheby & Co, 1981)
Sixth Report of the Royal Commission on Historical Manuscripts (London: HM Stationery Office, 1877)
Acker, Faith. 'John Benson's 1640 *Poems* and its Literary Precedents', in *Canonising Shakespeare: Stationers and the Book Trade, 1640–1740*, edited by Emma Depledge and Peter Kirwan (Cambridge: Cambridge University Press, 2017), pp. 89–106
Acker, Faith. *First Readers of Shakespeare's Sonnets, 1590–1790* (Abingdon: Routledge Press, 2020)

Albright, Evelyn May. 'To be Staied' in *PMLA* 30.3 (1915): pp. 451–99
Alexander, Gavin ed. *Sidney's 'The Defence of Poesy' and Selected Renaissance Literary Criticism* (London: Penguin Books, 2004)
Arber, Edward. *A Transcript of the Registers of the Company of Stationers of London, 1554–1640*, 5 vols (London: The Stationers' Company, 1875–84)
Auerbach, David Benjamin. 'Review of *The New Oxford Shakespeare Authorship Companion*', in *ANQ: A Quarterly Journal of Short Articles, Notes and Reviews* 33.2-3 (2020): pp. 236–41
Bald, R. C. 'Dr. Donne and the Booksellers', in *Studies in Bibliography* 18 (1965): pp. 69–80
Baker, J. H. 'The Third University 1450–1550: Law School or Finishing School?' in *The Intellectual and Cultural World of the Early Modern Inns of Court*, edited by Jayne Elisabeth Archer, Elizabeth Goldring, and Sarah Knight (Manchester: Manchester University Press, 2013), pp. 8–24
Barnard, John. 'The Financing of the Authorised Version 1610–1612: Robert Barker and "Combining" and "Sleeping" Stationers', in *Publishing History* 57 (2005): pp. 5–52
Barnard, John and Maureen Bell, 'Statistical Tables' in *The Cambridge History of the Book in Britain, Volume IV: 1557–1695*, edited by John Barnard and D. F. McKenzie (Cambridge: Cambridge University Press, 2002 [paperback edn 2014]), pp. 779–84
Bednarz, James. 'Canonizing Shakespeare: *The Passionate Pilgrim*, *England's Helicon*, and the Question of Authenticity' in *Shakespeare Survey* 60 (2007): pp. 252–67
Bednarz, James. 'Contextualising "The Phoenix and Turtle": Shakespeare, Edward Blount and the *Poetical Essays* Group of *Love's Martyr*', in *Shakespeare Survey* 67 (2014): pp. 131–49
Bell, Maureen. 'Women in the Early English Book Trade 1557–1700' in *Leipziger Jahrbuch zur Buchgeschichte* 6 (1996): pp. 13–45
Bellingradt, Daniel, Paul Nelles, and Jeroen Salman eds, *Books in Motion in Early Modern Europe: Beyond Production, Circulation and Consumption* (Basingstoke: Palgrave Macmillan, 2017)
Bennett, Stuart. *Trade Bookbinding in the British Isles 1660–1800* (London: The British Library, 2004)
Bergel, Giles and Ian Gadd eds, *Stationers' Register Online*. https://stationersregister.online
Blair, Ann. *Too Much to Know: Managing Scholarly Information before the Modern Age* (New Haven, CT: Yale University Press, 2010)
Bland, Mark. 'The London Book-trade in 1600' in *A Companion to Shakespeare*, edited by David Scott Kastan (Oxford: Blackwell Publishing, 1999), pp. 450–63
Blayney, Peter W. M. *The Bookshops in Paul's Cross Churchyard* (London: The Bibliographical Society, 1990)
Blayney, Peter W. M. *The First Folio of Shakespeare* (Washington, DC: Folger Shakespeare Library, 1991)
Blayney, Peter W. M. 'If It Looks Like a Register…' in *The Library* 20.2 (2019): pp. 230–42
Blayney, Peter W. M. 'Initials within Initials' in *The Library* 20.4 (2019): pp. 443–61
Blayney, Peter W. M. 'The Numbers Game: Appraising the Revised STC' in *Papers of the Bibliographical Society of America* 88.3 (1994): pp. 353–407
Blayney, Peter W. M. 'The Publication of Playbooks', in *A New History of Early English Drama*, edited by John Cox and David Scott Kastan (New York: Columbia University Press, 1997), pp. 383–422
Blayney, Peter W. M. *The Stationers' Company and the Printers of London 1501–1557*, 2 vols (Cambridge: Cambridge University Press, 2013)

Boeckeler, Erika. 'Left to their Own Devices: Sixteenth-century Widows and their Printers' Devices' in *Women's Labour and the History of the Book in Early Modern England*, edited by Valerie Wayne (London: Arden Shakespeare, 2020), pp. 95–114

Boulton, Jeremy. 'Wage Labour in Seventeenth-century London' in *Economic History Review* 49.2 (1996): pp. 268–90

Bourdieu, Pierre. *The Field of Cultural Production*, edited by Randal Johnson (Cambridge: Polity Press, 1993)

Bourdieu, Pierre. *Distinction: A Social Critique of the Judgement of Taste*, trans. by Richard Nice (Abingdon: Routledge Classics, 2010)

Bourne, Claire M. L. 'Shakespeare and "Textual Studies": Evidence, Scale, Periodization and Access' in *The Arden Research Handbook of Shakespeare and Textual Studies*, edited by Lukas Erne (London: Bloomsbury Arden Shakespeare, 2021), pp. 21–49

Bourne, Claire M. L. 'Vide Supplementum: Early Modern Collation as Play-reading in the First Folio' in *Early Modern English Marginalia*, edited by Katherine Acheson (New York: Routledge, 2018), pp. 195–233

Bourne, Claire M. L. *Typographies of Performance in Early Modern England* (Oxford: Oxford University Press, 2020)

Bowerbank, Sylvia. *Speaking for Nature: Women and Ecologies of Early Modern England* (Baltimore, MD: Johns Hopkins University Press, 2004)

Bowers, Fredson. 'Essex's Rebellion and Dekker's *Old Fortunatus*' in *Review of English Studies* 3.12 (1952): pp. 365–6

Brayman, Heidi, Jesse M. Lander, and Zachary Lesser eds *The Book in History, The Book as History: New Intersections of the Material Text* (New Haven, CT: Beinecke Rare Book & Manuscript Library with Yale University Press, 2016)

Brewerton, Patricia. 'Denham, Henry (*fl.* 1556–1590)'. *Oxford Dictionary of National Biography* (Oxford: Oxford University Press, 2004; online edn, 23 September 2004) [accessed 13 August 2020]

British Book Trade Index. http://bbti.bodleian.ox.ac.uk/

Bromilow, Pollie ed. *Authority in European Book Culture 1400–1600* (Abingdon: Routledge, 2016)

Carlson, David. 'Alexander Barclay and Richard Pynson: A Tudor Printer and his Writer' in *Anglia* 113 (1995): pp. 283–302

CERL Thesaurus. http://thesaurus.cerl.org/

Certeau, Michel de. 'Reading as Poaching' in *The Practice of Everyday Life*, trans. Steven F. Rendall (Berkeley and Los Angeles, CA: University of California Press, 1988), pp. 165–76

Cervantes, Fernando. '*Phronêsis* vs Scepticism: An Early Modernist Perspective' in *New Blackfriars* 91.1036 (2010): pp. 680–94

Chartier, Roger. *The Order of Books: Readers, Authors, and Libraries in Europe between the Fourteenth and Eighteenth Centuries*, trans. by Lydia G. Cochrane (Stanford, CA: Stanford University Press, 1994)

Chartier, Roger. 'Texts, Printing, Readings' in *The New Cultural History*, edited by Lynn Hunt (Berkeley: University of California Press, 1989), pp. 154–75

Chartier, Roger and Peter Stallybrass. 'Reading and Authorship: The Circulation of Shakespeare 1590–1619' in *A Concise Companion to Shakespeare and the Text*, edited by Andrew Murphy (Chichester: Wiley-Blackwell, 2010), pp. 35–56

Cheney, David. 'Edward Topsell's *The History of Four-Footed Beasts and Serpents*,' in *Books at Iowa* 10 (1969): pp. 31–4

Cheney, Patrick. *Shakespeare, National Poet-Playwright* (Cambridge: Cambridge University Press, 2004)

The Clergy of the Church of England Database 1540–1835. http://www.theclergydatabase.org.uk

Coker, Cait and Kate Ozment eds, *Women in Book History: A Bibliography.* http://www.womensbookhistory.org/

Collinson, Patrick. 'The Protestant Cathedral, 1541–1660' in *A History of Canterbury Cathedral*, edited by Patrick Collinson, Nigel Ramsay, and Margaret Sparks (Oxford: Oxford University Press, 1995): pp. 154–203

Connor, Francis X. *Literary Folios and Ideas of the Book in Early Modern England* (Basingstoke: Palgrave Macmillan, 2014)

Connor, Francis X. 'Preliminaries in the First Folio' in William Shakespeare, *The New Oxford Shakespeare: The Complete Works Critical Reference Edition*, 2 vols, edited by Gary Taylor, John Jowett, Terri Bourus, and Gabriel Egan (Oxford: Oxford University Press, 2017), vol. 2, p. lxxi–lxxxiii

Connor, Francis X. 'Shakespeare, Poetic Collaboration, and *The Passionate Pilgrim*' in *Shakespeare Survey* 67 (2014): pp. 119–30

Connor, Francis X. 'Shakespeare's Theatrical Folio' in *Philological Quarterly* 91.2 (2012): pp. 221–45

Consortium of European Research Libraries (CERL) Thesaurus: https://data.cerl.org/thesaurus/

Cummings, Brian ed. *The Book of Common Prayer: The Texts of 1549, 1559, and 1662* (Oxford: Oxford University Press, 2011)

Dahl, Folke. *A Bibliography of English Corantos and Periodical Newsbooks 1620–1642* (London: The Bibliographical Society, 1952)

Dane, Joseph A. and Alexandra Gillespie. 'The Myth of the Cheap Quarto' in *Tudor Books and Readers: Materiality and the Construction of Meaning*, edited by John N. King (Cambridge: Cambridge University Press, 2010), pp. 25–45

Darnton, Robert. *The Kiss of Lamourette: Reflections in Cultural History* (New York & London: W. W. Norton and Company, 1990)

Davies, David W. *The World of the Elseviers 1580–1712* (The Hague: Martinus Nijhoff, 1954)

DEEP: Database of Early English Playbooks. Edited by Alan B. Farmer and Zachary Lesser. Created 2007. http://deep.sas.upenn.edu

Depledge, Emma. 'Shakespeare for Sale, 1640–1740', in *Canonising Shakespeare: Stationers and the Book Trade, 1640–1740*, edited by Emma Depledge and Peter Kirwan (Cambridge: Cambridge University Press, 2017), pp. 17–25

Depledge, Emma. *Shakespeare's Rise to Cultural Prominence* (Cambridge: Cambridge University Press, 2018)

Depledge, Emma and Peter Kirwan eds, *Canonising Shakespeare: Stationers and the Book Trade, 1640–1740* (Cambridge: Cambridge University Press, 2017)

Donaldson, Ian. *Ben Jonson: A Life* (Oxford: Oxford University Press, 2011)

Dowling, Margaret. 'The Printing of John Dowland's *Second booke of songs or ayres*' in *The Library* S4.12.4 (1932): pp. 365–80

Dutton, Richard. *Shakespeare, Court Dramatist* (Oxford: Oxford University Press, 2016)

Eckhardt, Joshua. *Religion around John Donne* (University Park, PA: Penn State University Press, 2019)

Eisenstein, Elizabeth. *The Printing Press as an Agent of Change: Communications and Cultural Transformations in Early Modern Europe*, 2 vols in 1 (Cambridge: Cambridge University Press, 1980)

BIBLIOGRAPHY 265

Eisenstein, Elizabeth. *The Printing Revolution in Early Modern Europe*, 2nd rev. edn (Cambridge: Cambridge University Press, 2012)
Engle, Lars and Eric Rasmussen. 'Review of *The New Oxford Shakespeare*' in *Review of English Studies* 69.289 (2018): pp. 356-412
Erne, Lukas. *Shakespeare as Literary Dramatist*, 2nd edn (Cambridge: Cambridge University Press, 2013)
Erne, Lukas. *Shakespeare and the Book Trade* (Cambridge: Cambridge University Press, 2013)
Erne, Lukas and Tamsin Badcoe. 'Shakespeare and the Popularity of Poetry Books in Print, 1583-1622,' in *Review of English Studies* 65 (2014): pp. 33-57
Evans, Geraint. 'Heb Ddieu Heb Ddim: The Welsh Printer's Device on Shakespeare Quarto Title-pages' in *Studia Celtica* 44 (2010): pp. 155-64
Evenden, Elizabeth. *Patents, Pictures and Patronage: John Day and the Tudor Book Trade* (Aldershot: Ashgate, 2008)
Eyre, George E. B., H. R. Plomer, and Charles R. Rivington eds, *A Transcript of the Registers of the Worshipful Company of Stationers; From 1640-1708*, 3 vols (London: privately printed, 1913-14)
Fallon, David. 'Piccadilly Booksellers and Conservative Sociability' in *Sociable Places Locating Culture in Romantic-period Britain*, edited by Kevin Gilmartin (Cambridge: Cambridge University Press, 2017), pp. 70-94
Farmer, Alan B. 'Shakespeare as Leading Playwright in Print, 1598-1608/9' in *Shakespeare and Textual Studies*, edited by Margaret Jane Kidnie and Sonia Massai (Cambridge: Cambridge University Press, 2015), pp. 87-104
Farmer, Alan B. 'Widow Publishers in London, 1540-1640', in *Women's Labour and the History of the Book in Early Modern England*, edited by Valerie Wayne (London: Arden Shakespeare, 2020), pp. 47-73
Farmer, Alan B. and Zachary Lesser. 'The Popularity of Playbooks Revisited' in *Shakespeare Quarterly* 56.1 (2005): pp. 1-32
Farmer, Alan B. and Zachary Lesser. 'Vile Arts: The Marketing of English Printed Drama, 1512-1660' in *Research Opportunities in Renaissance Drama* 39 (2000): pp. 77-165
Farmer, Richard. *An essay on the learning of Shakespeare* (Cambridge, 1767)
Felski, Rita. *The Limits of Critique* (Chicago, IL: University of Chicago Press, 2015)
Ferguson, W. Craig. 'The Stationers' Company Poor Book, 1608-1700' in *The Library* S5.31.1 (1976): pp. 37-51
Fincham, Kenneth ed. *Visitation Articles and Injunctions of the Early Stuart Church, Volume 1* (Woodbridge: The Boydell Press and Church of England Record Society, 1994)
Fincham, Kenneth and Peter Lake. 'The Ecclesiastical Policy of James I,' in *Journal of British Studies* 24.2 (1985): pp. 169-207
Fish, Stanley. 'Interpreting the *Variorum*', in *Critical Inquiry* 2.3 (1976): pp. 465-85
Fish, Stanley. *Is There a Text in This Class?: The Authority of Interpretive Communities* (Cambridge, MA: Harvard University Press, 1980)
Fletcher, Reginald. *The Pension Book of Gray's Inn: 1569-1669* (London: Gray's Inn, 1901)
Foster, Joseph. *Alumni Oxonienses: the members of the University of Oxford, 1500-1714*, 4 vols (Oxford: Parker & Co, 1891-2)
Foucault, Michel. 'What Is an Author?' in *Textual Strategies: Perspectives in Post-Structuralist Criticism*, edited by Josué V. Harari (Ithaca, NY: Cornell University Press, 1979), pp. 141-61
Frazer, Paul. 'Performing Places in Thomas Dekker's *Old Fortunatus*' in *Philological Quarterly* 89.4 (2010): pp. 457-80

Furnival, Frederick James. *The Shakspere Allusion-Book: A Collection of Allusions to Shakspere From 1591 to 1700*, 2 vols (London: Oxford University Press, 1932)

Galbraith, Steven K. 'English Literary Folios 1593-1623: Studying Shifts in Format' in *Tudor Books and Readers: Materiality and the Construction of Meaning*, edited by John N. King (Cambridge: Cambridge University Press, 2010), pp. 46-67

Gallagher, John. *Learning Languages in Early Modern England* (Oxford: Oxford University Press, 2019)

Gants, David L. 'A Quantitative Analysis of the London Book Trade 1614-1618' in *Studies in Bibliography* 55 (2002): pp. 185-213

Gaskell, Roger. 'Printing House and Engraving Shop: A Mysterious Collaboration' in *The Book Collector* 53.2 (2004): pp. 213-51

Genette, Gérard. *Paratext: Thresholds of Interpretation*, trans. Jane E. Lewin (Cambridge: Cambridge University Press, 1997)

Gillespie, Alexandra. 'Poets, Printers, and Early English *Sammelbände*' in *Huntington Library Quarterly* 67.2 (2004): pp. 189-214

Gillespie, Alexandra. *Print Culture and the Medieval Author: Chaucer, Lydgate, and their Books 1473-1557* (Oxford: Oxford University Press, 2006)

Girling, F. A. *English Merchants' Marks: A Field Survey of Marks Made by Merchants and Tradesmen in England between 1400 and 1700* (Warwick Sq, London: Oxford University Press, 1964)

Graheli, Shanti ed. *Buying and Selling: The Business of Books in Early Modern Europe* (Leiden: Brill, 2019)

de Grazia, Margreta. 'The First Reader of *Shake-speares Sonnets*' in *The Forms of Renaissance Thought*, edited by Leonard Barkan, Bradin Cormack, and Sean Keilen (London: Palgrave Macmillan, 2009), pp. 86-106

de Grazia, Margreta. *Shakespeare Verbatim: The Reproduction of Authenticity and the 1790 Apparatus* (Oxford: Clarendon Press, 1991)

Greg, Walter Wilson. *A Bibliography of the English Printed Drama to the Restoration*, 4 vols (London: The Bibliographical Society, 1939-59)

Greg, Walter Wilson. 'On Certain False Dates in Shakespearian Quartos' in *The Library* S2.9.34 (1908): pp. 113-31

Greg, Walter Wilson. *The Shakespeare First Folio: Its Bibliographical and Textual History* (Oxford: Clarendon Press, 1955)

Greg, Walter Wilson and E. Boswell eds, *Records of the Court of the Stationers' Company 1576 to 1602 from Register B* (London: The Bibliographical Society, 1930)

Hackel, Heidi Brayman. *Reading Material in Early Modern England: Print, Gender, and Literacy* (Cambridge: Cambridge University Press, 2005)

Hadfield, Andrew. *Lying in Early Modern English Culture: From the Oath of Supremacy to the Oath of Allegiance* (Oxford: Oxford University Press, 2017)

Hailey, Carter. 'The Best Crowne Paper' in *Foliomania! Stories behind Shakespeare's Most Important Book*, edited by Owen Williams and Caryn Lazzuri (Washington, DC: The Folger Shakespeare Library, 2011), pp. 8-14

Hailey, R. Carter. 'The Dating Game: New Evidence for the Dates of Q4 *Romeo and Juliet* and Q4 *Hamlet*' in *Shakespeare Quarterly* 58.3 (2007): pp. 367-87

Hailey, R. Carter. 'The Shakespearian Pavier Quartos Revisited,' in *Studies in Bibliography* 57 (2005/6): pp. 151-95

Hall, Stuart. 'Encoding/Decoding' in *Culture, Media, Language: Working Papers in Cultural Studies, 1972-79*, edited by Stuart Hall, Dorothy Hobson, Andrew Lowe, and Paul Willis

(London: Routledge in association with the Centre for Contemporary Cultural Studies, University of Birmingham, 2005), pp. 117–27

Halsey, Katie and Angus Vine eds. *Shakespeare and Authority: Citations, Conceptions and Constructions* (London: Palgrave Macmillan, 2018)

Hamlin, William M. *Montaigne's English Journey: Reading the Essays in Shakespeare's Day* (Oxford: Oxford University Press, 2013)

Hardy, Nicholas. *Criticism and Confession: The Bible in the Seventeenth Century Republic of Letters* (Oxford: Oxford University Press, 2017)

The Hartlib Papers, edited by M. Greengrass, M. Leslie, and M. Hannon. https://www.dhi.ac.uk/hartlib

Helgerson, Richard. *Forms of Nationhood: The Elizabethan Writing of England* (Chicago, IL: University of Chicago Press, 1994)

Hellinga, Lotte. '"Less than the Whole Truth": False Statements in 15th-century Colophons' in *Fakes and Frauds: Varieties of Deception in Print and Manuscript*, edited by Robin Myers and Michael Harris (Winchester: St Paul's Bibliographies, 1989), pp. 1–29

Hentschell, Roze. *St Paul's Cathedral Precinct in Early Modern Literature and Culture* (Oxford: Oxford University Press, 2020)

Hester, M. Thomas, Robert Parker Sorlien, and Dennis Flynn eds. *John Donne's Marriage Letters in The Folger Shakespeare Library* (Washington, DC: The Folger Shakespeare Library, 2005)

Higgins, Ben. '"The Book-sellars Shop": Browsing, Reading, and Buying in Early Modern England' in *The Oxford Handbook of the History of the Book in Early Modern England*, edited by Adam Smyth (Oxford: Oxford University Press, forthcoming 2022)

Higgins, Ben. '*Judith* and *Lucrece*: Reading Shakespeare between Copy and Work' in *English Literary Renaissance* 52.1(2022): pp. 34–71.

Higgins, Ben. 'The Library of James Marsh, DD. (1593–?1645), with "Shackspeers playes" and "Donnes Poem"' in *The Library* 22.1 (2021): pp. 33–56

Higgins, Ben. 'Printing the Folio', in *The Cambridge Companion to Shakespeare's First Folio*, edited by Emma Smith (Cambridge: Cambridge University Press, 2016), pp. 30–47

Hind, A. M. *Engraving in England in the Sixteenth and Seventeenth Centuries*, 3 parts, part 2: 'The Reign of James I' (Cambridge: Cambridge University Press, 1955)

Hinman, Charlton. *The Printing and Proof-Reading of the First Folio of Shakespeare*, 2 vols (Oxford: Clarendon Press, 1963)

Hooks, Adam G. 'Royalist Shakespeare: Publishers, Politics and the Appropriation of *The Rape of Lucrece* (1655)' in *Canonising Shakespeare: Stationers and the Book Trade, 1640–1740*, edited by Emma Depledge and Peter Kirwan (Cambridge: Cambridge University Press, 2017), pp. 26–37

Hooks, Adam G. *Selling Shakespeare: Biography, Bibliography, and the Book Trade* (Cambridge: Cambridge University Press, 2016)

Hooks, Adam G. 'Shakespeare at the White Greyhound,' in *Shakespeare Survey* 64 (2011): pp. 260–75

Hooks, Adam G. and Zachary Lesser eds, *Shakespeare Census*. Created 2018. http://www.shakespearecensus.org

Hunter, Michael. *Robert Boyle (1627–91): Scrupulosity and Science* (Woodbridge: The Boydell Press, 2000)

Inderwick, F. A. ed. *A Calendar of the Inner Temple Records, Volume 2: 1603–1660* (London: The Inner Temple, 1898)

Ingram, Anders. 'Bishop, George (*b.* in or before 1538, *d.* 1610/11), bookseller'. *Oxford Dictionary of National Biography*. (Oxford: Oxford University Press, 2004; online edn, 30 May 2013) [accessed 16 Aug 2019]

Jackson, MacDonald P. 'Authorship Attribution and *The New Oxford Shakespeare*: Some Facts and Misconceptions' in *ANQ: A Quarterly Journal of Short Articles, Notes and Reviews* 33.2–3 (2020): pp. 148–55

Jackson, MacDonald P. *Determining the Shakespeare Canon: Arden of Faversham and a Lover's Complaint* (Oxford: Oxford University Press, 2014)

Jackson, William A. ed., *Records of the Court of the Stationers' Company, 1602–1640* (London: The Bibliographical Society, 1957)

Johns, Adrian. *The Nature of the Book* (Chicago, IL: University of Chicago Press, 1998)

Johnson, Gerald. 'Nicholas Ling, Publisher 1580–1607,' in *Studies in Bibliography* 38 (1985): pp. 203–14

Johnson, Gerald. 'Thomas Pavier, Publisher, 1600–25,' in *The Library* S6.14.1 (1992): pp. 12–50

Jowett, John. 'Exit Manuscripts: The Archive of Theatre and the Archive of Print' in *Shakespeare Survey* 70 (2017): pp. 113–22

Jowett, John. *Shakespeare and Text* (Cambridge: Cambridge University Press, 2007)

Jowett, John. 'The Writing Tables of James Roberts,' in *The Library* 20.1 (2019), pp. 64–88

Kastan, David Scott. 'Humphrey Moseley and the Invention of English Literature' in *Agent of Change: Print Culture Studies after Elizabeth L. Eisenstein*, edited by Sabrina Alcorn Baron, Eric N. Lindquist, and Eleanor F. Shevlin (Amherst and Boston, MA: University of Massachusetts Press, 2007), pp. 105–24

Kastan, David Scott. 'Plays into Print: Shakespeare to his Earliest Readers,' in *Books and Readers in Early Modern England: Material Studies*, edited by Jennifer Anderson and Elizabeth Sauer (Philadelphia, PA: University of Pennsylvania Press, 2002), pp. 23–41

Kastan, David Scott. *Shakespeare after Theory* (New York: Routledge, 1999)

Kastan, David Scott. *Shakespeare and the Book* (Cambridge: Cambridge University Press, 2001)

Kathman, David. 'Roberts, James (*b.* in or before 1540, *d.* 1618?), bookseller and printer'. *Oxford Dictionary of National Biography* (Oxford: Oxford University Press, 2004; online edn, 28 September 2006) [accessed 18 December 2019]

Keighren, Innes M. 'Geographies of the Book: Review and Prospect' in *Geography Compass* 7 (2013): pp. 745–58

Kennedy, D. E. 'King James's College of Controversial Divinity at Chelsea,' in *Grounds of Controversy: Three Studies in Late 16th and Early 17th Century English Polemics*, edited by D. E. Kennedy, Diana Robertson, and Alexandra Walsham (Parkville, Australia: University of Melbourne Press, 1989), pp. 97–119

Kenny, Neil. *The Palace of Secrets: Béroalde de Verville and Renaissance Conceptions of Knowledge* (Oxford: Clarendon Press, 1991)

Kewes, Paulina. '"Give Me the Sociable Pocket-books…": Humphrey Moseley's Serial Publication of Octavo Play Collections' in *Publishing History* 38 (1995): pp. 5–21

Kidnie, Jane and Sonia Massai eds, *Shakespeare and Textual Studies* (Cambridge: Cambridge University Press, 2015)

Kingsley-Smith, Jane. *The Afterlife of Shakespeare's Sonnets* (Cambridge: Cambridge University Press, 2019)

Kirschbaum, Leo. *Shakespeare and the Stationers* (Columbus, OH: Ohio State University Press, 1955)

Kiséry, András. 'Companionate Publishing, Literary Publics, and the Wit of Epyllia: The Early Success of *Hero and Leander*' in *Christopher Marlowe, Theatrical Commerce, and* the Book Trade, edited by Kirk Melnikoff and Roslyn L. Knutson (Cambridge: Cambridge University Press, 2018), pp. 165–81

Kiséry, András. 'An Author and a Bookshop: Publishing Marlowe's Remains at the Black Bear' in *Philological Quarterly* 91.3 (2012): pp. 361–92

Knight, Jeffrey Todd. *Bound to Read: Compilations, Collections and the Making of Renaissance Literature* (Philadelphia, PA: University of Pennsylvania Press, 2013)

Knight, Jeffrey Todd. 'Economies of Scale: Shakespeare and Book History' in *Literature Compass* 14.6 (2017): e12393

Knight, Leah. 'Lady Anne Clifford' in *Private Libraries in Renaissance England*, vol. 9, edited by Joseph L. Black (Tempe, AZ: ACMRS, 2017), pp. 348–63

Knight, Leah. 'Reading Proof: Or, Problems and Possibilities in the Text Life of Anne Clifford' in *Women's Bookscapes in Early Modern Britain: Reading, Ownership, Circulation*, edited by Leah Knight, Micheline White, and Elizabeth Sauer (Ann Arbor, MI: University of Michigan Press, 2018), pp. 253–73

Knight, Leah, Micheline White, and Elizabeth Sauer eds, *Women's Bookscapes in Early Modern Britain: Reading, Ownership, Circulation* (Ann Arbor, MI: University of Michigan Press, 2018)

König, Jason and Greg Woolf eds, *Encyclopaedism from Antiquity to the Renaissance* (Cambridge: Cambridge University Press, 2013)

Landels-Gruenewald, Tye. 'Georeferencing the Early Modern London Book Trade: 1. Theory without Practice' in *The Map of Early Modern London*, edited by Janelle Jenstad. University of Victoria, 20 June 2018: mapoflondon.uvic.ca/BLOG16.htm

Lander, Jesse M. *Inventing Polemic: Religion, Print, and Literary Culture in Early Modern England* (Cambridge: Cambridge University Press, 2006)

Lawrence, Jason. *'Who the Devil Taught Thee So Much Italian?': Italian Language Learning and Literary Imitation in Early Modern England* (Manchester: Manchester University Press, 2005)

Lesser, Zachary. *Ghosts, Holes, Rips and Scrapes: Shakespeare in 1619, Bibliography in the Longue Durée* (Philadelphia, PA: University of Pennsylvania Press, 2021)

Lesser, Zachary. *Hamlet after Q1: An Uncanny History of the Shakespearean Text* (Philadelphia, PA: University of Pennsylvania Press, 2015)

Lesser, Zachary. 'The Material Text between General and Particular, Edition and Copy' in *English Literary Renaissance* 50.1 (2020): pp. 83–92

Lesser, Zachary. *Renaissance Drama and the Politics of Publication* (Cambridge: Cambridge University Press, 2004)

Lesser, Zachary. 'Shakespeare's Flop: John Waterson and *The Two Noble Kinsmen*' in *Shakespeare's Stationers: Studies in Cultural Bibliography*, edited by Marta Straznicky (Philadelphia, PA: University of Pennsylvania Press, 2012), pp. 177–96

Lesser, Zachary and Peter Stallybrass. 'Shakespeare between Pamphlet and Book' in *Shakespeare and Textual Studies*, edited by Sonia Massai and M. J. Kidnie (Cambridge: Cambridge University Press, 2015), pp. 105–33

Levy, Michelle. 'Women and the Book in Britain's Long Eighteenth Century' in *Literature Compass* 17.9 (2020): pp. 1–13

Lidster, Amy. 'At the Sign the Angel: The Influence of Andrew Wise on Shakespeare in Print' in *Shakespeare Survey* 71 (2018): pp. 242–54

Lidster, Amy. *Publishing the History Play in the Time of Shakespeare: Stationers Shaping a Genre* (Cambridge: Cambridge University Press, 2022)

Lindley, David. 'Campion, Thomas (1567–1620), poet and musician'. *Oxford Dictionary of National Biography* (Oxford: Oxford University Press, 2004; online edn, May 2006) [accessed 27 November 2019]

Loewenstein, Joseph. *Ben Jonson and Possessive Authorship* (Cambridge: Cambridge University Press, 2002)
Loewenstein, Joseph. 'The Script in the Marketplace,' in *Representations* 12 (1985): pp. 101–14
Loewenstein, Joseph. 'Wither and Professional Work' in *Print, Manuscript, and Performance: The Changing Relations of the Media in Early Modern England*, edited by Arthur F. Marotti and Michael D. Bristol (Columbus, OH: Ohio State University Press, 2000), pp. 103–23
Lyons, Tara L. 'Serials, Spinoffs, and Histories: Selling "Shakespeare" in Collection before the Folio' in *Philological Quarterly* 91.2 (2012): pp. 185–220
Maguire, Laurie E. *Shakespearean Suspect Texts: The 'Bad' Quartos and their Contexts* (Cambridge: Cambridge University Press, 1996)
Malay, Jessica. 'Reassessing Anne Clifford's Books: The Discovery of a New Manuscript Inventory' in *The Papers of the Bibliographical Society of America* 115.1 (2021): pp. 1–41
Malone, Edmond. *Supplement to the edition of Shakspeare's plays published in 1778 by Samuel Johnson and George Steevens* 2 vols (London, 1780)
Manley, Lawrence. *Literature and Culture in Early Modern London* (Cambridge: Cambridge University Press, 1995)
Marino, James. *Owning William Shakespeare: The King's Men and their Intellectual Property* (Philadelphia, PA: University of Pennsylvania Press, 2011)
Marotti, Arthur. *Manuscript, Print, and the English Renaissance Lyric* (Ithaca, NY: Cornell University, 1995)
Marotti, Arthur. 'Shakespeare's Sonnets as Literary Property' in *Soliciting Interpretation: Literary Theory and Seventeenth-century English Poetry*, edited by Elizabeth Harvey and Katharine Maus (Chicago, IL: University of Chicago Press, 1990), pp. 143–73
Martin, Charles ed. *Minutes of the Parliament of the Middle Temple, Volume II: 1603–1649* (London: Middle Temple, 1904)
Massai, Sonia. 'Editorial Pledges in Early Modern Dramatic Paratexts' in *Renaissance Paratexts*, edited by Helen Smith and Louise Wilson (Cambridge: Cambridge University Press, 2011), pp. 91–106
Massai, Sonia. 'Edward Blount, the Herberts, and the First Folio', in *Shakespeare's Stationers: Studies in Cultural Biography*, edited by Marta Straznicky (Philadelphia, PA: University of Pennsylvania Press, 2012), pp. 132–46
Massai, Sonia. *Shakespeare and the Rise of the Editor* (Cambridge: Cambridge University Press, 2007)
Mayer, Jean-Christophe. *Shakespeare's Early Readers: A Cultural History from 1590–1800* (Cambridge: Cambridge University Press, 2018)
Mays, Andrea E. *The Millionaire and the Bard: Henry Folger's Obsessive Hunt for Shakespeare's First Folio* (New York: Simon and Schuster, 2015)
McCabe, Richard. *'Ungainefull Arte': Poetry, Patronage, and Print in the Early Modern Era* (Oxford: Oxford University Press, 2016)
McClure, Norman ed. *The Letters of John Chamberlain*, 2 vols (Philadelphia, PA: The American Philosophical Society, 1939)
McGann, Jerome J. *A Critique of Modern Textual Criticism* (Chicago, IL: University of Chicago Press, 1983)
McGann, Jerome J. *The Textual Condition* (Princeton, NJ: Princeton University Press, 1991)
McKenzie, D. F. *Bibliography and the Sociology of Texts* (Cambridge: Cambridge University Press, 1999)
McKenzie, D. F. *The Cambridge University Press 1696–1712: A Bibliographical Study*, 2 vols (Cambridge: Cambridge University Press, 1966)
McKenzie, D. F. 'The London Book Trade in 1644,' in *Making Meaning: 'Printers of the Mind' and Other Essays*, edited by Peter McDonald and Michael F. Suarez, S.J. (Amherst, MA: University of Massachusetts Press, 2002), pp. 126–43

McKerrow, Ronald B. 'Edward Allde as a Typical Trade Printer,' in *The Library* S4.2 (1929): pp. 121-62

McKenzie, D. F. *Printers' and Publishers' Devices in England and Scotland 1485-1640* (London: Bibliographical Society, 1949)

McKitterick, David. '"Ovid with a Littleton": The Cost of English Books in the Early Seventeenth Century' in *Transactions of the Cambridge Bibliographical Society* 11.2 (1997): pp. 184-234

McMillin, Scott and Sally-Beth MacLean. *The Queen's Men and their Plays* (Cambridge: Cambridge University Press, 1998)

Melnikoff, Kirk. *Elizabethan Publishing and the Makings of Literary Culture* (Toronto, ON: University of Toronto Press, 2018)

Moretti, Franco. *Graphs, Maps, Trees: Abstract Models for a Literary History* (London: Verso, 2005)

Muldrew, Craig. *The Economy of Obligation: The Culture of Credit and Social Relations in Early Modern England* (Basingstoke: Palgrave Macmillan, 1998)

Murphy, Andrew. *Shakespeare in Print: A History and Chronology of Shakespeare Publishing*, 2nd rev. edn (Cambridge: Cambridge University Press, 2021)

Myers, Robin, Michael Harris, and Giles Mandelbrote, eds *The London Book Trade: Topographies of Print in the Metropolis from the Sixteenth Century* (London: British Library, 2003)

Neidig, William. 'The Shakespeare Quartos of 1619,' in *Modern Philology* 8.2 (1910): pp. 145-63

Nelson, Alan H. *Records of Early English Drama: Cambridge*, 2 vols (Toronto, ON: University of Toronto Press, 1989)

Nelson, Alan H. 'The Universities and the Inns of Court' in *The Oxford Handbook of Early Modern Theatre*, edited by Richard Dutton (Oxford: Oxford University Press, 2011), pp. 280-91

Newman, Harry. *Impressive Shakespeare: Identity, Authority and the Imprint in Shakespearean Drama* (Abingdon: Routledge, 2019)

North, Marcy L. 'Anonymity's Subject: James I and the Debate over the Oath of Allegiance' in *New Literary History* 33.2 (2002): pp. 215-32

Nuovo, Angela. *The Book Trade in the Italian Renaissance*, trans. Lydia G. Cochrane (Leiden: Brill, 2013)

Oastler, C. L. *John Day: The Elizabethan Printer* (Oxford: The Bibliographical Society, 1975)

Ogborn, Miles and Charles W. J. Withers eds *Geographies of the Book* (Farnham: Ashgate, 2010)

Olson, Rebecca. 'The Continuing Adventures of *Blanchardyn* and *Eglantine*: Responsible Speculation about Early Modern Fan Fiction' in *PMLA* 134.2 (2019): pp. 298-314

Ozment, Kate. 'Rationale for Feminist Bibliography' in *Textual Cultures* 13.1 (2020): pp. 149-78

Pantzer, Katherine, A. W. Pollard, and G. R. Redgrave eds. *A Short-title Catalogue of Books Printed in England, Scotland, and Ireland and of English Books Printed Abroad 1475-1640*. 2nd rev. edn, 3 vols (London: The Bibliographical Society, 1976-91)

Pearson, David. *English Bookbinding Styles, 1450-1800: A Handbook* (New Castle, DE: Oak Knoll Press, 2014)

Pettegree Andrew. *The Invention of News: How the World Came to Know about Itself* (New Haven, CT: Yale University Press, 2014)

Pettegree Andrew. 'A Whole New World? Publishing in the Dutch Golden Age' in *Negotiating Conflict and Controversy in the Early Modern Book World*, edited by Alexander S. Wilkinson and Graeme J. Kemp (Leiden: Brill, 2019), pp. 73-87

Pitcher, John. 'Daniel, Samuel (1562/3-1619), poet and historian'. *Oxford Dictionary of National Biography* (Oxford: Oxford University Press, 2004; online edn, September 2004) [accessed 27 November 2019]

Plomer, Henry R. 'The 1574 Edition of Dr. John Caius's *De Antiquitate Cantebrigiensis Academiæ Libri Duo*' in *The Library* S4.7.3 (1926): pp. 253–68

Pollard, Alfred W. 'A Literary Causerie: Shakespeare in the Remainder Market' in *The Academy* (2 June 1906): pp. 528–9

Pollard, Alfred W. *An Essay on Colophons with Specimens and Translations* (Chicago, IL: The Caxton Club, 1905)

Pollard, Alfred W. *Shakespeare Folios and Quartos: A Study in the Bibliography of Shakespeare's Plays 1594-1685* (London: Methuen and Company, 1909)

Pratt, Aaron T. 'Stab-stitching and the Status of Early English Playbooks as Literature' in *The Library* 16.3 (2015): pp. 304–28

Prest, Wilfred R. *The Inns of Court under Elizabeth I and the Early Stuarts 1590-1640* (London: Longman, 1972)

Private Libraries in Renaissance England, edited by R. J. Fehrenbach, Joseph L. Black, and E. S. Leedham-Green. https://plre.folger.edu/

Questier, Michael C. 'Loyalty, Religion and State Power in Early Modern England: English Romanism and the Jacobean Oath of Allegiance' in *The Historical Journal* 40.2 (1997): pp. 311–29

Quitslund, Beth. '"A Second Bible": Liturgy and Interpretation in the *Expositions* of John Boys' in *Reformation* 23.1 (2018): pp. 79–99

Rasmussen, Eric. 'Publishing the Folio' in *The Cambridge Companion to the First Folio*, edited by Emma Smith (Cambridge: Cambridge University Press, 2016), pp. 18–29

Rasmussen, Eric and Anthony James West. *The Shakespeare First Folios: A Descriptive Catalogue* (Basingstoke: Palgrave Macmillan, 2012)

Raven, James. *Bookscape: Geographies of Printing and Publishing in London before 1800* (London: British Library, 2014)

Raven, James. *The Business of Books: Booksellers and the English Book Trade 1450-1850* (New Haven and London: Yale University Press, 2007)

Raven, James. 'The Economic Context' in *The Cambridge History of the Book in Britain: Volume IV: 1557-1695*, edited by John Barnard and D. F. McKenzie (Cambridge: Cambridge University Press, 2002 [paperback edn 2014]), pp. 568–82

Raven, James. 'Jobbing Printing in Late Early Modern London: Questions of Variety, Stability and Regularity' in *Forms, Formats and the Circulation of Knowledge: British Printscape's Innovations, 1688-1832*, edited by Louisiane Ferlier and Benedicte Miyamoto (Leiden: Brill, 2020), pp. 27–49

Razzle, Lucy. '"Like to a title leafe": Surface, Face, and Material Text in Early Modern England' in *Journal of the Northern Renaissance* 8 (2017): http://northernrenaissance.org

Richardson, William. 'Boys, John (*bap*. 1571, *d*. 1625), dean of Canterbury'. *Oxford Dictionary of National Biography*. (Oxford: Oxford University Press, 2004; online edn, 2004) [accessed 16 August 2019]

Roberts, Sasha. *Reading Shakespeare's Poems in Early Modern England* (Basingstoke: Palgrave Macmillan, 2003)

Rogers, Shef. 'Imprints, Imprimaturs, and Copyright Pages' in *Book Parts*, edited by Dennis Duncan and Adam Smyth (Oxford: Oxford University Press, 2019), pp. 51–64

Rose, Hugh James ed., *A New General Biographical Dictionary*, 12 vols (London: B. Fellowes et al., 1848)

Rudman, Joseph. 'Review of *The New Oxford Shakespeare Authorship Companion*' in *Digital Scholarship in the Humanities* 34.3 (2019): pp. 703–5

Saenger, Michael. *The Commodification of Textual Engagements in the English Renaissance* (Abingdon: Routledge, 2016)

'Sale 579: Rare Books and Manuscripts', lot 99. Accessed 15 May 2021. https://www.pbagalleries.com/view-auctions/catalog/id/384/lot/119215/Mr-VVilliam-Shakespeares-Comedies-Histories-and-Tragedies-Published-according-to-the-true-originall-copies

Sanders, Julie. *The Cultural Geography of Early Modern Drama, 1620–1650* (Cambridge University Press, 2011)

Schlueter, June. 'Droeshout, Martin, the younger (*b.* 1601, *d.* in or after 1640), engraver'. *Oxford Dictionary of National Biography* (Oxford: Oxford University Press, 2004; online edn, 2018) [accessed 3 December 2019]

Scott-Warren, Jason. 'Milton's Shakespeare?' on the *Centre for Material Texts* website (https://www.english.cam.uk/cmt/), entry of 9 September 2019

Scott-Warren, Jason. 'News, Sociability, and Bookbuying in Early Modern England: The Letters of Sir Thomas Cornwallis' in *The Library* 1.4 (2000): pp. 381–402

Scott-Warren, Jason. *Shakespeare's First Reader: The Paper Trails of Richard Stonley* (Philadelphia, PA: University of Pennsylvania Press, 2019)

Scragg, Leah. 'Edward Blount and the History of Lylian Criticism' in *Review of English Studies* 46.181 (1995): pp. 1–10

Shaaber, M. A. 'The Meaning of the Imprint in Early Printed Books' in *The Library* S4. 24.3-4 (1944): pp. 120–41

Shakeosphere: Mapping Early Modern Social Networks. shakeosphere.lib.uiowa.edu/

Shakespeare Documented. https://shakespearedocumented.folger.edu/

'Shakespeare Second Folio'. Accessed 15 May 2021. https://www.peterharrington.co.uk/blog/shakespeare-second-folio-john-smethwick-imprint-1632

Sharpe, Kevin. *Reading Revolutions: The Politics of Reading in Early Modern England* (New Haven, CT: Yale University Press, 2000)

Sheavyn, Phoebe. 'Writers and the Publishing Trade, circa 1600,' in *The Library* S2.7 (1906): pp. 337–65

Sherman, William H. 'The Social Life of Books' in *The Oxford History of Popular Print Culture, Volume I: Cheap Print in Britain and Ireland to 1660*, edited by Joad Raymond (Oxford: Oxford University Press, 2011), pp. 164–71

Sherman, William H. and Heather Wolfe, 'The Department of Hybrid Books: Thomas Milles between Manuscript and Print' in *Journal of Medieval and Early Modern Studies* 45.3 (2015): pp. 457–85

Silva, Andie. *The Brand of Print: Marketing Paratexts in the Early English Book Trade* (Leiden: Brill, 2019)

Smith, Emma. *The Making of Shakespeare's First Folio* (Oxford: Bodleian Library, 2015)

Smith, Emma. *Shakespeare's First Folio: Four Centuries of an Iconic Book* (Oxford: Oxford University Press, 2016)

Smith, Emma. 'A New Corrected Proof Sheet from Shakespeare's First Folio (1623)' in *The Library* 19.1 (2018): pp. 69–72

Smith, Helen. '"Imprinted by Simeon such a signe": Reading Early Modern Imprints' in *Renaissance Paratexts*, edited by Helen Smith and Louise Wilson (Cambridge: Cambridge University Press, 2011), pp. 17–33

Smith, Helen. *Grossly Material Things: Women and Book Production in Early Modern England* (Oxford: Oxford University Press, 2012)

Smith, Helen. '"To London all"? Mapping Shakespeare in Print, 1593–1598' in *Shakespeare and Textual Studies*, edited by Margaret Jane Kidnie and Sonia Massai (Cambridge: Cambridge University Press, 2015), pp. 69–86

Smith, Helen. '"A unique instance of art": The Proliferating Surfaces of Early Modern Paper' in *Journal of the Northern Renaissance* 8 (2017): http://www.northernrenaissance.org

Smyth, Adam. *Material Texts in Early Modern England* (Cambridge: Cambridge University Press, 2018)

Smyth, Adam. 'The Scale of Early Modern Studies' in *English Literary Renaissance* 50.1 (2020): pp. 145–52

Spirgatis, Max. 'Englische Litteratur Auf Der Frankfurter Messe Von 1561–1620' in *Beitrage Zur Kenntnis des Schrift-, Buch- und Bibliothekswesens* 7 (1902): pp. 37–89

Spufford, Margaret. *Small Books and Pleasant Histories: Popular Fiction and its Readership in Seventeenth-century England* (London: Methuen, 1981)

Stallybrass, Peter. 'Books and Scrolls: Navigating the Bible' in *Books and Readers in Early Modern England*, edited by Jennifer Andersen and Elizabeth Sauer (Philadelphia, PA: University of Pennsylvania Press, 2002), pp. 42–79

Stallybrass, Peter. '"Little Jobs": Broadsides and the Printing Revolution' in *Agent of Change: Print Culture Studies after Elizabeth L. Eisenstein*, edited by Sabrina Alcorn Baron, Eric N. Lindquist, and Eleanor F. Shevlin (Amherst, MA: University of Massachusetts Press, 2007), pp. 315–41

Steele, Robert. 'Printers and Books in Chancery,' in *The Library* S2.10.37 (1909): pp. 101–6

Stern, Tiffany. *Documents of Performance in Early Modern England* (Cambridge: Cambridge University Press, 2009)

Stern, Tiffany. *Making Shakespeare: From Stage to Page* (London: Routledge, 2004)

Stern, Tiffany. 'Watching as Reading: The Audience and Written Text in Shakespeare's Playhouse' in *How to Do Things with Shakespeare: New Approaches, New Essays*, edited by Laurie Maguire (Oxford: Blackwell, 2008), pp. 136–59

Straznicky, Marta. *Shakespeare's Stationers: Studies in Cultural Bibliography* (Philadelphia, PA: University of Pennsylvania Press, 2012)

Straznicky, Marta. *The Book of the Play: Playwrights, Stationers, and Readers in Early Modern England* (Amherst, MA: University of Massachusetts Press, 2006)

Straznicky, Marta. 'What Is a Stationer' in *Shakespeare's Stationers: Studies in Cultural Bibliography*, edited by Marta Straznicky (Philadelphia, PA: University of Pennsylvania Press, 2012), pp. 1–16

Sullivan, Ceri. *The Rhetoric of Credit: Merchants in Early Modern Writing* (London: Associated University Presses, 2002)

Swift, Daniel. *Shakespeare's Common Prayers: The Book of Common Prayer and the Elizabethan Age* (Oxford: Oxford University Press, 2013)

Swinbourne, Algernon Charles. *Studies in Prose and Poetry* (London: Chatto & Windus, 1894)

Tankard, Paul. 'Reading Lists' in *Prose Studies* 28.3 (2006): pp. 337–60

Taylor, Gary. 'Blount [Blunt], Edward (*bap.* 1562, *d.* in or before 1632), bookseller and translator'. *Oxford Dictionary of National Biography* (Oxford: Oxford University Press, 2004; online edn, January 2008)

Taylor, Gary. '*Comedies, Histories, & Tragedies* (and Tragicomedies and Poems): Posthumous Shakespeare, 1623–1728', in *The New Oxford Shakespeare: The Complete Works Critical Reference Edition*, 2 vols, edited by Gary Taylor, John Jowett, Terri Bourus, and Gabriel Egan (Oxford: Oxford University Press, 2017), vol. 2, pp. xvii–lxix

Taylor, Gary. 'Making Meaning Marketing Shakespeare 1623,' in *From Performance to Print in Shakespeare's England*, edited by Peter Holland and Stephen Orgel (Basingstoke: Palgrave Macmillan, 2006), pp. 55–72

Taylor, Gary and Gabriel Egan eds, *The New Oxford Shakespeare: Authorship Companion* (Oxford: Oxford University Press, 2017)

Thomas, Max W. 'Eschewing Credit: Heywood, Shakespeare, and Plagiarism before Copyright' in *New Literary History* 31.2 (2000): pp. 277–93

Thompson, James Westfall. *The Frankfort Book Fair: The Francofordiense Emporium of Henri Estienne* (Chicago, IL: The Caxton Club, 1911)
Todd, William B. 'The Issues and States of the Second Folio and Milton's Epitaph on Shakespeare' in *Studies in Bibliography* 5 (1952): pp. 81–108
Tromans, Philip. 'The Business of Browsing in Early Modern English Bookshops' in *Buying and Selling: The Business of Books in Early Modern Europe*, edited by Shanti Graheli (Leiden: Brill, 2019): pp. 111–35
Vickers, Brian. *Shakespeare, Co-Author: A History of the Study of the Five Collaborative Plays* (Oxford: Oxford University Press, 2002)
Wayne, Valerie. 'The First Folio's Arrangement and its Finale' in *Shakespeare Quarterly* 66.4 (2015): pp. 389–408
Wayne, Valerie ed. *Women's Labour and the History of the Book in Early Modern England* (London: Arden Shakespeare, 2020)
Welch, Charles. 'The City Printers' in *The Library: Transactions of the Bibliographical Society* 14.1 (1917): pp. 175–242
West, Anthony James. 'The First Shakespeare First Folio to Travel Abroad: Constantine Huygens's Copy' in *Foliomania! Stories behind Shakespeare's Most Important Book*, edited by Owen Williams and Caryn Lazzuri (Washington, DC: The Folger Shakespeare Library, 2011), pp. 40-4
West, Anthony James. *The Shakespeare First Folio: The History of the Book*, 2 vols (Oxford: Oxford University Press, 2001)
Willard, Oliver. 'Jaggard's Catalogue of English Books' in *Stanford Studies in Language and Literature* (1941): pp. 152–72
Williams, Franklin B. *Index of Dedications and Commendatory Verses in English Books before 1641* (London: Bibliographical Society, 1962)
Williams, Franklin B. 'An Initiation into Initials' in *Studies in Bibliography* 9 (1957): pp. 163–78
Willoughby, Edwin. *The Printing of the First Folio of Shakespeare* (Oxford: The Bibliographical Society, 1932)
Willoughby, Edwin. *A Printer of Shakespeare: The Books and Times of William Jaggard* (London: Philip Allan & Co, 1934)
Wing, Donald Goddard ed. *Short-title Catalogue of Books Printed in England, Scotland, Ireland, Wales, and British America, and of English Books Printed in Other Countries, 1641–1700*. 2nd edn revised and enlarged by John J. Morrison and Carolyn Nelson. 4 vols (New York: Modern Language Association of America, 1982–98)
Wolkenhauer, Anja and Bernhard F. Scholz eds *Typographorum Emblemata: The Printer's Mark in the Context of Early Modern Culture* (Berlin: Walter de Gruyter, 2018)
Wood, Anthony à. *Fasti Oxonienses: or, Annals of the University of Oxford*, continued by Philip Bliss (London: Printed for F. C. and J. Rivington, 1815)
Woolf, Virginia. *Selected Essays* (Oxford: Oxford University Press, 2008)
Woudhuysen, Henry. 'From Duck Lane to Lazarus Seaman: Buying and Selling Old Books in England during the Sixteenth and Seventeenth Centuries' in *The Oxford Handbook of the History of the Book in Early Modern England*, edited by Adam Smyth (Oxford: Oxford University Press, forthcoming 2022)
Woudhuysen, Henry. *Sir Philip Sidney and the Circulation of Manuscripts 1558–1640* (Oxford: Clarendon Press, 1996)
Yamada, Akihiro. *Peter Short: An Elizabethan Printer* (Tsu, Mei Prefecture: Mei University Press, 2002)
Yamada, Akihiro. *Thomas Creede, Printer to Shakespeare and his Contemporaries* (Tokyo: Meisei University Press, 1994)

Yates, Frances. *John Florio: The Life of an Italian in Shakespeare's England* (Cambridge: Cambridge University Press, 1934)

Yeandle, Laetitia ed. *Sir Edward Dering, 1st bart., of Surrenden Dering and his 'Booke of Expences' 1617–1628*. The Kent Archaeological Society Papers, no. 20. Web. http://www.kentarchaeology.ac/authors/020.pdf

Index

Note: Tables and figures are indicated by an italic "*t*", "*f*", and notes are indicated by "n." following the page number.

1619 collection, *see* Jaggard Quartos

Abbot Hall 75, 76*f*
Acker, Faith 30, 175 n.17, 199 n.93
Acosta, Jose de
  The naturall and Morall Historie of the East and West Indies 16 n.43
actors 10, 31, 43 n.8, 69, 72, 75, 111–12, 135, 139, 157, 160
Adams, Joseph Quincy 100 n.76
Adams, Thomas 98 n.67, 212
  The Blacke Devill 239*t*
advertising of books 8–9, 18 n.49 n.52, 26 n.78, 33, 35–7, 41–5, 77, 82, 85, 90–9, 104, 107–11, 114–15, 131, 153, 156, 164–6, 176–7, 180–1, 190–1, 195–6, 202, 217, *see also* marketing of books; First Folio publicity
advice books 15, 51, 97
Aesop
  The fabulous tales of Esope the Phrygian 179
aesthetics 65 n.93, 92
agency 10, 32, 83, 91, 94, 106–7, *see also* booksellers; publishers
Aggas, Edward 55
Albertus Magnus
  The Secrets of Albertus Magnus 238*t*, 240*t*
Albright, Evelyn May 20 n.55
Aldine Press 28 n.85
Aldus Manutius 70 n.112
Aleman, Mateo
  The Rogue 61, 74
Alexander, William
  A Paraensis to the Prince 15 n.38
Allott, Mary 25 n.73
Allott, Robert 15, 25 n.73, 61, 173, 208 n.116, 248*t*
almanacs 49, 129, 145
Alsop, Nicholas 146 n.65
Andrewes, John
  The Brazen Serpent 96 n.60
Andrewes, Launcelot 144
annotations, *see* reading
Anon.
  A warning for faire women 131
  The cobler of Canterburie 177

apprentices, *see* Stationers' Company
Arber, Edward 19 n.54
Ariosto, Ludovico
  Orlando Furioso 176 n.21
aristocracy
  as patrons 10, 38, 54
  as readers, 53–4
Aristophanes 64
Armin, Robert 179–80, 196
Aspley, William 11, 13, 15, 17–18, 26, 32, 37–8, 50*t*, 51, 54 n.48, 60 n.73, 67 n.96, 74 n.124, 126, 133*t*, 136, 137*t*, 139–40, 143, 145–6, 152–3, 154*f*, 158, 166, 168, 172–3, 176, 210, 213–14, 217, 244*t*, 246*t*, 247*t*, 248*t*
  apprenticeship 143 n.50
  bequests 130
  biography 143, 168
  bookseller's guarantee 149*f*
  bookselling interests 129–32, 138–50
  bookshop 142, 144, 147, 149–51, 165, 183
  business trouble 57 n.61
  collaboration with Andrew Wise 16, 19, 22, 62 n.78, 127, 131–2, 75, 203
  decision to join First Folio syndicate 149
  first encounter with Shakespeare 125–6
  First Folio titles owned 22, 130–32
  interest in religious conformism 143–7
  interest in Shakespeare 127–9
  investment in John Boys 129, 142–7, 151–69
  legal issues 130
  loyalty to the state 146–8
  prefatory addresses 66*t*, 148
  status as minor Shakespearean 38, 127–9, 130, 132–3, 136–8, 166–8, 217
  wife 212
  will 129, 167–8, 212
Attersoll, William
  A Commentarie upon S. Paul 102, 239*t*
  A Commentarie upon the Fourth Booke of Moses 91 n.47, 240*t*
  A Continuation of the Exposition 239*t*
  The Badges of Christianity 238*t*
  The New Covenant 239*t*
  The Pathway to Canaan 239*t*

278   INDEX

Attingham Park 163
attributions, see authorial; Shakespeare
Aubrey, John 207
  'Naturall Historie of Wiltshire' 48
  'The Life of Mr Thomas Hobbes' 47 n.24
Austen, Ralph
  A Treatise of fruit-trees 8, 9 n.18 n.20
authorial
  attributions 22 n.63, 87 n.27, 110, 125,
    153, 157
  branding 1, 3, 7, 77–8, 101–4, 117–18, 149,
    153–67, 202 n.96
  collaboration 117–20, 159–60, 202, 206
  collections 17, 19–28, 42, 44, 77–8, 82–4,
    104–12, 117–20, 150–67, 183–4, see also
    sammelband volumes; Shakespeare
  corrections 54 n.49, 55*f*
  geography, see Shakespeare

Babington, Gervase
  *The Works of the Right Reverend Father in God,
    Gervase Babington* 16 n.43, 145 n.60
Bacon, Francis 112
  *A briefe discourse, touching the happie union of
    the kingdomes of England, and
    Scotland* 144 n.52
  Essayes 55
Badcoe, Tamsin 102 n.82
Baker, J. H. 187 n.51
ballads 1, 49, 134, 179
Bankworth, Richard 58, 203 n.99, 212
Barclay, Alexander 146 n.65
Barker, Christopher 148, 149*f*
Barrett, William 133*t*, 137*t*, 246*t*
Basta, Giorgio
  The Government of Light Cavalry 235
Baudier, Michel
  *The history of the imperiall estate of the grand
    seigneurs* 235
Beale, John 92 n.50, 188
Beaumont, Francis 26, 52 n.38, 73, 111, 202 n.97
Beck, Randall 60
Bednarz, James 68, 101 n.77
Belcamp, Jan van
  'The Great Picture' 75, 76*f*
Bellingradt, Daniel 181 n.41
Bell, Jane 175 n.18
Bell, Maureen 211 n.1
Bell, Thomas
  The Jesuites Antipast 91 n.47, 238*t*
  The Tryall of the New Religion 238*t*
Belvedere 125
Benson, John 119 n.133, 174–5, 198–9, 203–4,
    206, 249*t*

Beza, Theodore 236
bibliographers 80, 82–3, 104, see also New
  Bibliography
bibliographic
  communities 178–81, 186, 191, 196, 198
  conventions 157–8, see also authorial
    branding
  ego 91
  personality 67–8
bibliography 2 n.5, 10 n.21, 61 n.77, 211,
    216–17, see also New Bibliography
Bill, John 41 n.2
binding, see bookbinding
Bingham, John 234
biography 17, 70, 80–1, 113–14, 136, 143, 158,
    163–4, 207–8, 217
Bird, Robert 248*t*
Bishop, George 143
Blackfriars theatre 183, 195 n.81
Blair, Ann 98 n.67
Bland, Mark 14 n.32
Blayney, Peter W. M. 2 n.5, 11 n.23, 13 n.28,
    15 n.33, 18 n.50, 19 n.54, 20, 27 n.82, 32, 35,
    47, 59 n.67, 80, 88 n.37, 89 n.40, 90 n.42,
    95 n.59, 136 n.34, 142 n.47, 175,
    185 n.47, 237 n.1
Blount, Edward 10–11, 13, 15–16, 19, 28 n.87,
    29, 37, 41–4, 49, 50*t*, 51, 53–5, 63–5, 66*t*,
    73–4, 78–9, 84, 107–8, 111 n.108, 129, 133*t*,
    137*t*, 143, 146 n.65, 147 n.70, 151, 168,
    172–3, 203, 208, 216, 247*t*, see also Blount,
    Elizabeth Bankworth
  bill of complaint 58–9, 211
  biography 45 n.14, 59–60
  bookshop 16, 18, 46, 58, 67 n.97, 70–3, 142, 212
  collaboration with Jaggards 17, 20, 21*f*, 22,
    26–7, 153
  collaboration with John Smethwick 15
  collaboration with William Aspley 16, 75, 149
  correspondence 69–72, 221, 223–36
  financial difficulties 56–61
  importation of books 57
  influence over First Folio
    preliminaries 22, 73–6
  investment strategies 49–61, 56, 58
  literariness of 32, 45–6, 49–51, 52, 56, 61,
    62–70, 77–8, 216
  personal seals 221, 222*f*
  prefatory addresses by 65, 66*t*, 67–9
  reputation of 56, 67 n.97, 69–70, 71–2
Blount, Elizabeth Bankworth 58, 211–12
Blower (Blore), Ralph 86 n.24
Boccaccio, Giovanni
  The Decameron 84, 240*t*

Bodleian Library 7–8, 15, 30 n.93, 88, 103 n.84, 125 n.2, 139, 161 n.107, 177 n.24
Bonian, Richard 50*t*, 133*t*, 137*t*, 157, 199, 246*t*
Book of Common Prayer 142–5, 156, 158
bookbinding, 16, 47, 54 n.48, 89 n.39, 93 n.54, 104–6, 134, 145 n.60, 148, 160, 161 n.107, 163, 189, 205
booksellers 9, 15–18, 22–5, 28, 33–4, 36–8, 77, 86–7, 103 n.84, 104–5, 114, 168, 173, 175–8, 184–5, 191, 208, 212–13, 242, *see also* printers; publishers
  as correspondents 18, 33, 69–73, 145 n.60, 221–36
  bills 89, 145 n.60, 177 n.24
  collaborations and partnerships 14 n.31, 16–17, 18, 32, 50*t*, 51–2, 168, 194
  critical approaches to 28–32, 211, 215–17
  economic concerns 47–9, 50*t*, 51–2
  guarantees 148–9, 149*f*, 198 n.90
  of St Dunstan's in the West 38, 185, 197–9, 206
  ownership of Shakespeare's work 19–26, 132, 133*t*, 134–6, 137*t*
  prefaces 30, 65–70, 66*t*, 73, 91, 100, 199, *see also* paratext
  range of activities 17–19, 29–30, 56, 67 n.97, 72 n.117
  relationships with authors 70–6, 146–7, 150–1
  women 9, 17 n.45, 25 n.73, 58–60, 106 n.92, 208 n.114, 211–15
bookshops 8*f*, 9, 18, 36, 38, 58, 59 n.67, 142, 144, 151, 165, 213–14, 242–9*t*
  and reading 47, 67
  as social hubs 70–3
  customers of 16, 28, 35–6, 47, 69 n.107, 107, 158, 161, 188 n.59, 207, 213
  maps of 182*f*, 192*f*, 200*f*, 201*f*
  range of activities in 18–19, 47, 67
  significance of location 172–85, 194–6
bookshop signs
  Angel 243*t*, 244*t*, 245*t*
  Bell 246*t*
  Bible 248*t*
  Bishop's Head 142 n.47
  Black Bear 18, 46, 57, 59 n.67, 67 n.97, 70–6, 212, 229, 234, 247–8*t*
  Cat and Parrot 244*t*, 246*t*, 247*t*
  Crown 202, 249*t*
  Eagle and Child 247*t*
  Fleur de Luce and Crown 245*t*
  Fox 242, 245*t*, 246*t*, 247*t*, 248*t*
  Golden Unicorn 249*t*
  Green Dragon 244*t*
  Greyhound 86–7, 243*t*, 244*t*, 245*t*
  Gun 18 n.52, 243*t*, 244*t*, 246*t*
  Holy Ghost 245*t*, 246*t*
  Parrot 125, 127, 142 n.48, 144, 165, 167, 246*t*, 247*t*, 248*t*
  Pied Bull 245*t*
  Spread Eagle 246*t*
  Sun 245*t*
  Three Pigeons 246*t*, 247*t*
  Tiger's Head 244*t*
  White Greyhound 174, 184, 243*t*
  White Hart 186, 244*t*
  White Lyon 36
book trade 47 n.26, 56, 75, 102–3, 166–7, 172, 181, 185, 187
  collaborations 14 n.31, 16–18, 22, 26–7, 31, 49, 50*t*, 51, 75, 85–6, 106, 126–7, 129 n14, 131–2, 138, 146 n.65, 186, 193, 198–9, 208, *see also* First Folio syndicate
  competition 24, 138, 165, 166, 168
  critical approaches to 29–37, 211, 215–17
  genealogy 74–5, 143
  geography 172–85, 199–203, *see also* London
  labour 2, 9–10, 27, 53, 76, 80, 87–90, 175–6, 194, 212–13
  networks 16, 18, 32, 33, 69–71, 74–5, 157, 164–5, 168, 194, 221
  scale 14, 216
  second-hand trade 148 n.75, 149, 198 n.90
  wives 211–15
Boston Public Library 139
Bourdieu, Pierre 34–5, 37, 52, 77, 196
Bourne, Claire M. L. 120
Bourne, Nicholas 52
Boyle, Robert
  Some receipts of medicines 218
Boys, Anthony 163 n.115
Boys, Dorothy 163 n.115
Boys, John
  creation of folio *Workes* 150–1, 159*f*, 167–9
  marketing of authorial persona 153–64
  relationship with William Aspley 129–31, 142–50
  religious views 145–7
  popularity in print 142–6, 167–9
Boys, John (works)
  An exposition of the dominical Epistles and Gospels 144 n.55, 154*f*, 156 n.89
  An exposition of the festivall Epistles and Gospels 155*f*
  An exposition of the last Psalme 147 n.67, 156
  An exposition of the proper Psalmes 144 n.55, 156

Boys, John (works) (*cont.*)
  The Autumne Parte from the Twelfth Sunday after Trinitie 142 n.48, 164f
  The Workes of John Boys Doctor in Divinitie 142, 149, 151, 159, 163–4, 169
Branche, Dame Helen 218 n.27
Brathwait, Richard 52 n.39
Brewerton, Patricia 86 n.23
British Library 69, 221, 222f
Bromfeilde, Arthur 142 n.47
Brooke, Ralph 99–100
  A Catalogue and Succession of the Kings 113, 240t
Browne, Christopher 235–6
Browne, John 198 n.91
Browne, Sir Richard 235–6
Browne, Sir Thomas 28 n.86
Browne, Sir William 28
Browne, Thomasine Gonson 236
Brown, Thomas 178
Brussels 69, 71–3, 226, 233–4
Bryskett, Lodowick
  A discourse of civill life 16 n.43
Buck, Sir George 136, 188 n.56
Budge, John 25
Bulman, James C. 128 n.11, 138 n.35
Bunny, Edmund
  Of the Head-Corner-Stone 99, 102, 239t
Buoni, Thomasso
  Problemes of beautie and all humane affections 16 n.43, 65 n.93
Burby, Cuthbert 25, 133t, 134, 137t, 184–5, 191, 193–5, 243t, 244t
Burrow, Colin 82 n.11, 101 n.79, 103 n.84
Burton, Francis 95, 96f, 112
Burton, Robert 33, 112, 128 n.10
Burton, William
  The description of Leicester shire 81
Busby, John 133t, 137t, 197 n.88, 198 n.91, 244t
Butter, Nathaniel 15 n.35, 18 n.52, 23 n.67, 49, 50t, 51–2, 66t, 67, 103 n.86, 105, 133t, 137t, 195, 234, 245t, 246t
Buxton, John 27
Byford, Mark 148 n.74, 149f, 163 n.111

Caius, John
  De antiquitate Cantebrigiensis Academiæ 9 n.18
Calvert, George 232
Cambridge 28, 67 n.97, 98 n.67, 158, 187–8, 190, 208 n.114, 227
  Corpus Christi College 160
  St John's College 54 n.48
Campion, Thomas 64
  Observations in the Art of English Poesie 8 n.17, 62

Canterbury Cathedral 130, 158, 163
capital
  alternative forms in book trade 15, 25, 33–6, 52, 77
Carey, Elizabeth (Lady Berkeley) 54 n.48
Carleton, Sir Dudley 69 n.104, 71–2, 221, 224–5, 236
Casaubon, Isaac
  The answere of Master Isaac Casaubon to the epistle of the most reverend Cardinall Peron 147
catalogues *see* advertising of books; First Folio catalogue page; Frankfurt catalogues
catechisms 107–8, 239t, 240t, 241t
Catholicism/Catholics 43, 145, 147–8, 226–8, 234
Cavendish, Margaret 218 n.27
Cavendish, William
  Horæ subsecivæ 16 n.39, 68 n.101
Cecil, Lord Robert 88–9
censorship 138–42, 140f, 141f
Certeau, Michel de 181
Cervantes, Fernando 97 n.63
Cervantes, Miguel de 29
  Don Quixote 45, 75 n.130
Chamberlain, John 69 n.104
chapbooks 49
Chapman, George 44, 161
  Eastward Hoe 140, 142 n.45
  The Divine Poem of Musæus 17 n.44, 84, 240t
chapmen 177
Charde, Thomas 86 n.23
Charles I, King 48 n.31, 128 n.10, 147, 236
Charlewood, John 92
Charron, Pierre
  Of Wisdome 16, 54 n.48, 75, 129
Chartier, Roger 34, 161, 178
Chaucer, Geoffrey 73
  The assemblie of foules 49 n.33
Chelsea College 146–7
Cheney, Patrick 100
Chester, Robert
  Loves Martyr 44, 68, 74 n.125, 74, 102, 132 n.23, 181 n.43
Chetwood, William 128 n.12
Church of England 92 n.50, 93 n.55, 94, 108, 130, 147–8
Chytraeus, David 143
circulation
  of dramatic texts 135, 167
  spurring textual change 72–3, 191–6
city printing, *see* Printing for the City of London
clergymen 17, 25, 55 n.54, 56, 93 n.55, 107, 129, 130, 143 n.49, 144–6, 150, 152, 159f, 162–3, 171, 188, 228, 236

INDEX 281

Clifford, Lady Anne 75, 76f
Cokain, Aston 36
Coke, Sir Edward 188
Coles, Francis 248t, 249t
collaboration, *see* book trade collaborations
collections, *see* authorial collections; sammelband volumes
College of Arms 96
Collier, John Payne 45 n.15
colophons 37 n.119, 129 n.14, *see also* First Folio colophon; Second Folio colophon; imprints, First Folio imprint
commonplace books 11, 125, 161, 190
communities, *see also* bibliographic communities
  of readers 31–2, 72–3, 178 n.31, 179–80
  of stationers 173, 179–80, 185, 199, 203, 206, 210, 215–16
  of writers 62–5, 72–3
compositors 9, 23 n.68, 27, 80, 90, 102, 157, 176, 179 n.36 *see also* book trade labour
Condell, Henry 10, 110, 183
consortium, *see* book trade collaborations; First Folio syndicate
Constable, Francis 59 n.67, 146 n.65
Constable, Henry
  The Catholike moderator 234
copyright 19 n.54; *see also* Stationers' Register
Corbett, Richard 218
Corbett, Vincent 218
Corney, Bolton 45 n.15
Cornwallis, Sir William
  Essayes 55
Coryate, Thomas 33, 218
  Thomas Coryate, Travailer 240t
Cotes, Richard 20 n.57, 208 n.116, 211
Cotes, Thomas 20 n.57, 208 n.116, 211, 214, 249t
Cotton, Sir Robert 233
Court of Assistants 15, *see also* Stationers' Company
Court of Chancery 57–9, 173 n.12, 211–12
Cowley, Abraham 119, 204
Cowper, William
  Works 86 n.21
Creede, Thomas 80 n.5, 103 n.86, 194, 245t, 246t
Crompton, William
  A wedding-ring 236
Crooke, Helkiah
  Mikrokosmographia 93 n.57, 102, 240t
  Sōmatographia Anthrōpinē 91 n.48, 240t
Crosley, John 177 n.24
cryptograms 95–6, *see also* woodblock devices
customers, *see* bookshops customers of

Dahl, Folke 66t
Dallington, Sir Robert 71, 226–8, 234
  Aphorismes Civill and Militarie 15 n.38, 61 n.74
d'Andilly, Arnauld
  The manner of ordering fruit-trees 202 n.97
Daniel, Samuel 146 n.65
  A Defence of Ryme 62, 64 n.89
  Musophilus 62
  The Civil Wars 62
Danter, John 133t, 134–5, 137t, 157, 176 n.21, 191, 193, 195, 243t
Darnton, Robert 215
Davies, David W. 28 n.85
Davies, John
  A discoverie of the state of Ireland 16 n.41
  A scourge for paper-persecutors 52 n.39, 179 n.35
  Orchestra or A poeme of dauncing 134
  Yehovah Summa Totalis 238t
Day, John 80 n.5
dedications, *see* booksellers prefaces; paratext
de Grazia, Margreta 199 n.93
Dekker, Thomas 47, 205
  The guls horne-booke 205 n.105
  The Magnificent Entertainment 97 n.64
  The Pleasant Comedie of Old Fortunatus 138
  The Pleasant Comodie of Patient Grisill 47 n.23
  West-ward Hoe 238t
Delamothe, G. 18 n.52
  The French Alphabet 15 n.36
Denham, Henry 86 n.23, 98 n.67, 143
Depledge, Emma 30, 175 n.17
Dering, Edward 108
  A Briefe and Necessarie Catechisme 107, 239t, 240t, 241t
  Workes 17
Dering, Sir Edward 150
Devereux, Robert (Earl of Essex) 138 n.36, 142
devices, *see* woodblock devices
Dewe, Thomas 18, 23 n.67, 49 n.34, 50t, 66t, 67, 103 n.86, 146 n.65, 198 n.92
dictionaries 45, 53–4, 56, 63–5, 81–2, 98 n.67, 102, 145, 239t, 240t, 241t
Digges, Leonard 18, 74–5
  'To the memorie of the deceased Authour' 1, 75, 205
  'Upon Master William Shakespeare' 128 n.9
Donne, John 7, 144, 150, 171, 173, 223, 234
  Poems 11
Dove, John
  A sermon preached at Pauls Crosse the 3. of November 1594 86 n.23, 238t
Downe, John 67 n.97
dramatic manuscripts 136 n.34

dramatists 26, 64, 83, 161, 207
Drayton, Michael
  Englands heroicall epistles 186 n.49
  Poems: by Michael Drayton Esquire 16 n.41
  Poly-Olbion 198
Dring, Thomas 36
Droeshout, Martin 3, 6, 8, 9 n.18
Droeshout, Martin (elder) 3 n.7
Dryden, John 7–8, 132
Duncan-Jones, Katherine 101, 242
Dutton, Richard 138 n.35
Dyce, Alexander 45 n.15

Earle, John
  Micro-cosmographie 57, 60
economics, *see* booksellers economic concerns; capital; First Folio costs; publishing economics
Edgar, John 60
Edinburgh 181, 182f, 201f, 248t
edition sheets 47, 49, 50t, 51–3, 86 n.21, 87, 90, 99, 102–3, 143
Egerton, Sir Thomas 54 n.48
Eisenstein, Elizabeth 70
Eld, George 103 n.86, 176
Elizabeth I, Queen 56, 89, 138, 143, 170
Ellis, G.
  The Lamentation of the Lost Sheepe 238t
Elsevier publishing house 28–9
encyclopaedias 87, 98–9, 239t, 240t
Englands Helicon 197
Englands Parnassus 125
engravings 3, 6, 8–9, 73, 91, 129 n.14, 153, 159, 171f, 198
epyllia 17, 60
Erasmus, Desiderius 28 n.85
Erne, Lukas 10 n.21, 102 n.82, 103, 116 n.124, 125, 132 n.23, 157 n.93, 158, 165 n.116, 176 n.21, 181 n.43, 242
essay form 45, 53–6, 68, 180
Evenden, Elizabeth 80 n.5

Fallon, David 70 n.112, 180 n.37
Faret, Nicolas
  The honest man: or, The art to please in court 236
Farewell, Christopher 48 n.31
Farmer, Alan B. 51 n.35, 67 n.96, 132 n.21, 166, 195, 206 n.109, 212
Farmer, Richard 117, 161 n.107
Favyn, Andre
  The Theater of Honour and Knight-hood 86 n.21, 98, 241t
Featley, Daniel 228

Felski, Rita 53
Fenton, Roger
  Treatise of Usurie 129
Field, Richard 132, 133t, 137t, 243t
Fincham, Kenneth 93 n.55, 144 n.54, 147 n.70
First Folio 1–3, 4f, 6–11, 13–15, 17–20, 22–8, 30–5, 37–8, 41–7, 49, 50t, 56–8, 60 n.73, 61, 65, 71, 73–86, 90–1, 94, 99 n.72, 100–1, 105, 107, 110–21, 126–7, 128 n.12, 130–2, 134–5, 138 n.35, 142, 148–53, 156, 158, 164–7, 169–70, 172–5, 179, 183, 186–7, 194, 196–7, 199, 202–8, 211, 213–15, 217–19, 230, 232
  assembling the collection 19–28
  authority of texts 84–5, 110–12, 115–21, 167–9, 205–6, 217
  Bodleian copy, 7–8
  catalogue page 26, 112–14, 128 n.10
  colophon 2, 11–13, 12f, 26–7, 35–7, 56, 79–80, 127, 170, 173, 208, 215
  costs 11, 20, 25–6, 27, 47, 56–8, 59 n.67, 61
  critical approaches to 2 n.5, 13–14, 30–1, 215
  edition size 27 n.82
  Fourth Folio (fourth edition, 1685) 6, 78
  imprint 2, 10–11, 35–7, 56, 79–80, 110, 173, 208–10, 215
  ownership of copy 19–24
  publicity 8–9, 26 n.78, 33, 37, 41–5, 114–15
  Second Folio (second edition, 1632) 1, 3, 15, 20 n.57, 61, 127, 128 n.10, 134, 167, 173, 187, 193, 202, 204, 208, 209f, 210, 214
  colophon 208, 209f, 210
  Stationers' Register entry for 20–1, 21f
  syndicate 2, 11, 14–19, 26–7, 80, 149, 151, 202–3, 208–10, 215–19
  Third Folio (third edition, 1663–4) 167, 175, 206
  timeline of printing 24–5, 79, 81–2
  title page 3–11, 4–5f
Fisher, George 228
Fisher, Thomas 23 n.67, 133t, 136, 137t, 186, 244t
Fish, Stanley 178
Fletcher, John 26, 52, 111, 118–19, 202, 206
  Henry VIII 118, 152
  The two noble kinsmen 202
Florio, John 45, 54, 56, 61–2, 64–5, 74
  A Worlde of Wordes 53, 55, 63
Folger, Henry 100
Folger Shakespeare Library 15, 26 n.78, 100f, 104 n.87, 139, 141f, 160, 198 n.90
forensic photography 105, 117
Foucault, Michel 34
Foxe, John 25

INDEX 283

Foxe, Simeon 234
Foxe, Thomas 234
Frankfurt Book Fair 26 n.78, 37, 41, 77
Frankfurt catalogues
  Catalogus universalis pro nundinis Francofurtensibus autumnalibus de anno M.DC.XXIIII 44 n.11
  Catalogus universalis pro nundinis Francofurtensibus vernalibus 26 n.78, 37 n.120, 41 n.3, 42 n.6, 43*f*
Free Library of Philadelphia 4*f*, 12*f*, 120, 121 n.137

Galbraith, Steven K. 53 n.45
Gants, David L. 51, 90, 92, 98 n.67
Gaskell, Roger 3 n.8
Gaultier, Jacques
  Rodomontados 239*t*
Genette, Gérard 6, 8 *see also* paratext
Gentleman, Tobias 18 n.52
geography, *see* book trade geography; London; maps
ghost impressions 82, 109, 117
Gilbertson, Will 175 n.18
Globe Theatre 23, 157, 183, 195
Glover, Robert
  Nobilitas Politica vel Civilis 98, 239*t*
Goad, Thomas 227-8
Goodwin, John 33-4, 49
Gosson, Alice 25 n.75
Gosson, Henry 20, 245*t*
Granada, Luis de
  Of prayer and meditation 25 n.75
Great Fire of London 6, 175
Greene, Robert 161, 176 n.21
Greenham, Richard 25, 152 n.86
Greg, W. W. 2 n.5, 19 n.53, 23 n.67, 27 nn.79-80, 85, 105, 126 n.6
  A Bibliography of the English Printed Drama 47 n.22, 216
Griffin, Edward 107, 154*f*
Grigge, Francis 197-8
Guez de Balzac, Jean-Louis 28
Gunpowder Plot 147 n.70
Gwinne, Matthew 54 n.48, 64

Hailey, R. Carter 25 n.71, 47 n.22, 81 n.9
Hall, Joseph 152-3
Hamlin, William M. 53 n.44, 54 n.48
Hamond, Walter 240*t*
Hampton Court Conference 145
Hanmer, Thomas 78
Harington, Sir John 161
Harris, Michael 174 n.14
Harrison (1), John 133*t*, 134, 137*t*, 243*t*, 244*t*, 245*t*

Harrison (4), John 89 n.39, 249*t*
Hartman, G. 37 n.117
Harvey, Gabriel 191
Haviland, John 248*t*, 249*t*
Hawkins, Richard 173, 191, 193, 202, 248*t*
Hayes, Lawrence 23 n.67, 50*t*, 51, 66*t*, 133*t*, 137*t*, 249*t*
Hayes, Thomas 133*t*, 136, 137*t*, 244*t*
Heath, Robert 114, 115 n.121
Hellinga, Lotte 37 n.119
Helme, John 103 n.86, 197, 198 n.91
Heminge, John 10, 22, 46 nn.18-19, 110-14, 116, 183
Hemmingsen, Niels 143
Henry, Prince of Wales 54 n.48, 56
heraldry/heralds 26 n.78, 81, 96, 99, 113, 215, 239*t*, 240*t*, 241*t*
Herbert, Philip (Earl of Montgomery) 10, 56, 74-5
Herbert, William (Earl of Pembroke) 10, 56, 74, 113
Herrick, Robert 67 n.97
Herrick, Sir William 67 n.97
Herringman, Henry 208 n.116
Heywood, Thomas 83, 98, 101, 104, 117, 119, 135, 136 n.34, 207
  A Woman Kilde with Kindnesse 84, 106-9, 113, 162, 238*t*, 240*t*
  Troia Britanica 103, 239*t*
Hieron, Samuel
  The workes of Mr. Sam. Hieron 152
Higgons, Theophilus 148
Hill, Thomas
  A Pleasant History 239*t*
  The Schoole of Skil 93 n.57, 238*t*
Hinman, Charlton 2 n.5, 24, 58, 80, 81 n.9
Hobbes, Thomas 47, 68
Hodson, Phineas 235
  The king's request 236
Holinshed, Raphael
  Chronicles 98 n.67
Holland, Abraham 52 n.39
Holland, Hugh 113-14
Hollyband, Claudius 18 n.52
Holy Trinity Church 1
Hooks, Adam G. 29-30, 41 n.3, 107, 131, 150, 184 n.46, 217
Howard, Henry
  A Defensative Against the Poyson 240*t*
Huggins, Thomas 16, 160
Humfrey, Richard
  Lady Pecunia 238*t*
  The Anathomie of Sinne 238*t*
  The Conflict of Job 238*t*
  Two Guides to a Good Life 86 n.24, 238*t*, 239*t*

Hunnis, William
 Hunnies Recreations 238t
Huntington Library 109, 160

Ibbitson, Robert 176 n.20
impressions, *see also* ghost impressions
 definition 23 n.68
 sale of 23–5, 151–3
imprints 10–11, 35–7, 75, 84, 88, 92, 153, 170, 175–8, *see also* First Folio imprint, First Folio colophon
 false or unreliable 82, 105, 109, 176 n.21, 183–4, 237, 242
 industrial purpose of 35, 90, 92
 used as adverts 36–7, 37 n.117
 Jaggard use of 90–2, 94, 109, 114
ink, *see* printing ink
inns of chancery 187, 188
 Clifford's Inn 187
 Serjeants' Inn 173 n.13, 181, 182f, 187, 201f, 202, 249t
inns of court 9, 170, 179
 Gray's Inn 27, 180, 187, 203
 Inner Temple 175 n.18, 187
 Lincoln's Inn 187
 Middle Temple 146, 173 n.13, 175 n.18, 181, 182f, 187, 201f, 204, 248t
 readership 186–91
inscriptions, *see* presentation copies
Islip, Adam 98 n.67
Italian language learning 18 n.52, 53–5

Jackson, Roger 133t, 137t, 164, 196, 246t, 247t
Jackson, Thomas 205
Jaggard, Dorothy 208 n.114, 211, 214
Jaggard, Isaac 10–11, 15, 79–85, 107, 109, 213–14
 City Printer 79, 89
 death and will 208, 208 n.114
 list of publications 237–41
 role played in First Folio 13 n.28, 20, 21f, 26 n.78, 27, 42, 58, 60, 84–5
Jaggard, Jane 106 n.92, 213–15
Jaggard, John 17, 90 n.46, 171, 203
Jaggard Quartos 82–4, 92–4, 104–10, 116–17, 119–20, 162, 182f, 183–4, 237
Jaggard, Thomas 106 n.92, 208, 213
Jaggard, William 10–11, 14–17, 26 n.78, 32, 37–8, 79–121, 130, 151–3, 172, 175, 183, 208, 216–17, 244t, 246t, 247t
 A Catalogue of Such English Bookes 93, 108, 112–13, 131, 160 n.101, 240t
 A View of All the Right Honourable the Lord Mayors 91 n.48, 98, 238t

City Printing 79, 88–90, *see also* Printing for the City of London
 critical anxiety about 13–14, 101, 107, 110, 115–21, 216–17
 death 79, 208, 213–14
 identity as printer 80–5
 identity as publisher 50t, 80, 86–100, 110–15
 interest in reference books 96–100, 110–11
 Jaggard Quartos (1619), *see* Jaggard Quartos
 jobbing printing 87–90, 114–15
 links to John Smethwick 16, 17, 203
 list of publications 237–41
 ownership of Shakespeare's work 19–20, 102, 104
 printing and publishing premises 87, 101, 172, 175, 180, 181, 183–4
 promotion to livery 15
 textual legitimacy 32, 37–8, 82–4, 100–1, 104, 115–21, 216–17
 The passionate pilgrime 82, 86, 100–4, 116–17, 119
 woodblock devices 92–8, 107–9
James I, King 89, 97, 126, 130, 140, 143–4, 146–8, 195, 228, 232
 Basilikon Doron 45, 51, 60t
 Daemonologie 144
 Directions for Preachers 145
Johns, Adrian 34, 177
Johnson, Arthur 23 n.67, 50t, 51, 53 n.41, 66t, 90, 105, 133t, 137t, 152–3, 245t, 247t
Johnson, Rob
 Essaies, or rather Imperfect offers 55 n.54
Johnson, Samuel 78
Johnstoune, William 13 n.27
Jones, Richard 108
Jones, Thomas 197–9
Jones, William 103 n.86, 180
Jones, William (2) 108
Jones, William (3) 108
Jonson, Ben 1, 6–7, 9, 23, 52, 61, 73–4, 113, 114, 161, 207
 'An Epitaph on Master Vincent Corbet" 218
 Argenis 61
 Eastward Hoe 140, 142 n.45
 'Epigram, to my Book-seller' 213
 Every Man in his Humour 134
 links to Edward Blount 73–4
 The Workes of Benjamin Jonson 23 n.66, 44, 144, 218 n.24, 219
journeymen, *see* printers
Jowett, John 136 n.34
Justinus, Marcus
 The Historie of Justine 94, 95f, 97, 99 n.72, 113, 238t

Kastan, David Scott 81 n.7, 111 n.107, 116 n.124
Kenny, Neil 98 n.69
King, John 228
Kingsley-Smith, Jane 30
King's Men 22–3, 26, 83–5, 107, 110, 135, 183
King's Printing House 14 n.32
Kingston, Felix 155*f*, 151 n.80
Kirkman, Francis 9
Kirschbaum, Leo 116 n.123
Kirton, Joshua 92 n.50
Kirwan, Peter 30
Kiséry, András 64, 70 n111
Knight, Jeffrey Todd 106, 109 n.101, 110, 162 n.108
Knight, Leah 75 n.130

labour, *see* book trade labour
Lambe, Sir John 85 n.17, 214
Landels-Gruenewald, Tye 174 n.14
Lanier, Emilia
   Salve Deus rex Judaeorum 236
Lanier, Nicholas 236
Law, Matthew 23 n.67, 24–5, 50*t*, 65, 66*t*, 126 n.5, 133*t*, 134, 137*t*, 151, 199, 208, 242, 245*t*, 246*t*, 247*t*, 248*t*
lawyers 146, 187–91, 204, *see also* inns of court
Lead, Jane 218
Leake, William 86, 133*t*, 137*t*, 175 n.18, 242, 244*t*, 245*t*, 246*t*
Legat, John 98 n.67
legitimacy of Shakespeare's texts, *see* Jaggard, William textual legitimacy
Lesser, Zachary 30, 43 n.7, 51 n.35, 67 n.96, 83 n.12, 93 n.54, 106–7, 109–10, 117, 186 n.50, 202 n.97
   Renaissance Drama and the Politics of Publication 29
Lily, William 130 n.15
Ling, Nicholas 22, 95, 133*t*, 136, 137*t*, 158, 186–91, 193, 208, 245*t*
Lisle, Laurence 152–3, 203
Lisle, William
   The faire Æthiopian 190 n.69
literariness, *see* Blount, Edward literariness of
literary property, *see* Stationers' Register
Lloyd, Richard 163, 164*f*
Loewenstein, Joseph 47 n.26, 91
London, *see also* book trade geography; maps
   Aldersgate 214
   Barbican 37, 81, 85, 90, 91 n.48, 94, 98, 101, 105, 136, 172, 175, 179, 181, 182*f*, 183–4, 186, 200*f*, 201*f*, 202, 213–14, 245*t*, 246*t*, 247*t*, 249*t*
   Bishopsgate 8*f*
   Blackfriars 114, 183, 195
   Britain's Burse 182*f*, 200*f*, 247*t*
   Carter Lane 182*f*, 200*f*, 244*t*
   Chancery Lane 173 n.13, 181, 182*f*, 187, 201*f*, 202, 248*t*
   Cheapside 182*f*, 201*f*, 248*t*
   Christ Church Gate 182*f*, 183, 200*f*, 246*t*
   Cornhill 165, 173, 181, 182*f*, 184, 186, 200*f*, 243*t*, 244*t*
   Fleet Bridge 175 n.18, 182*f*, 201*f*, 202, 249*t*
   Fleet Street 17, 38, 101, 170, 171*f*, 173 n.11, 175 n.18, 178–80, 182*f*, 184–7, 190 n.69, 196, 200*f*, 201*f*, 212, 217, 244*t*, 246*t*, 247*t*
   Foster Lane 182*f*, 201*f*, 202, 249*t*
   Holborn 173
   Hosier Lane 182*f*, 200*f*, 243*t*
   Ivy Lane 182*f*, 185, 246*t*, 247*t*
   Little Britain 183
   Ludgate 178, 180, 196
   Middle Temple Gate 173 n.13, 181, 182*f*, 201*f*, 248*t*
   Newgate 182*f*, 201*f*, 248*t*, 249*t*
   Old Bailey 182*f*, 201*f*, 248*t*, 249*t*
   Paternoster Row 177, 181, 182*f*, 183, 200*f*, 234, 243*t*, 244*t*, 245*t*, 249*t*
   Paul's Cross Churchyard 8 n.17, 38, 52, 58, 86, 127, 142, 147–8, 165, 172–3, 175–6, 179–81, 182*f*, 184–6, 191, 195, 199, 200*f*, 201*f*, 203, 205–6, 229, 242*t*
   Paul's Wharf 194
   Piccadilly 180 n.37
   Pope's Head Alley 183
   Royal Exchange 115*f*, 173, 181, 182*f*, 184–6, 191, 192*f*, 194, 195, 200*f*, 243*t*, 244*t*
   Serjeants' Inn 173 n.13, 181, 182*f*, 187, 201*f*, 248*t*
   Smithfield 191, 192*f*, 195
   Snow Hill 183
   St Augustine's Gate 242, 245*t*, 246*t*, 247*t*, 248*t*
   St Dunstan's Churchyard 17, 38, 101, 170–1, 173–4, 180–1, 182*f*, 185–7, 190–1, 192*f*, 194–9, 200*f*, 201*f*, 202–4, 206, 210, 217, 245*t*, 246*t*, 247*t*, 248*t*, 249*t*
   St Peter's Church 182*f*, 184, 200*f*, 243*t*, 244*t*
   Strand 165, 173 n.11 173, 178, 181, 182*f*, 185 n.47, 199 n.93, 201*f*, 202, 249*t*
   Stratford 132
   Temple Church 187
   Warwick Lane 182*f*, 200*f*, 246*t*
   Westminster 165, 181, 182*f*, 191, 200*f*
Lord Chamberlain 84, 110
Lord Chamberlain's Men 131
Louis XIII, King 71, 235–6
Lownes, Humphrey 53 n.41, 87

Lownes, Matthew 44, 90, 102, 186, 198 n.91, 213, 228
Lunn, Robert 167–8
Lupton, Donald 178, 188 n.56
Lydiat, Thomas 41, 44, 48
Lyly, John 45, 73, 77
  Sixe court comedies 68
Lyons, Tara 30, 162, 184 n.46

Mabbe, Edward 17
Mabbe, James 17, 61 n.74, 71, 74–5, 114, 230, 232, 234
Mabbe (Mab), Ralph 234
Macky, John 178
Maguire, Laurie 105
Malay, Jessica 75 n.130
Malone, Edmond 45 n.15, 100, 103 n.84, 117, 161 n.107
Mandelbrote, Giles 174 n.14
Manley, Lawrence 178 n.27
Manning, Francis 37 n.117
Man, Thomas 59 n.67
manuscript, *see also* reading annotations
  circulation 18, 38, 68, 72–3, 136 n.34, 166
  cost of 25, 135
  publication 218, 230
maps 174–85, 182f, 192f, 200f, 201f, *see also* book trade geography; London
marginalia, *see* reading annotations
Marino, James 19 n.53, 106
marketing of books 8–9, 43–4, 92, 103 n.84, 104, 126–7, 156–8, 165–6, 185, 206–7
  see also advertising of books; First Folio publicity
Marlowe, Christopher 29, 45, 56, 70, 77, 100, 118
  Hero and Leander 16–17, 60, 65, 67 n.96, 69
Marotti, Arthur F. 53 n.45
Marriot, John 11, 146 n.65, 197–8, 199 n.93
Marsh, James 150
Marshall, Edward 197–8
Marston, John 44, 161
  Eastward Hoe 140, 142 n.45
  The Malcontent 138–9, 140f, 177
Martin, John 208 n.116
Massai, Sonia 54 n.47, 74–5, 110 n.102, 127 n.8, 194
Matthew, Tobias 54 n.48
McGann, Jerome 35
McKenzie, D. F. 29
McKerrow, Ronald B. 81 n.7, 92 n.52, 93 n.53, 94 n.58
Meighen, Richard 173, 187, 197–8, 202, 235, 248t
Meisei University 13 n.27
Melchiori, Giorgio 138 n.35

Melnikoff, Kirk 29, 30, 44 n.10, 65, 95 n.59, 216 n.21
Melzo, Lodovico
  Millitary Rules 236
Ménage, Gilles 28 n.85
Mexia, Pedro 91
  The imperiall historie 86 n.21
Middleton, Thomas 118
  The Changeling 36
  The ghost of Lucrece 177 n.24
  The Roaring Girle 23
Millenary Petition 145
Milles, Thomas 87 n.27, 91, 218 n.27, 237
  A Catalogue of the Kings of Scotland 113, 239t
  Archaio-ploutos 91 n.49, 111 n.103, 240t
  The Catalogue of Honor 102, 112, 239t
  The treasurie of aunciency and moderne times 98
  Times Store-House 91
  Treasurie of aunciency and moderne times 98, 102
Millington, Thomas 133t, 137t, 176 n.21, 184–5, 243t, 244t
Milton, John 119 n.133, 120–1
  Areopagitica 36 n.115
Minshull, Geffray
  Essayes and characters 180
Montagu, Richard
  Diatribæ 228
Montaigne, Michel de 16, 29, 61, 77
  Essayes 45, 53–6, 55f, 75 n.130
Montenay, Georgette de
  A booke of armes 11 n.24
Moore, Richard 146 n.65, 197, 198 n.92
More, Thomas 25 n.73
Moretti, Franco 206, 207 n.110, 208 n.115
Moseley, Humphrey 26, 45 n.16, 111, 156 n.92, 202
Muldrew, Craig 35 n.110
Munday, Anthony
  A Briefe Chronicle 239t
  Chruso-thriambos 239t
  The Triumphes of Re-united Britania 88 n.34, 238t
Murphy, Andrew 10 n.21, 83 n.12, 110 n.102
Musaeus 16
  The Divine Poem of Musæus 84, 240t
music books 18 n.52, 51, 177
Myers, Robin 174 n.14

Nashe, Thomas 36, 64, 118, 172
  Pierce Penilesse his supplication to the divell 108
  The Terrors of the Night 35
Neidig, William 105
Nelson, Alan H. 190, 204 n.100

networks *see* book trade networks
New Bibliography 38, 71, 81, 94, 100, 105–7, 110, 115, 184, 216
newsbooks 49, 52, 66*t*
Nichols, Josias
  Abrahams faith 43
Norden, John
  A Pensive Mans Practice 129
Norton, Bonham 130
Norton, John 199, 248*t*
Norton (2), John 181, 249*t*

Oastler, C. L. 80 n.5
Oath of Allegiance 144–5, 147–8, 228
Ogborn, Miles 174 n.14
Olsen, Rebecca 213
Overall, John 147
Ovid 117 n.127
Oxford 9 n.20, 16, 47, 64, 71, 145, 158, 160, 163, 177, 187, 190, 227
  All Soul's College 143 n.49
  Corpus Christi College 209*f*
  Magdalen College 232, 234
  Worcester College 55*f*
Oxinden, Henry 161

Paddy, Sir William 226, 228
Paget, William 38
Page, William 167
Pagitt, Justinian 146
paper 11, 13 n.27, 16, 86 n.21, 89–90, 105
  see also printed waste
  cost of 47, 49, 136 n.34
  merchants 9, 157
paratext 10, 23, 30, 54, 56, 63–5, 66*t*, 67–70, 72, 73, 74, 82, 91, 97–8, 100, 111–13, 115–16, 156, 157 n.93, 180, 199, *see also* Genette; booksellers prefaces
  epitext 8
  peritext 6–7
Paré, Ambroise
  Method of Curing Wounds Made by Gunshot 84, 240*t*
Paris 71, 212, 235–6
Parker, John 133*t*, 137*t*, 247*t*
Parker, Martin 1, 3
Parker, Matthew 9 n.18
Parrot, Henry 188 n.59
  Cures for the Itch 199 n.93
Parry, Henry 56
partnerships, *see* book trade collaborations, First Folio syndicate
patents 98 n.67, 130 n.15
Paternoster Row, *see* London

patrons/patronage 10, 34, 38, 54, 56, 65, 67, 71, 74–5, 218 n.27, 235
Paul's Cross Churchyard, *see* London
Pavier Quartos, *see* Jaggard Quartos
Pavier, Thomas 20, 23 n.67, 49, 50*t*, 65, 66*t*, 83, 87 n.27, 103 n.86, 104–6, 129, 130 n.15, 132, 133*t*, 136, 137*t*, 172 n.8, 182*f*, 183–5, 208, 216, 244*t*, 246*t*, 247*t*
Payne, John 47, 48 n.27, 52
Pearson, David 16 n.40
Peele, George 118
Pepys, Samuel 33
Percy, Henry (Earl of Northumberland) 56
Perry, Hugh 181, 249*t*
Peter Martyr
  Loci communes 11
Philip II, King 131
Philos and Licia 17
Piper, John 150
Piper, Thomas 16
Plantin, Christophe 49 n.33, 70 n.112
Plantin-Moretus Museum 175
playbills 86 n.24, 87, 114, 115
playbooks, *see also* Jaggard Quartos
  binding 106, 161
  cost 46–7, 89 n.40, *see also* First Folio costs
  edition size 90 n.42
  William Aspley interest in 138–42, 150
players, *see* actors
Playfere, Thomas 144, 150
playhouses, *see* Globe Theatre; theatres
Plomer, Henry R. 9 n.18
Pollard, Alfred W. 22, 104–6, 116, 237 n.1
Ponsonby, William 63 n.83, 75, 143
Pope, Alexander 78, 204
  The Dunciad 65
Portugal 68
Potter, Lois 202 n.96
Powell, Thomas 3
prayer books 129, 145, *see also* Book of Common Prayer
preachers, *see* clergymen
prefaces, *see* booksellers prefaces; paratext
presentation copies 26 n.78, 54, 55*f*, 100*f*
Preston, Roland 226, 228
Primroes, W.
  A funerall poeme 239*t*
printed waste, 15–6, 27, 176 n.20
printers *see also* printing for the City of London; Stationers' Company
  compositors 9, 23 n.68, 27, 80, 90, 102, 157, 176, 179 n.36
  journeymen 76, 80, 86n.23
  master printers 27, 70, 85, 85 n.17, 92 n.51

printing
   abundance of 33–4
   costs 9 n.18, 25, 89, *see also* First Folio costs
   for the Church of England 93 n.55, 94
   for the City of London 79, 88–90, 93 n.57, 114
   ink 3, 9, 18, 82, 89 n.39, 109, 139
printing houses 14, 37, 70 n.112, 80–1, 85–6,
   90 n.45, 97, 175, 194, 214
Privy Seal 89
profits, *see* publishing economics
Prynne, William 204
publicity *see* advertising of books; First Folio
   publicity; marketing of books
publishers 10–19, 23–7, 176, 180, 185, 208
   see also booksellers; printers
   critical approaches 28–32, 215–19
   influence of 33–7, 67–70
   literary publishers 32, 45–6, 49–51, 52, 56, 61,
      62–70, 77–8, 216
   minor Shakespeareans 126–8, 132, 133t,
      134–6, 137t, 165–8
   prefaces 66t
   printer-publishers, 86–90
   women 9, 17 n.45, 25 n.73, 58–60, 106 n.92,
      208 n.114, 211–15
publishing
   and belief 33–6
   economics 25, 46–54, 132, *see also* First
      Folio costs
Pudsey, Edmund 125
Purfoot, Thomas 18 n.52, 247t
Puritans 144–5, 204
Purslowe, Elizabeth 25 n.74
Pynson, Richard 146 n.65, 185

Quarles, Francis 146 n.65, 198

Raleigh, Walter 100
Rasmussen, Eric 10 n.21, 14 n.30, 152 n.82
Raven, James 14 n.31, 35 n.108, 47 n.25, 87 n.29
Raworth, Robert 242, 245t
reading
   annotations 7, 26 n.78, 54, 55f, 69–70, 100,
      100f, 120–1, 134, 139, 141f, 162, 163–4,
      164f 194
   in bookshops 47, 67
religious
   writings of John Boys 131, 142–8
   dictionary 81
Richelieu, Cardinal 71, 236
Roberts, James 20, 80, 87, 92 n.52, 105, 133t,
   136, 137t, 188, 247t
Robinson, Humphrey 26
Rowe, Nicholas 77–8, 119–20, 204

Rowlandson, Thomas 236
Roydon, Roger 57–9
Rudman, Joseph 118
Ryder, John
   Dictionary 60

Saenger, Michael 205
Sallust 98
   Two Most Worthy and Notable Histories 239t
Salman, Jeroen 174 n.14, 181 n.41
sammelband volumes 104–10, 160–4, *see also*
   authorial collections; bookbindings;
   Jaggard Quartos
San Pedro, Diego de 18 n.52
Sanford, Hugh 63–4
Savile, Sir Henry 49 n.33
Savile, Thomas
   The Prisoners Conference 238t
Schlueter, June 3 n.7
Scott-Warren, Jason 29 n.90, 69 n.104, 120, 217
Scott, William 125
Scragg, Leah 68
Selden, John 218, 233
   Historie of tithes 228
Seneca 28
   Works 75 n.130
sermons 52, 67 n.97, 86, 142, 144–5, 147–8, 150,
   156, 167, 171, 235–6, 238t, 239t, 240t
   reading of 162–4, 164f
Shaaber, M. A. 35 n.112
Shakespeare, William, *see also* First Folio
   attributions 24, 82–3, 100–1, 103–5, 116–19,
      125, 126f, 158, 166, 197
   geography of publication 172–3, 174–85,
      191–6, 200f, 201f
   ownership of works 19–26, 126–9, 132, 133t,
      134–6, 137t, 151–3, 156–8, 168
   sammelband collections 104–10, 161–2
   textual authority 82–5, 111–12, 115–21,
      165–7, 207–8
Shakespeare, William (works)
   1 Contention (2 Henry VI) 93 n.54, 105, 133t,
      137t, 184–5, 243t, 244t, 247t
   1 Henry IV 23 n.67, 24, 126 n.5, 132, 133t,
      134, 137t, 181, 182f, 184, 199, 201f, 202,
      242, 243t, 244t, 245t, 246t, 247t, 248t, 249t
   1 Henry VI 118
   2 Contention (3 Henry VI) 93 n.54, 105, 133t,
      137t, 184–5, 247t
   2 Henry IV 22, 62 n.78, 125, 126f, 127–8,
      131–2, 133t, 137t, 138, 244t
   2 Henry VI 23 n.67, 105, 133t, 137t, 208 n.116
   3 Henry VI 23 n.67, 105, 133t, 137t, 157,
      172 n.8, 184, 185

INDEX 289

A Midsummer Night's Dream 23 n.67, 105, 133*t*, 136, 137*t*, 186, 244*t*, 247*t*
A Yorkshire Tragedy 105, 162, 208 n.116
All's Well That Ends Well 81
Antony and Cleopatra 20, 133*t*, 137*t*
Arden of Faversham 118
As You Like It 19–20, 134
Cymbeline 11, 12*f*, 13, 20, 58, 79, 81, 170, 204
Edward III 118, 132 n.23, 133*t*, 134, 137*t*, 181 n.43, 185, 243*t*
Hamlet 22, 25, 95, 102 n.83, 120–1, 126, 131, 133*t*, 136, 137*t*, 144, 158, 172, 186–91, 196–9, 202, 208 n.116, 245*t*, 246*t*, 247*t*, 249*t*
Henry V 23 n.67, 104–5, 109, 133*t*, 134, 137*t*, 184, 244*t*, 246*t*
Henry VIII 118, 152
Julius Caesar 22
King John 23 n.67, 49 n.34, 197
King Lear 11, 23 n.67, 133*t*, 135, 137*t*, 245*t*, 246*t*
Love's Labour's Lost 22, 125, 133*t*, 137*t*, 172, 188, 202, 242, 243*t*, 248*t*
Macbeth 20, 22, 118
Measure for Measure 118
Much Ado About Nothing 22, 62 n.78, 125, 126*f*, 127–8, 131–2, 133*t*, 134, 137*t*, 244*t*
Othello 23 n.67, 24, 81, 133*t*, 137*t*, 157, 175 n.18, 181, 182*f*, 191, 193, 195 n.81, 200*f*, 202, 247*t*, 248*t*
Pericles 20, 30, 93–4, 102 n.83, 105, 117, 133*t*, 137*t*, 202, 206, 208 n.116, 245*t*, 246*t*, 247*t*, 248*t*, 249*t*
Poems (1640) 119 n.133, 128, 174–5, 198, 203–4, 206, 249*t*
Richard Duke of York 184, 243*t*, 244*t*
Richard II 23 n.67, 24, 82 n.10, 125, 126 n.5, 132, 133*t*, 134, 137*t*, 184, 243*t*, 245*t*, 246*t*, 249*t*
Richard III 23 n.67, 24, 125, 126 n.5, 132, 133*t*, 134, 137*t*, 199, 243*t*, 245*t*, 246*t*, 247*t*, 248*t*, 249*t*
Romeo and Juliet 22, 25, 120, 125, 133*t*, 137*t*, 158, 172, 188, 191, 192*f*, 193–5, 198, 202, 243*t*, 244*t*, 245*t*, 247*t*, 249*t*
Sonnets 30, 42, 73, 104, 116, 127, 133*t*, 137*t*, 157, 165, 176, 183, 229, 246*t*
The Comedy of Errors 203
The Merchant of Venice 23 n.67, 105, 133*t*, 136, 137*t*, 157 n.93, 175 n.18, 202, 244*t*, 247*t*, 249*t*
The Merry Wives of Windsor 23 n.67, 81, 105, 133*t*, 137*t*, 153, 187, 202, 245*t*, 247*t*, 248*t*
The Passionate Pilgrim 82–4, 86, 100–4, 116–17, 119–20, 238*t*, 239*t*, 244*t*, 246*t*, *see also* Jaggard, William

The Rape of Lucrece 30, 87, 133*t*, 134, 153, 157, 161 n.107, 164, 175 n.18, 177, 184, 195–6, 243*t*, 244*t*, 245*t*, 246*t*, 247*t*, 249*t*
The Spanish Tragedy 118, 177
The Taming of the Shrew 22, 172, 188, 202, 248*t*
The Tempest 7, 22, 204
The Two Noble Kinsmen 117, 202, 249*t*
The Winter's Tale 151–2, 204
Timon of Athens 152, 202 n.96
Titus Andronicus 23 n.67, 102 n.83, 118, 133*t*, 134, 137*t*, 172, 176 n.21, 208 n.116, 243*t*, 244*t*, 246*t*
Troilus and Cressida 23 n.67, 26, 49 n.34, 58 n.65, 79 n.1, 128 n.12, 133*t*, 137*t*, 152, 157, 199, 204 n.100, 246*t*
Twelfth Night 22, 151, 203–4
Venus and Adonis 14, 17, 29 n.90, 86, 132, 133*t*, 134, 137*t*, 153, 157, 161 n.107, 174, 181, 182*f*, 184, 201*f*, 217, 242, 243*t*, 244*t*, 245*t*, 246*t*, 247*t*, 248*t*, 249*t*
Sharpe, Kevin 178
Sheares, William 25 n.73, 248*t*
Sheavyn, Phoebe 45 n.15
Sheldon, Richard
  Certain general reasons, proving the lawfulnesse of the Oath of allegiance 147–8
Sherman, William 215, 218 n.27, 237
Shirley, James 73, 207
Short, Peter 80 n.5, 133*t*, 137*t*
Sidney, Philip 1
Silva, Andie 46 n.17
Silver, George
  Paradoxes of defence 54 n.48
Simmes, Valentine 132
Sinklo, John 139
Sir John Oldcastle 105, 162, 208 n.116
Smethwick, Francis (son) 148 n.74, 171–2
Smethwick, Francis (wife) 212
Smethwick, George 198
Smethwick, John 15–19, 38, 50*t*, 66*t*, 67 n.96, 74 n.124, 133*t*, 137*t*, 152, 170–210, 212, 217, 245*t*, 246*t*, 247*t*, 248*t*, 249*t*
  address of bookshop 38, 170–4, 171*f*, 185–99, 202–10
  collaboration with William Aspley 17, 152
  First Folio titles owned 22
  links to Edward Blount 15, 203
  links to Jaggards 16, 17, 203
  ownership of Shakespeare's work 22, 25, 133*t*, 137*t*, 172, 188

Smethwick, John (*cont.*)
  prefaces 65, 66*t*
  promotion to livery 15
  publication of *Romeo and Juliet* 191–6
  publishing output 50*t*
  role in First Folio 11, 13, 26, 126 n.6, 127, 166, 172, 203, 208–10, 217
  woodblock device 95
Smethwick, Richard 170
Smith, Emma 2 n.5, 7, 13 n.27, 14 n.30, 20, 30, 73 n.122, 99 n.72, 150 n.76, 202 n.96, 211
Smith, Helen 13 n.27, 35, 175 n.16, 176 n.22, 211 n.1
Smith, Sir Thomas 189 n.61
  The common-wealth of England 188
Smyth, Adam 16, 54 n.49, 61 n.77, 216 n.20
Snodham, Thomas 103 n.86, 133*t*, 137*t*
Socrates 64
Speed, John
  The Historie of Great Britaine 86 n.21
Spenser, Edmund 73
Spufford, Margaret 177 n.26
Stafford, John 175 n.18
Stafford, Simon 246*t*
Stallybrass, Peter 43 n.7, 83 n.12, 87, 89, 99, 106, 110, 161
Stansby, William 41 n.2, 75 n.130, 152, 233, 235
stationers, *see* booksellers; printers; publishers; Stationers' Company
Stationers' Company 14–15, 19 n.54, 21*f*, 23–5, 27, 41, 48, 59, 60*f*, 84, 88, 92 n.51, 93, 125–6, 130, 135*f*, 152–3
  apprentices 9, 14–15, 80, 86 n.23, 87, 98 n.67, 143, 161, 173, 185, 194, 214 n.12
Stationers' Hall 15, 58
Stationers' Register 19–20, 125, 188, 212
  description of 19 n.54
  First Folio entry 21*f*, 84–5
  Shakespeare entries 132–5, 137*t*
Staveley, Leonard 162, 163 n.111
Steevens, George 126*f*
Stempe, John 198
Stern, Tiffany 23, 136 n.34
Stow, John 188
  Chronicles of England 98 n.67
  Survay of London 187
Straznicky, Marta 29 n.89, 57
Strode, William 163
Sutcliffe, Matthew
  The supplication of certaine masse-priests 147
Swift, Daniel 145
Swift, Jonathan
  A Tale of Tub 65
Swinburne, Algernon Charles 14 n.29, 83

Swynnerton, John
  A Christian Love-Letter 91 n.47, 238*t*
syndicate, *see* book trade collaborations; First Folio syndicate

Tankard, Paul 99
Taylor, Gary 13 n.28, 45 n.14–15, 57, 69 n.105, 71 n.114, 73, 118 n.131, 119 n.133, 221
Taylor, John 44, 67 n.97
The Annals of Great Britain 44
theatre companies 10, 22, 31, 72, 131, 136 n.34, 179, 203, *see also* King's Men
theatres 22–3, 38, 75, 87, 112, 114–15, 128, 136 n.34, 153, 157, 158, 183, 195, 203–4, 207
The fierie tryall of Gods saints 96*f*
Theobald, Lewis 78, 204
The Returne from Pernassus: or The scourge of simony 135
The Taming of a Shrew 22, 133*t*, 137*t*
The troublesome raigne of John King of England 18, 24, 49 n.34, 102 n.83, 197
The whole volume of statutes at large 148, 149*f*
Thomas, John 60
Thompson, James Westfall 41 n.1
Thorpe, Thomas 56, 72–3, 127, 133*t*, 137*t*, 140, 176, 229, 232, 246*t*
Todd, William B. 208 n.116
Tonson, Jacob 128 n.12
Topsell, Edward
  The Historie of Foure-Footed Beastes 93 n.57, 98, 113, 238*t*
  The Historie of Serpents 98, 239*t*
Tromans, Philip 67
Trumbull, Sir William 69, 71–3, 74 n.127, 226, 229–34
Trundle, John 158, 179, 186, 245*t*
Tuvill, Daniel 55 n.54

Ursinus, Zacharias
  The summe of Christian religion 53 n.41

Vecellio, Cesare
  The True Perfection of Cutworks 238*t*
Venice 69 n.104, 72, 224–5, 235–6
Venner, Tobias 233
Vesalius, Andreas 236
Victoria and Albert Museum 139, 141*f*
Vincent, Augustine 26 n.78, 85, 100
  A Discoverie of Errours 99, 100 n.75, 113, 241*t*

Wake, Sir Isaac 71, 225, 235–6
Walker, Robert 128 n.12
Walkley, Thomas 23 n.67, 24, 50*t*, 66*t*, 133*t*, 137*t*, 182*f*, 191, 193, 202, 247*t*

Walley, Henry 23 n.67, 26, 49 n.34, 50*t*, 66*t*, 133*t*, 137*t*, 152, 157, 199, 246*t*
Wallis, Thomas
    The Path-way to Please God 240*t*
Walsingham, Sir Thomas 65, 69
Warburton, William 78
Washington, Philip 18
Washington, William 197–8
waste, *see* printed waste
watermarks 105, 117
Waterson, John 202, 206, 249*t*
Waterson, Simon 62, 63 n.83, 90, 146 n.65
Wayne, Valerie 13 n.27, 111 n.108, 211
Weaver, Edmund 43, 130 n.15, 203
Webster, John
    The Malcontent 138–9, 140*f*, 177
    The white divel 204
Wechel, André 70 n.112
Welby, William 25 n.74, 133*t*, 137*t*, 151 n.80, 152 n.86
Wellington, Richard 37 n.117
West, Anthony J. 2 n.5, 10 n.21, 33 n.102
West, Robert 8*f*
White, Edward 25 n.75, 176 n.21, 243*t*, 244*t*, 246*t*
Whitehall 165, 195 n.81
White, John 81
White, R. 115*f*
Wilkins, George 20 n.57, 94, 108
Wilkinson, Robert 147
Willoughby, Edwin 2 n.5, 80–1, 88, 101 n.81

Wilson, Thomas
    A Christian Dictionarie 81 n.9, 102, 239*t*, 240*t*, 241*t*
    A Commentarie Upon S. Paul 239*t*, 240*t*
    Saints by Calling 240*t*
Wimbledon, Thomas
    A Sermon No Lesse Fruitfull then Famous 240*t*
Winder, George 198 n.92, 233
Windet, John 194
Windsor Castle 128 n.10
Wise, Andrew 125–6, 128, 130, 133*t*, 134, 136, 137*t*, 168, 208, 216, 243*t*, 244*t*, 245*t*
    collaboration with William Aspley 22, 62, 127, 131–2
Wither, George 1, 47–8, 52, 61, 97
Withers, Charles W. J. 174 n.14
Wolfe, Heather 237
Womock, Laurence 38
woodblock devices 82, 94–7, 153, 157, 186
    Half Eagle and Key 90, 92–4, 108–9
    Heb Ddieu 92–4, 107–9
    Prudentia 94, 95*f*, 96–7, 101
Woodfall, Abraham 214 n.12
Woudhuysen, Henry 54 n.49, 86 n.23, 148 n.75, 173 n.12, 242
Wreittoun, John 248*t*
Wright, John 127, 176, 183, 246*t*

Yamada, Akihiro 80 n.5, 87
Yates, Frances 63 n.84, 64
Young, Robert 89, 152